replied, earnestly, "Mister, I was already fooled once today by those mountains. Now, by damn, I'm going to swim this river even if it takes all day."

Johnson

The old ghost town of Johnson sits a few miles north of Interstate 10 on the east side of Dragoon Pass. The town was founded in 1883 by the Russell Gold and Silver Mining Company. The company had a prosperous mine called the Peabody, and the town of Johnson, named for the general manager of the mine, was established as a convenience to the company and its 150 employees.

Johnson was primarily a copper town, and most of the miners were family men. It couldn't boast of "gunfights at somebody's corral" or of anything that might qualify for Hollywood's silver screen. In fact, this writer came across only two shooting scrapes, and neither would put the participants in the Valhalla of western heroes.

The first involved an attempted ambush on the road between Johnson and Dragoon Station. Unknown parties, figured to be saloon bums from Johnson, fired a fusillade at two residents and succeeded only in wounding both horses. The other had to do with the popular Mrs. Hanson, who ran the town boardinghouse. Apparently she was working on her fast draw and suffered a gunshot wound in the foot.

Willcox

Willcox was one of those "off the beaten path" towns a few years ago, when US 80 ran south from Benson to Bisbee and then around the east side of the Chiricahua Mountains to Lordsburg, New Mexico. Later, the highway took a more direct route between Tucson and Lordsburg, and Willcox's economy became heavily dependent on tourists. Motels, gas stations, cafes, and truck stops sprang up along Haskell Avenue, the town's main street. Today many of the old buildings, including what is said to be Arizona's oldest continuously operated mercantile store, still stand as a reminder of the town's bygone days.

The history of Willcox, like that of other towns of similar size along transcontinental routes, has seen three major phases. The first came with the arrival of the railroad in the 1880s when the merchants and saloon keepers built along Railroad Avenue. Phase II came during the second quarter of the twentieth century, when transcontinental highways like Route 66 and US 80 stretched across the state. A new "main drag" would be established a block or two away from the older section, and businessmen would have to pick up and establish again

Railroad Avenue in Willcox in the 1880s
Courtesy
Southwest Studies

along the new thoroughfare. Usually the old section became a skid row rendezvous for transients, winos, and other ne'er-do-wells. Phase III came with the completion of the Interstate Highway System in the 1980s. Once again, merchants were forced to relocate closer to the freeway off-ramps or go out of business.

Community leaders were faced with finding ways to lure tourists off the fast-paced freeways to stop long enough to stimulate the local economy. In some cases civic-minded or tourist-oriented enterprises are attempting to renovate the nostalgic old buildings that sprang up along the railroad tracks and to create a Wild West-type setting as a way of attracting tourists.

In 1854 Lieutenant John G. Parke of the Army Corps of Topographical Engineers surveyed a route for a transcontinental railroad through Apache Pass at the north end of the Chiricahua Mountains. This road was later used by the famous Butterfield Overland Stage Line. The pass had too steep a grade and too many arroyos for a railroad to cross, so the following year Parke found a much easier way around the north side of the Dos Cabezas Mountains, but the Civil War caused years of delay. The Southern Pacific, building east, finally reached the site of Willcox in August 1880. For the next quarter century the town enjoyed a steady business growth. Before the railroads built branch lines to Bisbee and Globe, Willcox was second only to Tucson as the major shipping point in southern Arizona. The dusty streets were crowded continuously with deep-bellied ore wagons hauling processed ore from mining camp smelters. Until 1935 forty to fifty thousand head of cattle were shipped out of Willcox annually. After the district was split, the average has been about thirty thousand a year.

The original site of Willcox was called Maley (sic), for James H. Mahley, whose ranch straddled the Southern Pacific's right of way. According to local legend, the first train to arrive on the new line carried the department military commander, General Orlando B. Willcox. He was given such a warm reception by residents that someone suggested changing the name of the new station to Willcox.

Willcox lies in the heart of the Sulphur Springs Valley, or "Sufferin' Springs Valley" as some residents call it. The valley is about fifteen miles wide and one hundred miles long, stretching from Douglas on the south to Fort Grant on the north. When cattlemen first arrived in the early 1870s the lush native grasses were "stirrup high," and it was said to be the richest cattle country in the West. Tragically, that changed over the next twenty years as droughts and overgrazing nearly turned the area into a desert.

Like most of southern Arizona, the land around Willcox is basin and range country characterized by islands of lofty mountains with lyrical-sounding names like Peloncillo, Pinaleno, Pedregosa, Dos Cabezas, Chiricahua, Galiuro, and Dragoon, rising majestically off the valley floors.

Willcox in its early days attracted settlers from a wide gamut of frontier society with all its virtues and vices. Like most cowtowns, it had a colorful, wild and wooly history. One of the Old West's most humorous train robberies took place five miles west of Willcox on January 30, 1895. Cowboys Grant Wheeler and Joe George decided to raise their station in life by holding up the Southern Pacific. They purchased a large box of dynamite in Willcox, ostensibly to go prospecting, and went out to meet the Southern Pacific. They stopped the train, uncoupled the passenger cars, and ordered the engineer to take the mail and baggage cars several miles down the track. They broke open the express car but found the messenger had gone out the opposite side and escaped. Undaunted, the amateur train robbers placed sticks of dynamite around the two safes. The first blast demolished the small safe but the big, sturdy Wells Fargo safe remained intact, so they tried again without success. Finally, the frustrated punchers packed the rest of the dynamite around the safe and piled eight sacks, each containing $1,000 in Mexican silver pesos, on top to act as ballast. The blast that followed shook the mountains nearby. The Wells Fargo safe was blown apart but so was the express car. The air was filled with flying shrapnel as 8,000 "dobe dollars" were hurled in all directions, impregnating everything they hit, including nearby telegraph poles. It was said that for the next thirty years folks were still picking up silver pesos in the surrounding desert. The damage created far exceeded the loot, which was estimated at between $200 and $1,500.

Although the heist left a lot to be desired, Wheeler and George were happy with their handiwork and decided to continue their new careers. On the evening of February 26, they stopped another Southern Pacific train at Steins Pass, near the New Mexico line. To their surprise, the engineer and fireman looked familiar. "Well, here we are again," the two erstwhile cowpunchers grinned. Following their previous plan, Wheeler and George uncoupled the cars and ordered the engineer to head down the tracks to where the horses were staked. In their haste, the two would-be badmen unhitched the wrong car. When they got to the horses and dynamite it was discovered that the express car—the one with the *dinero*—was still hooked up to the passenger cars. With resigned frustration, they ordered the engineer to reverse his engine and rejoin his train. They then lit the fuse to the unused dyanmite and rode off in disgust.

Another spectacular train robbery took place a few miles from Willcox on the evening of September 11, 1899. The heist was planned by none other than the good-humored Willcox town marshal, Burt Alvord. Alvord, a swarthy-looking, bald-headed man was a "good ole boy" if there ever was one. He had a big broad grin, coupled with a sense of humor, and he was an accomplished prankster. The popular constable made friends easily, ranging from judges and merchants to cattle rustlers; however, he wasn't blessed with a great deal of intelligence, his entire tenure of formal education having been gleaned in the pool halls of Tombstone, the town where he was raised. Burt Alvord was also good with a gun, and he was absolutely fearless. John Slaughter, the legendary sheriff of Cochise County from 1886 to 1892, deputized him, placing great stock in his prowess in the pursuit of outlaws.

Alvord had befriended an ornery bunch of cohorts that included the deputy constable at Pearce, Billy Stiles, along with Bill Downing, Matt Burts, Three-finger Jack Dunlap, and Bravo Juan Yoas. Collectively their IQs wouldn't have added up to a hundred, but they were as mean and nasty as any bunch that ever rode the Arizona scene.

At about 11:30 P.M., on September 11, 1899 Billy Stiles and Matt Burts climbed aboard the westbound Southern Pacific just as it was pulling into the station at Cochise, ten miles west of Willcox. While one of the gunmen covered the fireman and engineer, the other uncoupled the engine and express car from the rest of the train. The Wells Fargo messenger was ordered to open the door and vacate the premises. Next, they ordered the engineer to take the train down the track a few miles. At a pre-arranged point, the outlaws jumped off and picked up a box loaded with sticks of dynamite. Then they climbed into the express car and piled explosives around the safe, lit the short fuse, and hightailed it for cover.

The stillness of the night was shattered by a resounding blast as the interior of the express car was blown to splinters. The blast blew open the Wells Fargo safe, and the outlaws quickly emptied the contents. Estimates of the loot ranged from $3,000 to $300,000 in gold. An educated guess would put the figure at $30,000. They loaded the gold on horses and rode off into the night toward Willcox.

Meanwhile the engineer rejoined his train and backed to Willcox to give the alarm. The town marshal, Burt Alvord, was sitting innocently in the back room of Schwertner's saloon playing poker with his pals. He deputized Bill Downing, and they rode out to Cochise, cut the trail of the robbers and followed it back to the outskirts of Willcox, where the tracks were lost in a herd of horses. Feigning great frustration, the two returned to their poker game.

Obviously, the card game had been a clever ruse to establish an alibi. During the evening Alvord and friends exited through a window and headed to the outskirts of town, where Downing had left some horses. Burts and Stiles then rode to a spot two miles west of Cochise, where a cache of dynamite was waiting. They then hobbled the horses and jumped on the train as it slowed on the long uphill grade to the station.

The porter at Schwertner's had been bribed to take drinks to the room every few minutes and return with empty glasses, creating the illusion that the long-running poker game was still in progress. By the time the train returned to Willcox, Alvord and friends had returned through the back window and had resumed their poker game.

Just to make sure the boys didn't start squandering their new wealth around town and arouse suspicions, Burt took the gold to a secret hiding place and buried it. He was feeling pretty good about his perfectly executed train robbery and the alibi he'd established.

However, he hadn't counted on the persistence of Wells Fargo detectives and a lawman named Bert Grover. Grover suspected Alvord early on—perhaps the marshal had acted a little too innocent. Grover cajoled the porter at the saloon into confessing his role in establishing Burt's alibi, but before he could bring charges, his star witness got cold feet and left the territory.

Burt and the boys felt so good about their debut as train robbers they decided to plan another; this time they let Bravo Juan, Three-finger Jack, Bob Brown, and the Owens brothers do the dirty work, but the robbery at Fairbank didn't go as planned. They didn't reckon on the legendary gunfighter Jeff Milton being in the express car. Milton opened fire on the gang from inside the express car, mortally wounding Three-finger Jack and sending the rest away empty-handed. The outlaws left Jack on the trail to die, and when lawmen found him, he bitterly gave all the details of both robberies.

Burt Alvord and his pals righteously proclaimed their innocence, claiming Dunlap had tried to frame them. Since Burt was so likable and nobody considered him intelligent enough to plan and execute a daring train robbery, many people believed his story, but dissension was building within the gang. Downing, a quarrelsome, morose fellow was disliked and not trusted by the others; and since Alvord was the only one who knew where the gold was buried, the others feared they wouldn't get a fair share. Finally, Billy Stiles, a treacherous and pugnacious hoodlum broke under pressure and confessed in exchange for his freedom.

With Billy Stiles's confession, the Alvord gang was locked up in the county jail at Tombstone. Since the gold had not been found Burt and the boys were charged with tampering with the United States Mail.

On the morning of April 8, 1900, for reasons known only to himself, Billy Stiles walked into the Tombstone jail, shot the jailer in the leg, and opened the cell doors for Alvord and Bravo Juan. Not surprisingly, he left the troubled Bill Downing sitting in his cell cursing as they ran out the door to waiting horses.

Burt Alvord and Billy Stiles hid out in Mexico for a couple of years until Arizona Ranger Captain Burt Mossman, working undercover, enlisted their help in capturing the notorious bandit Augustine Chacon. In return they were to surrender to authorities and be given light sentences. Despite their short jail terms, Alvord and Stiles broke out of the Tombstone jail again, this time digging their way out. Alvord was later captured and served a term at the Yuma Territorial Prison, but Stiles was never caught. He moved to Nevada, took the name Larkin, and was killed in a gunfight. Matt Burts served his time and then went back to being a cowboy at his brother's ranch near Willcox. Burt Alvord did his time, returned to Willcox for a few days, said howdy to all his old cronies, and then left town for good. Old timers say he dug up his gold and moved to Honduras, where he married and settled down.

Before he got crosswise with the law, Downing had married a pretty young lady from a good family in Texas. While he was in prison, she'd been forced to sell their ranch and move to Tucson, where she worked as a domestic. Before his ten-year term (three years off for good behavior) was up, she died. The coroner's report said heart failure—perhaps it was heartbreak.

Bill Downing came out of the Yuma prison in 1907, as despicable and mean as ever. He returned to Willcox and became proprietor of the Free and Easy Saloon. It became a gathering place for prostitutes, brawlers, tin horn gamblers, and other riff-raff. Customers complained of having their wallets picked by the ladies, but nobody in town was brave enough to press charges. Downing frequently boasted he'd kill anyone who got in his way and that lawmen would never take him alive. Finally the Arizona Rangers were called in. Captain Harry Wheeler dispatched Ranger Billy Speed to Willcox to keep an eye on the Free and Easy Saloon.

In 1907 the Territorial legislature had passed a law against allowing women in a saloon. Downing was charged with violation of this law and fined $50. He went home and beat up his live-in girl friend to vent his anger. She went to Willcox Constable Bud Snow and gave evidence about the customers being robbed at the Free and Easy. Snow asked Ranger Speed to help arrest Downing.

At 8:00 A.M., on the morning of August 5, 1908 Ranger Billy Speed, armed with a .30-.40 Winchester, stood in the street in front of the Free and Easy and ordered Downing to step outside with his hands up. Downing, who'd been drinking heavily and feeling mean, ignored the ranger's command. When Speed called a second time, Downing headed for the back door. As he moved past some fellow early-morning imbibers, one reached over and snatched the revolver out of Downing's holster. The outlaw went out the door, around the corner, only to meet the ranger coming the other way.

"Throw up your hands," the ranger yelled. Downing, a left hander, reached for his pistol but came up with nothing but an empty holster. At the same time, Speed fired, putting a bullet into Downing's chest. The outlaw fell to the ground mortally wounded. Nobody in Willcox was remorseful over the demise of Bill Downing.

Some historians, who probably got their information from self-styled "old timers," say Bill Downing once rode with the Sam Bass gang in Texas and escaped to Arizona when Texas lawmen shot the gang to pieces.

Warren Earp, youngest brother of the legendary brothers, lies buried in an unmarked grave in the Willcox cemetery. For a long time nobody knew or cared where the grave was located, but during the 1980s some of Willcox's citizens have suggested relocating Earp's grave and erecting some sort of a shrine in hopes of attracting tourists.

The younger brother seems to have lacked the charisma of his older siblings. According to some historians, he was generally known around town as a bully. He was shot and killed in a Willcox bar, and although Earp was unarmed, the coroner's jury found the defendant's actions justified. Other accounts claim Earp as a decent, law-abiding citizen. It seems Earp had a long-running feud with a fellow-cowboy named John Boyett. Both worked for Henry Clay Hooker's Sierra Bonita Ranch at the north end of the Sulphur Springs Valley. They'd had a barroom argument, and Boyett had pulled a gun and killed Earp. Whatever the case, Boyett was turned loose. One historian mentions that Boyett later went insane in remorse over the killing of Warren Earp.

The mountains around Willcox served for years as a refuge for cattle rustlers who hung out on the fringes of the ranches in the area. Others were wanted for outlawry someplace else and were hired out as cowpunchers. They could get nervous when a stranger rode into camp. Cowboy-writer Ross Santee tells about an old timer who hired out to work on a cow-outfit near Willcox:

> "I'd hired out to a man in Willcox," said an old timer, "an' was looking fer the camp his outfit was workin' from when I happened onto a puncher huntin' horses. From the brand on his horse I knowed he was workin' for the spread I was huntin'. When I asked where the camp was located an' didn't mention I was goin' to work I could see he had me pegged for an officer. Finally he pointed out the camp an' rode on.
>
> "When I rode into camp there was saddles an' bed rolls layin' all about the place. Supper was just ready an' there was bread in the Dutch ovens for at least twenty men, but there wasn't a man in sight except the cook.
>
> "He laughed when I rode up; it happened I knowed him. When he yelled they all come sneakin' in a looking kind of foolish. For it seems this puncher I had met had rode ahead and spread the word that an officer was on his way to camp. Not knowin' which man was wanted the whole doggone outfit had took to the brush."

Willcox was becoming modernized in 1897 when the first ice plant was opened. Four years later a local brewery was turning out one thousand bottles of beer a day to help wash the alkali dust down the parched throats of cowboys and freighters. The electricity age arrived in Willcox briefly in 1899 when a generating plant was built, and for a time the boisterous cowtown was literally lit up all night. Three years later, hard times came, and the customers couldn't pay their light bills so the equipment was sold to a location in Mexico, causing the town to be without electricity until 1926. In 1902 Willcox had its first automobile but it was several years before the horseless carriage caught on in this cowtown.

The vast, dusty, wind-swept alkali sink that lies southwest of town is known as the Willcox Playa. Lt. John G. Parke in 1854 called it the Playa de los Pimas. Playa is a Mexican word for a dry lake with no vegetation. It's been called, probably with tongue-in-cheek, Dry Lake, Lake Cochise, and Alkali Flats, but playa is the most descriptive. The huge, shallow lake bed has given off some spectacular mirages and from a distance gives the illusion of being a deep-water lake. It is said that during World War II the pilot of a Navy flying boat decided to make a landing during a cross-country flight. Not only did it prove embarassing, but it was a mighty choppy landing.

Rex Allen, the best of Hollywood's "singing cowboys" and the only one who could lay claim to being a real cowboy, hailed from Willcox. Allen wasn't a native but moved there in the 1920s when he was a youngster. He was a likable, talented lad but was afflicted with crossed eyes. The Allen family was too poor to have the problem corrected, so local friends took up a collection to send Rex back east for treatment. He never forgot their kindness, and after becoming a movie star, he continued to return annually for "Rex Allen Days."

Historically, farming has been important to Willcox's economy— irrigation from deep wells produced barley, alfalfa, maize, and cotton. Despite its reliance on the highway tourist business and farming, Willcox is, at heart, a cattle town.

Bowie

The townsite of Bowie was first homesteaded by Captain James Tevis, an adventurer who came to Arizona before the Civil War. His true life adventures read like an action-packed novel. As a youth, he rode with William Walker's *filibusteros* in Central America. In 1857 he joined a party of twenty-four adventurers bound for Arizona. Later that year, he became agent for the Butterfield Overland Stage Line at Apache Pass. At the time, several thousand Chiricahua Apaches lived in the mountains around the pass. Open warfare between the whites and Apaches hadn't begun at that date, but the unpredictable nature of the warriors made life precarious around the station. Tevis made friends with some of the bands, but others regarded him as hostile. Evidence of this came when Tevis was captured and about to be put to death by Cochise and his warriors. Another Apache chieftan, named Esconolea, whom Tevis had befriended, saved his life with a daring rescue. In 1886 Tevis wrote *Arizona in the Fifties*, which later was the basis for a Walt Disney movie. During the war, Tevis became an officer in the Confederate Army. After mustering out in 1865, he settled in Austin, Texas, but in 1880 he returned to Arizona and opened a store in Apache Pass at the site of the old Butterfield station. When Tevis learned the Southern Pacific Railroad was building across the plains some fourteen miles north of Fort Bowie, he filed on some land near the proposed route. When he and some friends organized the Cochise Mining and Milling Company to work claims located in the Dos Cabezas Mountains, he donated land for a mile near the railroad line, and a small town sprang up nearby. A post office was established, and the residents wanted to call the place Teviston. However, a railroad superintendent named Bean wanted to name the place after himself. Tevis told him that since the residents ate beans three times a day, they already had a bellyful. The humorless Mr. Bean was insulted and named the town Bean anyway. Three months later the postmaster changed it to Teviston. Undaunted, Bean insisted on calling the town Bowie Station. For a time both Teviston and Bowie Station were used, but in 1908 the name was changed to just plain Bowie.

US 80 replaced this road in San Simon in 1939. Courtesy Arizona Historical Foundation

San Simon

A little over a hundred and twenty-five years ago, the San Simon Valley was described as having some of the richest cattle grazing lands in the entire West. A few years earlier, in 1847, members of the Mormon Battalion reported the area carpeted with native grasses that reached stirrup-high and crowded with game such as antelope and deer. The San Simon River was a living stream in those days and Sonoran beaver were found in large numbers. During the early 1890s some 50,000 head of Mexican cattle were moved into the valley, grazing it "down to the rocks." A three-year drought began in 1902, followed by heavy rains in 1905-06. The rich fertile soil, with no grass to hold it, washed into the Gila River. During these same years, ruts made by the wheels of stagecoaches and freight wagons crisscrossed the valley and became small arroyos. More droughts, followed by heavy rains in 1916 and 1920, continued the massive erosion process, rendering the area useless for ranching. Since the 1930s there has been a continuous effort to restore the land to its former condition.

During the 1840s the San Simon River was known to some locals as the San Domingo. Others called it the Rio de Suaz (River of Willows) after the trees that grew along its banks. Other maps prepared in the 1850s by road builders and surveyors called it the "Cienega de Suaz," or Willow Swamps.

The Butterfield Overland Stage Line built a relay station in the area in 1859. Following the arrival of the Southern Pacific Railroad in 1881, a post office was established, and a town called San Simon came into existence. Wells Fargo opened a station in 1885. The San Simon station was one of the most remote in Arizona. Just west of the New Mexico line, travelers entering Arizona had their first glimpse of the territory at San Simon and those leaving, their last. The job of running the station at San Simon was not suited to the timid or weakhearted—it was right in the path of a major Apache plunder trail leading into Mexico. In 1895 Black Jack Ketchum and his gang held up the Wells Fargo agent, Adolph Langlotz. The strongbox was low on cash and the outlaws didn't make much of a haul. Agent Langlotz took a personal loss in the robbery when Black Jack stole his brand new mail order jacket that had just arrived from Sears and Roebuck. It was said the agent was more irate over the loss of his coat that he was over the theft of Wells Fargo's money.

Nogales in the 1920s Courtesy Arizona Historical Foundation

Interstate 19
Nogales to Tucson
The "Cradle" of Arizona's History

Nogales

The city of Nogales is a newcomer, relatively speaking, to southern Arizona. Recorded history begins with the arrival of Father Eusebio Kino in 1691, but the city dates from the arrival of the Arizona and Southwestern Railroad from Benson to Guaymas, Sonora in 1882. Jacob Isaacson, a traveling salesman, arrived and saw the opportunities for a store near the railroad. The community consisted of a few tents, mud huts, and a boxcar railroad station. The store was located on the international boundary. On May 31, 1882 a post office was opened in the store and the place became known as Isaacson. Jacob Isaacson stayed only three years, but in that time became a respected community leader, successful entrepreneur, linguist, and musician. In September 1882 he was given the honor of driving the last ceremonial railroad spike in the line that connected the cities of Guaymas and Benson.

After a year, the town decided on a name change. Someone suggested Line City, but fortunately the citizens had the good sense to name the town Nogales. The Los Nogales de Elias land grant,

Major William Emory, soldier-scientist, led several boundary surveys in the 1850s.
Courtesy Arizona Historical Foundation

totaling nearly 33,000 acres, had been awarded to Don José Elias in 1843. The ranch had no streams running through it, so the selling price of $113 was inexpensive at the time.

The Los Nogales de Elias grant was rich in gold and silver, but the family didn't exploit the mineral wealth beneath the soil. They were ranchers, and the grass-carpeted hills provided feed for as many as 4,000 head of cattle. The ranch headquarters was for many years a stopover for weary travelers between Tucson and Sonora, and like most of the other ranches in southern Arizona and Sonora that lay along the Apache plunder trails, it was raided frequently.

Actually, the name Nogales had been around a long time. In the early 1850s Major William Emory, of the Army Corps of Topographical Engineers, camped on the site while surveying the land acquired through the Gadsden Purchase. Two big walnut trees were straddling the border, providing the inspiration for the camp name, Dos Nogales (Nogales means walnuts in English).

Spain had tried, unsuccessfully, during the fifteenth century to conquer the Indians that inhabited the American Southwest. The horseback *conquistadores* were among the greatest combat soldiers of the time, and the native peoples further south were pacified with relative ease by the fearless soldiers in their quest for glory, God, and gold.

But this was a harsh, inhospitable land, and it bred a tough, indestructible people. This was the home of the Ah-kee-mult O'Odham, the River People, or Pima, and the Tono (Toh-oh-no) O'Odham, People of the Desert, commonly called the Papago. They spoke a common language but had marked cultural differences. One group lived in *rancherias*, or widely scattered brush huts, and farmed the Santa Cruz and San Pedro river valleys. The other group were nomadic food gatherers inhabiting the dry desert lands west of the Santa Cruz River. These Piman peoples were the first natives encountered by the Spanish missionaries, and the area would be marked on maps as the Pimeria Alta, or Land of the Upper Pima, whose boundaries were the Gila River on the north, the Colorado River on the west, the San Pedro River to the east, and the Rio Altar, in Sonora, on the south.

The dreaded adversaries of the Piman peoples and soon to be the most feared enemies of the Spanish were a group calling themselves the Dine, or, in our language, "The People." Neighboring tribes had other names for these nomadic raiders, who swarmed down out of the mountains, raided their crops, and stole their young women. The Pueblo Indians called them Apaches or "enemies," and the name stuck. The Apaches proved to be unconquerable, although they never saw themselves as one political entity. Military defeats or peace treaties with one band weren't considered binding by any of the others. Free-spirited nomads, they had no prime minister to speak for all and no capital city or state to capture, and they fiercely resisted European attempts to change their independent lifestyle.

The Mission San Gabriel de Guévavi

By the early 1600s the Spanish had given up their plan for a military conquest of these intractable tribes, thus marking the dawn of the "Great Missionary Period." Missionaries wearing the black robes of the Jesuit Order and the Franciscans in their brown robes were to be the harbingers of Christian religion and Spanish culture to the natives. In theory the padres would locate among the native villages and *rancherias*, build missions and *visitas* (branch missions), and over a ten-year period, indoctrinate the natives into the Spanish culture. At the end of a decade, the missions would be secularized or taken over by regular clergy, and the zealous missionaries would venture out into the next frontier to reap a new harvest of souls. It was also assumed that mission-villages would be self-sustaining, and natives, taxpaying Spanish citizens.

The responsibility for the religious pacification of the Pimeria Alta fell to the Jesuits. Long known for their militancy, the Jesuits have been called the "storm troopers" of the Catholic faith. There is much historical evidence to bear this out, but the Jesuits couldn't have selected a more gentle, kindly man to build a chain of missions in the Pimeria Alta than Father Eusebio Francisco Kino.

Eusebio Kino, born in a small town in northern Italy, was truly the outstanding figure of his time on the Spanish frontier. A brilliant student of mathematics, Kino might have become one of the great scholars of Europe except for a serious illness while attending college. He attributed his miraculous recovery to the divine intervention of St. Francis and decided to dedicate his life to missionary work. He joined the Society of Jesus (Jesuits) and studied in European universities for fourteen years before applying for duty in the Orient. By some twist of fate, he was assigned to Mexico. He arrived in Mexico in 1681, and six years later, at the age of forty-two, he was sent to the Pimeria Alta. His family name in Italy was Chinus and was pronounced "Chino." Chino in Spanish referred either to a Chinese or to a person of low caste. To avoid any misunderstanding, he changed his name to Kino.

In January 1691, Kino first set foot in what is Arizona today. For the next twenty-four years this so-called "Padre on Horseback" criss-crossed Arizona, covering some 75,000 miles in all. At one stretch the indefatigable padre rode an average of forty miles a day for twenty-six consecutive days. He was fifty-five at the time. A few years earlier he rode a 1,500-mile journey to Mexico City in just fifty-three days. Kino was truly a man for all seasons—humanitarian, explorer, cartographer, mathematician, geographer, cattleman, farmer, and "Arizona promotor el grande." His greatest gift was the manner in which he dealt with the natives. He was a merciful, kind, sensitive, and humble man, always defending the Indians in his charge. They, in turn, worshipped him and, in troubled times, saw that no harm came his way. During a Pima rebellion in 1694, many Spaniards, including another padre, were killed. Kino, alone in his mission at Dolores, stoically awaited martyrdom, but the natives refused to harm the good padre. Later, Kino was able to bring the rebels and Spanish authorities to a parley, ending the further slaughter of innocent victims. When the shooting stopped, Kino resumed his missionary work. Historians generally agree that if Spanish authorities had called upon Kino to intervene at the outset of the revolt, he could have prevented the bloodshed altogether. One characteristic of the Spanish system that hindered efforts to colonize the Pimeria Alta was the rivalry and bickering among the civil authorities, the military, and the missionaries. Each was quick to blame the other for periodic native rebellions. And the natives were quick to sense the disarray and take advantage of the situation. The major troublemakers among the tribes were the *hechiceros*, or medicine men, who resented the competition from the padres. More than one priest had his dinner salted with poison herbs by some vindictive medicine man.

Father Kino seems to have always been a welcome visitor to the Piman *rancherias* and villages. He firmly believed that Christianity was easier to swallow on a full stomach than an empty one. He introduced animal husbandry, and planted fruit trees and crops of vegetables, thus insuring his converts of a regular food supply.

Kino's chain of missions and *visitas* covered such a wide range of territory that he rarely stayed in one place very long. This, no doubt, endeared him to the natives because he didn't remain long enough to impose any restrictions on their time-honored lifestyle. Many years later, resident priests would take a dim view of plural marriages and wild drinking binges during the harvest of the cactus fruit. Kino was always careful to play down the negative habits of his charges for fear the Spanish crown would use this lifestyle as an excuse to close down his missions.

Kino first set foot in Arizona in January 1691 after receiving an invitation from natives along the Santa Cruz River. He stopped at Guévavi, two miles south of Sonoita Creek (ten miles north of Nogales); then he continued north to Tumacacori. He visited again in January 1697 with a herd of cattle, which he distributed among his new *visitas*, and missions.

In 1701 Kino established the Mission San Gabriel de Guévavi at the Pima village of Guévavi and added a *visita* some five miles north at Tumacacori, called San Cayetano (later San José) de Tumacacori.

Statue of Father Kino at Tucson's Arizona Heritage Center. Another stands in the rotunda at the Capitol building in Washington, D.C.

Herds of cattle and sheep were driven to the new mission and *visita* by native drovers from the *cabecera*, or head mission, at Dolores.

In 1701 Father San Juan de Martin was assigned as a resident priest to Guévavi and the *visita* at Tumacarcori. However, that same year Spain became involved in a thirteen-year war in Europe, and the remainder of Kino's life was spent trying to maintain his missions with limited help from the Crown.

Spain's entanglements in European wars caused the Pimeria Alta to be neglected for more than twenty years after Kino's death. On May 4, 1732 a forty-two-year-old Austrian named Father Juan Grazhoffer arrived at Guévavi. For a brief time, the 1,400 Pimas living in villages along the river became his responsibility for salvation. Apparently hard feelings developed between the German padre and his proteges. He resented their boozing and wenching, and they took exception to his piety. Somebody poisoned his dinner, and he died on May 26, 1733.

Perhaps the observations of another German priest in the Pimeria Alta, Philipe Segesser, help to explain some of the cultural misunderstandings. When he questioned the practice of polygamy, they shrugged and replied that the rooster keeps several hens and the stallion manages to satisfy a brood of mares.

A third German priest, Gaspar Stiga, remained at Guévavi and Tumacacori until 1736 but had no more success than his predecessor. Ignacio Keller, Jacob Sedelmayr and Ignaz Pfefferkorn, all German Jesuits in the service of Spain, spent time at Guévavi and Tumacacori over the next few years. The free-spirited lifestyle of the Pimas continued to be a source of frustration for the black-robed padres for the remainder of their tenure in the Pimeria Alta.

By 1766 the native population at Guévavi had dropped to fifty. Four years earlier, Spanish authorities had recommended the evacuation of friendly Sobaipuri Pimas in the San Pedro Valley to strengthen the Santa Cruz area. These hard-fighting warriors had borne the brunt of Apache attacks, acting as a barrier for the *rancherias* and missions further west along the Santa Cruz. However, the plan backfired; their removal made it easier for Apache war parties to reach the villages and missions at Guévavi and Tumacacori.

In 1767 a royal decision by King Carlos III of Spain would have great impact on the Pimeria Alta. With the stroke of a pen he expelled the Jesuits from the Spanish Empire. It was a period of reform, and the king believed that absolute control was a prerequisite. The powerful, militant Jesuits were a threat to royal control over the Church, so on February 27, 1767 he banished some 5,000 Jesuits. In the Pimeria Alta, orders were carried out in secrecy. Soldiers would appear at the doors of the missions and the padres taken into custody. Missionaries, some aged, were put in chains and marched to the seaport at Guaymas and deported. Fifty padres were arrested in the Pimeria Alta, and of those, twenty died on the march. It was interesting that the Jesuits who had been in Sonora were not allowed to leave Spain. A war with England was imminent, and the King feared the British might gather strategic information on the geography of the Pacific Coast.

The Jesuit Expulsion in 1767 has been the inspiration for dozens of lost-treasure stories. Rumors that the padres had hidden caches of gold in the walls and floors of missions have caused modern-day treasure seekers to destroy parts of these historic relics in search of riches. Two basic truths refute this senseless quest and destruction. The missions of the Pimeria Alta were poor and had no gold or silver; secondly, the arrest of the padres was conducted in secret—there wouldn't have been time to bury a treasure if one had existed.

The following year saw the *entrada* of the brown-robed Franciscan friars in Arizona. The best known (sometimes referred to as the "Franciscan Kino") was Francisco Tomás Garcés. Apache war parties greeted the friars in typical fashion with a series of mission-destroying raids. Finally, in 1773 the besieged mission of Guévavi was abandoned for good. Two years earlier Tumacacori became the *cabecera*, or head mission, and was renamed San José.

The Pimeria Alta saw plenty of activity over the next few years. In the late 1700s, mines were opened and land grants awarded, and mission life at nearby Tumacacori flourished. The reason for this was a new Spanish policy in dealing with the Apaches. During the 1780s hardriding Spanish troops led by talented, aggressive officers went on the offensive. At the same time, rations, liquor, and inferior weaponry were issued to to the Apaches. Despite complaints by some that these policies had a degenerative effect, the Apaches did go off the warpath for some thirty years.

Mexico won its independence from Spain in 1821, and for a time the peace treaty remained in effect. However, a series of revolutions in Mexico City diverted attention away from the Pimeria Alta, and the Apache payoffs stopped coming. The frontier citizens bore the brunt of this neglect, and by 1831 the Apaches had resumed their warring ways. Once again, the area was abandoned.

War between the United States and Mexico, 1846-1848, had little effect on the Pimeria Alta. The Treaty of Guadalupe Hildalgo, ending the conflict, left the boundary separating the two countries at the

Gila River, far to the north. The primary reason for the war from the United States point of view was the acquisition of California. After the treaty was signed, however, the experts in Washington hadn't taken enough land to build a southern railroad to the Pacific; therefore, Mr. James Gadsden was sent to Mexico City to acquire more land. He might have been able to purchase most of northern Mexico for the tidy sum of 50 million dollars if some American pirates under William Walker didn't make an independent invasion of Mexico, thus blocking Arizona's chance for a sea coast along the Gulf of California. As it turned out Gadsden spent ten million dollars and acquired some 29,670 square miles, but without a sea coast.

Old timers like to say that the diagonal line running from Nogales toward Yuma resulted because of some thirsty surveyors—it is said they reached the desert west of Nogales before they realized the nearest saloon was northwest at Yuma; turning and heading in that direction, they thus deprived Arizona of its sea coast.

Calabazas

Calabazas, located on the Santa Cruz about ten miles north of Nogales and near today's Rio Rico, was originally a Pima pueblo. Calabazas is Spanish for pumpkins, and probably the name was given because of the number of pumpkin plants growing in the area. In the late 1600s Father Kino established a Calabazas *visita* that was abandoned about a century later.

In the early 1800s Calabazas was a stock farm for the mission at Tamacacori; however, the mission went into decline during the early days of the Mexican Republic—the Apaches had resumed raiding and plundering when the Mexicans abandoned Spain's policy of providing rations for the Indians. When the government began selling church lands in 1842, Calabazas was sold at auction to Manual Maria Gándara. In 1853 Gándara converted the old Calabazas church into a headquarters and started running thousands of goats and sheep on the ranges.

The following year an old Apache woman notified the commandant at Tucson, Colonel Gilanin García, that about two hundred warriors were planning a raid on Calabazas. When the war party arrived, Garcia's troops were there to meet them with sixty dragoons and forty Apache allies from Tucson. These Apache allies were descendants of those who had made peace with the Spanish between 1786 and 1820. They spoke Spanish and were considered Mexican citizens. The surprised band of raiders was completely routed, and no quarter was asked or given in the one-sided battle. Two American surveyors, A. B. Gray and Pete Brady, were camped nearby and watched the donnybrook. Afterwards the Mexican officer invited the visitors to view the grim aftermath. Brady, who later became one of Arizona's leading citizens, described what he first thought was a long string of dried apples but which turned out to be the ears of dead warriors. The Mexicans won that round, but persistent Apache attacks forced the abandonment of the ranch in 1856.

Major Enoch Steen and his First U.S. Dragoons camped at Calabazas in November 1856 on their way to establish Fort Buchanan on Sonoita Creek. A few settlers were known to be farming around Calabazas in 1860, but when the outbreak of the Civil War caused the abandonment of Ft. Buchanan and withdrawal of Federal troops, the ubiquitous Apaches took control again. But by the mid-1870s most of the wild Apache bands had been subdued and located on reservations. With the area relatively secure from attack, real estate values increased dramatically. The Tumacacori-Calabazas mission ranch, which Señor Gándara had purchased for $499 in 1869, was sold to a Californian named Charlie Sykes for $12,500 ten years later. Sykes, who knew something about promotion, sold a small parcel to another Californian for $9,000; then both sold out to an Eastern group for $75,000.

The new outfit was called the Calabazas Land and Mining Company, and Charlie Sykes was hired as director. His promotional schemes are reminiscent of twentieth century Arizona developers, one brochure depicting a line of steamers hauling ore on the tiny and oftentimes dry Santa Cruz River.

Sykes built a fancy two-story brick hotel dubbed the Santa Rita. Newspapers at the time described it as the most elegant in the West. Next, he imported a dozen pretty Boston girls as hostesses and started calling himself "Colonel." Apparently "Colonel" Sykes was a good salesman. A Tucson newspaper noted in 1882 that 2,500 of the town's 2,800 lots had been sold. Obviously they had not been built on, for the town had only 150 residents. The paper also mentioned that the town had sixteen saloons, six gambling tables, two dance houses, two Chinese gambling casinos, an opium den, five stores, and a boarding house.

Others referred to Calabazas as "Hell's Hollow" because of its raucous ways. Calabazas represented all those vices Easterners generally expected a frontier town to have—shooting, brawling, boozing, and whoring. The Tombstone *Epitaph* advised: "Calabazas wants to be incorporated. If the inhabitants keep on 'removing' each other at the rate they have been doing, there won't be enough left to fill the city offices."

Calabazas's notoriety was short-lived. Its promoters had great expectations that the railroad would locate a terminal point in the town, but Nogales became the port of entry, shattering the promoters' dreams of a thriving metropolis. The once opulent Santa Rita Hotel was last used by a rancher for storing hay, before it burned down with the rest of the town in 1927. The townsite was plowed under in the 1930s and became a cotton field.

Pete Kitchen's Ranch

The junction of Potrero Creek and the Santa Cruz River was the ranch headquarters of Pete Kitchen, one of Arizona's most illustrious pioneers. Kitchen, born in Kentucky in 1822, arrived in Arizona in 1855. His first ranch was at Canoa, a few miles further down the Santa Cruz River. Like most settlers, he evacuated the area when the Civil War broke out and the troops were withdrawn. After the war, he found the unclaimed land around Calabazas to his liking and built "El Potrero," a fortified ranchhouse on a hill with a commanding view on all four sides. The main ranchhouse was a five-room adobe with walls twenty-five inches thick—enough to stop any assailants' bullets—and a ceiling twelve feet high. A trap door and stairway provided quick access to a flat roof surrounded by a four-foot high parapet with portholes, a safe fort from which to fend off Apache attacks. "Pete's Stronghold," as he called it, provided refuge for many a harried rider between Tucson and Magdalena. Pete coined a phrase during those years—"Tucson, Tubac, Tumacacori, Tohell."

Kitchen's *vaqueros* had to be as handy with a rifle as they were with a lariat. Manual Ronquillo, his trusty *caporal* (foreman), and Fran-

Pete Kitchen
Courtesy Arizona
State Library

Pete Kitchen's original ranch house. The one room adobe structure was the first ranch house built by an American in Arizona. Courtesy Arizona State Library

cisco "Pancho" Verdugo were his most dependable defenders against the raiders. Pete, or Don Pedro as he was known to his Mexican friends, Manuel, and Pancho used to practice quickshooting at targets while blindfolded, all three being expert shots with or without the blinds. Kitchen married Verdugo's beautiful dark-eyed sister Rosa. She too was an expert shot with a pistol and rifle, and her ability to ride an outlaw horse and her expert marksmanship were almost as legendary as her husband's.

Apache bands on the prowl were constantly probing for some weakness in the defense. They killed so many of Kitchen's ranch hands a cemetery had to be built on the property. On one blitz, Apaches swept down on a field and slit the throat of his twelve-year-old stepson. Another time, the ranch was attacked three times in twelve hours, but Kitchen stubbornly refused to be driven out.

A story appearing in the "Personal" section of the Arizona *Citizen* on June 6, 1872 presents an interesting contemporary account of life at El Potrero:

Our friend Pete Kitchen was in town this week from Potrero. He reports that his crops are excellent. He has about 20 acres of potatoes planted and has made this year about 14,000 pounds of No. 1 bacon and hams which he has sold at an average of .35 per pound. Also 5,000 pounds of lard sold at the same price. Mr. Kitchen's farm is located near the Sonora line, and at one of the most exposed points for Apache depredations in Arizona. The Apache had endeavored to take his place many times; one partner and all his neighbors have been murdered, and last summer his boy was killed within gun-shot of his door. Instead of being frightened or discouraged by these bold and numerous attacks he seems only more determined to stand his ground and take his chances. The

Indians have learned to their sorrow that in him they have no insignificant foe. He never travels the same road twice, and he always sleeps with one eye open, therefore, ambushes do not win on him worth a cent. He has been on the picket line now for over fourteen years and he has buried nearly all of his own acquaintances and should his luck continue he may be truly called the first and last of Arizona's pioneers.

High casualties finally caused the Apaches to avoid El Potrero. Occasionally they rode in close enough to lob a few arrows into his thick skinned hogs—someone said they resembled four-legged pincushions—but the warriors tried to avoid combat with the tenacious Don Pedro and his straight-shooting *vaqueros*.

Apaches weren't the only menace to ranchers in the 1860s. Rustlers hung around the perimeters like hungry wolves. Don Pedro was a gregarious and kindly man who loved children, but when it came to rustlers stealing livestock, he could be hardbitten. He used to tell a story about a time he pursued some rustlers into Sonora. He captured one of the thieves and recovered his stolen horses. On the way back, Pete had gone about twenty hours without sleep and needed to stop to rest. Knowing that if he dozed off his prisoner would crush his skull with a rock, he found a solution to his dilemma. The outlaw was left astraddle his horse, hands and feet tied, a noose draped over a tree limb and placed over the outlaw's head, the other end of the rope anchored to the trunk of the tree. Then Pete took his siesta. Invariably someone would ask what happened next. "You know," Pete would reply, "while I was asleep that damned horse walked off and left that fellow hanging there." Pete was a reknowned storyteller in his later years, and no doubt there is much truth in the preceding story. It illustrates the fact that during the 1860s in raw, lawless Arizona a man had to be his own judge, jury, and, at times, executioner.

Pete and Rosa Kitchen spent their last years in Tucson. Magnanimous, generous, and free-spending, he gradually lost the fortune he had accumulated, but he never lost his friends and admirers. When Pete Kitchen died on August 5, 1895, the following article appeared in the Arizona *Daily Citizen*:

The funeral was one of the largest ever seen in this city, for Pete Kitchen's name has long been a household word in Southern Arizona. And so closes the earthly career of one of the most remarkable men that ever faced the frontier dangers of the far Southwest. . . . Keenly alert to his surroundings, a quick and ready shot, he bore nothing else than a charmed life and died in peace, and full of years, surrounded by the comforts of civilization and friends.

The Mission San José de Tumacacori

Ten miles downstream from Calabazas is the historic Mission San José de Tumacacori. During the Jesuit period in Arizona (1691-1767) Tumacacori, which means curved peak in the Piman language, was a *visita* for Guévavi, which Father Kino first visited in January 1691. Being favorably impressed with the natives, he built a church at the site. In 1701 Father San Juan Martín was appointed resident priest, but apparently the natives resented his presence, for the padre left after a year. Spain was preoccupied with a European war during the next few years, and the missions of the Pimeria Alta received little attention or support. When Guévavi began to decline in the 1770s, the newly-arrived Franciscans elevated Tumacacori to mission status.

The missions underwent great construction during the so-called "golden years—1786-1821," when peace prevailed with the Apaches. In 1807 the government issued a grant of nearly 7,000 acres to the Tumacacori mission. But when Mexico gained its independence from Spain in 1821, the new republic began expelling Franciscans, ending the years of prosperity. The mission declined further when the Apaches resumed the warpath in 1831, Mexico having repudiated the peaceful coexistence treaty with the Apaches that had been so successful during the last days of the Spanish empire.

Tubac

During the period of the Jesuits, 1691-1767, Tubac was a *visita* for the mission at Guévavi. Tubac, like the other missions, fell on hard times during periods of neglect. Jesuit padres who followed in Kino's footsteps didn't fare so well in their relationships with the natives. The mild-mannered Kino never remained in one place long enough to make any impositions on his charges, but zealous padres who set up residence in Arizona during the 1730s were critical of the free-spirited lifestyles of the natives. Father Segessor, for example, took a dim view of the Pima method of selecting a bride. The ceremony took place at an all-night dance. Several women would put on a dance performance, and the one who endured the longest would be taken home as a bride. Divorces were even more simple—the couple just separated. These were time-honored customs as were the rituals of the *hechicero* (shaman), whose paganistic rituals the padres condemned as communication with the devil.

In 1736 a great silver strike occurred near a *rancheria* called Arisoona about twenty-five miles southwest of Nogales. The rush to riches that followed brought a large number of Europeans into the

Pimeria Alta. The inevitable conflicts among civilians, military, church, and natives set the stage for the great Pima Revolt in 1751. The rebellion began in Sonora and quickly spread to the Santa Cruz Valley. The church at Tubac was burned and ransacked, and by the time Spanish troops quelled the revolt, more than a hundred settlers and miners had been killed. Among the dead were two padres.

In March 1752 Captain José Diaz established a military post at Tubac, while launching forays against hostile Pimas in the nearby mountains. Later that year fifty Spanish soldiers under the command of Captain Tomás de Belderrain established a *presidio*, the first in Arizona. That same year the first European community and the first white woman arrived in Arizona.

The origin of Tubac's name is disputed. Some say it means "place of brackish water" while others insist it means "low ruins or house." The towering Santa Rita Mountains provide a picturesque panoramic backdrop, giving Tubac one of Arizona's most spectacular settings. Since the Spanish established a *presidio* at the site in 1752, Tubac has had a violent and bloody history. Written off as dead several times, it has been called a city with nine lives.

The first settlers were the soldiers, their wives, and children. Rich minerals in the nearby mountains and a fertile valley with an abundance of water brought a rush of miners and farmers to the area.

It was from Tubac that one of Spain's greatest soldiers, Captain Juan Bautista de Anza, launched his expedition to find an overland road to California. De Anza, born on the Sonoran frontier in 1735, was a third generation soldier. While De Anza was still an infant, his father was killed in battle by an Apache lance. Later, the dashing young officer was fearless in battle and subscribed to the soldier's code of fidelity. During an inspection of the Pimeria Alta by the Marquis de Rubi, a member of King Carlos III's high ranking military mission, de Anza was proudly proclaimed the "complete soldier."

"Lt. Col. Juan Bautista de Anza," oil on board by Theresa Potter. The son of the Presidio Captain of Fronteras, Juan Bautista de Anza lived and served on the frontier for 36 years.

Father Francisco Garcés, the priest-explorer, had confirmed Father Kino's earlier claims that a land route was possible. In 1774 he traveled across the dreaded El Camino del Diablo (along today's international boundary) to the Yuma crossing and on to California. In October 1775 on a second expedition to California, de Anza and Garcés led 240 colonists, this time along the less-forbidding Gila Trail to Yuma, thence across to the Pacific Coast and north to found a colony at San Francisco. The earliest census of the City by the Bay shows that one-third of the population listed Tubac as their birthplace.

That same year the *presidio* of Tubac was moved to Tucson, leaving the remaining citizens without military protection. Eventually, some soldiers were stationed at Tubac, and during the prosperous "golden years" of peace with the Apaches, the village was a thriving community, but during the unstable early years of the new Mexican Republic, Tubac once again fell upon hard times.

The first recorded *visita* of American immigrants came during the gold rush to California in 1849. A well-traveled route across Sonora and down the Santa Cruz River to Tucson brought thriving business to the community, but roving bands of Apache warriors were still a constant threat.

In October 1849 an emigrant party from Missouri sensed something ominous as they approached the village. The noise and rush of activity that usually preceded the arrival of a wagon train was curiously absent. The Missourians' most foreboding thoughts became reality when they found Tubac in smouldering ruins and all the inhabitants murdered.

Tubac remained deserted until 1854 when two prospectors, Charles Poston and Herman Ehrenberg, came looking for gold and silver. They found rich ore specimens in the mountains, and Poston, who is known as the "Father of Arizona," went east and raised capital for a mining venture. He founded the Sonora Mining and Exploring Company and set up residence in the old Tubac *presidio*.

Once again Tubac came to life. Mexican miners went to work digging out the ore. A thriving trade was established with both Tucson and the Sonorans, and more than a few dark-eyed señoritas came riding in on the hurricane deck of a mule to seek employment and perhaps find a husband.

Poston became the *alcalde*, magistrate, patron, and a self-styled "Marrying Sam." He not only married the young couples but baptized their babies and probably would have granted divorces if asked. Father Josef Machebeuf, a representaive of Archbishop Lamy at Santa Fe, visited Tubac and was horrified at the happenings. In a fit

*Charles D. Poston,
promoter,
entrepreneur, and
leader in the fight for
territorial status, is
known today as the
"Father of Arizona."*
Courtesy Sharlot
Hall Museum

of anger he declared all marriages null and void. The locals were much distressed to learn they'd been living in sin; however, Poston was a persuasive man, and the padre was an understanding one. They struck a bargain—Poston made a contribution to the Church, and the priest re-married all the couples in a "mass" ceremony.

Arizona's first newspaper, the *Weekly Arizonan*, was first printed at Tubac in 1859. In those raw, untamed days a journalist had to be as good with a sixgun as he was with a type case. Soon after the paper opened for business, local mining magnate and promoter Sylvester Mowry took exception to some of editor Ed Cross's written comments and challenged him to a duel. People came from as far as Tucson to watch two of Arizona's best known citizens shoot it out. Bets were piled high as the two men, armed with Burnside rifles, squared off at forty paces. Each fired three times, missing each time. On the fourth try, Cross folded his arms and grimly faced his adversary. Mowry, feeling his honor vindicated, gallantly fired over the editor's head. The affair was consummated with a forty-two gallon barrel of whiskey, the contents of which were shared by duelists and spectators. Afterwards, Mowry purchased the newspaper and moved it to Tucson.

Tubac's tranquil times under the benevolent dictatorship of Poston ended with the outbreak of the Civil War, the troops being removed and the military posts abandoned. The Apache bands became even bolder, and settlers began to flee the area once more. Poston closed his mining company and just barely escaped with his life.

About forty residents who stubbornly refused to leave Tubac found themselves besieged on one side by two hundred Apaches and on the other by seventy-five Sonoran bandits. The timely arrival of a rescue party from Tucson was all that prevented another massacre.

J. Ross Browne, a writer who inspired the style of Mark Twain, traveled through Arizona in 1864. In *Adventures in Apache Country*, he described Tubac's intrepid citizens as ". . . harassed on both sides by Apaches and Mexicans and without hope of future protection, the inhabitants of Tubac for the last time have abandoned the town; and thus it has remained ever since, a melancholy spectacle of ruin and desolation."

After the war, when the army returned, settlers moved back into the fertile valley. Still, Apache war parties kept up their endangering attacks. During January 1869 Apaches raided Tubac five times, and by 1871 the town had been abandoned once more.

The building of a railroad from Tucson to Nogales, and the end of the Apache wars brought new life to Tubac, but it never regained its stature as one of Arizona's largest communities. In the 1950s Tubac seemed on the verge of becoming a ghost town again. This time the cause was the exodus of its young people to Tucson, Nogales, and Phoenix. Old Lady Luck once again lent a hand, when a group of artists and art fanciers took up residence, and the town with nine lives lived on.

San Ignacio de la Canoa

The old Canoa Ranch was located along the west side of the Santa Cruz River, twelve miles north of Tubac, in a fertile well-watered valley between the Santa Rita Mountains on the east and the Sierrita on the west, near the river crossing on the road to Tucson. The name Canoa comes from a hollowed out log that was used as a watering trough. Franciscan Padre Garcés noted a Papago *rancheria* on the site in 1775, which was used as a regular campsite by Spanish military expeditions. In 1821 Tomás and Ignacio Ortíz, prosperous owners of the Arivaca Ranch, were issued a grant under the name San Ignacio de la Canoa—the price $250, or about nine dollars a section.

Apache raids devastated the area in the 1840s and '50s. Charles Poston reported an attack in 1857 saying, "When we reached the Canoa . . . the place looked like it had been struck by a hurricane. The doors and windows were smashed, and the house a smoking ruin. . . . We buried seven in a row in front of the burnt houses." The victims of the Canoa raid had unwittingly joined a party of Mexicans who were in pursuit of some Apaches who had stolen some livestock. The livestock was recovered, but the Apaches returned later to take their vengeance on the settlers at Canoa.

William Hudson Kirkland, 1909. For him, the proudest of his many achievements was hoisting the American flag over Tucson in 1856.
Courtesy Ben and Fern Allen

Two of Arizona's best known *Anglo* pioneers, Bill Kirkland and Pete Kitchen, ranched at Canoa in the late 1850s. Kirkland was the first American to drive cattle into Arizona, the first of three cattle drives from Sonora for the tall Virginian, all three driven off by Apaches. Kitchen remained until 1862 when Washington diverted its attention to the Civil War and withdrew troops stationed in Arizona.

San Xavier del Bac

Arizona's first and principal mission was founded by Father Eusebio Kino in 1700. The legendary "Padre on Horseback" first stopped at Bac in 1692. The natives had sought him out and invited the missionary-explorer to visit their *rancheria*. Kino's journal reports: "I found the natives very affable and friendly, and particularly so in the principal *rancheria* of San Xavier del Bac, which contains more than 800 souls." He returned again in 1697 with a herd of livestock to distribute among the villages. On April 28, 1700 he laid the foundation for a church at Bac.

San Xavier del Bac, named by Kino to honor his patron saint, the illustrious "Apostle to the Indies," Saint Francis Xavier, would remain one of the padre's favorites. He tried many times to have his *cabecera* (head mission) moved there so he could be closer to the unexplored regions of the Pimeria Alta.

Kino had observed the natives using blue abalone shells as trade items. He'd seen these shells on the Pacific Coast of Baja, California, and wondered if the shells had come from a land route. At the time, map makers believed California was an island, but Kino believed it to be a peninsula. He assembled the native headmen at Bac and determined that the blue shells had indeed come from the Pacific Coast. He then made some exploratory journeys to prove his theory, then proclaiming that California was not an island. Despite his insistence that a land route to California was possible, it would be more than sixty years after Kino's death before an expedition would prove his proclamation correct. Kino's last visit to Bac was in 1702, most of his work during the remainder of his life being in Sonora. Those last years were frustrating ones for the hardriding padre, since Spain was involved in a costly war in Europe and paid little attention to a padre's pleas for more missions in Arizona. After Kino's death in 1711 the region was neglected for more than twenty years.

In the 1730s more Jesuits arrived at Bac to take up the missionary movement. Lacking Kino's patience and spiritual persuasion, they were generally unsuccessful. Since San Xavier del Bac was on the extreme rim of Christendom, the *rancheria* and mission bore the brunt of Apache attacks.

During the Pima Rebellion in 1751 the San Xavier Mission was sacked by local Indians. Following the revolt, Spanish civil authorities blamed the Jesuits, accusing them of brutalizing the Pimas, causing them to rebel. After a lengthy investigation into the matter, the missionaries were exonerated, but bad feelings continued among the padres and the military and civil officers.

Following the infamous Jesuit Expulsion by King Carlos III in 1767 the Franciscan Order was requested to fill the void in the Pimeria Alta. On June 30, 1768 Father Francisco Garcés arrived at San Xavier. Garcés, a humble, quiet man has been called the "Franciscan Kino." He lacked Kino's administrative ability and scientific background, but what Garcés lacked in those areas he more than made up in others: he was a tireless explorer and a zealous missionary, with deep feelings of affection for the neophytes and gentiles in his charge. The gregarious friar was in his glory among the natives, sitting on the ground, eating their food, and socializing. Another Franciscan Father wrote: "God, in his infinite wisdom, must have created Garcés for the place in which he served."

When he wasn't being sent into the wilderness to harvest souls, Garcés was happiest at San Xavier, where there were no Spaniards. He expressed these feelings when he wrote simply: "I am very content. There are plenty of Indians. I like them and they like me." This

San Xavier del Bac
in 1890
Courtesy Arizona
Historical Foundation

great missionary would be murdered in an Indian uprising on the Colorado River in 1781.

The "White Dove of the Desert," the beautiful Mission San Xavier as we know it today, a blend of baroque, Moorish, and Byzantine architecture, went into construction in 1783 but wasn't completed until fourteen years later. The unexplained tower without a cap has inspired many stories and legends. The best story is that when the Crown placed a tax on any finished building, the Franciscans left the tower uncapped to avoid the tax.

The mission flourished during Spain's "golden years" of peace with the Apaches (1786-1821), but hard times came after the Mexican Revolution. The unstable Republic took a vindictive attitude toward the Franciscans, expelling many to Spain. When the Apaches resumed warfare in 1831 the mission was abandoned.

Americans passing through in the 1840s and '50s were duly impressed by the statuesque beauty of the neglected mission, once noting that the natives were in awe of the church and wouldn't dare deface it.

During this period, Americans controlled the area, and when Father Josef Machbeuf visited San Xavier and noted the sad condition of the old mission, it was soon reopened. In 1861 Bishop Lamy of Santa Fe appointed Father Salpointe bishop of the new diocese. Salpointe, who continued the renovation of the mission, became one of the territory's most influential citizens.

In the early 1900s the old church was once again in need of repairs. The ancient adobe walls were deteriorating so badly the government was threatening to close the church school. The new bishop, Henri Granjon, another man of ability and determination, completed the renovation of the church, thus preserving one of Arizona's greatest historic and cultural treasures.

*Ed Schieffelin
located rich silver
lodes at Tombstone*
Courtesy
Southwest Studies

US 80
Benson to Tombstone

A few miles south of Benson is the small Mormon community of St. David. Just how the place got its name is a matter of conjecture. The village was settled in 1877 by a colony of Mormons led by Philemon Merrill. Merrill had been a member of the Mormon Battalion some thirty years earlier. Following a disagreement with fellow church members at Lehi, on the Salt River east of Phoenix, Merrill took his group south to colonize the fertile farmland on the flood plains of the San Pedro River.

The Benson to Tombstone highway roughly parallels the old stage-coach road that linked the two communities before the railroad reached Fairbank in 1881. Some of the old adobe ruins remain but are on private land and it's not advisable to trek off to any of these without first getting permission from the owner.

When prospector Ed Schieffelin set out to explore the Apache-infested mountains of southeast Arizona, he was warned that all he would find there would be his own tombstone. He found instead a veritable mountain of rich silver a few miles east of the San Pedro River. It was only fitting that the town that sprang up nearby be named Tombstone.

The story of Tombstone's spectacular rise to fame and riches is an

Arizona classic. There's no doubt that if Schieffelin hadn't made the strike, some other incurable sourdough would have, for burro men were scouring every square foot of Arizona's mineral belt, and the turbulent history of the town wouldn't have been any different.

Ed Schieffelin represented the best qualities one expects to find but seldom does in the colorful prospectors of Arizona's past. He was honest, hardworking, persistent; he struck it rich, but didn't squander his wealth on booze, whores, and faro tables.

He'd come west to Oregon while still in his teens and taken up prospecting with his father. By the time he reached twenty, Schieffelin had seen most of the West's gold camps. Tall, lean, and broad-shouldered, he thrived on the backbreaking toil of panning for gold in cold mountain streams—he was hooked on prospecting. While others invested in successful farm and business ventures, he eked out a meager living searching for gold. After a few years, his rigorous lifestyle began to take its toll. While still in his twenties, he looked like a man well past forty. His shoulders stooped, and his unkempt hair hung past his shoulders. His full beard was a tangle of dark knots. At one time he tried another line of work but quit after a year and a half, saying he was "no better off than I was prospecting and not half so well satisfied." He held fast to a passionate faith that someday he would strike it rich.

When Ed Schieffelin heard about the gold and silver strikes in the Arizona territory, he set off once more in search of the illusive rainbow's end. His quest for a big strike led him to the San Pedro Valley, a hostile land virtually uninhabited by white men. His keen prospector's eye, based on years of experience, led him to a geologic upheaval in the area north of the Mule Mountains. These upheavals often brought rich minerals near the surface. The dominant rock protruding up through a thin layer of limestone was porphyry, a formation where large bodies of ore are known to occur. Schieffelin's instincts told him this drab, greyish mantle of limestone was hiding one of the West's greatest treasures.

Schieffelin spent the summer of 1877 scouring the hills, gathering ore specimens and staking two claims, which he called the Tombstone and the Graveyard. When supplies ran low, he headed west to Tucson. The people around Tucson had come to look on the shaggy prospector as eccentric; therefore, nobody would grubstake him, although his ore sample looked promising.

Undaunted, he took his specimens and headed for Globe, where his brother Al was working as a hardrock miner. At Globe, he learned Al had moved on to McCracken, near the Colorado River, 250 miles west. Schieffelin took his last thirty cents and bought a plug of tobacco—his only vice, for he neither drank, smoked, nor swore—and set out on foot for McCracken. Brother Al wasn't impressed with his brother's ore samples either—he suggested Ed throw away his rocks and take a regular job in the mines.

Fortunately for Ed, fate was there to lend a hand. Also living in McCracken was an assayer of some reknown named Richard Gird. Gird assayed some of the specimens at $2,000 to the ton, and that night a three-way partnership was formed. Although Al was still unenthused, he was persuaded to go along. Gird's reputation was such that the threesome had to sneak out of camp, for Gird's absence would have alerted others that something was up. The three men went east to Wickenburg, then southeast to the settlement at Phoenix. They crossed the Salt River at Hayden's Ferry and then went south to Tucson. They remained at the old pueblo only long enough to re-equip for the trek to the San Pedro Valley. At the Pantano stage station, they saw bullet scars on the adobe walls, evidence of a recent Apache attack. A few miles further they came upon the shallow graves of two unlucky travelers, victims of Victorio's Chiricahua warriors. Undaunted, they turned south at the tiny Mormon hamlet of St. David and followed the San Pedro River twenty miles upstream to the Narrows. Nearby on a hilltop was an old abandoned cabin. The adobe structure had been used twenty years earlier by Frederic Brunchow, another prospector. Here, the resourceful Gird built an assaying furnace out of the fireplace.

Unfortunately, Ed's ore specimens had come from a rich, but shallow pocket that soon played out. It looked for a time that the Graveyard claim was well-named, for they had nearly "buried their hopes," Schieffelin later wrote.

They spent the next few days prospecting with little luck. Al was getting impatient, but his older brother persisted, so they agreed to give it another few days. Several days later Ed uncovered a ledge of ore-bearing granite that assayed out at $15,000 to the ton of silver and $1,500 to the ton of gold. Richard Gird's face broke into a wide grin as he exclaimed, "Ed, you are a lucky cuss. You have hit it," and that's how this fabulous lode came to be called the Lucky Cuss.

Ed began tracking another outcropping through some tricky faulting. This one was named appropriately enough the Tough Nut. Soon after, he staked out another winner, the Grand Central.

In the meantime, other prospectors were in the area staking claims. Hank Williams, struck a deal with Gird whereby he would split everything fifty-fifty if Gird would do his assaying free. When Williams struck paydirt, he conveniently forgot to include Gird's name on the claim. The two Schieffelins and Gird confronted Williams and joggled his memory, but physical violence was averted when Williams agreed to keep his end of the bargain. They named this strike the Contention in honor of the confrontation. The Contention turned out to be one of the richest mines in the whole Tombstone area.

The major producing lodes were the Grand Central, Contention, and Lucky Cuss; however, the Schieffelins and Gird would not have been able to develop their mines without the financial backing of ex-governor A. P. K. Safford and Tucson businessman John Vosburg, along with the Corbin brothers of Connecticut. The Tough Nut and its related properties became the Tombstone Mine and Milling Company, and the Lucky Cuss and its related properties became the Corbin Mill and Mining Company.

Schieffelin sold the Contention for $10,000 in 1880. Three years later the mine produced five million dollars. Soon after, he sold all his interests in the Tombstone area. People no longer snickered when Ed Schieffelin walked down the street, and his words were no longer subject to ridicule but were quoted as prophetic. From Wall Street to San Francisco, everyone had heard of the man who had made the biggest silver strike in Arizona history. Through it all he remained genial, generous, honest, and as reliable as a railroader's timepiece. He married, settled down, and bought a mansion in San Francisco.

He could have lived out his life in comfort and luxury as befitting a man who was a legend in his own lifetime, but the lure of the wilderness beckoned. He missed the smell of sizzling bacon, of boiling coffee, and of an open campfire. Most of all he missed the quest for buried treasure. He never passed up an opportunity to don his red flannel shirt, floppy hat, and corduroy trousers tucked into hob-nailed boots and to go off in search of the mother lode. Schieffelin died in the wilds of Oregon on May 12, 1897. His last written words tell us much about the man. "I am getting restless here in Oregon and wish to go some-

The Ed Schieffelin Monument, Tombstone, Dragoon Mountains in background Courtesy Southwest Studies

Tombstone in the 1880s Courtesy Southwest Studies

where that has wealth for the digging of it. I like the excitement of being right up against the earth, trying to coax her gold away and scatter it."

There is a narrow dirt road meandering past the old cemetery at the west end of Tombstone. About two and a half miles from town, on a gentle rock-strewn slope, stands a lofty monument marking the final resting place of the discoverer of the Tombstone treasure. Ed Schieffelin's final wishes were that he be dressed in prospector's clothing, pick and canteen included, and taken to Tombstone for burial. His burial site was at a spot where he had camped for two nights just prior to his fabulous silver strike.

During the 1880s Tombstone was the West's most notorious boomtown. Although Hollywood has portrayed it exclusively as a frontier Sodom and Gomorrah that claimed a "man before breakfast" each day, Tombstone, larger than San Francisco, had a relatively nonviolent history. Like most mining towns, the wealthy citizens imported the best culture and entertainment money could buy. Everyone pitched in to build churches and schools, and miners labored ten hours a day in the mines and raised families. However, like all boomtowns, Tombstone had its share of growing pains. The vast riches uncovered by the Schieffelins and others attracted representatives of a wide gamut of frontier society, including gamblers, lawyers, ladies of easy virtue, merchants, real estate dealers, stock swindlers, and con artists.

Most intermingled on Allen Street, the main thoroughfare, named for John B. Allen, one of Arizona's earliest Anglo settlers. Allen was already living in Arizona when Mexican troops evacuated in 1856 following the Gadsden Purchase. He had nearly gone broke panning for gold at Gila City before going into the pie business. "Pie" Allen, as he became known, baked tasty, dried apple pies and sold them to the soldiers and miners at a dollar each. Taking his earnings, he moved to Tombstone, where he became one of the town's first merchants.

Allen Street had two sides. On the south side were merchandise stores, cafes, and other similar enterprises, while the north side was a Barbary Coast, Old West style. The bars and casinos, with their faro tables and spinning roulette wheels, boisterous laughter, and rinky-tink pianos, went non-stop twenty-four hours a day. No self-respecting lady would have been caught dead strolling down the boardwalk on the north side lest she be mistaken for such boomtown belles as Dutch Annie, Crazy Horse Lil, Lizzette the Flying Nymph, or Little Gertie the Gold Dollar. The crib houses and fancy brothels were located in the vicinity of 6th Street and Allen. Two blocks west, at 4th Street between Allen and Tough Nut, were lawyers' offices, conveniently situated only two blocks from the courthouse and less from local watering holes, the area known as Rotten Row.

The original settlement had been at Watervale, about two miles west of Tombstone, but in mid-1879 a townsite was established on Goose Flats and called Tombstone. The earliest settlers set up house-keeping in canvas tents, brush wickiups, and flat board shanties, if they could get the lumber. By 1880 the town boasted telegraph service and gas lighting.

At the corner of Safford and 3rd streets stands St. Pauls Episcopal Church, the oldest Protestant church in Arizona, built in 1882 mostly through the efforts of a big, strapping, charismatic preacher, named Endicott Peabody. During his brief six-month stay in Tombstone, Peabody became one of its most unforgettable characters. A fine athlete, he starred in baseball and as a pugilist—he could hold his own in the boxing ring with the toughest of miners. His congregation included some of the wayward men and women of Allen Street, who always contributed generously to his many fund-raising activities.

Another of Tombstone's unforgettable characters was Nellie Cashman. Nellie was an incurable argonaut if there ever was one. With her sister, she immigrated to San Francisco from Ireland during the California gold rush. Nellie never did get the gold fever out of her system, her goldseeking ventures taking her from Mexico to the Arctic Circle. An attractive woman, there's no record of the number of marriage proposals she turned down; Nellie was too adventuresome to be tied down. During the time she spent in Tombstone, Nellie ran the Russ House on Tough Nut and 5th streets. Most of her boarders were hardrock miners.

*Nellie Cashman,
"Angel of the Mining
Camp"*
Courtesy
Southwest Studies

Kind hearted and generous almost to a fault, she never refused to help someone down on his luck. When Red Sample, Dan Dowd, Bill Delaney, Tex Howard, and Dan Kelley were about to be legally hanged at the county courthouse for their part in the infamous "Bisbee Massacre," an enterprising but ghoulish carpenter decided to build a grandstand overlooking the walls and to charge admission. The condemned men called upon Nellie to prevent their execution from becoming a public spectacle. She obliged by rounding up a few friends and destroying the structure the night before the hanging.

Two major fires destroyed the business district of Tombstone. The first occurred on June 22, 1881 when a bartender tried to measure the contents of a whiskey barrel with a cigar in his mouth. The resulting explosion engulfed the saloon in flames, and within minutes more than sixty stores, saloons, restaurants, and businesses were destroyed. The industrious citizens went to work immediately to rebuild the town, and within two weeks business was booming again.

The second major fire came less than a year later, on May 26, 1882. Once again a saloon was the culprit. The fire started in the Tivoli Saloon and quickly spread, once again destroying the business district and this time doing an estimated half-million dollars in damage.

City fathers wisely decided to rebuild with brick and adobe, since the lack of an adequate water supply made firefighting futile despite the herculean efforts of volunteer firemen. Eventually the Huachuca

Water Company was organized, and a seven-inch iron pipeline was laid in from the Huachuca Mountains, twenty-one miles to the southwest.

Most of Tombstone's notoriety stemmed from the "Gunfight at the OK Corral," so-called by Hollywood, although the shootout actually took place near the corner of Fremont and 3rd streets. The gunfight grew out of a long and bitter struggle for power in Cochise County among the Earp brothers, who were enforcers for the Citizens' Safety Committee, supported by Mayor John Clum and leading businessmen; sheriff Johnny Behan, who was the leader of the Democratic Party machine; and the Clanton gang, who rustled cattle under the guise of honest ranchers. Johnny Behan sided with this gang because he had never forgiven Wyatt Earp for stealing the affections of his friend Josephine Sarah Marcus, an attractive San Franciscan who fell in love with the charismatic Wyatt Earp at first sight and remained with him until his death in 1929.

When the shooting started, Ike Clanton, the instigator, turned tail and ran. Two other cocky gunslingers, Billy Claiborne and Wes Fuller, ducked out, leaving young Billy Clanton and Tom and Frank McLaury to face the three Earps and Doc Holliday. All hell broke loose for a few moments, and when the smoke had cleared, all three "cowboys" lay dead. Two of the Earps, Virgil and Morgan, were down with wounds, and Doc had been creased. The "cowboys," severely whipped in a stand-up gunfight, turned to ambush tactics. On December 14, an unknown assailant fired at Mayor John Clum. Two weeks later Virgil Earp took a full load of buckshot that left him crippled for life.

The final blow against the Earps occurred on March 18, 1882 when Morgan Earp was shot to death in a pool hall on Allen Street. Witnesses pointed the finger at Frank Stilwell, Curly Bill, Pete Spence, and Florentino Cruz, but all were able to produce alibis and were released by Sheriff Behan. Wyatt knew he could expect no help from Sheriff Behan and his friends, so he went on a personal vendetta outside the law. Within a week he had gunned down Stilwell, Cruz, and the outlaw leader, Curly Bill Brocius.

The turmoil in Cochise County was such that United States President Chester A. Arthur was threatening to proclaim martial law. Wyatt's life was in danger as long as he remained in Arizona, so he left for Colorado. It has been said Wyatt never returned to Cochise County. Others believe he returned in July and stayed long enough to gun down another old nemesis, Johnny Ringo. Ringo's body was found in Turkey Creek, but the crime was never solved.

Outlawry and cattle rustling didn't end with the closing of the

Cochise County War, but the outlaw leadership was gone and some of the underlings had headed for Mexico.

In 1887 a no-nonsense rancher named John Slaughter became sheriff. He issued a terse edict—rustlers get out or get killed. Slaughter, an ex-Texas Ranger, was a man of action and few words. Those who didn't heed his advice contributed to the population increase in the Boot Hills of Cochise County.

By 1901 rustling had increased again, so a new force, the Arizona Rangers, was organized. The rangers could cross county lines in pursuit of outlaws, and a few bold ones even crossed the international boundary to get their man. The rawhide-tough, hardriding rangers were effective against rustling until their demise in 1909.

Tombstone was typical of many boomtowns in that it attracted numerous colorful characters. One of the most colorful was Doctor George Goodfellow, the famous "gunshot physician." Doc Goodfellow opened an office over the Crystal Palace Saloon in the early 1880s, and he quickly established a reputation as an expert in the treatment of gunshot wounds, publishing articles on the subject. Whether it was commandeering and driving a steam locomotive to rush a gunshot victim to a hospital in Tucson, riding horseback to some remote mountain hideaway to treat a cattle rustler suffering from lead poisoning, or crawling into a smoke-filled mine shaft to rescue hard-rock miners, Doc Goodfellow was always the man of the hour.

During the great earthquake in northern Sonora in 1887 Goodfellow was one of the first outsiders in the stricken area and was given a special medal by Mexican President Porfirio Diaz. But perhaps his greatest notoriety came in connection with a case involving outlaws who, after they had robbed the Goldwater Store in Bisbee, murdered five citizens. Four men were captured and subsequently hung legally for their sins. An accomplice named John Heith was given only a prison sentence for his part. This so outraged the local citizens that they took Heith from jail and administered the Old West's rendition of a suspended sentence. Ironically, considering Tombsone's reputation as a rough-and-ready town, that was the only lynching in the town's raucous history.

Even though Heith probably deserved his punishment, lynching was illegal and charges were pressed against the vigilantes, pending a report by the county coroner—none other than Doc George Goodfellow. A lot of Doc's friends were members of the vigilance committee; it was even said he had been there himself. He resolved the difficult issue with all the aplomb of a frontier Solomon by ruling that John Heith came to his end by emphysema, or shortage of breath at high altitude.

Silver-rich Tombstone could afford the finest that money could buy. An endless array of acting troupes and other performers played in theaters like the Bird Cage and Schieffelin Hall. The Bird Cage, which according to legend was the inspiration for the old-time ditty "She Was Only a Bird in a Gilded Cage," offered a variety of entertainment ranging from vaudeville to prostitution. Built in 1881 for only $600, it was a saloon, brothel, burlesque theater, and dance hall all rolled into one, and it was an immediate success, attracting a wide gamut of Tombstone society. Comedian Eddie Foy appeared there in the '80s and later described the narrow, oblong adobe building as more like playing in a coffin than a theater.

One of the Bird Cage's most memorable shows occurred in 1882 when a troupe performing "Uncle Tom's Cabin" came to town. During the dramatic scene where little Eliza is being pursued across an icy river by vicious bloodhounds an unsophisticated cowboy in the audience stood up, drew his revolver, and shot one of the dogs. Bystanders pounced on the puncher and hauled him off to jail. The next day the repentent young man apologized and offered his horse and bankroll as compensation.

Schieffelin Hall, built in 1881 by Al Schieffelin in honor of his brother Ed, was Tombstone's most impressive legitimate theater. It was the tallest adobe building in the United States and during its heyday the civic, social, and cultural center of the town.

Miners following rich veins of silver drilled a labyrinth of passages beneath the town itself. It is said a million dollars worth of silver was taken out in the 1880s earning the town the name "Million Dollar Stope." On Tough Nut and 5th streets, a great gaping hole was created in 1907 when a stope collapsed, forming what is known in mining lingo as a glory hole. The cave-in engulfed a horse and delivery wagon. The wagon was a wreck, but the horse walked out two miles through a tunnel to the other side of town.

Almost from the beginning, Tombstone's days were numbered. Some said Ed Schieffelin bailed out too soon. Perhaps he did, but not by much. At the 500 foot level they hit water. The companies installed pumps to lift the water out, but in 1886 fires destroyed the pumps at the Contention and Grand Central, flooding the mines. By 1890 the town was nearly dead. The Panic of 1893 and the demonitization of silver were other blows.

In 1901 the Tombstone Consolidated Mines Company secured title to most of the properties, and new pumps were installed. That same year, the El Paso and Southwestern Railroad ran a spur line in from Fairbank. For a time it looked like Tombstone would prosper once more. In 1909 the pumps failed again, and two years later Tombstone

Consolidated was bankrupt.

Tombstone, "the town too tough to die," was barely hanging on, the final humiliation coming in 1929 when Bisbee took the county seat away. Today, at the corner of Tough Nut and 3rd streets, stands one of the most classic looking buildings in Arizona, the old Tombstone County Court House. Built in 1882, this venerable red-brick structure looks much the same as it did the day it was dedicated. It is now in the capable hands of the State Park Commission and will remain the best reservoir of Tombstone's rich and illustrious past. It holds the distinction of being the smallest state park in Arizona.

Diamond A Outfit, Cochise County. A few punchers from the Diamond A ham it up for the cameraman. They bear little resemblance to the Hollywood version. Courtesy Southwest Studies

Bisbee, looking west up Tombstone Canyon
Courtesy Arizona
Historical Foundation

US 80
to Bisbee

Bisbee

Those brawny mountains east of US 80 aren't as awesome as the Huachucas, across the San Pedro Valley on the west, or the Chiricahuas, forty miles to the east. They're only about thirty miles long and half that distance wide, reaching a height of 7,400 feet. The rough-hewn range with its twisting rocky canyons was a favorite sanctuary for the Apaches during the nineteenth century. At the southern end, a trail led through a pass and out into the San Pedro River valley. In this steep-sided canyon were seeps and springs where men and animals could be watered. The Mexicans called the place *Puerto de las Mulas* (Mule Pass), and that's how the Mule Mountains acquired their name.

Beneath those granite mountains was a wealth of gold, silver, and copper that defied the wildest imagination of even the most incurable prospector. But the mountains guarded their secrets well, and it was late in the nineteenth century before a government scout named Jack Dunn stumbled across some rich outcroppings in the spring of 1877. Dunn, an Irishman, was a civilian scout with Company C, Sixth Cavalry, under the command of Lieutenant John A. Rucker. Company C was chasing hostile Apaches and had stopped to camp in Mule Pass. Dunn went off in search of water, and, in the vicinity of today's Castle Rock, found rich outcroppings of ore. He collected some specimens, showing them to Lieutenant Rucker and T. D. Byrne, another member of the scouting expedition. They agreed to go partners and file a claim, but the demands of the Apache campaigns kept them on the trail for the next several months. Meanwhile, at Fort Bowie, Dunn made the acquaintance of George Warren, a forty-two-year-old prospector of dubious integrity. Dunn and his partners grubstaked

Warren, the latter agreeing to file claims on their behalf. On his way to the Mule Mountains, Warren got sidetracked in a saloon and lost his grubstake. When the drunken prospector revealed his mission, he was quickly re-equipped but with new partners. Eventually Warren filed several claims in Mule Pass, but Dunn, Rucker, and Byrne were not included.

Dr. James Douglas, mining engineer, pioneered many mining techniques. The town of Douglas is named for him.
Courtesy Arizona
State Library

George Warren was a hard worker but that was the only virtue he seems to have possessed. He'd led a rough life: his mother had died when he was an infant, his father had been killed by raiding Apaches, and young George had been captured by the same band. Later he was sold back to some miners for twenty pounds of sugar. The youth grew up among the rough-and-tumble miners and became something of a reprobate himself. By the time Warren met Jack Dunn, "ole John Barleycorn" had gained control.

Two years after the discovery of rich ore in Mule Pass, a drunken George Warren wagered, on a footrace, his share of what was to become the legendary Copper Queen Mine. Warren firmly believed

he could outrun a man on horseback, but lost the race and with it millions of dollars, dying in poverty, alone and forgotten. Years later he was reburied with a headstone honoring him as "Father of the Camp." A more lasting memorial is the nearby town of Warren, named in his honor. The miner pictured on the Arizona State Seal bears a striking resemblance to an old photograph of Warren.

The reputation of Warren's mining camp, nestled in what was being called Tombstone Canyon, quickly spread to the far reaches of the mining West. A smelter was erected in 1880, and the place changed from a hand-to-mouth existence to steady income. Earlier, the ore had to be freighted by wagon over to the railroad at Fairbank on the San Pedro River and then shipped by rail to Pennsylvania for smelting.

The Copper Queen ran day and night, mining an endless supply of rich ore. In early 1881 famed metalurgist and geologist Dr. James Douglas, paid a visit to the boom camp. The forty-four-year-old Douglas, a brilliant visionary, had been commissioned by some eastern speculators to examine mining properties around Jerome. While in Arizona, he decided to check out the place that would become known as Bisbee.

Dr. Douglas was so impressed with the area he convinced a New York-based import-export company named Phelps-Dodge to go into the mining business. They purchased 51% of the Copper Queen Mine and, on Douglas's strong recommendation, several adjacent properties. Dr. Douglas was given a choice of taking a commission in cash or a piece of the action. He wisely chose the latter, acting as consultant to Phelps-Dodge until 1885 when he was named president of Copper Queen Consolidated, a position he held until 1908. When Douglas died in 1918 he left behind a fortune valued at more than 20 million dollars. Dr. Douglas, a man of rare qualities and varied interests, was trusted and respected by mine workers and investors alike for his honesty, integrity, and loyalty.

In 1889 the long-awaited railroad arrived in Bisbee, ending the mule-driven hauls to Fairbank. When the Arizona and South Eastern's Engine #1 came chugging up the final stretch from Fairbank on its first run, the whole town turned out to give a rousing welcome.

Later, the Southern Pacific acquired the spur line in an exchange with the Santa Fe Railroad. When the Southern Pacific jacked up the freight rates, Dr. Douglas declared war and built a new railroad line. The resourceful president of Copper Queen Consolidated, anxious to get out from under the thumb of the Southern Pacific, succeeded in building a new and more direct line east to El Paso. Dr. Douglas renamed his railroad the El Paso and Southwestern and built a spur line joining the Santa Fe at Deming, New Mexico. In 1924 Phelps-Dodge sold the line to the Southern Pacific. Old Engine #1 escaped the scrap pile and was given an honorary resting place near the Southern Pacific headquarters in El Paso.

Soon after the prospector's pick struck paydirt, a town sprang up nearby, called Bisbee after Judge DeWitt Bisbee of San Francisco, a financial backer of the Copper Queen. Despite the fact that Bisbee eventually became known as the most cultured and gracious city between San Francisco and New Orleans, Judge Bisbee never visited it.

Bisbee was rough around the edges in those pristine 1880s. The woodframed homes were perched precariously on the steep, terraced hillsides—it was said you couldn't spit tobacco juice off your front porch without hitting your neighbor on the level below; and small children had to be tethered to fence posts lest they fall onto a neighbor's roof.

Bisbee was a two-canyon city, the main thoroughfare being Tombstone Canyon, later called Main Street, and a confluent canyon, called Brewery Gulch, coming in from the north. Tombstone Canyon became the central business district, and Brewery Gulch became notorious for its saloons and shady ladies, catering to a more raucous crowd. Old-timers used to say that the farther up Brewery Gulch one went, the rougher were the saloons and the wilder the women.

Brewery Gulch got its name when General George Crook's legendary scout, Al Sieber, dug a hole in one side of the gulch and opened a brewery, embellishing the front with a bar later called Brewery

Gulch. The "Gulch" went down in Western history as one of America's rowdiest avenues of pleasures.

However, action began to slow down along Brewery Gulch in 1910 when prostitution was outlawed. Five years later, Prohibition became law, and anyone with some wild oats to sow had to go across the Mexican border at Naco.

Bisbee, like all mining towns, had its share of violence. The worst occurred during the Christmas season of 1883 when five men held up the Goldwater-Casteneda Store on Main Street. During the robbery, the men stationed outside the store opened fire, killing five people, including a pregnant woman. The five outlaws— Red Sample, Bill Delaney, Tex Howard, Dan Dowd, and Dan Kelley—jumped on their horses and rode swiftly down Tombstone Canyon and off into the night. They were all captured after a lengthy manhunt and sentenced to hang. A sixth man, John Heith, was later implicated in the heist. Heith owned a dance hall in Bisbee, where he was arrested and charged with planning the robbery. Since Heith didn't want a murder rap hanging over his head, he demanded and received a separate trial. The jury found him guilty of robbery, not murder, and sentenced him to the Yuma Territorial Prison. So outraged were the residents that they broke into the Cochise County jail at Tombstone, took Heith out, and strung him up to a telegraph pole on Tough Nut Street. A few weeks later, the rest of the gang were legally hanged, the largest mass hanging in Arizona history. Surprisingly, the illegal hanging of John Heith was the only lynching in Tombstone's turbulent history.

In 1901 investors from Calumet, Michigan, formed the Calumet and Arizona Mining Company, hitting an immense body of high grade ore, which became one of the richest mines in the world, paying out 47 million dollars in dividends. Bisbee's major mines were the Calumet and Arizona and Phelps-Dodge—they thrived in friendly competition until the Great Depression, when Phelps-Dodge bought out the Calumet and Arizona, which had fallen on hard times.

By 1975 the Bisbee area, one of the richest mineral sites the world has ever known, had produced a staggering wealth of 6.1 billion dollars, from nearly 3 million ounces of gold, over 97 million ounces of silver, over 8 billion pounds of copper, 304 million pounds of lead, and nearly 273 pounds of zinc.

Not all of those early-day entrepreneurs went away with their pockets full. Hugh Jones, Joe Halcro, and Hank McCoy located a claim they called the Halcro Mine, hoping for a rich silver bonanza but finding instead "copper stains." Discouraged, they mounted their mules and rode away. The next developer came along and renamed the mine the Copper Queen, and the rest is history. During the peak years of the Copper Queen, 10,000 people occupied the 640 acres of livable hillside land nearby, and the greater Bisbee area once supported a population of 20,000 people. Actually it was officially called the Warren Mining District and included Bisbee, Warren, Lowell, San José, and a humble Mexican community called Tintown. Amazingly, the ore-bearing land lay in an area two by three miles on the surface and ran to a depth of 4,000 feet.

During World War I, the development of new techniques for reducing low-grade ore at a profit and the advent of large trucks and earthmoving equipment made open pit mining a reality. Mountains were turned into terraced canyons. Sacramento Hill, just east of Buckey O'Neill Hill and southeast of Bisbee was a classic example. The destruction of the cone-shaped mountain began in 1917 when tons of explosives literally blew its top off.

A new operation was begun in the mid-1950s that overwhelmed the

The Copper Queen Hotel in Bisbee, circa 1900
Courtesy Arizona Historical Foundation

Sacramento Pit. Called the Lavender Pit in honor of Harrison Lavender, Manager of the Copper Queen Branch of Phelps-Dodge, the huge pit reached a depth of more than 900 feet before it shut down in 1974.

The most traumatic twentieth century event to take place in Bisbee and, perhaps all Arizona, was the infamous Bisbee Deportation of 1917. For years a bitter power struggle ensued between the unions and the copper companies. The price of copper and company profits skyrocketed with the advent of World War I; because it was wartime, the allies desperately needed copper. The unions felt the time was ripe for a strike, and rumblings were felt in mining towns throughout the state. One union, the Industrial Workers of the World (I. W. W.s or "Wobblies") was more vocal than the rest, quickly gaining a reputation as a troublemaker. The copper companies, especially Phelps-Dodge, waged a clever propaganda war against the union. Since Phelps-Dodge controlled several newspapers, not to mention a number of legislators, it wasn't hard to arouse the general public's ire against any group that preached strike during these critical times.

The climax came on July 12, 1917 at 6:30 A.M. when 2,000 armed men with white handkerchiefs tied around their arms took to the streets of the Warren Mining District and rounded up more than 2,000 suspected I. W. W. members and sympathizers. They were herded to the baseball park at Warren, and by the day's end nearly 1,200 had been loaded into boxcars and shipped to Columbus, New Mexico. By some miracle only two men died that day—one a suspected I. W. W., the other a vigilante.

Like so many Arizona mining towns, Bisbee exudes a rich turn-of-the-century history. The Copper Queen Hotel, built in 1902, was as opulent as any big city hostelry. Celebrants spending the night and dining in its elegant restaurant included President Teddy Roosevelt and General John "Blackjack" Pershing. One early-day couple was skeptical of the four-story hillside hotel. The gentleman came back to

Bisbee in 1908
Courtesy
Southwest Studies

the desk after inspecting his room on the third floor. "I can't keep that room," he asserted; "my wife's nervous and afraid of fire." The inn-keeper, without any change of expression, replied, "Oh, my friend, if fire breaks out, just raise your window and step out onto the hillside."

Entering picturesque, mile-high Bisbee from the west end, through Mule Pass, is something like entering a mythical Shangri-la. The highway enters Mule Pass Tunnel, the longest highway tunnel in the state, and after a brief period of darkness, as if by magic appears a turn-of-the-century community. The old buildings and landmarks include the elaborate Phelps-Dodge general offices, now the Bisbee Mining Museum; the Copper Queen Hotel; Mulheim's Brewery; the Pythian Castle, with its magnificent green dome; Castle Rock, a natural landmark; and a host of other tourist attractions.

The entrance to the old Copper Queen Mine is on the north side of Buckey O'Neill Hill. The original excavations at Bisbee lie just up this slope at what is called the "Glory Hole." Here, a monument marks the spot where, in 1877, Jack Dunn picked up a few rich ore specimens to show to his friends. Open pit mining ended in 1974, and underground operations shut down a year later.

Today's US 80 rolls across the slope of Buckey O'Neill Hill, and today it may be the only place in the world where visitors, under the guidance of ex-hardrock miners, can don hard hats and slickers and venture deep into what was once a working mine.

Bisbee as it looked in 1979.

74

Douglas in 1938. On the left is the Gadsden Hotel.
Courtesy Arizona State Library

US 80 to Douglas

Douglas

Leaving Bisbee, US 80 eases down the eastern slope of the Mule Mountains and out across Sulphur Springs Valley—"Sufferin' Springs Valley," the old timers like to call it. The land not under cultivation is high desert, the vegetation mostly chaparral and mesquite. The elevation is around 4,000 feet. Twenty-four miles across the flat, open plain lies the city of Douglas. One can see smoke billowing out of the tall chimneys of the Phelps-Dodge smelter long before spotting the town.

It was the smelter that led to the town's founding by Phelps-Dodge in 1901. It was named for Dr. James Douglas, a man whose scientific prowess had done much to advance mining techniques. Dr. Douglas's new El Paso and Southwestern railroad from Bisbee to El Paso passed through the new town, and ore from both Bisbee and Nacozari, Sonora, was shipped in for smelting. The company built a hospital and residences for employees at the smelter. Among the city fathers was John Slaughter, an ex-Texas Ranger and sheriff of Cochise County, who owned the San Bernardino ranch, seventeen miles east of the new town.

The site was originally called Black Water because the water was so rank one had to shut his eyes and hold his nose to drink it; however, water was so scarce no one complained too much. The city of Agua Prieta, on the Mexican side of the border, kept the old name of Agua Prieta, meaning black water.

The area around Douglas was, and still is, some of the most remote in Arizona, well off the beaten path of most travelers. In the 1880s and '90s it was mostly rangeland. Thousands of cattle grazed on the rich carpet of native grasses. The sprawling valley was the site of roundups in the spring and fall as ranchers gathered their cattle to mark, brand, and move to a shipping point on the railroad.

A famed Douglas landmark was, and still is, the fabulous Gadsden Hotel. The stately, five-story, 160-room structure was built in 1907, and no expense was spared in making the Gadsden the "best hotel in the West." The spacious lobby was highlighted by four towering marble columns, a winding marble staircase, an exquisite stained glass skylight, and a gold-leaf ceiling.

The Gadsden became the social, financial, and social center for cattle barons and mining magnates. It's been said that million-dollar deals were made there with nothing more than a handshake. Next to the lobby was the Saddle and Spur Saloon, where, for a fee, cattlemen could have their ranch brands painted on the walls.

A favorite gathering place for Douglas residents during the Mexican Revolution was the roof of the Gadsden, which provided a ringside view of General Francisco "Pancho" Villa's army battling the Federales at Agua Prieta. Occasionally a stray bullet sent the spectators scurrying for cover. Douglas residents piled bales of hay or sandbags around their homes to stop the bullets, not always successfully. One bullet shattered the window of a house, went through a birdcage, and knocked the tailfeathers off a parakeet.

The Gadsden caught fire and burned in 1927, and Douglas wasn't the same without it. The owner decided to rebuild an exact replica with one exception—steel and concrete were used in place of wood. At 1929 gold prices, the new gold-leaf ceiling cost $20,000. In 1929 the Gadsden, billed as "the last of the Grand Hotels," resumed its role as the key landmark of Douglas.

During the early 1900s Douglas gained a notorious reputation for lawlessness. When the Arizona Rangers were organized in 1901 orders were to headquarter where the most crimes were being committed. The following year they centered their operations in Douglas.

Tom Rynning, one of Teddy Roosevelt's ex-Rough Riders and a Captain of the Arizona Rangers, said of Douglas: "I've been in many a rough town in my day, but from Deadwood to Tombstone I've never met up with a harder formation than Douglas was when we made the Arizona Rangers' home corral there in 1902." The row of saloons on 6th and 10th streets was where most of the hard-core border ruffians gathered, the Cowboy's Home Saloon being one of the favorite watering holes.

In the early 1900s, cattle thieves had gained the upper hand again in Cochise County, and the ringleaders were the Taylor family. It was difficult to get a conviction, unless the rustlers had been caught in the act; otherwise, it wasn't hard to convince a jury that there had been an honest mistake. The Taylor cattle herd was growing too fast for natural gestation. Old timers used to say of such situations, "His cows always produce twins" or "His cows have a calf every wash day." Other ranchers knew the Taylors were stamping their brands on neighbors' cows, but nobody could catch them in the act.

Tom Rynning devised a clever scheme to trap the rustlers. He and one of his men roped thirteen young calves that had been recently weaned; then he took his pocketknife and slit open the gullet of each calf and inserted a Mexican silver coin, then sewing up the incision and turning the animals loose on the open range. Captain Rynning waited about six months and then went back to check Taylor's place. Sure enough, there were the thirteen calves, all wearing Taylor's brand. The rancher was arrested, and the calves were impounded in a stock pen in Douglas. At the trial, the jury was led out to the pen, where Rynning deftly reopened each incision and removed the coins.

"You got me this time, boys," muttered Taylor. The judge gave the rustler and his relatives just twenty-four hours to sell the ranch, lock, stock, and barrel and get out of the territory. Captain Rynning personally escorted them to the New Mexico line and pointed them eastward.

East of Douglas US 80 bends its way in a northeasterly direction around the southern end of the Chiricahua Mountains on its way to the New Mexico line. Seventeen miles due east of Douglas is the old San Bernardino land grant. There was a natural spring on the site that provided water dating back before the days of the Spanish missionaries. Father Kino had a *visita* at the springs in the early 1700s, and in 1773 Captain Juan Bautista de Anza located a military camp at the site while scouring the country for Apaches. Two years later, Captain Hugo O'Conor proposed a *presidio* at San Bernardino.

In 1821 Lieutenant Ignacio Peréz purchased four *sitios* (about twenty-seven sections) from the Mexican government for $90. He ran cattle in the area until 1830 when the Apaches in the area went on the warpath. Peréz and his *vaqueros* had to make a hasty retreat, and the cattle were left to run wild. Following the Gadsden Purchase in 1854 the new international boundary ran through the Peréz property, only about 2,400 of the 70,000 acres remaining on the American side. side.

In 1884 John Slaughter drove a large herd of longhorns from Texas into southeastern Arizona. Near Tularosa, New Mexico, the forty-year-old drover met a beautiful nineteen-year-old girl named Viola Howell. She was helping her father move a herd of cattle along the same trail. It was love at first sight, so the couple stopped at a small church and were married just two days later. Viola Howell was Slaughter's second wife. His first wife had died of smallpox, leaving him with two youngsters to raise. The second Mrs. Slaughter, a pretty, high-spirited brunette, was a remarkable woman. An expert horsewoman, she could work cattle with the best of men.

The Slaughters branded the San Bernardino cattle with a Z, one of the first brands registered in Cochise County, and went on to put together one of the largest ranches in Arizona history. Slaughter raised a small army of cowboys, who could handle a Winchester as well as a lariat, and went on the warpath against the rustlers in southeast Arizona. Before long the word was out among the rustling fraternity to stay away from cattle with the Z brand. So great was his success, Slaughter was persuaded by his neighbors to run for sheriff in 1886. He ran a quiet campaign and was easily elected. Slaughter, a short man with piercing, coal-black eyes, enforced the law in Cochise County as he interpreted it, using a 12-gauge shotgun to back his play. A quiet, unassuming man, he didn't care much for lawyers or trials by jury. He'd seen swaggering outlaws like Curly Bill hauled before a court in Tombstone—they hired eloquent lawyers to sway juries and loaded the courtroom with cronies to intimidate anyone who might testify against them. Most of the time Slaughter acted alone—as judge, jury, and executioner, but he didn't always execute the outlaws he captured. All he needed to say was, "Get out of Cochise County or I'll kill you!" Usually that was enough to get the desired results.

"He shot Tombstone full of law and order," one historian said admiringly.

After retiring from office in 1892 Slaughter remained an honorary deputy sheriff in the county until his death in 1922. John Slaughter was one of the true cattle kings of Arizona. His sprawling ranch extended deep into Mexico and he ran thousands of cattle on the high plains. Artesian wells were drilled on the ranch, and a concrete dam was built to create a lake. On the edge of the lake, he built a low, rambling adobe house. The self-sustaining San Bernardino ranch became a veritable feudal barony, complete with store, school, blacksmith shop, and post office.

Geronimo's Monument

US 80 moves in a northeasterly direction toward the New Mexico line. On the north are the Chiricahua Mountains. Reaching a maximum height of nearly 10,000 feet, these mountains are named for the Apache group that roamed these ranges for several hundred years. Independent of all authority except their own, they were the scourge of Mexico, Spain, and the United States before finally surrendering in 1886.

The Geronimo Monument is a sixteen-foot high pyramid located on US 80, thirty-nine miles northeast of Douglas. Dedicated in 1934, it commemorates the final Apache surrender, at Skeleton Canyon, ending twenty-five years of bitter warfare between the United States Army and the Chiricahua Apaches.

Overshadowed by other Apache headmen, Geronimo didn't emerge as a prominent leader until about 1881. In battle he was intelligent and resourceful, a dreaded enemy. During peace he was a troublemaker and a liar. Untrustworthy and despised by many of his own people, he was feared by settlers on both sides of the border. Humble Mexican peasants in Sonora perceived him as the personification of the Devil, up from Hell to punish them for their sins.

War first broke out between the Chiricahua Apaches and the Army in 1861 over an alleged kidnapping. Lieutenant George Bascom accused Cochise, a prominent Apache headman, of raiding a ranch near Fort Buchanan and of taking a child captive. Cochise denied the charge, and evidence later revealed the Apache was telling the truth. The incident is described elsewhere in this work and it suffices to say that a ten-year war ensued. In 1871 the war ended, and the Chiricahua Apaches were allowed to remain in their favorite stamping grounds, the Chiricahua Mountains. In 1874 Cochise died, leaving the group without a strong leader. The proximity of the Chiricahua Reservation to the Mexican border made it a favorite staging area for Apaches launching raids against their traditional foe, the Mexicans. In the mid-1870s the Federal government decided to consolidate the numerous Apache groups at the San Carlos and White Mountain agencies. This proved unwise as the tribes battled each other with as much zeal as they did the whites.

The restive Apaches, especially the Chiricahua, detested reservation life. Meager rations and boredom didn't suit a people regarded as the most independent and warlike of all the Southwestern tribes. Admittedly, conditions on the reservation were atrocious, but it's doubtful if even the most idyllic conditions would have kept the Chiricahua happy for long.

The discovery of rich minerals in the area and the dramatic increase of the white population also made the Apaches uneasy. The natives watched encroachments on their lands with growing apprehension. In addition, rumors that all Apaches would be moved to

General George Crook, the greatest "Indian fighting General" in the army. He was also one of the few to win the trust and respect of the Indians.
Courtesy Sharlot Hall Museum

Oklahoma had the Indians in such a querulous mood that it would take only a minor incident to spark the Chiricahuas into open revolt.

The spark that ignited the Geronimo Campaign came when the Agency chief of police tried to arrest a Chiricahua. The suspect ran, and the officer fired into a crowd of people, killing a woman. Apologies were given, but the Chiricahuas wanted justice their own way. They patiently waited for the right opportunity, then seized the police chief, decapitated, him, and played a game of soccer with his head.

Afterwards, seven hundred men, women, and children bolted the reservation and headed for Mexico's towering Sierra Madre Mountains. For centuries this wild range of snow-capped mountains with awesome rock-strewn canyons had been an impenetrable fortress. Very few who dared pursue the Apaches into their lair ever came out alive.

On September 4, 1882 General George Crook was recalled to Arizona. Crook had won the respect of both the Apaches and the whites during his 1871-72 campaign in Arizona's central mountains when in a matter of months of hard winter warfare he had subjugated the Yavapai and Tonto Apaches. The quiet, unpretentious officer was regarded by many as being more Indian than white. Unlike many of his genre, Crook sympathized with the Apaches but felt that the only way to save them from total extermination was to force them to give up their nomadic ways, to stop raiding, and to learn ranching and farming. Crook had the greatest respect for his formidable foe. "The adult Apache," he wrote, "is an embodiment of physical endurance—lean, well-proportioned, medium sized, with sinews like steel, insensible to hunger, fatigue, or physical pains."

One of Crook's favorite campaign tactics was to use Apache scouts to hunt down those designated as hostiles (ones who refused to accept reservation life). "Regular troops," he said, "are as helpless as a whale attacked by a school of swordfish . . . The only hope of success lies in using their own methods—Apache vs. Apache."

Crook's campaign of 1883 into the Sierra Madre was both clever and daring. After receiving permission from the Republic of Mexico to cross the border, Crook gathered his force at San Bernardino Springs. He took 193 Apache scouts and one troop of cavalry. Strapped to the backs of his sturdy pack mules were enough supplies and ammunition to last sixty days. The use of mule teams rather than less mobile wagons was a characteristic Crook stratagem.

The invasion of their "natural fortress" in the Sierra Madre dealt the Chiricahua a psychological defeat. When a large band was defeated and their *rancheria* burned, the Chiricahua called for a truce. Crook's terms were terse—return to the reservation at once. Grudgingly they agreed, and within a few months Geronimo and his people were back at San Carlos.

The uneasy truce at San Carlos lasted until the early part of 1885, when Geronimo, always the malcontent, led a disgruntled group to protest Crook's policy against wife-beating and alcohol. Because of some bureaucratic bungling, the General wasn't made aware of the protest, and the situation became tense. On May 17, 1885 Geronimo, with forty-two warriors and ninety-two women and children, bolted again. The army spent the rest of 1885 campaigning in the Sierra Madre against the elusive Chiricahua band.

When supplies ran low, the Apaches made daring raids into southern Arizona and New Mexico. One such raid by Josanie and a dozen warriors lasted a month, the band traveling over 1,200 miles and leaving thirty-eight dead settlers in their wake.

Crook's Mexican Campaign suffered a severe setback in early 1886 when Captain Emmett Crawford, one of his most valued officers, was

Apache scouts. Courtesy Southwest Studies.

killed. Crawford, leading a group of Apache scouts, had defeated Geronimo's band. During the peace talks that followed, a group of Mexican militia arrived and fired on the parley. Crawford climbed on a rock pedestal to show his blue United States uniform and was shot through the head. Also wounded in the gunfire was scout Tom Horn. Further tragedy was averted by the quick action of Horn and Lieutenant Marion Maus, who rallied the troops to action. In the face of a strong show of arms and will, the Mexicans backed down, and the parley was resumed.

A meeting with Crook at San Bernardino was arranged in "two moons." Two months later, on March 25, 1886 at Canyon de los Embudos, about twelve miles south of the border, Crook and Geromino had their historic meeting. Famous Tombstone photographer C. S. Fly was present, recording on film for the first time, hostile Indians still on the warpath. Earlier, officials in Washington had given the general authority to set terms for surrender—a key point in the months to follow. Crook's terms were as follows: two years confinement with their families in Florida before being allowed to return to the reservation. Crook sat patiently while Geronimo and the other headmen gave orations on past transgressions. Finally, the wily warriors agreed to terms, and Crook headed back to his headquarters at Fort Bowie to wire the news to Washington.

In the meantime, a whiskey drummer visited Geronimo's camp. After getting the war chief well oiled, the peddler informed Geronimo that the soldiers planned to kill him. The next morning Geronimo and a few of his party were missing. When word reached Washington that Geronimo had bolted once more, General Crook was removed and General Nelson Miles named to replace him.

General Miles had proved to be a successful Indian fighter, but in personality, he made a startling contrast to Crook. Vain and politically ambitious, Miles was keenly aware of what the capture of Geronimo could do for his career.

Essentially, his tactics differed little from Crook's. Crook had been accused of relying too much on his Apache scouts. Miles still used the scouts but gave major credit to his white troops. Miles firmly believed white troops could locate and defeat the hostile bands in the Sierra Madre as well as the Apache scouts, but he was proved wrong. A much more effective tactic was the removal of the Chiricahua from Arizona. On August 29, 1886, the last of the peaceful Chiricahua were rounded up, marched to Holbrook, loaded on trains, and shipped to Florida.

At about the same time, Lieutenant Charles B. Gatewood, a Crook protegé and the only officer on Miles's staff that was known and trusted by Geronimo, was sent to Mexico for another parley. Accom-

Noted Tombstone photographer C.S. Fly took this picture of Geronimo at the time of his surrender in September, 1886.

panying Gatewood was Tom Horn and two Chiricahua scouts, Martine and Kayitah. In a field of canebreaks near Bavispe, Gatewood met with Geronimo and stated the terms—two years in Florida before a return to the reservation. Geronimo stubbornly refused to accept. Then Gatewood pulled his ace card—the Apache families had already been shipped to Florida. This news broke the stalemate, since the Apaches traditionally had strong family ties. Geronimo insisted on surrendering to Miles personally, and he also demanded permission to retain his weapons and to keep Gatewood as a hostage until they were safely in General Miles's custody.

On September 4, 1886 Geronimo surrendered to General Miles at Skeleton Canyon, a few miles southeast of the Geronimo Monument. Five years earlier, the canyon had been the scene of a massacre of Mexican smugglers by Curley Bill Brocius and Old Man Clanton. The smugglers' bones were left to be picked clean by vultures, giving the place its macabre name.

Geronimo and his band were held at Fort Bowie for a few days, then loaded into wagons and hauled a few miles north to the railroad at Bowie Station. As the wagons were rumbling out the front gates of the post, the military band struck up "Auld Lang Syne."

The Geronimo Campaign had a bittersweet ending for the victors and the vanquished. Arizona was rid of the intractable Chiricahua Apaches, but the military pulled out soon after, causing severe economic loss. Some merchants would have preferred the wars to go on indefinitely as long as they weren't in harm's way. The loyal Chiricahua, including Gatewood's two scouts, Martine and Kayitah, were shipped east along with the prisoners. General Miles grabbed his share of the glory and eventually rose to the rank of Army Chief of Staff. Several of his loyal protegés, Captains Leonard Wood and Henry Lawton, were praised by their commander and rose in rank, each becoming a general. Conspicuously absent was the real hero, Lieutenant Charles Gatewood.

While the careers of the others blossomed, Gatewood was relegated to obscurity. Injured in an accident and his health broken by the arduous Sierra Madre campaigns, Gatewood was dropped by the army. He died without ever receiving the recognition he so richly deserved. General Crook died in 1890, his last years spent trying to get his government to honor the terms of Geronimo's surrender.

At the time of his surrender, Geronimo came close to being hanged in Arizona. A few vengeful Arizonans pressed President Grover Cleveland to turn the war chief over for trial in a civilian court. Believing Geronimo had surrendered unconditionally, the President agreed. The train carrying Geronimo was halted at San Antonio, and plans were made to return him to Arizona. General Miles acquiesced in the matter, and for a time it looked as though Geronimo would be hanged for murder. At this juncture, General Crook informed the President that Geronimo had surrendered with terms. General Miles was publicly embarassed, and an angry President ordered Geronimo's train on to Florida.

However, the terms of surrender were never honored. In Florida, the prisoners were kept separated from their families, and many died in the fierce tropical climate. Two years of confinement stretched into eight. Finally, despite Miles's objections, the Apaches were moved to a more suitable climate at Fort Sill, Oklahoma, in 1894. United States Senator James Fair suggested that the Apaches be given a permanent home on Catalina Island, off the coast of California, but his proposal never jelled. In 1913, less than two hundred were allowed to move to the Mescalero Reservation in New Mexico, the rest remaining in Oklahoma.

General Nelson Miles, the "man who captured Geronimo," bungled the war with Spain in 1898 so badly that his hopes for the Presidency were dashed forever. A nemesis named Teddy Roosevelt found military glory in that war and went on to occupy the Oval Office. Two giant egos had clashed, and Miles was unceremoniously retired during Roosevelt's administration.

US 80 leaves Arizona and heads into Rodeo, New Mexico; it then joins Interstate 10 thirty miles north. However, if one wants to see the back of the beautiful Chiricahua Mountains, about three miles north of Rodeo there is a road leading west to Portal. A few miles past Portal, the pavement ends. Nearby is the old mining town of Paradise, which gained its name when a pair of newlyweds moved into the isolated area. It remained a paradise until 1901 when a rich vein of silver was discovered and the place was overrun with rough-and-tumble miners. Up the road is another ghost town, Galeyville. The town was laid out in 1880, and two years later had four hundred residents. Some gold and silver were found nearby, but Galeyville, named for John Galey, owner of the Texas Mine and Smelter, is best known as the favorite hangout of the outlaw Curly Bill, who was "unofficial" town mayor during his brief heyday. From Galeyville, a dirt road crosses the Chiricahuas and comes out on the outskirts of the Chiricahua National Monument.

Main Street in Florence around 1900
Courtesy Arizona Historical Foundation

US 89
Tucson to Florence Junction

Oracle Junction

A fork in the road to Florence was known in the 1880s as Represso and was used as a *la posta*, or place to change horses on the road from Tucson to the mine at Mammoth. Curley Bill Neal, one of the most successful and enterprising blacks in territorial history, held the stock contract for the stage line. Neal and his wife owned the famous resort hotel, the Mountain View, at Oracle (see Oracle, Arizona 77).

Tom Mix Memorial

On an October day in 1940, cowboy movie idol Tom Mix crashed his Cord automobile in a shallow arroyo near Florence. Before Tom Mix became one of Hollywood's greatest movie stars, he was a horse wrangler and rodeo performer. His amazing stunts and horsemanship gave him an edge over others of the same genre and made him the most illustrious "shooting" star of the Roaring Twenties. During that decade Mix was earning $17,500 a week turning out B Westerns. His material was mechanical, gimmicky, and predictable, but his fans adored him. Equally popular was Tony, the "wonder horse." Mix,

The Tom Mix Memorial on US 89 between Tucson and Florence
Photo by Jeff Kida

like most real cowboys, had great respect for a good horse. Once, in 1923 a dynamite charge went off prematurely and almost blew Mix and Tony into the next county. While recuperating in a hospital from the near-fatal accident, Mix said he didn't mind risking his own neck to make a movie but he wouldn't take a chance with Tony. From that time on, he used a double named Buster for the dangerous stunts.

At one time or another, Mix was said to have been a Texas Ranger; a hero in the Spanish American War who charged up San Juan Hill with Roosevelt's Rough Riders; an adventurer who stormed the Great Wall of China and fought Boers in South Africa; a performer in Zack Miller's famous 101 Ranch Show; and, for a time, a rider with Pancho Villa. These bigger-than-life adventures were great stuff for his hero-worshipping fans, but the story has obviously been embellished by his publicity agent. As a matter of record, Mix had an unglamorous military career before deserting his post at Fort Hancock, New Jersey, in 1902. In 1910 he was arrested in Knoxville, Tennessee, for stealing a horse. These revelations tarnished Mix's reputation, but no one can deny that he loved horses, knew how to ride, and was a marvelous showman.

Florence

Florence was born on a piece of land laid claim to by Levi Ruggles, who came there as an Indian agent in 1866. In 1875, he transferred title over to the town, already established several years earlier. Florence took its name from one of his two daughters.

Florence is an important freighting and supply center for the mines located in the mountains to the northeast. The town is unique in that the business district is still located on Main Street and, with the exception of pavement and a few modern fixtures, the place hasn't changed much since 1880, when the population was about nine hundred.

Florence became the Pinal County seat in 1875, and the old courthouse, completed in 1891, is still in use. The venerable structure represents a classic piece of architecture not seen much in Arizona any more. The town's clock stands frozen at 9 o'clock; in fact, it never ran from the beginning, as the funds for a working clock were diverted to construct what citizens felt was more necessary—a jail.

Ernest W. McFarland State Park, on the north end of Main Street, honors one of Arizona's most distinguished politicians. McFarland, whose hometown was Florence, is the only Arizonan to have served in the U.S. Senate (in the early 1950s he was Senate Majority Leader); as governor of the State (1955-59); and a Chief Justice of the State Supreme Court.

Pinal County Courthouse in 1895. Built in 1890-1891 for $29,000, the American-Victorian style building is still in use today. The "clock" never moves past 9 o'clock.
Courtesy Arizona State Library

In its earlier days, Florence was a small agricultural area, but after the completion of the Ashurst-Hayden Diversion Dam in 1921 the town became known as the agricultural center of Pinal County. Seven years later, Coolidge Dam, on the Upper Gila, increased this reputation. Soon after Coolidge's construction, Lake San Carlos slowly formed behind the dam, taking over fifty years to reach capacity. American humorist, Will Rogers gazed out on the weed-grown area behind the dam in the early 1930s and remarked with a wry grin, "If that was my lake, I'd mow it."

Pauline Cushman, notorious Union spy during the Civil War, called Florence home for a spell. Captured by Confederates, she was supposed to hang, but her life was spared when the Southern troops, who had to make a hasty retreat, abandoned her. President Abraham Lincoln praised her as a bona fide American heroine for her service to the Union cause. Billed by her press agent as "Major Cushman," she sustained a good living on the lecture circuit. In 1879 she married Pinal County Sheriff Jere Fryer. Cushman later moved to San Francisco, where in 1893 she committed suicide.

Florence was the setting in 1888 of the famous "Six-gun Classic." Joe Phy and Pinal County Sheriff Pete Gabriel were personal and long-standing political enemies. One day Phy walked into a bar where Gabriel was having a glass of redeye and opened fire, hitting the sheriff twice. Before he hit the floor, Gabriel put three bullets into Phy, one of them a mortal wound in the stomach. Dr. William Harvey rushed to the scene and treated his friend Phy, who then died. The doctor refused to treat Gabriel, whom he disliked. Although one of the bullets just missed hitting Gabriel in the heart, he survived the shootout.

Jim Sam was the rarest of individuals—a Chinese gunfighter. his name and reputation became immortal the day a bunch of rowdies decided to have a furniture-breaking fracas in his restaurant. Up to then, everyone thought the timid Chinese was a pushover. Suddenly, all turned quiet as Jim Sam appeared in the doorway with a look of grim determination. In each hand was a six-shooter, and clenched between his teeth was the largest butcher knife the boys had ever seen. The bullies tumbled all over themselves trying to get out the door, and none dared start trouble in Jim Sam's place ever again.

Florence is best known today as the site of the State Prison, which was a political plum in the early 1900s when the town was chosen as the prison site. The old Territorial Prison at Yuma, first opened in 1876, was closed in 1909, and the prisoners were transferred to the new facility at Florence.

Just across the Gila River is a cone-shaped mountain known as

Poston's Butte. The "Father of Arizona," Charles Poston, spent many of his twilight years here. During his world travels he had become a worshipper of the sun. He'd planned to erect a temple to the sun on top of this butte but spent his last days living in poverty in Phoenix. The former entrepreneur and Arizona promoter died on June 24, 1902, and was buried in the capital city. Earlier, he'd requested he be buried on top of Poston's Butte, and in 1925 a group of citizens granted his last wish.

Back in 1885, the citizens of Florence petitioned the Territorial Assembly for a bridge across the erratic Gila River. The stream was usually dry, but on those occasions when water did materialize, it was impossible to cross. The legislators were sympathetic to the bridge plea and granted $1,200 for this purpose. Soon after the bridge's completion, however, the river changed its course, meandering around the structure and flowing merrily on its way to Yuma.

Crossing the Gila River at Florence Courtesy Arizona Historical Foundation

US 666
Cochise to Douglas
(turn off Interstate 10 at milepost 331)

Cochise (four miles south of Interstate 10)

The community of Cochise came into existence on August 28, 1886 when a post office was established. A few months later the Southern Pacific built a railroad station. The settlement was named for the noted Chiricahua leader. Around the turn of the century, Cochise was a thriving community. Hard times came with the Great Depression, and the railroad lines that extended from Cochise all the way to Douglas were finally abandoned in 1933. The most notable reminder of the early days is the historic adobe-walled Cochise hotel. This handsome hostelry is still renting rooms and serving meals.

During the heyday of the mining boomtowns of Pearce, Courtland, and Gleeson, in the Turquoise Mining District, Cochise was the shipping point for the Arizona Eastern Railroad. As late as the 1920s the Arizona Eastern line was running three trains a week to Courtland and Gleeson. There were so many trains running that one could board at Globe in the morning and reach Bisbee that evening. The journey involved making six changes and depended on each train arriving at the station in time to make connections with the next. The area was bustling with activity, perhaps with the exception of a brief time in Courtland when the Anti-Sunday Work Law Ordinance was in effect. Apparently the law was so popular among local residents that it was usually extended into the middle of the following week. Perhaps the most spectacular event to take place in Cochise was the Burt Alvord train robbery of 1899, mentioned elsewhere.

Main Street of
Pearce in 1912
Courtesy Arizona
Historical Foundation

The Ghost Town Trail

Pearce

Jimmy Pearce lived a prospector's dream one day in 1894 when he picked up some rich ore specimens. The young Cornishman had been a hardrock miner in Tombstone until he and his industrious wife saved enough money to buy a small cattle ranch in the Sulphur Springs Valley. One day, while moving some cattle, he stopped to rest on the side of a hill. Like any hardrock miner, he couldn't resist examining the rocks near where he sat despite the fact that for some twenty years prospectors had been scouring those hills, inch by inch. He shattered a piece of ore, exposing a golden interior. Ore specimens were taken to Tombstone, where they assayed out at $22,000 to the ton in silver and $5,000 to the ton in gold. Pearce quickly staked a claim for each member of his family and named the mine Commonwealth. Almost overnight the town of Pearce materialized at the foot of the slope.

A short time after the Commonwealth went into operation, a banker from New Mexico named John Brockman talked Pearce into selling out for a quarter of a million dollars. Most prospectors lacked the capital to develop their claims and often sold a rich prospect for a few dollars, but Pearce was a notable exception. Regardless, Mrs. Pearce was taking no chances. She demanded and received an exclusive on the hostelry business in the town. Since running a boardinghouse was a prosperous enterprise (many people considered the hotel business a more reliable profit maker than the mines), this industrious lady wasn't about to miss out on a golden opportunity.

It wasn't long before people began to drift in, looking for get-rich-

92

Pearce in 1912. In the foreground is the Commonwealth Mine, the source of wealth for the boom town.
Courtesy Arizona Historical Foundation

quick opporunities and employment in the mine. Several residents of Tombstone dismantled their homes and businesses, packing them over to the east side of the Dragoons and reconstructing them in the new town.

The boom times for Pearce lasted several years, peaking in 1919 with a population of some 1,500. The prosperous town had the usual assortment of stores, saloons, and restaurants, and even a movie theater. Pearce began to decline in the 1930s, as the Great Depression took its toll and the railroad pulled up its tracks. Worst of all, the supposedly inexhaustible Commonwealth mine played out.

Courtland

Courtland's boom began in 1909 when several large copper companies began operations in the area. By the middle of February, six weeks after the town was born, the local clarion boasted a population of two thousand residents living in tents and shacks. "No other camp in Arizona Ever Nade (sic) Such A Showing In So Short A Time," the same edition proclaimed with a burst of civic pride. It was estimated that the mines would produce two million pounds of copper per month.

During its heyday this rough mining town boasted such amenities as telephones, newspapers, movie theaters, an ice cream parlor, an automobile dealership, and five miles of underground water pipes. A branch line of the Southern Pacific linked Courtland to the rest of the world.

In their rush to construct a town, the boisterous miners overlooked building a jail, and for a time, a tunnel with a wooden door sufficed.

One day a prisoner tried to burn his way out by placing his mattress against the door and setting it afire. All he got for his trouble was a tunnel full of smoke. Fortunately someone came along in time to save him.

Courtland boomed for about ten years, until the end of World War I, when the copper market declined; however, it held on for twenty-three more years before most of its citizens drifted on to other places.

Gleeson

Gleeson dates back to prehistoric times when natives mined turquoise, giving the name Turquoise to the area. Copper, lead, and silver were found here during the late 1870s, about the same time as the strikes around Tombsone, sixteen miles to the west. John Gleeson, a native of Ireland, was working as a hardrock miner in Pearce during the 1890s and doing some prospecting on the side when he located a rich copper deposit near Turquoise. Gleeson called his strike the Copper Belle, and between 1896 and 1901 the mine produced $300,000 in copper. A new camp was located closer to water and named for Gleeson. Growth was slow; by 1909 the town had only five hundred residents, but boasted a hospital. Three years later, the town of Gleeson burned, a rather common occurrence in Arizona mining camps. The industrious citizens were out rebuilding before the last embers died, but post-World War I depression in the copper industry sounded the death knell of the little mining town.

Courtland, 1914
Courtesy Arizona
Historical Foundation

Kelton, Caliente (Webb), Sparks, McNeal, and Small were all small sidings on the shortline Mexico and Colorado Railroad, which ran from Douglas to Kelton. At Kelton the line joined another shortliner, the Arizona Eastern. The M & C ran a spur to the bustling town of Courtland, and the Arizona Eastern extended its line from Cochise Station to Gleeson. All these small lines were absorbed by the Southern Pacific Railroad by 1925.

At the height of the prosperity of the Turquoise District (Gleeson, Courtland, and Pearce), these small railroads did a prosperous business hauling ore to Douglas and Clifton. By the early 1930s when the market fell off and the mines began to play out, rail traffic decreased dramatically. McNeal and Kelton were shipping points for cattle destined for the feedlots in Los Angeles, but they couldn't keep the railroads busy enough. By the early 1930s the Southern Pacific had been granted permission from the I.C.C. to suspend operations and pull up the tracks.

Swisshelm Mountains

The mountains a few miles east of Elfrida and McNeal are the Swisshelm, named after John Swisshelm, who prospected in the area in the 1870s.

The noted gunslinger Buckskin Frank Leslie had a ranch in the Swisshelms in the 1880s. He was a handsome, dashing, ex-cavalry scout-turned-bartender and was regarded as Cochise County's number one ladies' man. Leslie had been courting May Killeen. May's estranged husband, Mike Killeen, was a jealous man, and he had been following her in and out of the saloons at Tombstone, threatening anyone who tried to make a pass. One night he caught Leslie and May in a fond embrace on the front porch of the Cosmopolitan Hotel. Killeen pulled his revolver and fired twice, hitting Leslie. The two grappled momentarily before Leslie drew his trusty .44-.40 and put several holes in Killeen. The jury ruled self-defense, and a short time later Buckskin Frank took May for his bride. The marriage was stormy—Leslie might have been a dashing lover but he was a poor husband. May divorced him not long after the honeymoon.

Buckskin Frank had taken a long string of lovers, no small feat in a land of few women, when he met Mollie Williams. Soon she was keeping house at Frank's ranch in the Swisshelms. He was drinking heavily and using Mollie for a punching bag, something that inspired her to seek solace in a young ranch hand named Jim Neal. This time it was Leslie's turn to be jealous. In a drunken rage he shot Neal and left him for dead. Then he turned his six shooter on Mollie. After he sobered up, Leslie planned to ride into Tombstone and tell the sheriff that Neal had killed Mollie and that he had killed Neal. Unknown to Leslie, Neal had survived the shooting and had made it to Tombstone, where he reported the incident to the sheriff. Imagine Leslie's surprise when he arrived to tell his tale of woe and found young Neal had beaten him to town.

Buckskin Frank Leslie was given a long term at the Yuma Territorial Prison, where his reputation as a lady killer had taken another turn. While he was in prison, a lady named Belle Stowell, of Stockton, California, read a story about the famed gunfighter and began sending him fruits and flowers. A romance blossomed, and she went to Yuma and begged that he be released to her custody. Leslie was pardoned after serving eight years. He married Belle, and they moved to California. He probably went back to his old ways, for old timers say that Buckskin Frank never lived up to his romantic image and that Belle tossed him out not long after the honeymoon. Buckskin Frank was reportedly last seen sweeping floors in a San Francisco saloon.

*Mountain View
Hotel at Oracle in
1900*
Courtesy Arizona
Historical Foundation

Arizona 77
Oracle to Dudleyville

Oracle

Bill Neal, better known as "Curley Bill," rode with another Bill, the legendary Buffalo Bill Cody, during the Indian Wars on the Plains. Neal, born in Oklahoma Territory, was the son of a black father and a Cherokee mother. His Indian name was "Bear Sitting Down," but the energetic young man spent little time sitting except on the back of a horse. After the war, he moved to Tucson and worked as a cook for a time and learned the hospitality business from the ground up. Next, he opened a prosperous freight business, supplying fuel for the charcoal smelters at nearby mines and hauling ore on his return trip. Bill took up ranching in his spare time, and within a few years his 3-N outfit at Oracle was running thousands of head of cattle over the ranges on the north slopes of the Santa Catalinas.

During those years, Curley Bill Neal found time to marry his girlfriend, Ann. In 1895 they opened the Mountain View Hotel in Oracle. The cool, scenic Santa Catalina Mountains were a favorite summer tourist attraction, and the hotel quickly gained a lofty reputation. Winter visitors and Tucsonians were hauled out to Oracle by Curley Bill's stagelines; then Ann took over and organized outings, parties, and picnics. Bill died in 1936, and Mrs. Neal continued to operate the hotel until her death in 1950.

Mammoth

Mammoth took its name from the old Mammoth Mine, located above the town in the 1870s. It was said the gold ore deposits were of mammoth proportions, hence the name. A mill was located at the settlement, and the ore was lowered to the mill in tramway buckets. Before being sent back up the mountain, the empty ore buckets were filled with drinking water for the thirsty miners.

Dudleyville

William Dudley Harrington, a native of Ireland, was one of the first settlers to arrive in this area in 1877. Dudleyville is located close to the site of old Camp Grant, a primitive military post described by Lieutenant John G. Bourke in 1870 as ". . . the most thoroughly God-forsaken post of all those supposed to be included in the annual Congressional appropriations. Beauty of situation or of construction it had none; its site was the supposed junction of the sandbed of the Aravaypa with the sandbed of the San Pedro."

On April 30, 1871 this desolate army post provided a name for one of the most brutal massacres in Arizona history. Perhaps encouraged by General George Stoneman's remarks that settlers should adopt a "do-it-yourself" policy toward Apache depredations, a group of Tucsonians and their Papago allies rode into an Apache village located near Camp Grant and slaughtered eighty-five Aravaipa Apaches. President Ulysses S. Grant was horrified and ordered the leaders to be brought to trial. A trial was held and a jury immediately found them innocent. In the 1870s it would have been difficult to find a white person in Arizona who would prosecute another for killing Apaches.

In the aftermath, President Grant replaced General Stoneman and ordered General Oliver O. Howard to attempt a peace policy with the Apaches—those Indians who were willing would be peacefully located on reservations. The President had another ace card up his sleeve for those who continued their warlike ways. He was holding General George Crook, the "greatest Indian fighter in the history of the United States," in reserve. That story is told elsewhere in this *Roadside History*.

Arizona 82
(three miles north of Tombstone)
Fairbank to Nogales

Six miles west of US 80, Arizona 82 crosses the old Arizona and Southeastern Railroad tracks and the San Pedro River. Just off the north side of the highway is an old, ramshackle, whitewashed adobe building. Above the door is the barely visible word "Fairbank." Not much else remains of the old town that came into existence in 1882 when the railroad established a station. It was named for N. K. Fairbank, a stockholder in the railroad that was laying track from Benson to Nogales and an organizer of the Grand Central Mining Company.

Fairbank became an important supply point for Tombstone and was a bustling community well into the twentieth century. The town carved a permanent niche for itself in the wild and wooly West on the evening of February 15, 1900 during a spectacular train robbery. Five desperados, including the notorious Three-finger Jack Dunlap and Bravo Juan Yaos, tried to rob the Wells Fargo express car while the train was stopped at the Fairbank station. What the outlaws did not count on was that the shotgun messenger on the run was the legendary ex-Texas Ranger, Jeff Milton.

When the train pulled into the station, the outlaws, pretending to be drunken cowboys, were mingling among the crowd. Milton, not expecting trouble, was standing in the open door of the baggage car. The outlaws opened fire with lever-action Winchesters, shattering his left arm and severing the artery. Milton was unable to return fire lest he hit innocent bystanders who were scurrying for cover. The gang took advantage of the confusion and charged the express car. Milton grabbed his Wells Fargo shotgun in one hand and opened fire, catching Three-finger Jack full bore. Bravo Juan saw the scattergun and turned to run just as Milton opened fire. He took a load of buckshot in the seat of the pants.

Milton slammed the door shut, tossing the keys to the strong box into a dark corner of the baggage car. Then he tore a piece of his shirt to make a tourniquet for his nearly severed left arm. He collapsed between two large trunks from loss of blood, and that probably saved his life because the three remaining outlaws riddled the car with rifle shots.

When the outlaws looked inside the baggage car, Milton was lying in a pool of blood. Believing the great gunfighter to be dead, they searched his body for the keys but couldn't find them. Frustrated, the outlaws mounted their horses and rode away empty-handed.

Jeff Milton, one of the last of the old-time lawmen, recovered from his wounds and continued his illustrious career. He died in Tucson on May 7, 1947 at the age of 85—one of the few of his kind to die with his boots off.

On the opposite side of the San Pedro River from Fairbank is the site of an old Sobaipuri Indian village called Santa Cruz that dates back to the 1600s. About two and one half miles farther north is another village, called Quiburi. These villages were first visited in 1692 by the legendary Jesuit missionary Father Eusebio Kino. The battle-toughened Sobaipuris were related to the Pimas and were located on the eastern frontier of Pimeria. Consequently these fierce fighters bore the brunt of Apache attacks. Kino established a *visita* (part-time mission) among the natives, but the Apaches forced its abandonment in 1698.

In 1775 a *presidio* (fort) was established at Quiburi and called Santa Cruz de Terrenate. Five years later the rampaging Apaches drove the Spanish soldiers out, the fortress then being relocated further south at its original site in Sonora.

About a mile and a half north of the ancient ruins of Quiburi lay Contention City. Located on the east bank of the Santa Cruz River, the town took its name from the Contention Mine at Tombstone. Lack of water at the Contention mine caused the owners to locate the mill on the banks of the San Pedro about ten miles north of Tombstone in 1879.

During its heyday in 1882 Contention City had several stamp mills in operation, pulverizing the ore and grinding out the gold and silver hauled in by ore wagons. It also had a few rowdy saloons boasting names like Dew-drop and Headlight. Also present were the usual soiled doves and gamblers to help separate some sucker from his poke sack.

Most of the surrounding country is rangeland for the old Boquillas Cattle Ranch. The San Juan de las Boquillas y Nogales Grant was issued in 1833 to Captain Ignacio Elías Gonzales and Nepomucino Felix. The two men paid $240 for the grant, about two miles wide and sixteen miles long, straddling the San Pedro River. The Boquillas, which means "little mouth" in Spanish, was later owned by Americans, including William Randolph Hearst. Because the range was heavily overgrazed in the 1880s, erosion set in, and a land that once ran stirrup-high with sacaton grass and groves of trees was overrun with scrubby mesquite and deep-cutting arroyos. Today the ranch is owned by Tenneco West Incorporated.

The sprawling, grass-carpeted rangelands that run all the way to Sonoita lie on the old San Ignacio del Babocomari grant. The grant stretched out along both sides of Babocomari Creek for about twenty miles. The elevation is around 4,000 feet, and the abundance of rainfall made it one of the best places to raise cattle in southern Arizona. The creation of Santa Cruz County in 1899 split the ranch into equal halves with Cochise County. Near the headquarters was the site of an old Pima village called Huachuca. It was visited by Father Kino in 1697 during his journey to the villages of Quiburi and Santa Cruz, at the junction of Babocomari Creek and the San Pedro River. Eventually the Apaches drove the Pima further west. Some relocated in the Santa Cruz Valley near the present location of Tucson, while others settled along Sonoita Creek.

In 1827 Don Ignacio Elías Gonzales and his wife Dona Eulalia filed for a grant of eight *sitos*, or nearly 35,000 acres. They paid a total of $380 for over 54 square miles of rich, well-watered grazing land. For almost twenty years the Elías family ran over forty thousand head of cattle, along with a large horse and mule herd, from the Santa Rita Mountains on the west to the San Pedro River on the east.

Fairbank is a ghost town today, but it was at one time a thriving rail supply point for Tombstone.
Courtesy
Southwest Studies

The family built an adobe fort with a fifteen-foot wall surrounding the ranch buildings, but the Babocomari ranch was abandoned during the 1840s, following Apache attacks in which two Elias brothers were killed. A troop of U.S. Cavalry occupied the old Babocomari fort in 1864, renaming it Camp Wallen. From here they launched campaigns against Cochise and his Chiricahua Apaches.

The rugged mountains on the north are called the Whetstones. Here, on March 23, 1882 Wyatt Earp and Curly Bill Brocius had their famous shotgun duel. Wyatt caught up with Curly Bill at Mescal Springs and in the ensuing gunfight, the famous outlaw leader died with his boots on.

On May 5, 1871 somewhere in the maze of arroyos west of the Whetstones, Lieutenant Howard Cushing and his troops were ambushed by a large band of Chiricahua Apaches. Cushing, one of the Army's boldest young officers, was killed in the fight. The actual site of the battle has not been located.

During the 1870s Dr. Edward Perrin began buying up the rights to the Babocomari. The former Confederate soldier from Alabama also purchased over 200,000 acres along the Santa Fe line in northern Arizona and the 100,000-acre Baca Float #5, south of Seligman. These acquisitions made him one of the largest landowners in Arizona.

After fifty years of overgrazing, intensified by severe droughts, the Babocomari range deteriorated. When hard rains did come, there wasn't enough grass left to hold the topsoil, and tons of precious earth washed down into the San Pedro River.

In the 1930s the Brophy family acquired the land. They waged a thirty-year war against the elements, building check dams to slow or divert the water. Wells were dug, the ranges reseeded, and gradually the land returned to its natural state.

Traveling west, one crosses the continental divide, and the watershed now flows into the Santa Cruz River, its major tributary Sonoita Creek. The Sonoita Creek area is rich in Arizona history. Almost completely surrounded by picturesque mountains, the rolling hills sprawl across grass-carpeted hills studded with groves of live-oak. Nestled along the creek are tall stands of ash, sycamore, black walnut, and cottonwood. During the 1950s the area was chosen for the filming of Rogers and Hammerstein's "Oklahoma." The land had all the natural beauty of turn-of-the-century Oklahoma except for golden fruit, and corn standing "high as an elephant's eye." Special projects personnel created cornfields and orchards with simulated fruit made of wax. A steady supply of fruit was needed during filming as the fruit kept melting in the hot Arizona sun.

The first recorded mention of Sonoita, a Papago word meaning "place where corn will grow," was by Father Kino in 1700. The Sobaipuri Indians had settled along Sonoita Creek after they abandoned their villages at Quiburi and Santa Cruz. Earlier they had whipped the Apaches and feared retaliation, so Chief Coro moved his people further west. The site of Coro's village was two or three miles southwest of Patagonia. It was called Sonoita (not to be confused with the present-day town). In 1701 the Jesuits established a mission nearby called San Gabriel de Guévavi.

Today's Sonoita owes its existence to the Benson-to-Nogales railroad line in 1882. The smallest of the Arizona land grants, San José De Sonoita lies just west of the town of Patagonia, near the Guévavi Mission. By the 1780s the Apaches had driven out both the missionaries and the Pima.

In 1821 Leon Herraras, a *ranchero* at Tubac, requested two *sitos* (over 8,000 acres) around the abandoned Sonoita village. He paid $105 plus fees for the parcel. Like most Spanish land grants, the land was to revert to the public domain if it was to be abandoned for more than a year. Fortunately, there was a clause in the legal document that made allowances for Apache raids.

Apache attacks drove the Herraras family out in the 1830s, and in 1857 their heirs sold the property. The grant was in litigation for much of the last half of the nineteenth century, but surprisingly, much of the old Sonoita grant is still intact today.

The ratification of the Gadsden Treaty in 1854 secured for the United States all the land (29,670 square miles) in Arizona south of the Gila River to today's international boundary. Mexican troops continued to protect settlers in the area until March of 1856. The following November, the First United States Dragoons, under the command of Major Enoch Steen, arrived in Tucson. Apparently Major Steen didn't find the old pueblo a suitable place to locate a military post, for soon after his arrival, he moved his troops to Sonoita Creek and established Fort Buchanan about ten miles northeast of today's Patagonia.

One of early Arizona's most colorful characters, James "Paddy" Graydon, was a member of Steen's Dragoons. Born in Ireland, the plucky youngster immigrated to America in 1853. He joined the army and because of his size, was assigned to the cavalry. His first assignment was to the New Mexico Territory, considered to be the roughest assignment in the army. His commander was Captain Richard Ewell, a rawhide-tough disciplinarian. Ewell, from a prominent Southern family, would later join the South to become one of the Confederacy's greatest generals. With reference to Ewell's receding hairline, and in

Richard Ewell, commandant at Fort Buchanan. He became a Confederate general during the Civil War. Courtesy Southwest Studies

his honor, his troopers named a towering timberless peak in the Santa Rita Mountains Old Baldy.

Graydon admired Ewell and served his commander well for five and a half years. When his tour of duty was up, Graydon resigned and opened the U.S. Boundary Hotel, about three miles from Fort Buchanan. Paddy's place was a tough hangout, providing off-duty soldiers with everything from prostitutes to whiskey, wine, cigars, and sardines. The tough little Irishman was also the self-appointed regulator of law and order in time of trouble.

In October 1860 a band of Apaches swooped down on the ranch of another Irishman, John Ward, driving off livestock and kidnapping a youngster. The most noteworthy chief in the area was Cochise, and it was assumed he was the culprit. The following January a small force under the command of Lieutenant George Bascom was sent to Cochise's camp in Apache Pass, at the north end of the Chiricahua Mountains, to parley. Cochise denied the charges, and when the soldiers tried to take him prisoner, the wily Chiricahua escaped into the brush, but three of his relatives were captured and held hostage. Cochise retaliated by attacking the Butterfield Overland Stage station in Apache Pass and taking three employees captive.

Meanwhile, reinforcements from Fort Buchanan arrived. Paddy Graydon, because of his experience on Apache campaigns, accompanied the troops. On the way he singlehandedly captured three more Apaches. Cochise upped the ante by taking three more hostages, each side now holding six prisoners. The white captives pleaded with the officers to relinquish the Apache captives, but Bascom stubbornly refused to deal unless the kidnapped youngster was returned.

Finally, Cochise grew tired of the eyeball-to-eyeball diplomacy and butchered his captives. In retaliation, the six Apaches were all hanged from the same tree limb. Cochise was outraged by the events at Apache Pass and commenced a bloody ten-year war. Conditions worsened a few months later, when the Civil War broke out and the army abandoned Fort Buchanan, leaving the settlers along Sonoita Creek at the mercy of Cochise's marauding raiders.

It turned out that in the Bascom affair, Cochise had been innocent of the kidnapping charges—the youngster, a Mexican, had been stolen by a band of Pinal Apaches. He grew up among the Pinals and later took the name "Mickey Free." During the Geromino Campaign of the 1880s he was one of General Crook's most valuable "Apache" scouts.

During the Civil War, Paddy Graydon rejoined the Union Army as captain of an independent spy company. Graydon and his charges were responsible for sneaking through Confederate lines to gather information and create havoc. He was described by Union Officers in New Mexico as "an enterprising, fearless leader of a desperate band," but not all of Paddy's imaginative schemes ended in success. During the Battle of Valverde, he proposed a daring raid on the Confederates that literally backfired. The Texans were camped on the east side of the Rio Grande, and Paddy devised a plan to sneak across the river with several pack mules loaded wth kegs of black powder to blow up the whole camp. That night Paddy forded the Rio Grande with his mules, reached the outskirts of the rebel camp, then lighted the fuses and pointed the animals toward the Texans. Paddy turned and headed back toward the river. He looked back once and much to his dismay saw the mules trotting along behind him. Paddy lit out in a hurry trying to outdistance his misguided missiles, leaping into the river just as the powder exploded.

Paddy Graydon never returned to Sonoita Creek—he was killed in a gunfight at Fort Stanton, New Mexico, a few months after the Battle of Valverde.

Another of Arizona's prominent pioneers, Bill Kirkland, ranched along Sonoita Creek in the 1860s. The tall frontiersman from Virginia was the first American to drive a herd of cattle into Arizona. He was fearless and more than once stood his ground against Apache raiders, but he also had the good sense to pull up stakes and leave when the warriors gained the upper hand. He'd help bury friends who'd said defiantly, "I've got as much right to be here as the Apaches."

The pesky Apaches harvested his crops by night and rustled his livestock by day. Once they stole a dozen mules, and Kirkland was so furious he jammed his Colt revolver into his belt, grabbed his Spencer carbine, and chased them several miles on foot. After the incident, Kirkland packed his family and moved to Yavapai County.

The army returned to Sonoita Creek after the Civil War. In 1867 a new military post, Fort Crittenden, was established on a hill overlooking the melted adobe ruins of old Fort Buchanan. The post remained active for a few years, closing in 1872 because of what was described as "unhealthy conditions."

The Patagonia Mountains, southeast of Arizona 82, were the site of several rich mining ventures in the 1860s. One of the most famous mines was the old Patagonia Mine, which dated back to Spanish times. Lieutenant Sylvester Mowry, a flamboyant officer stationed at Fort Crittenden, purchased the mine in 1859. He left the army and became a mining entrepreneur, changing the name of the Patagonia to Mowry. Under Mowry's ownership the mine employed over a hundred workers and produced $1,500,000 in silver and lead ore; in the early 1860s it was one of the nation's richest mines.

During the Civil War, Mowry was arrested as a Confederate sympathizer and detained at Fort Yuma. During this time his mine was gutted by highgraders. Mowry spent the remainder of his life trying to raise money in the East and in Europe to reopen his mine.

Although Apache war parties closed the area to mining during the rest of the 1860s, the Mowry Mine saw a brief flurry of activity at the turn of the century. However, Mowry soon joined the list of ghost towns in the area. Other ghost towns or mining camps in the area include Harshaw, Washington Camp, and Duquesne. All thrived in the latter part of the nineteenth century and supported prosperous communities before the mines played out in the early 1900s. Local legend has it that George Westinghouse, the future inventor of electric appliances, once resided at Duquesne. He amazed his neighbors by designing for his home a bathroom equipped wth hot and cold running water.

In those halcyon days of the open highways and few cars one never knew who'd you'd run into
Courtesy Arizona
Historical Society

Arizona 83
Sonoita to Interstate 10

Greaterville

The short stretch of highway from Sonoita to Greaterville, with the picturesque Santa Rita Mountains on the west and passing through rolling rangeland dappled with clusters of oak trees, offers some of Arizona's most scenic vistas.

Placer gold was discovered in the Santa Ritas in 1874 by A. Smith, and the town of Greaterville sprang up at the site. The peak population was about five hundred, only about a fifth Anglo, the rest Mexicans. During the 1870s prospectors were mining about $10 a day in placer gold. The town had several dance halls, saloons, and mercantile enterprises. The local jail was a deep hole in the ground, tenants being installed in their new abode by rope. Patrick Coyne, the local magistrate, also acted as school teacher. The cowboys working at the Empire Ranch frequently went to the dances to court the pretty señoritas of Greaterville. One night the miners decided not to share the ladies and locked the door. One resourceful cowboy, not to be denied, climbed on the roof and dropped a handful of cartridges down the chimney. A few seconds later all hell broke loose. The doors burst open as the miners ran for cover. The cowboys quickly moved in and took over the dance hall. One jealous miner followed his girlfriend with his knife as she was swept around the dance floor by a cowboy. Just to keep matters even, one of the puncher's friends shadowed the miner with his six-shooter drawn and cocked. It was a standoff that evening, as neither side inflicted any more damage.

Water was scarce and had to be hauled by burro in canvas and goatskin bags from Gardner Canyon, four miles away. Roaming bands of Apaches were a constant threat until Geronimo surrendered in 1886, after which the area engaged in a brief revival. Greaterville was located on a road known as Renegades Route—men fleeing the law camped in the area on their way to and from the Mexican border. The town had a relatively long life, the post office remaining open until 1946.

Total Wreck

About nine miles south of Pantano is the ghost town of Total Wreck. The unusual name came when John Dillon was asked what he planned to call his new silver-lead mine in the Empire Mountains. He said he didn't know, but the ledge where the claim was located looked like a total wreck, so that's what they decided to call it.

Two years after Dillon made his discovery, the Southern Pacific reached Pantano, and a seventy-ton mill was built at the site. By 1883 the population reached two hundred, and there were four saloons, a barber shop, lumber yard, three stores, and three hotels.

In 1883 Geronimo's band attacked a party of Mexican woodcutters, killing six. Total Wreck's most outlandish gunfight occurred during an argument when one man drew his revolver and shot another in the chest. Fortunately, the bullet lodged in a packet of love letters stashed in the victim's breast pocket. The lucky fellow went home and married the girl—whether out of love or gratitude is not recorded.

Davidson Canyon

Davidson Canyon, located between the Santa Rita and Empire mountains, was named for O. Davidson, a special Indian agent headquartered at Tubac. He was later killed by Apaches. This area was a dangerous place to travel in the 1860s and '70s. Several freighters and prospectors died at the hands of the Apaches during those years. Corporal Joe Black, mail carrier between Fort Crittenden and Tucson, had made the trip safely on many occasions, but always at night, when the Apaches wouldn't attack. On August 27, 1872 he was escorting Lieutenant Reid Stewart and a party of green troops to Tucson. Stewart and Black were riding in a buckboard, while the others rode behind. Near Davidson Canyon, Black urged the Lieutenant to wait until dark before proceeding, but the officer wouldn't listen because he had to get to Tucson to testify in a court martial case. Before long the faster-paced buckboard was an hour ahead of the escort.

When the escort reached the top of the divide, they discovered the body of Stewart with a bullet through his head and five other body wounds. The mail bags had been emptied and the contents scattered on the ground; the mules, harness, and Corporal Black were missing. Apparently he'd tried to make a break and had been captured. The soldiers picked up the trail, soon coming on a war party; the Apaches tied the corporal to a dead tree and set it ablaze. The soldiers rushed toward the horrifying scene but arrived too late to save Black from a brutal death. Afterwards they recovered the body and counted more than a hundred wounds made by lances, knives, and firebrands.

Arizona 85
Lukeville to Cashion

Organ Pipe National Monument

The Organ Pipe National Monument sprawls across five hundred square miles of desert. During the summer months it is one of the most forbidding, yet intriguing places in America. Here desert plants and animals have developed unique ways to survive. Some animals in the desert go their entire lives without taking a drink of water, taking in moisture from the succulent desert plants. Seeds lie dormant in the sand for years; then, after just the proper amount of rainfall, they spring to life in a dazzling array of wild flowers. Other plants grow life-preserving thorns as a protective device to keep from being eaten by hungry animals.

The unique Organ Pipe Cactus was so named because its curled arms cluster together at the ground and spread upward like the pipes of an organ. This area was set aside as a national monument in 1937.

Why

Why might be called Arizona's curiosity community. The town, a product of the 1960s, is situated on a junction, or "Y" in the road—one road leads to Ajo, another to Lukeville, and the third to Tucson. According to some, residents wanted to call it "Y" and tourists thought they said "Why." The most reliable and believable explanation is that tourists keep asking, "Why do you want to live out here?" Nowadays the most common question is, "Why is it called 'Why'?" and local people feel compelled to give a tedious explanation. Recently they've shortened their reply to "Why not?" Now, presumably, the tourists know why.

Ajo

Ajo means "garlic" in Spanish, but contrary to popular myth, the town wasn't named for the pungent plant. Papago Indians used a red ore pigment to paint their bodies. *Au'auho* is the Papago word for paint.

Spanish miners found a rich deposit of silver ore in the area around

1750. The discovery created a furor in Mexico at the time. Charles Poston and Herman Ehrenberg, inspired by the story of such deposits, prospected around Ajo in 1854. They took ore specimens to San Francisco; however, when Poston returned two years later, he set up operations at Tubac instead.

Pete Brady, another fabled Arizona pioneer, also explored around Ajo in 1864. He reported finding rich silver ore deposits, and the American Mining and Trading Company was organized. The high-grade surface stringers were not as rich as those found around Bisbee, Jerome, and Clifton, and technology hadn't advanced enough to operate stringers at a profit. Still, Ajo claims the distinction of having the first American-operated mine in Arizona. Despite traces of rich ore, the deposits around Ajo would lie dormant until the twentieth century.

About 1900 a smooth-talking promoter named A. J. Shotwell, picked up a few ore specimens and took them to St. Louis. He had little trouble raising capital from usually skeptical Missourians. After all, this was Arizona, where every coyote hole was a potential gold mine. When these investors lost their money, another group was waiting to take their place. The second group, more doubting than the first, wanted a first-hand look at Ajo, so Shotwell wisely chose the rainy season, and the investors were suitably impressed. On the way back to St. Louis, the Cornelia Copper Company was organized. The water holes around Ajo, so necessary for mining, soon evaporated, and so did the money and the investors' enthusiasm.

In 1911 John C. Greenway, ex-Rough Rider and manager of the Calumet and Arizona Company of Bisbee, along with some business associates, picked up the Cornelia Copper Company. The re-organized and re-financed company brought in new technology and geological expertise. They discovered a huge underground reservoir of water and began an open-pit operation. Soon Ajo became one of Arizona's richest copper camps, peaking in time for the copper boom of World War I. In 1916 the town of Cornelia, just north of Ajo, had a population of over five thousand.

In 1917 old Ajo burned. It was said that the only thing salvaged was a phonograph record—"There'll be a Hot Time in the Old Town Tonite."

Local opposition to living in a company town inspired Sam Clark to lay out his own town. By 1917 the population reached a thousand. The company tried to get even by refusing to sell water, but the free-spirited citizens sank a well in a mining shaft. In 1918 in a surge of patriotism the citizens tried to name their town either Woodrow or Wilson for the wartime president, but the post office refused. They next submitted Rowood (Woodrow pronounced backwards), which satisfied the bureaucrats.

Buckeye

In 1888 M. Jackson of Sydney, Ohio, built a canal in the west valley and named it Buckeye for his home state. In 1899 Tom Clanton donated a quarter section near the canal for a townsite. For a time the community was called Sidney, but it was incorporated as Buckeye in 1931, following a special order from the State Supreme Court. Buckeye called itself, in those early days, the Alfalfa Seed Capital of Arizona, not exactly the kind of promotion to land it in a Ned Buntline dime novel.

Avondale

Billy Moore ran a freight station east of here in the 1890s. He called the place Coldwater, the English translation for the Agua Fria River, which flowed nearby (when it flowed). When the railroad established a station further west at the Avondale Ranch, Billy's place declined. However, each October they still celebrate "Billy Moore Days" to honor the Arizona pioneer. Local legend has it that in his younger days Billy Moore rode with the notorious William Quantrill's raiders during the Civil War.

Liberty

In 1895 mail was being delivered at the Toothaker Farm, but the post office was established as Altamount. The farm was a little out of the way, so a new post office was located at a more central location and named Liberty.

Cashion

About 1910 a small settlement grew up around the railroad station established a decade earlier and named for Jim Cashion. Cashion was in charge of railroad construction and owned the parcel of land where the station was located.

Arizona 86
Tucson to Why

Roblés Junction

Roblés Junction is named for pioneer Bernabé Roblés, who had a ranch in the area around the turn of the century and also ran a stage line from Tucson to Gunsight. Bernabé's six-year-old granddaughter, June Roblés, was the victim of a sensational Tucson kidnapping in 1934. The youngster was on her way home from school on a late April afternoon when she was abducted. A couple of hours later her father received a ransom note demanding $15,000. The following day another note arrived, this time to Bernabé, reducing the amount to $10,000 and demanding that the police be taken off the case.

The family heard nothing from the kidnappers for several days, and with each passing day hope faded for June's safe return. Crowds of anxious citizens waited outside the Roblés's home for some word of her fate.

Nineteen days after the kidnapping, Governor Ben Moeur received a letter postmarked Chicago and giving instructions as to where June Roblés could be found. Searchers combed the desert outside town and were about to give up when a long sheet-iron box was found buried in the sand. The little girl was found alive, chained to an iron stake inside the box. She was exhausted from the terrible ordeal but glad to be alive.

The sensational story was given national attention in the press, and little June was even invited out to Hollywood. Investigaton turned up several leads, but police couldn't gather enough evidence to press charges. The promised release of the "complete story" on what had happened was never forthcoming. Some believe that the kidnapper was a vindictive relative in Mexico, trying to get even with Bernabé Roblés for some alleged transgression many years earlier.

Kitt Peak National Observatory

Fifteen miles west of Roblés Junction is the turnoff to Kitt Peak. One version says the town was named by George Roskruge in 1893 for an Indian named Kit, who cooked and ran errands for a surveying party in the area. Another story says it was named for George Roskruge's sister, whose married name was Kitt. The name appears on maps with both spellings. A national observatory, boasting the largest concentration of facilities in the world for stellar and solar research, was located here in 1958.

Sells

Back in 1909 Sells was called Indian Oasis. The town began when Joe and Louis Menager opened a store and post office, and dug a well. In 1919 the name was changed to honor Cato Sells, Commmissioner of Indian Affairs.

Sells is the agency headquarters for the Papago Indians. The nearly 2.8 million-acre reservation is exceeded in size only by the Navajo lands. About 7,500 Papago Indians occupy this sprawling desert reservation, which parallels a large section of the Mexican border.

The Papago Indians, properly known as the Tono O'Odham (Tohono O-otam), or "People of the Desert," are closely related to the Pima. Father Eusebio Kino first visited them in 1694. Until recently their lifestyle had changed little from the descriptions given by the Jesuit padre. The arid land made them less agrarian than the Pima. Traditionally they were a semi-nomadic, or *rancheria* people, moving to favorable climates in Papagueria as the season changed. Rainfall in this area varies from four to twelve inches, and elevation runs from 1,400 to 3,000 feet.

The Tono O'Odham were first introduced to cattle ranching by Father Kino in the 1600s, and cattle still graze the sparse grasslands of Papagueria today, these hardy people and their cattle having survived difficult periods of drought. During drought, cattle had to subsist on a diet of prickly pear and other desert plants, for there wasn't a single permanent stream or lake on the entire reservation. Most of the villages had only one well, and residents had to haul water to their homes in oil drums.

This inhospitable environment has been a blessing in disguise for the desert dwellers. Since no one else wanted to live here, there wasn't a need to establish reservation boundaries until the twentieth century.

Quijotoa

Quijotoa takes its name from a Papago word which means "carrying basket mountain" and refers to nearby Ben Nevis Mountain. The top looks like a basket, and the name was passed on to the Anglo-American newcomers.

As early as 1774 Spanish *gambusinos* worked the mines, shipping the ore to Baja, California. The area boomed again in 1883 when Alexander McKay found an outcrop of silver and copper on Ben Nevis Mountain. When the high rollers in San Francisco heard of the strike, they sent their experts out to investigate, and soon there were several mining companies setting up operations.

A well was dug on the east side of the mountains, and at that site a camp called Logan sprang up. Nearby, another camp, New Virginia, came into existence, and soon the two merged. Shortly thereafter, two more camps, Virginia City and Brooklyn, blossomed and joined the first two. The four towns, consisting of about two hundred buildings, merged, and the desert megalopolis took the name Quijotoa.

Real estate was a sure bet to prosperity. One man reportedly spent $500 to erect a building and then turned around and rented space for $75 a month. Drinking water sold for 75 cents a bucket, making it almost cheaper to wet a parched throat with whiskey. Lots of money was made here, but most of it came from mining the miners rather than the ore.

Mine promoters, including John Mackey of Comstock Lode fame, had a field day promoting Quijotoa, surrounding the place with a magical air of mystery and promise. It was said, however, that Mackey gouged a tunnel through the mountain and all he found was daylight at the other end.

In 1885 the ore played out, and the several thousand residents began to move on to greener pastures. On June 26, 1889, a fire broke out and swept throgh the town, almost finishing off Quijotoa.

About six miles west of town was the town of Allen, or Quijotoa City. During the silver rush to Ben Nevis Mountain, John B. "Pie" Allen was one of the first to arrive. The Tucson pioneer, who made his first fortune selling pies in Tucson for a dollar apiece, built a fine hotel on the opposite side of the mountain, about six miles by road from Quijotoa. The site was known informally as "Allen's Side." It was said Allen's hotel was well known throughout the territory for its cuisine, fine liquor, and gourmet cooking. He probably sold a few pies too, just for old times sake.

Covered Wells

Covered Wells, located about four miles west of Quijotoa, was a water supply place for the mining towns during the 1880s. The name comes from a wooden cover used at the well.

Gunsight

About five miles southwest of Why, on the road to Quijotoa, was the town of Gunsight. Silver was discovered here in 1878 near a mountain resembling a gun sight. During the early 1890s the Silver Gert Mining Company had forty miners digging ore. For a time the mine proved prosperous, and the town of Gunsight had several buildings. A stage coach left Tucson at 7 A.M., every Monday and Thursday for "Picacho, Quijotoa, and Gunsight." The Gunsight Ranch, located nearby, provided meat, dairy products, and produce for the hungry miners. Gunsight began its inevitable decline in the mid-1890s. About all that's left are a few crumbled ruins on the north slope of the Gunsight Mountains.

Arizona 87
Eloy to Chandler

Coolidge and Casa Grande National Monument

In 1924 President Calvin Coolidge signed the bill authorizing the building of Coolidge Dam on the Upper Gila. Two years later, a farming community sprang up on lands once occupied by the ancient Hohokam Indians. The name Coolidge was suggested, and Coolidge it became.

Just north of town is the Casa Grande National Monument, so designated in 1918. The four-story building, made of mud and caliche, was visited and named by Father Kino in 1694. It is considered one of the best preserved prehistoric dwellings in southern Arizona. Lieutenant Juan Mateo Manje, traveling with Kino, described it as a ". . . large ediface whose principal room in the middle is of four stories, those adjoining being of three. Its walls are two *veras* (about five feet) thick, made of strong cement and clay and are so smooth on the inside that they resemble planed boards and are so polished that they shine like pueblo pottery." Nearly a hundred years later, in 1775, Father Garcés described the Casa Grande as being in a state of near-ruin.

During the 1820s James Ohio Pattie reported passing by the ruins, and during the next decade somebody carved Pauline Weaver's name on one of the walls. Major Willam Emory mentions the site in his notes in 1846, while he was crossing Arizona with the Army of the West.

Dr. J. Walter Fewks, of the Smithsonian Institution, conducted the first scientific excavations in 1892, returning again in 1906 and 1908. Many other scientists have studied the site, yet much of it remains a mystery.

The eleven-room Casa Grande was built sometime around 1300 A.D. by Hohokam Indians living in the area. The upper floors were made of logs floated down the Gila from the high country. The calendar holes are of particular interest. Two small openings in the east and center rooms are placed in such a way as to let the sun's rays through. The streak of light coming through both holes and lining up on a target occurs near the spring and fall equinoxes. This "calendar" could have suggested a time for planting and harvesting ceremonies.

By 1450 the monument, America's first skyscraper, was mysteriously abandoned. By the time the Spanish arrived, the natives were living in open villages. Casa Grande remains a puzzling enigma. The structure was used, no doubt, as a watchtower, as nomadic tribes frequently raided these industrious farmers after the harvest; or the soil might have become saturated with alkali or waterlogged; or perhaps it was the temple of some great leader, and when he died, the building was abandoned. Pima custom called for the abandonment and burning of a dwelling when its owner died. Kino reported the interior had been burned prior to his visit in 1694.

Adamsville

Before Florence sprang up and Maricopa Wells was on the decline, an energetic pioneer named Charles Adams dug an irrigation ditch in the area and started farming. He laid out a townsite and gave away land to anyone who wanted to live there. Adams next opened a saloon and store. A flour mill was built and was soon supplying some of the military posts in the area. By 1870 about four hundred residents lived in the area.

According to local legend, Territorial Governor Richard C. McCormick disliked Adams so that when a post office was established in 1871, the governor pulled some political strings to have the town named Sanford for his friend Captain George B. Sanford. Both Sanford and Adams left the town about the time of this controversy. Over the next few years, both names were used—the post office marked the mail Sanford, but residents insisted on calling the town Adamsville.

Adamsville was famed as a rough-and-ready town before its demise about 1876. The only part of Adamsville that hasn't been plowed under is the cemetery.

Sacaton (just south of Arizona 87)

Today Sacaton is the headquarters for the eight-thousand-member Gila River Indian Reservation. For hundreds of years the industrious Pima Indians farmed this rich valley and sold their excess crops to American travelers on the Gila Trail. Following the construction of dams on the Upper Gila, precious water that used to irrigate their fields was diverted to farms owned by whites. The vast area straddling both sides of the river and covering over 372,000 acres of land was occupied by both the Pima and Maricopa Indians. The Maricopa, a Yuman group, often allied with the Pima against their relatives living along the Colorado River. Finally, in the mid-1800s they moved further up the Gila River to the Sacaton area to escape the continuous warfare with their cousins. Early American explorers and soldiers wrote in glowing terms of these friendly natives.

The word *sacaton* means "tall, rank herbage, unfit for forage." Ironically, the sacaton grass found in Arizona is good forage for grazing animals. It is also said to mean a "broad, flat land." The second meaning is more suitable for this area. Kino understood the Pima name to be "Sudason," and this probably explains how it came to be Sacaton.

The old Butterfield Stage Line ran through here in 1858 on its way from Tucson to Yuma. Near the center of town, in an unkempt patch of weeds, is a monument that deserves better care. It honors Mathew B. Juan, the first Arizonan and the first Native American to die in World War I.

Chandler

During the latter part of the nineteenth century, Dr. A. J. Chandler was Arizona's first veterinarian surgeon. During the 1890s he bought about eighteen thousand acres in the eastern part of the Salt River Valley that became known as the Chandler Ranch. In 1911 he subdivided the land and offered irrigated plots for sale. In 1913 Dr. Chandler built the elaborate San Marcos Hotel, complete with Southwestern architectural design, golf course, swimming pool, horseback rides, and desert outings as a lure to attract buyers to his Chandler Ranch. The first response was great, and Chandler was born; however, growth was slow, and by 1940 the population was only thirteen hundred. The San Marcos continued to be the cultural hub of the community, attracting winter visitors from all over the country. Chandler remained a quiet agricultural community until World War II, when Williams Air Force Base was established east of town. By the 1980s high-tech industry had discovered Chandler, and the end of growth is nowhere in sight.

An early day caravan of tourists
Courtesy
Southwest Studies

Arizona 90
Fort Huachuca

Fort Huachuca

By the mid-1870s the Apache wars in Arizona were winding down. In 1872 General Oliver O. Howard, with help from Tom Jeffords, had worked out a peace treaty with Cochise and his Chiricahua Apaches. That same year General George Crook ordered a relentless winter campaign against the Tonto Apaches and Yavapais in the mountains of central Arizona. In an effort to centralize the administration of these tribes, the federal government relocated them to San Carlos. Cochise died in 1874, and two years later his people were moved from their traditional lands around Apache Pass to San Carlos. Relocating the restive Chiricahus among the Western Apaches and Yavapais was something akin to inviting a group of sheepmen to a cattlemen's convention. Warriors, unaccustomed to the confines of the reservation, began to rally around leaders such as Chatto, Nana, Victorio, and Geronimo. War parties broke from the reservation and resumed raiding and plundering. Many of these forays crossed the border into old stomping grounds in Mexico.

When the Mexican Republic signed the Treaty of Guadalupe Hidalgo in 1848, ending the war with the United States, it gave up more than half a million square miles of territory. The United States also inherited more than 120,000 natives, some of whom were nomadic and had no respect for boundary lines set by newcomers. The treaty stipulated that the United States be responsible for the actions of their new charges. When war parties residing on reservations in Arizona raided south of the border, the Mexicans were understanda-

Fort Huachuca in the mid-1880s
Courtesy Arizona
State Library

bly upset and insisted the *Norte Americanos* restrain the Apaches. The establishment of Fort Huachuca a few miles north of the border was part of the attempt to keep the Apaches out of Mexico.

On March 3, 1877 Captain Sam Whitside and Company B Sixth Cavalry located a site for a temporary military post at the foot of the lofty Huachuca Mountains.

Almost immediately the military presence in the San Pedro Valley made it possible for settlers, ranchers, and miners to develop Ed Schieffelin's fabulous silver strike at Tombstone, and Jack Dunn's discovery at Bisbee came about the same time, when Captain Whitside's troops erected tents on the banks of Huachuca Creek. The saloons of rough towns like Tombstone, Charleston, and Bisbee became favorite watering holes for off-duty soldiers anxious to spend their hard-earned thirteen dollars a month.

The climate around Fort Huachuca is ideal, and the scenery is some of the best in southern Arizona. However, living conditions at the fort during the early years were described as dreary and primitive. The steady rains that lasted from early July through September were followed by a prolonged drought. Someone complained that the wind began its incessant howling on the first day of January and didn't stop until the last day of December.

In 1882 a resurgence of Apache warfare caused Fort Huachuca to be upgraded to a permanent military post. Living conditions improved as buildings were constructed and a railroad spur linked the post to the new line between Benson and Nogales. General William T. Sherman visited the post and personally selected the site for a new parade field, which is still the center for ceremonies and activities.

The peak of military activity during Fort Huachuca's early history came in 1885-86. On May 17, 1885 Geronimo and Nachez led a large band of disgruntled followers to Mexico. They were rounded up after a tough ten-month campaign in the Sierra Madre of Mexico. General Crook and Geronimo met at Cañon de los Embudos, near the Mexican border, and the Apaches accepted Crook's terms to return to Arizona. However, that evening a whiskey peddler dispensed his trade goods in Geronimo's camp and convinced the wily warrior that the Americans were planning to execute him. That night the Apaches slipped quietly out of camp and returned to the Sierra Madre.

The incident rankled the desk jockeys in Washington, who suggested Crook had placed too much trust in the Apaches. Crook was replaced by General Nelson Miles, who made his headquarters at Fort Bowie and designated Fort Huachuca as the advance base for expeditions into Mexico. Miles continued Crook's policy of hard campaigning, choosing Captain Henry Lawton, Commander of B Troop, 4th Cavalry, Fort Huachuca, to lead a summer campaign into the mountains and deserts of Mexico. Lawton, a Civil War recipient of the Medal of Honor, firmly believed in the quality of American soldiers as well as that of Crook's highly-touted Apache scouts. On May 5, 1886 while the 4th Cavalry band struck up "The Girl I Left Behind Me," Lawton led his troops out the fort's gates and turned south toward Mexico.

The exhausting campaign took its toll. Two-thirds of the officers and men failed to finish the campaign. Trails led up and down the jagged mountains laced with steep-sided canyons and gorges. Geronimo and his band continued to evade their pursuers with relative ease. Assisting Lawton in the campaign was Surgeon Leonard Wood, also of Fort Huachuca.

Geronimo and his band of Chiricahua Apaches prior to their departure for Florida in 1886
Courtesy Arizona State Library

Wood, a graduate of Harvard, put aside his medical bag and hit the campaign trail with the troops. He was awarded the Medal of Honor for bravery and deserves some recognition for common sense when it came to proper desert attire. He ordered his troops to strip down to their underwear and don straw hats to combat the hot desert weather.

By the middle of the summer, General Miles had backed down from his demands for unconditional surrender and agreed to offer terms if the elusive Geronimo would agree to come in. Lieutenant Charles Gatewood, interpreter Tom Horn, and a pair of Apache scouts rode into Geromimo's camp and presented the terms, which were accepted by the band, and for all practical purposes the Apache wars came to a close.

The legendary 9th and 10th Cavalry regiments, popularly known as the "Buffalo Soldiers," were stationed at Fort Huachuca off and on for several years. The black troopers of the 9th arrived in 1898, remained until 1900, and then returned for another tour in 1912. The 10th remained at Huachuca longer than any other regiment, arriving during the early days of the Mexican Revolution and staying until 1931. On March 9, 1916 the 10th launched an expedition into Mexico from Huachuca as a part of General John J. Pershing's Punitive Expedition. The expedition was the result of bandit chieftain Pancho Villa's earlier raid on Columbus, New Mexico.

Two other black regiments, the 24th and 25th Infantry Regiments, were also stationed at Fort Huachuca, the latter from 1928 to 1942. Despite the fact that these combat infantry regiments aren't as well remembered as their counterparts in the horse cavalry, the 24th and 25th established a proud tradition.

Life at Fort Huachuca was relatively peaceful until the outbreak of the Mexican Revolution in 1911. The strong military presence was necessary to keep the warring factions from carrying the war onto the United States side of the border.

The post reached its greatest importance during World War II, when more than thirty thousand soldiers and civilians were stationed there. After the war, the situation quieted down again, and the post was turned over to the Arizona National Guard. About 1950 the post was temporarily abandoned, but the outbreak of the Korean War brought new life to the fort. Fort Huachuca is the only active military post in Arizona that traces its roots back to the Apache Wars.

Sierra Vista

The small community at the entrance to Fort Huachuca was originally called Garden Canyon because produce was grown at the site. A post office was established in 1919 for civilian employees at the fort. In 1937 the settlement's name was changed to Fry, honoring Oliver Fry, an early settler. During World War II the black soldiers at Fort Huachuca called the town "Hook" because of the numerous prostitutes who hung out there. Apparently the name "Fry, Arizona," didn't sit well with the new wave of post-World War II settlers, not to mention the tourist-oriented Chamber of Commerce. In 1955 the town was incorporated with the more appropriate name of Sierra Vista.

An Arizona ranch girl
Courtesy
Arizona Historical Society

Arizona 92
Huachuca Mountains to Bisbee

Huachuca Mountains

Arizona 92 stretches across the eastern slope of the Huachuca Mountains. As it bends around and heads east toward Bisbee, it joins Arizona 83. The Coronado National Memorial is located five miles south and west of the junction. The site commemorates the approximate *entrada conquista* (expedition of conquest) into Arizona of the Spanish conquistador Francisco Vasquez de Coronado. American historian Samuel Elliot Morrison wrote of this expedition in *The Growth of the American Republic*: "There is no other conquest like this one in the annals of the human race. In one generation the Spaniards acquired more new territory than Rome conquered in five centuries."

Spanish and Aztec legends about fabulous cities of gold provided the inspiration for this epic four-thousand-mile journey that lasted from 1540 to 1542. The mythical stories were easy to believe, for the Spanish had already found vast treasures of gold and silver in Mexico, and in Central and South America. More mineral wealth could just as easily exist in the unexplored areas to the north.

The seeds of optimism that eventually led to the germination of a great expedition had been planted several years earlier, in 1528, when a Spanish expeditionary force was shipwrecked off the west coast of Florida. The survivors tried to make their way back to New Spain (Mexico) by sailing along the Gulf Coast. They landed somewhere near Galveston Bay, Texas. The few remaining survivors were taken prisoner, and of these, only four survived, the four being Alvar

Nuñez Cabeza de Vaca, Alonzo del Castillo, Andres Dorantes, and Dorantes's Moorish slave, Esteban. The castaways began an incredible eight-year odyssey that eventually led them to the west coast of Mexico, where they emerged from the wilderness with tales of large cities to the north.

Gold fever was beginning to engulf the young *hildagos* who had come to Mexico City from Spain to seek their fortunes. The Viceroy, Antonio Mendoza, seeking to maintain control over the situation, began making plans to sponsor an expedition to see if the legendary Seven Cities of Gold and the mythical Northwest Passage, or shortcut to the Orient, could be located and claimed. But first he needed to send a small party north to verify the cities' existence. Since none of the Spanish survivors wanted to venture north again, Mendoza sent the slave Esteban, accompanied by a Franciscan priest, Fray Marcos de Niza.

The small expedition reached Arizona in 1539, heading down the San Pedro River. At some point along the way, the two separated, and Esteban went ahead. He reached a Zuni pueblo called Hawikuh, located near the Arizona-New Mexico line and south of today's Zuni, New Mexico.

The Zunis gave Estaben a frosty reception; one word led to another, and finally the natives killed him and sent his Indian allies scurrying back down the trail to rejoin de Niza. The Friar claimed to have seen the pueblo before making a hasty retreat. This is unlikely, but his courage and imagination expanded the closer he came to Mexico City. By the time he met with the Viceroy, the mythical cities of gold, not to mention thousands of heathen souls, were out there waiting to be harvested.

It wasn't hard to find recruits for the expedition. The city was crawling with dashing young adventurers, eager for the chance to venture forth into the great unknown to conquer vast new lands and treasure for the Crown. Mendoza chose Coronado as leader—a handsome young man recently married into a wealthy family.

Pedro de Casteneda, chronicler of the expedition, described the group's picturesque quality: ". . . there were so many men of such high quality among the Spaniards, that such a noble body was never collected in the Indies." In reality, they were similar in their lust for wealth and adventure. Most were in their early twenties and included battle-toughened professional soldiers and a number of ne'er-do-wells described as "vicious young men with nothing to do."

The expedition, decked out in all its splendorous regalia, left Compostela in February 1540. Among the group were 225 *caballeros*, or horsemen, sixty infantry, two white women, a thousand native helpers, and some black slaves.

The expedition stretched for miles as it crawled northward along the west coast of Mexico, the shimmering blue Pacific Ocean on the west and the towering pinnacles of the Sierra Madre on the east.

They found the going much rougher than expected. Part of the journey took them across 150 miles of desolate, uninhabited desert. The party entered what is Arizona today a few miles west of Bisbee and traveled down the San Pedro Valley; they then bore eastward toward the Gila River. Coronado and his beleaguered army rested for several days on the south bank of this "deep and reedy" river, preparing to make a crossing. The men and animals that could swim did so. The others were carried across on rafts. For another sixteen days the colorful horde moved northward toward Cibola, through the rugged White Mountains. At last the weary and half-starved vanguard reached the open plains and on July 7, 1540 they reached Cibola. Again we rely on the vivid descriptions of Casteneda:

> . . . when they saw the first village, which was Cibola, such were the curses that some hurled at Friar Marcos that I pray God may protect him from them. It is a little, crowded village, looking as if had been crumpled all up together.

De Niza's blooming metropolis had fallen far short of expectations. Smoke signals on a distant hill told the Spanish their arrival had not gone unnoticed. The Zunis had moved their women, children, and aged to safety in the nearby mountains. Warriors from other villages had gathered in support. Wielding bows and arrows, shields, and clubs, they glared menacingly at the newcomers. Messages were carried through a native interpreter. At the same time, the Spanish pantomimed the interpreter's words by laying down their arms. Their gestures were greeted with jeers and yelling complemented with the symbolic scattering of corn meal followed by a barrage of arrows. Coronado, wearing a gilded helmet, rode forward with an offering of gifts. He too was given a shower of arrows for his efforts. The soldiers pressed for attack, but the captain-general said no. The natives, perceiving a weakness when the Spaniards hesitated, mounted an attack of their own. Some ran up almost to the heels of the horses before discharging their arrows. By this time, Coronado's patience had worn thin. "Santiago y a ellos!" (St. James and at them), he shouted, and the donnybrook was on. The Spanish soldiers at that time were among the most formidable horse soldiers in the world. They routed the Zuni warriors with ease, the natives retreating to the sanctuary of their pueblo. The walled city had only one entrance—a narrow, crooked passageway. On the first terrace they had positioned sharpshooters armed with bows and arrows. The first Spanish charge was driven back in a hail of arrows. Coronado next dispatched his crossbowmen and harquebusiers forward to provide cover fire while he and his dismounted cavalry charged the entrance. Again his forces met fierce resistance as arrows rained down upon them from the terrace. To make matters worse, the strings on the crossbows broke, and the musketeers did not have the strength to stand. Scaling ladders were leaned against the walls, but the soldiers were too weak from hunger to climb them.

Coronado, in his gilded helmet, was a favorite target for the Zunis. Twice he was knocked to the ground by five-pound stones and would have been slain had not two gallant captains, Garcia López de Cardenás and Hernan de Alvarado, shielded his battered body with their own. They carried the unconscious leader from the confusion. Cardenás then returned to lead the final charge on the passageway. The Zunis, their rocks and arrows spent, were routed. The pueblo, known as Hawikuh, capitulated; it was found to be well stocked with food, something the Spanish prized more than gold and silver at the moment.

The battle of Hawikuh, fought on July 7, 1540 was symbolic in many ways. Although it is only a footnote in history, it marked the first clash between the white men and the natives in what is today the continental United States. It was the beginning of the so-called "inevitable clash of cultures" that remains to this day. The Spanish sought the riches the land held, but they also held a zealous desire to Christianize all the heathens of this world. They reckoned that each and every native was doomed to hell's inferno and the only way to avert this end was for them to be "saved" (whether they liked it or not). On the other hand, the natives appreciated some innovations brought in by the Spanish. They welcomed horses, cattle, weapons, farm implements, and the introduction of any new crops. However, the propensity of the newcomers to upset the native culture, call Indian religious services "communicating with the devil," and relegate Indians to second-class citizenship was cause for rebellion. The clashes between the two cultures, would be frequent and sometimes violent.

While Coronado was recovering from his wounds, he met with the village headmen. The gentleman from Salamanca bore the Indians no animosity for defending their villages. On the contrary, he hoped that both sides might co-exist peacefully. The Zunis told him of seven villages about twenty-five leagues west at a province they called Tusayan. There, on the high mesas, lived a "warlike people" who called themselves the Hopitu (the Peaceful People).

Coronado sent out an exploratory party led by Pedro de Tovar, along with twenty soldiers and a priest. They rode the 110 miles to the mesas, arriving in late evening. The soldiers crept up to the edge of the villages and waited for morning. At the first light of dawn, they were spotted by the villagers, who immediately formed for battle. The Hopi had already heard of the fierce, bearded men who rode atop "creatures that devoured people." The native messenger service was so efficient that within a fortnight of the Hawikuh battle, tribes ranging from the Lipan Apaches, four hundred miles out on the plains to the east, and the Yumas on the lower Colorado River, the same distance to the west, had already learned the exaggerated details.

Tovar, through his interpreter, demanded the village surrender and swear allegiance to Spain, audacity that drew jeers and catcalls from the villagers. They threw their corn meal on the ground in front of the soldiers. One particularly daring warrior approached the soldiers and clubbed a horse on the head. This transgression on the part of the Peaceful People was too much even for the most patient cavalrymen. Once again, it was "St. James and at them!"

The horses sprang forward, knocking the Hopi warriors to the ground, the skirmish lasting only a few minutes. There were no Spanish casualties and only a few Hopi were injured. As Tovar prepared to attack the village, the headmen appeared bearing gifts.

In the parlays that followed, Tovar learned of a great river to the west and that farther downstream lived people who were "very tall and had large bodies" (the Quechans, or Yumas).

When Tovar relayed the messages back to his captain-general, there was cause for optimism. Another expedition was sent immediately to locate this "river of giants" and explore the possibility that this great river might be the fabled Strait of Anian (the Northwest Passage), the mythical passage to the Orient.

Cardenás and twenty-five men set out in search of the river. Hopi guides led them down a twisting, hundred-mile trail heading northwest of the mesas until they came to the awesome depths of the Grand Canyon. Far below, between almost vertical walls, a thin rivulet wound its way, twisting and turning through the abyss like some reddish serpent. The soldiers spent the next three days gazing upon this geologic wonder, trying to find a way to get to the bottom. Three tried to descend, but went only a third of the way and gave up.

Cardenás returned to Coronado with the discouraging news. The captain-general decided on no future quests to the west and turned his attention toward the Rio Grande. Somewhere out on those vast plains seven golden cities were basking in the shining sun, and he quietly determined that he would claim them for the glory of Spain.

The dreams of cities of gold and of the Northwest Passage had not been realized. The expedition returned to Mexico City in disgrace. Coronado died a few years later, never dreaming that history would consider him one of Spain's greatest explorers. The vast, uncharted *terra incognita* had been opened for future exploration and settlement. Ironically, the riches Coronado sought were there all the time—his trek took him within rock-throwing distance of the rich mining regions of Bisbee, Tombstone, and Clifton-Morenci.

In the aftermath, Casteneda's prophetic words provide the real significance of Coronado's quest: "Granted they did not find the gold, at least they found a place in which to search."

Palominas

Palominas today is a fast-blink town on the highway to Bisbee. At one time the small community provided supplies for the mining and cattle ranches nearby. Ruby White lived at Palominas about 1915. She was a young teacher in a one-room school at the time, and most of her pupils lived on ranches. It wasn't unusual during roundup for twelve-year-old youngsters to come to school wearing spurs and chaps, and packing six-shooters. During school hours, the chaps and spurs were hung alongside wide-brimmed sombreros in the cloakroom, but the revolvers were kept in Ruby White's desk drawer.

At the time, Pancho Villa's army was trying to take Naco, Sonora, which was occupied by *federales*. West of the town is a cone-shaped mountain on which the *Villistas* had placed an antique cannon for the purpose of lobbing shots onto the entrenched *federales*. Each time the cannon fired, the recoil would jar the weapon loose and send it careening down the mountain. It took hours to get it in place for another shot. This allowed the *Villistas* only a few sporadic rounds a day. At first this cannon fire caused a stir among the school children at Palominas, but after a while they grew accustomed to the noise, and following a round, one of the students would look up from his book and casually observe, "Well, there goes that cannon again," and go back to reading.

Naco

A few miles south of Bisbee Junction is the border town of Naco. It was established in the 1890s when a railroad ran through to the mines at Nacozari, Sonora. Naco was a native word for the fruit of the barrel cactus; of this fruit, a tasty jelly is made from the meat and an alcoholic beverage from the fermented juices.

Few people outside Arizona (few people outside Cochise County, for that matter) have ever heard of Naco. Actually, there are two Nacos, one on each side of the Mexican border ten miles south of Bisbee. During Prohibition (1915-1933) these two communities were typical small border towns, with low-slung adobe buildings and dusty, unpaved streets—sleepy, quiet villages basking in the bright desert sun. After dark the similarity ended as Naco, Sonora, was transformed into a bibulous Babylon, its bistros lighting up like Christmas trees beckoning pleasure seekers much the same as the Sirens tempted Ulysses and his men. Thus thirsty residents of Bisbee and Fort Huachuca headed south to quench their thirst in the saloons and casinos that lined the streets of tiny Naco.

Today, both Nacos are quiet—the halcyon days are only a fading memory. Few can remember that Naco, Sonora was once a familiar haunt for the notorious Pancho Villa and other revolutionaries. Fewer still know that Naco, Arizona claims the distinction of being the only community in the continental United States to have been bombarded from an airplane by a foreign power.

The attack occurred in 1929 during the Topete Revolution. The *federales* were entrenched on three sides of the town with their backs to the American border while the rebel forces occupied the surrounding countryside. One skirmish blazed up when a number of the *federales* garrisoned at Naco switched to the rebel side and were planning to capture the town. Changing sides was common during these revolts—generals had been known to reverse the cause of entire armies if the price were right. The rebels had delayed their attack until the gambling houses closed, to allow the Bisbee residents to leave.

There was usually no major plan of attack; in fact, there seemed to be no organized plan at all. The rebels loaded a freight car with black powder and sent it hurtling down toward the center of town, but it picked up so much speed that it derailed and blew up before it reached its target.

It had been said that these two opposing armies engaged in combat only during daylight hours, reserving the nights for revelry as both sides converged on the bistros and bawdy houses of Naco to partake in the pleasures of *cervesa*, women, and the spirited *corridos* sung by wandering minstrels. No doubt there was much fraternizing and telling of tall tales at these festivities, which went on far into the night. Dawn would find both armies continuing the revolution "business as usual."

Pancho Villa once hired a movie company to film his revolution. He staged battles only when the lighting was right for the cameras. Unfortunately, his war movie was a box office disaster—the public did not think it realistic enough.

The *Norte Americanos* from Bisbee were not excluded from the conviviality as school children ditched their classes, housewives abandoned their kitchens, and businessmen locked up their shops. All headed for Arizona's Naco to watch the fighting. A railroad track ran parallel to the border, and the spectators climbed on top of the cars for a better view. Occasionally a stray bullet would send them dropping for cover, but for the most part, revolutionaries and *federales* alike avoided firing toward Naco, Arizona, lest they incur the wrath of the United States Army.

Some remnants of these turbulent times are still in evidence on the Arizona side. There is the "Bulletproof Hotel"—a tongue-in-cheek dubbing of a rooming house that had been armor-plated with corrugated tin. Standing forlorn in a state of ruin behind the customs station is a rundown red brick building that was the Phelps-Dodge store. The old building marks the site of the infamous Naco "blitzkrieg" of 1929.

This "war" began when a roguish barnstorming pilot named Patrick Murphy offered his services to the rebel forces. "I can blow the *federales* right out of their trenches," he boasted. The revolutionary leaders were quick to seize the opportunity to blast the well-entrenched federal troops out of Naco, and the soldier of fortune and his nondescript biplane became the Rebel Air Force.

The bombs were primitive affairs, leather pouches loaded with explosives, scrap iron, and sundry metal, ignited by a fuse which was left peeking out through the opening of the bag. The bombardier was usually a cigarette-smoking youngster whose primary responsibility was to light the fuse with his cigarette and toss the suitcase-size pouch over the side. Whether these bombs did any real damage is a matter of conjecture; however, they did provide much entertainment for the spectators. Whatever the reason, several of the hand-guided missiles landed in Arizona. One went through the roof of a local garage, destroying an automobile that was parked inside, while another went through the roof of the Phelps-Dodge store. The bombing runs ended when one of the *federales* shot down Murphy's plane with a 30.06 Springfield rifle.

Arizona 186
Willcox to the Chiricahua Mountains

Dos Cabezas

Dos Cabezas is Spanish for "two heads" and is named for the two distinctive bald knolls that highlight the range of mountains that bears the same name.

A half mile east of Dos Cabezas was a spring that was a favorite watering place for travelers. The site was noted by a boundary-survey party in 1851. The "Jackass Mail," or San Antonio-San Diego Stage Line established a station at the springs in 1857. During the late 1850s the place was called Ewell's Springs, honoring Captain Richard Ewell, commander at Fort Buchanan. It is claimed that Ewell's Springs had the first school in Cochise County.

Prospectors filed gold and silver claims near the two bald summits in the late 1870s, and a town of about three hundred residents sprang up nearby. A reporter described Dos Cabezas in 1881 as having "upwards of fifty buildings, mostly adobe. The town has one hotel—not first class, three saloons, blacksmith shop, a post office, stamp mill for gold ore and several *arrastras* worked by private individuals."

Apache Pass

Apache Pass is located northeast of Arizona 186. The junction is near mile post 351. From the community of Bowie on Interstate 10,

Fort Bowie is about 14 miles south.

Apache Pass is a twisting, narrow passage separating the Dos Cabezas and Chiricahua mountains. Here desert grasslands merge with the piñon and juniper of mountain slopes. The rough-hewn mountains are streaked with sandy washes lined with oak, hackberry, willow, and black walnut. It is a biotic transition zone—to the east is the Chihuahua Desert; to the west the Sonora Desert. The six-mile trail through the pass connected Sulphur Springs Valley with San Simon Valley. The old stage line eastbound from Dos Cabezas crossed the summit at 5,115 feet and descended along arroyos and rocky slopes two miles to where the road entered Siphon Canyon. This point marks the site of the old Butterfield station. East of the station was a narrow defile that led out in a northerly direction to the San Simon Valley.

The pass was a well-traveled Indian trail and was used by early Spanish soldiers on campaigns against the Apaches. Lieutenant John G. Parke camped near Siphon Canyon in 1854 while surveying a proposed railroad route. It was determined that the grade was too steep, and a new route was surveyed north of the Dos Cabezas Mountains.

During the mid-1850s the area was the scene of one of the bloodiest massacres of Americans in Arizona history. A westbound wagon train was ambushed in Siphon Canyon by Nachi, the father of Cochise. More than thirty immigrants, including women and children, were murdered, their bodies horribly mutilated. Several women were taken captive and of these, two were sold in Mexico. The others were put to death.

In July 1858 the Butterfield Overland Mail Company opened a station in the pass. The stageline was a government-subsidized operation that ran from Tipton, Missouri to San Francisco, California. Because of the $600,000 subsidy, it cost the government $65 for a letter from Missouri to California. The 2,800-mile route, dubbed the "Ox-bow," dipped down through El Paso to Tucson, then across to Los Angeles and up to the City by the Bay. "Remember, boys," owner John Butterfield commanded, "nothing on God's earth must stop the United States Mail." The reliable stageline was run with clockwork efficiency. Butterfield was a genius at keeping the stages running on schedule. The cross-country trip took about twenty-six days; the fare was $200 plus meals, which usually consisted of coffee, beans, venison, mule meat, salt pork and plenty of mustard. The stage ran day and night, traveling at an average speed of five miles an hour and making about 120 miles in a twenty-four-hour period. The leather-slung coaches, described by Mark Twain as "cradles on wheels," offered a rough ride, rendering a night's rest nearly impossible. On

*Mickey Free, aka
Felix Telles. His
alleged kidnapping
by Cochise set off a
long and bitter war
in southwest
Arizona. He later
became a scout for
the army.*
Courtesy
Southwest Studies

steep grades, the able men were required to get out and push. In Arizona's hot desert, lighter, open-air Celerity wagons were used instead of the more familiar Concord coaches. Canvas curtains could be lowered to provide shade but did little to keep out the dust.

Newspapers published information advising wary passengers on proper conduct. Some of these instructions included: If a team runs away, don't jump out, just sit tight (some of the mules were so green they had to be blindfolded before they could be hitched); don't discuss politics or religion with your fellow passengers; don't drink hard liquor in freezing weather; and don't groom your hair with grease (too much dust).

Male passengers literally drank their way across Arizona, tossing their empties out along the road. Twentieth-century airplane pilots claimed they could easily follow the route of the old Butterfield line by the "dead soldiers" glittering in the sun.

At the time the Butterfield Overland Stage Line opened a station in Apache Pass, a large number of Chiricahua Apaches were living in *rancherias* scattered throughout the area. Among these were Cochise with about seven hundred warriors and their families, Jack with about five hundred warriors, and Esconolea with three hundred warriors and their families.

Relations between the Butterfield employees and the Apaches were relatively serene, but being surrounded by about 1,500 unpredictable warriors kept the ten employees at the station in a state of wariness.

Despite the fact that the Apaches living at the pass allowed the twice-weekly stages to pass through and tolerated the presence of the employees, they continued to raid Mexican and American ranches and settlements. There were several "incidents" that led to open warfare between United States troops and the Apaches near the pass, and it's safe to say that the "inevitable clash of cultures" would have occurred sooner or later.

The Bascom affair, involving the alleged kidnapping of a youth near Sonoita Creek, is generally credited as being the spark that set off the hostilities. Lieutenant George Bascom accused Cochise of the crime and then seized hostages to assure the safe return of the youngster. Cochise retaliated by capturing some white men, including an employee at the Butterfield station. When both sides refused to back down, Cochise executed his hostages. The army responded by hanging their captives.

During this time, both the eastbound and westbound stagecoaches survived death-defying rides through the Apache-infested defile. The eastbound was attacked just as it passed the summit and headed down the grade toward the station. Two mules were hit and went down, a passenger was hit in the chest, and the driver caught a bullet in the leg. While the passengers returned fire, two men ran forward and cut the traces from the wounded animals. The driver was able to get the stage moving again, but when they reached a small bridge crossing a deep arroyo, he saw the side planks had been removed by the crafty Apaches. He cracked his long whip and forged ahead, the belly of the coach literally sliding across the center of the structure and up the other side to the safety of the station.

Fortunately for the westbound stage, it was running two hours ahead of schedule. The Apaches had piled dried grass in a narrow passageway, intending to light the grass just before the stage arrived. It was a favorite trick to stop a team of horses or mules. Since the warriors weren't expecting the stage to arrive early, no one was there to set the fire, and the coach rolled into the station without further incident. The stage remained at the station, marking the only time something on "God's earth" stopped John Butterfield and the United States Mail.

The Bascom Affair has been romanticized and fictionalized. Cochise emerged a hero—he had been shamefully wronged by a "brash young army officer" and had taken vengeance on all whites in southern Arizona. In reality, the Chiricahua leader was known as a rogue long before the incident with Lieutenant Bascom.

The Civil War had more to do with increased Apache raiding in southern Arizona than Cochise's "outrage" at Apache Pass. The threat of an invasion by Texans caused the federal command to order the abandonment of Forts Breckenridge and Buchanan. The soldiers were ordered east to the Rio Grande, and the citizens of western New Mexico (Arizona) were left to fend for themselves.

In February 1862 fifty-four men under the command of Confederate Captain Sherod Hunter, rode through Apache Pass on their way to occupy Tucson for the Confederacy. Following Confederate defeats in New Mexico and the approach of the 2,000-man California Column, Hunter discreetly withdrew his troops to Texas. He passed through sometime in late April 1862, encountering only minor opposition from the Apaches. The arrival of advance elements of the California Column at Apache Pass set the stage for the largest battle between army troops and Indians on Arizona soil.

After raising the Stars and Stripes over Tucson, General James Carleton, commander of the California Column dispatched an advance force toward Apache Pass. On July 8, 1862 Captain Tom Roberts and 126 men and nearly 250 animals were ordered to proceed to the abandoned Butterfield station at San Simon, just east of Apache Pass. His mission was to fortify the station and give protection to the supply trains for the main column.

Meanwhile, at Apache Pass, the Chiricahuas were joining forces with the Mimbreños under their great chief, Mangas Coloradas (Red Sleeves). In the annals of Apache history there had never been such an overpowering figure. He stood six feet six inches and weighed over two hundred pounds. Daniel Conner, chronicler of the Joseph Rutherford Walker Expedition, met the great chief and gives this description:

> He had prominent bloodshot eyes, disdained to notice anyone, and was head and shoulders above any paleface present. His dress consisted of a broad-brimmed small crowned chip or straw hat of Mexican manufacture—a checked cotton shirt, breech cloth or clout, and a high pair of moccasins . . . with legs to them like boots, only that they fit the legs closely. Mangus (sic) was apparently fifty years of age and a large athletic man considerably over six feet in height, with a large broad head covered with a tremendously heavy growth of long hair that reached to his waist. His shoulders were broad and his chest full, and muscular. He stood erect and his step was proud and altogether he presented quite a model of physical manhood.

Mangas Coloradas possessed many attributes of greatness—he was soldier, statesman, diplomat, and considered the greatest of all Apache headmen. He was also said to have had no peer when it came to brutality and ferocity. That he was a skillful statesman is evidenced by the fact that he married his daughters to other Apache headmen. It was said that he once captured a beautiful Mexican girl and brought her home to join his family as wife number three. Wives number one and two were sisters and did not appreciate this encroachment on their rights by a beautiful rival, especially a hated Mexican. They encouraged their two brothers to "persuade" Mangas to rid himself of the young woman. In the melee that followed, Mangas slew both his brother-in-law adversaries. From that time on nobody took exception to his new bride.

From this union, Mangas raised several daughters, and like the feudal lords of old, married them off to leaders of nearby bands, including Cochise. Normally the Apache groups worked independently of each other and did not feel under any obligation to support one another if they chose not to. However, it was different if a father-in-law called for a joining of forces. The Apaches are a matriarchal society, and upon marriage the men become obligated to the woman's clan. So that summer of 1862, when Cochise and his father-in-law decided to join forces, other in-laws felt compelled to do the same; thus a band of seven hundred warriors assembled to meet the soldiers at the pass.

Meanwhile Captain Roberts divided his eastbound force to insure that there would be adequate water supplies at each camp. He advanced toward the pass while Captain John C. Cremony was left with a small detachment to follow up with the supply wagons.

On the afternoon of July 14, Roberts, accompanied by sixty infantry soldiers and seven cavalrymen, plus a battery of two twelve-pound prairie howitzers, set out for Apache Pass, about forty miles away, arriving at the entrance to the pass about noon the next day.

Roberts's men were only a half-mile from the abandoned stage station. The Apaches concealed in the surrounding hills opened fire on the rear of the column. The soldiers returned the fire, killing four and losing one. Roberts withdrew to the summit of the pass and regrouped his men. He sent skirmishers out on both sides of the road and loaded his howitzers. The thirsty soldiers were desperate in the knowledge that unless they took the spring a few yards beyond the station, they would surely perish, as the only other water supply was several miles to the rear. They literally bulled their way to the station walls. By now Roberts's men had undergone nineteen hours of march and six hours of fighting on one cup of coffee.

On the two hills just east of the station, the Apaches had built a breastwork of rocks, giving them a commanding view of the spring below. They had the advantage of firing down on the soldiers from a range of about four hundred feet, thus thwarting any attempt to rush the spring. Roberts brought up his howitzers in wagons and placed them in a dry wash. He opened fire, the shells exploding over the rock parapets and raining schrapnel on the warriors. This destructive new weapon forced the Apaches to abandon their position, the Apache leaders later saying that they could defeat the soldiers, but not the "wagon that shoots twice." They had noted the puff of smoke and the explosion at the wagon, but the monster had exploded a second time, right above their heads, scattering pieces of hot metal in all directions. The army won that round, and the thirsty troopers filled their canteens and drank heartily that night.

Later that evening Roberts dispached six cavalrymen to rejoin the supply train and escort it to the pass. As the six cavalrymen rode west of the summit and into the Sulphur Springs Valley to the west of the pass, they were attacked by a large number of well-armed Apaches. In the opening fire, one man was shot in the arm and two horses were wounded. Private John Teal fell behind and found himself cut off from the rest of the group. Realizing they could be of no help to Teal, the others rode on, and after a frantic chase reached the supply train safely. Teal, meanwhile, had turned his horse southward, heading down the valley in hopes of outdistancing the warriors, but to no avail. A well placed shot dropped his horse, but Teal jumped free and secured a position behind the dying animal, his only chance being to keep the enemy at a safe distance until darkness approached. The rapid firing of his breech-loading carbine confused the Apaches, who up to now had not encountered such a weapon. They circled cautiously, waiting for a chance to close in for the kill. The stand-off had lasted about an hour when a warrior rode within range of Teal's carbine. Teal took careful aim and fired, sending the bullet into the midsection of the Apache. The others lost interest in Teal at this point, riding away with the wounded warrior. Wasting little time, Teal swung his saddle over his shoulder, grabbed his bridle and rifle, and began the eight-mile trek to the supply train. He arrived late that same evening, much to the surprise of his friends who had given him up for dead.

It was later learned that the warrior Private Teal had shot was the notorious Mangas Coloradas. Carrying their wounded chieftain southward, the Apaches rode into the little Mexican settlement of Janos, woke up the local doctor and told him: "Mangas hurt. You make Mangas well and Janos lives. If Mangas dies, Janos dies." No physician has ever operated under more trying conditons. Luckily the good doctor was aided by the rawhide constitution of his patient. The bullet was extracted, the wound bound, and true to their word, the warriors left.

Old Mangas never recovered fully from his wound, and about a year later, he was taken prisoner by a party of prospectors. When the army

Fort Bowie at the time of Geronimo's surrender in 1886
Courtesy Arizona State Library

learned of his capture, they sent soldiers to take charge. Sometime during the night, Mangas was killed, the army claiming the old chief had been "shot while trying to escape." Civilian eyewitnesses claimed Mangas had been tormented into resisting, then brutally murdered.

Shortly after Teal came in from his ordeal, Captain Roberts and his infantry rejoined the supply train. After a brief pause, the column set out for the pass. When they reached the station, they learned that the Apaches were again in control of the spring and the high ground.

The previous day's battle had given Roberts an accurate knowledge of the terrain. The wagons and mules were protected in the stone corral, and the artillery and troopers were in place. To the sound of bugle, fife, and drum, which must have been something of a curiosity in the middle of Apacheria, the soldiers advanced toward the spring. Once again, the howitzers blasted the hilltop, filling the air with case shot and causing the Apaches to abandon their positions. The fleeing Apaches were an easy target for the riflemen. Those who escaped were cut down by the cavalry. It was to be an oft-repeated story in the latter days of the Indian wars.

When the battle ended, Roberts and his men had gained control of the spring. Roberts reported losing two men in the battle, while the Apaches loss was set at sixty-three. Recent historians have given a more realistic figure of ten Apaches killed, and the battle is generally regarded as a stand-off. The Apaches blamed most of their losses on the "wagons that shoot twice." This battle caused the Apaches to change their tactics to a guerilla-type warfare.

A few days later, Colonel Carleton arrived at the pass. It was decided that a post was needed there for the protection of military and civilians alike, so Fort Bowie was officially established on July 28, 1862. The post was named for Colonel George Washington Bowie, one of the California Volunteers.

The original site of Fort Bowie was on a knoll overlooking Apache Spring. It also gave a broad view of Siphon Canyon and the pass. But space was limited, and in 1868 a new fort was built a half mile east.

During the 1880s Fort Bowie became one of the most important military posts in the Southwest. Search and destroy missions would be launched into Mexico until the final surrender of Geronimo's band in 1886. The post was officially abandoned on October 17, 1894. In 1964 the old fort with its picturesque but crumbling adobe walls was designated a National Historic Site.

Arizona 186 to Arizona 181

Arizona 186 becomes Arizona 181 after it passes the junction at the Chiricahua National Monument. The imposing Chiricahua Mountains to the east are an awesome barrier separating Sulphur Springs Valley from San Simon Valley.

In 1872 a large part of this area was designated a Chiricahua Apache Reservation. A treaty was arranged between Cochise and General Oliver O. Howard ending the bloody ten-year war that had made the area unhabitable for settlers, miners, and ranchers. The reservation was closed in 1876 when the Chiricahua were moved to San Carlos, and the grass-carpeted valley was soon swarming with Texas cattle.

Ten miles south of the junction the highway turns west toward the picturesque and historical Dragoon Mountains on the west side of Sulpur Springs Valley. A dirt road leading east follows West Turkey Creek canyon 4.5 miles to the gravesite of notorious Tombstone gunfighter Johnny Ringo.

Ringo's overblown reputation was made during the Earp-Clanton feud in the early 1880s. The only man Ringo killed in a fight was Louis Hancock, who was shot to death in a Tombstone saloon after refusing to let Ringo buy him a drink. The fight didn't remotely resemble the classic western shootout, since Hancock was taking a drink at the time Ringo drew on him, and was not much to make a reputation on, but self-styled Western experts have a way of embellishing the reputations of the undeserving. Ringo was closely associated with the rustler element led by N. H. "Old Man" Clanton and later by Curly Bill Brocius.

In July 1882 Ringo's body, with a bullet in the temple, was found propped against an oak tree on the banks of west Turkey Creek. Some trophy hunter had removed a piece of his scalp with a pocketknife. A coroner's jury ruled it suicide, but many people thought otherwise. Ringo's rifle was propped against a tree, and his hand gripped his revolver. The six-gun carried only five cartridges but nearly everybody kept the chamber where the hammer rested empty to prevent accidental discharge. There is evidence that Wyatt Earp killed Ringo in revenge for the murder of his brother Morgan; however, some believe he was killed by Buckskin Frank Leslie, another well-known Tombstone gunman, while others say he was shot by a small-time gambler named Johnny-behind-the-deuce (John O'Rourke).

Cochise Stronghold

Due west of the community of Pearce is the Cochise Stronghold. The area was one of several used by the noted Chiricahua leader. When Cochise died in 1874, his body was taken to a secret place in these mountains and buried in the traditional custom of the Apaches, all traces of the grave having been eradicated.

The hazards of early-day travel on Arizona "highways"
Courtesy Southwest Studies

*Sam Heintzelman,
commanding officer
at Fort Yuma,
mining magnate,
and a leader in the
fight for territorial
status*
Courtesy Arizona
Historical Foundation

Arizona 286
Roblés Junction to Sasabe

Arizona 286 heads south toward the Mexican border, running parallel with Brawley Wash. Brawley is a corruption of Bowley, a stage station on the road to Quijotoa in the 1880s. Barnes mentions the site as being an abandoned ranch in the 1920s.

The Altar Valley is first mentioned by Father Kino in 1693. The valley runs southward from the Mexican border, but the Altar River, which has its headwaters in the same area, flows south, passing close to the site of the ancient Papago village of Ali-Shonak (Place of the Small Springs). In the 1730s, the fabulous *Planchas de Plata* silver strike took place near here. "Ali-Shonak" became "Arisoonac" to the Spanish but was changed to Arizona by the Anglos.

Located east of Arizona 286, Cerro Colorado, or "Red Hill," was the site of the famous Sam Heintzelman Mine. Heintzelman, commanding officer at Fort Yuma in the early 1850s, was an active promoter of and investor in Arizona mines. He and Charles Poston bossed operations here until the Apaches drove them out following the outbreak of the Civil War in 1861. The mines were re-opened after the Apache wars and worked into the early 1900s.

The history of the legendary Aquirre family runs deep in these parts. This ranching and freighting family, led by Epifanio, Yjinio, and Pedro, Jr., opened a stage line from Tucson to Altar in 1868. Two years later Don Epifanio was killed by Indians on the road near Sasabe.

In the early 1870s Don Pedro, Jr., built a horse relay station called the "La Posta de Aquirre" on the rolling hills of the Altar Valley. Soon after, he established the storied Buenos Aires Ranch. A dam was built at the fork of two washes, forming a lake that covered several hundred acres.

In 1863 Governor John Goodwin and his party traveled from Albuquerque to Prescott to set up a government in the new Arizona. They were delivered safely by Don Yjinio Aquirre and his capable muleskinners.

The border town of Sasabe, which in Tono O'Odham (Papago) means head, or parent valley, refers to the Altar. Apparently the community of Sasabe has had several locations. The "new border town" of Sasabe is located where the community of "La Osa" used to be. Modern Sasabe was the dream development of Carlos Escalante, who settled here in 1916 when a new port of entry was established. He called the private village San Fernando in honor of his uncle Don Fernando Serrano. Don Fernando had left Mexico during the Revolution of 1910 and established a cattle ranch nearby. The name of the village had to be changed in 1926 because there was a San Fernando in California.

II Central Arizona

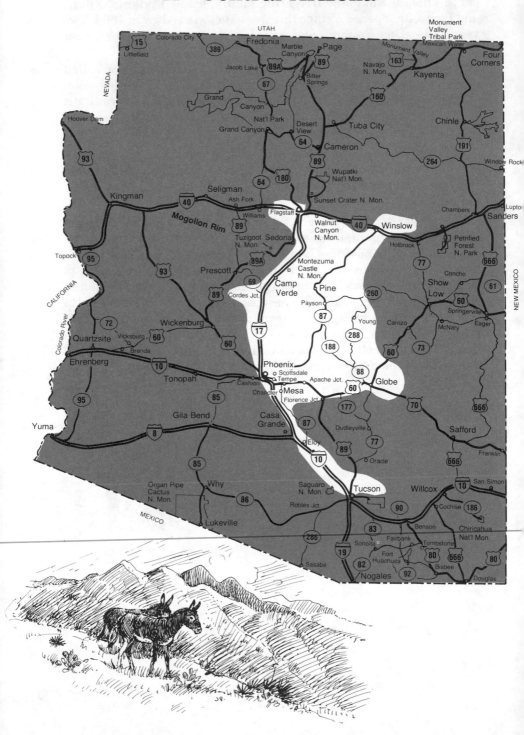

Interstate 10
Phoenix to Tucson

Phoenix

Once upon a time in Greek Mythology there lived a legendary bird who, every 500 years or so, flew to the Egyptian city of Heliopolis, the place of worship for the Sun God. Upon the great altar the bird built a nest from the twigs of spice trees then settling into the nest, set it on fire and was consumed by the flames. Then, when all that remained was ashes, the bird miraculously arose from its funeral pyre, reborn and beautiful once more and gracefully flew away. It was called phoenix.

—Storyteller

The earliest inhabitants of the Phoenix area were migrant big game hunters called Paleo-Indians. Dating back at least 15,000 years, they left no permanent mark upon the area. Climates changed, large animals like the mastodon and mammoth became extinct. Other peoples followed the Paleo-Indians but also left little evidence of their culture.

Then, about 300 B.C. a new people entered from Mexico and slowly spread along the river valleys of southern Arizona, including the Gila and Santa Cruz. By 700 A.D. they had reached the Salt River Valley. They brought with them a rich, highly developed culture that is surpassed in this hemisphere only by that of the Incas and Mayans. By 1100 A.D. they had created a network of cities and satellite communities with a population estimated as high as a hundred thousand. They left behind no written history, and since we don't know what they called themselves, we've given them the name Hohokam, a Pima Indian word for "all used up" or "vanished ones." During seven hundred years in the Salt River Valley, the Hohokam engineered the most extensive prehistoric canal system in the world. They introduced both cotton and barley to this area. Masters of creative arts, the Hohokam were using the lost wax process to make jewelry hundreds of years before the Europeans. Using an acidic juice from the cactus, they created elaborate etchings on seashells. The Hohokam introduced a game played with a rubber ball that had to be knocked through a hoop; it was played in open-air, sunken stadiums

147

and was undoubtedly Arizona's first experience with a spectator sport.

The Hohokam culture reached its zenith about 1200 A.D. About 1250 A.D. the Hohokam people began to leave the Salt River Valley, and by 1400 A.D. they had vanished completely. The reasons for their decline and departure remain a mystery. Some believe a great earthquake drove them away. Others are convinced a prolonged drought led to their demise. Some believe the soil became oversaturated with alkali. Another theory was that hostile, nomadic tribes caused them to emigrate. The most logical theory is that the Hohokam never left at all and that their descendants are the Pima and Papago (O'Odham) of today.

The Salt River Valley lay unclaimed for nearly 500 years. At the close of the Civil War in 1865, Fort McDowell was established near where Sycamore Creek joins the Verde River. Lieutenant John Y. T. Smith, mustered out of the army about that time, decided to stay on as a hay contractor and post sutler. He'd seen the fields of wild hay growing on the flood plains of the Salt River eighteen miles to the south and decided to set up a hay camp. The place became known as Smith's Station and was located on the road he built to Fort McDowell (near 40th and Washington streets of today's Phoenix).

Originally John Y. T. Smith was just plain John Smith, but he grew tired of meeting so many other people with the same name. Later he became active in territorial politics, and when he ran for Congress in 1874, a newspaper editor commented unfavorably on a man with a name like "John Smith" running for office. Smith didn't have a checkered past, and John Smith was his real name, so he went to the legislature and legally added the middle initials "Y. T.," which stood for "Yours Truly."

In September 1867 Smith's Station was visited by Jack Swilling, thirty-seven-year-old ex-Indian fighter, adventurer, hellion, Confederate officer, and most recently, a member of the famed Walker party which had discovered gold in the Bradshaw Mountains. Swilling was quick to note the opportunities for irrigating the rich, fertile soil by cleaning out the old Hohokam canals and ditches. He went to Wickenburg, a thriving mining community on the Hasayampa River, fifty miles to the northwest, and organized a company called the Swilling Irrigation Canal Company. The gregarious redhead also raised $400 to fund the project, then recruited a party of strong-backed visionaries and headed for Smith's Station. Swilling and sixteen companions arrived in December 1867, and began the laborious task of cleaning out the old canals. They began digging in the north bank of the Salt across from Tempe but hit caliche and rock, so they moved down the river to 40th Street and the riverbed near Smith's Station.

Jack Swilling,
adventurer,
Confederate officer,
Union scout,
argonaut, and
"father of irrigation"
in the Salt River
Valley
Courtesy Arizona
Historical Foundation

By March 1868 the wheat and barley crops were in, and the population had reached fifty. Swilling's Ditch, as the watering system was called, ran northwest across the desert for 1½ miles, then curved back toward the river. Eventually it would be called the Town Ditch and would run along the north side of Van Buren across to about 27th Avenue. During its heyday the ditch was multi-purpose—it was used to bathe in, drink, irrigate, and do the laundry in. One newspaper complained that saloonkeepers washed their spittoons in the ditch when nobody was looking. Nobody could have known at this time that from these humble beginnings the Salt River Valley would develop into one of the richest agricultural regions in the world. The first permanent farm in the valley was started by Frenchy Sawyer. That site is marked by a small plaque on the southeast corner of Washington and 24th streets.

The federal census of 1870 recorded a population of sixty-one women and 164 men. The ages of this hardy group ranged from twenty-one to thirty. Among the populace were ninety-six who listed themselves as farmers. There wasn't a single doctor, lawyer, banker, or teacher in the whole community.

On October 20, 1870 a committee of citizens gathered to select a townsite. Among the members of the selection committee was Bryan Philip Darrell Duppa, better known as "Lord" Duppa, reported to be a

British lord who'd been something of an embarassment to his family and had been exiled to the colonies. He received financial support on a regular basis as long as he remained out of England. The thirty-seven-year-old adventurer was strongly addicted to ardent spirits, probably the reason for his exile. "Lord" Duppa was also a well-traveled, educated man who spoke five languages fluently. His friends complained, however, that he was hard to comprehend because he remained in a drunken state most of the time and spoke all five languages at once.

Sometime between 1868 and 1872 "Lord" Duppa built a two-room adobe house at 116 W. Sherman, three blocks south of today's Central Avenue underpass. Today that simple little casa with a roof of cottonwood beams overlaid with salt-cedar poles and covered with arrowweed and mud seems overwhelmed by the towering skyscrapers of downtown Phoenix. It is the oldest house still standing in the capital city and is the most obvious link with the city's historic past. Duppa favored locating the townsite about four miles west of Smith's Station, near today's Central Avenue and Van Buren Street. Actually, there were three proposed sites: one group wanted to locate at the northeast corner of 16th and Van Buren; one at 32nd and Van Buren; and the third on a mesquite-covered parcel between 7th Street and 7th Avenue, the site finally chosen. The vote of the committee resulted in a victory for the "downtowners" over the "eastsiders"; that's why the center of Phoenix is at its present location and not further east. Jack Swilling, who wanted the 32nd Street site, was so angry at the voting results, he fired a round of birdshot, scoring a direct hit on one of those who had voted against him.

Swilling, a generous and big-hearted man, was the product of the violent frontier. Originally from South Carolina, he had fought in both the Mexican and Civil wars and had been involved in several scrapes with Apaches and Comanches. At one time his skull had been fractured by a gun barrel, and he was carrying a bullet in his left side from another shooting scrape. Because his old injuries caused a great deal of pain, he took morphine and whiskey to dull the pain, and at times became a little crazy. He would die in a Yuma jail in 1878, accused of a crime he didn't commit.

Not long after the townsite had been selected, a citizen came down from Wickenburg and planted the first tree, a cottonwood, on Washington Street. The first lot, located on the southwest corner of 1st and Washington streets, sold for the sum of $103. More than sixty lots, with prices ranging from $20 to $140, were sold by the end of the day.

The next task for the settlers was to chose a name. several were proposed, including Stonewall, Salinas, Pumkinville, and Millville. The eccentric, bibulous "Lord" Duppa is credited by some historians with providing the inspiration, but credit for naming the city after the mythical Phoenix bird that rose from its own ashes and flourished again should be given to Jack Swilling. He found the description in his Webster's dictionary and thought the name suited the place; thus, on October 26, 1870 the tiny community of adobe houses, reborn from the ashes of the great Hohokam civilization, had a name.

In 1871 Maricopa County was organized, and Phoenix became the county seat. Captain William Hancock, the man who surveyed the townsite and reputedly erected the first adobe building, was appointed sheriff on an interim basis.

The first election for Sheriff of Maricopa County set an early precedent for political fireworks. Three candidates tossed their hats into the ring, least conspicuous of the trio being Jim Barnum, who wisely sat back and let the other two, "Whispering Jim" Favorite and J. M. Chenowth, fight it out. Each claimed the other was immoral, hated kids, and was rude to little old ladies. The feuding between Favorite and Chenowth was giving the two so much attention that poor Jim Barnum was almost forgotten and didn't seem to have a chance. Then a day before the election, "Whispering Jim" and Chenowth grew tired of arguing politics and went for their six-shooters. When the smoke cleared, "Whispering Jim" lay dead, and the city fathers suggested Chenowth leave town. Jim Barnum was elected as the first sheriff of Maricopa County by a landslide.

In 1871 Bill Kirkland, another distinguished Arizona pioneer, moved to Phoenix. Kirkland, a Virginian, had been one of the first Anglo-Americans to arrive in Arizona after the Gadsden Purchase. It was he who took the American flag and planted it on the roof of Ed Miles's hardware store—the first time the colors had flown over this new United States territory that would one day be called Arizona. Kirkland was also the first Anglo-American to engage in cattle ranching in Arizona.

Kirkland, his wife Missouri Ann, and their two children moved into a small adobe house on Washington Street, between Central (Center) and 1st Avenue. On August 15, 1871, a daughter, May Ellen, was born. She was the first Anglo-American child born at the Phoenix townsite.

In 1872 Phoenix opened its first school. Fewer than twenty youngsters showed up for the opening class, which was held in a one-room adobe building with a mud-thatched roof. It did boast the first wooden floor in town. The first teacher was a lady named Ellen Shaver. The pretty young school marm didn't last long—none did in a town full of lonesome bachelors. John Yours Truly Smith promptly took her for his wife.

By 1877 funds had been appropriated for the construction of roads that would link Phoenix with the outside world. Not much more than dusty cattle trails extended toward Globe, Prescott, Wickenburg, and Yuma. By 1879 a road stretched south across the Salt and Gila rivers to Maricopa, linking Phoenix by stagecoach to the new Southern Pacific Railroad.

It was a dusty, jostling sixteen-hour ride from Maricopa to Phoenix, but the local people were happy and tolerant just to be so close to a railroad. In 1879 Sam Lount opened the first ice-making plant. He sold his ice for seven cents a pound, and anyone who has ever spent a summer in Phoenix before air conditioning will surely agree that there ought to be a monument dedicated to Lount. By 1880 Phoenix, zesty and full of optimism, boasted a population of 1,708.

Since both transcontinental railroads missed Phoenix, it looked as though the isolated community on the banks of the Salt River was destined to remain small and unimportant. Tucson had the railroad and all the amenities that came with it. At the time, not even the most prophetic could foresee what was about to take place in what would become known as the Valley of the Sun. Agriculture would be the key to Phoenix's growth, but it would take men of vision and fortitude to bring it about. Someone had to figure a better way to water the thirsty desert. Historically, lands located north of a canal were considered worthless. To change this, all one had to do was build bigger and better canals.

A bold visionary appeared in the person of William J. Murphy. In 1885 Murphy took on the difficult task of building the thirty-five-mile-long Arizona Canal, a project both massive and speculative, to open up irrigation north of the Grand Canal. The company that contracted Murphy went broke, so he took his pay in bonds. Self-interest groups tried to block his efforts with political obstacles, but Murphy was undaunted.

In June 1887 Murphy was able to meet his deadline, completing the project with just two hours to spare. The Arizona Canal was a reality, and agriculture on a much larger scale would now be possible. There were now four canals north of the Salt River, but delivery systems were poor and there was a lot of water loss. Murphy organized the Arizona Improvement Company and built a cross-cut canal connecting all four canals, minimizing water loss and improving delivery. Phoenix was now able to challenge Prescott and Tucson, perennial rivals for the territorial capital, and two years later, Phoenix succeeded in getting the capital.

The courthouse in Phoenix before 1900 Courtesy Arizona Historical Society Library

For years the "Capital on Wheels" had been the source of a bitter struggle between Tucson and Prescott. Prescott was named first capital in 1864. Three years later it was moved to Tucson, where it remained until 1877, when the Prescott politicos garnered enough votes to get it back. It remained in Prescott until 1889, until Phoenix could exercise enough clout to relocate it on the banks of the Salt River.

A story is told that on the evening before the final vote, one of Prescott's delegates went over to the red light district to pay a visit to one of the ladies on the line. He had a glass eye, of which he was self-conscious, and after blowing out the lamp, he removed the eye and placed it in a water glass next to the bed. Sometime during the night his friend became thirsty and turned the water glass bottoms up, swallowing the legislator's glass eye. The story goes on to say that when the delegate awoke the next morning and found his eye gone, vanity overcame him and he refused to attend the legislative session, so Phoenix won the capital by one vote.

Before the days of a Capitol building, the legislators met in the County Court House. Dedicated in 1901, the beautiful new Capitol building on West Washington Street was ready for occupancy. On top of the huge domed structure was a weather vane called "Winged Victory," designed as the figure of a beautiful woman. Cowboys in town on a spree used to take delight in racing their horses out to the Capitol to take pot shots at the shapely celestial creature on the dome. It was said that prevailing winds at certain times of the year caused her to face west, thus turning her backside to those approaching the Capitol steps. Apparently a few stuffy legislators took personal af-

153

front at this indignant lack of respect and had the lady welded in place facing the entrance. A few years ago the building underwent a remodeling and "Winged Victory" was freed again to expose her backside whenever the winds dictated.

Even with the completion of the Arizona Canal, Phoenix faced serious water problems. Disastrous floods in 1890 and 1891 nearly wiped out the town. These were followed by long droughts in the 1890s. There seemed to be too much or too little water to sustain life in Phoenix. Crops were withering in the fields, and livestock were dying of thirst. Discouraged farmers were abandoning their lands, packing up their families, and leaving the valley. A way had to be found to guarantee a permanent water supply.

There was a lot of politiking going on in Washington in 1900 by western states and territories seeking funding for water projects. The Newlands Act of 1902 called for reclamation projects in the West to be financed by money raised from the sale of public lands; by a stroke of luck and some hard lobbying by Arizonans, the Washington politicos decided that the best place in the West to demonstrate what reclamation projects could do in arid lands was to build a massive dam at the confluence of Tonto Creek and the Salt River, in the Arizona Territory.

The Theodore Roosevelt Dam was completed in 1911, and the future of Phoenix was assured. It marked the dawning of a new era—during the next few years four more dams would be built on the Salt and two on the Verde.

Before the building of Roosevelt Dam, the federal government wanted a guaranteed repayment plan before it would make such a huge loan (the original estimate was $3 million; the final cost was $10 million). Since Washington refused to deal with individual landowners, it became necessary for the Arizonans to unite; thus was born the

Phoenix in 1900 Courtesy Arizona Historical Foundation

Salt River Valley Water Users Association (today's Salt River Project), whose duties would include local management of the massive project. Men of vision like Ben Fowler, Willam J. Murphy, Dwight Heard, and John Orme were faced with the difficult task of convincing landowners to put their lands up as collateral and work for a common goal instead of following the prevailing attitude of "every man for himself." If the Arizonans would not unite, the funds would go to some other state or territory. The association was also given the responsibility of managing the 13,000-square-mile watershed in the mountains north and east of Phoenix. The government loan to build Theodore Roosevelt Dam was paid in full by 1955.

The growth of Phoenix has been spectacular as the rush to the sun belt followed World War II, and Phoenix, attractive to industry and a huge work force, has become the third largest high-tech area in the country.

Camelback Mountain (Phoenix) in 1915
Courtesy Arizona Historical Foundation

Phoenix is a young place in an ancient land. Thousands of new residents move here each year, most being young and well-educated. They come seeking employment in the growing fields of high technology. Others come to reside in a place where the sun shines 85% of the time. Not long ago the desert was perceived by most as a dry, forbidding place with desiccating heat, inhabited only by cowboys, Indians, cactus, coyotes, and rattlesnakes. Today desert living means laid-back lifestyle, wide-open spaces, spectacular scenery—lakes,

Completion of a Phoenix leg of Southern Pacific's second main line across Arizona touched off this celebration at the Union Station in Phoenix in October, 1926. Courtesy Arizona Historical Society

streams, canyons, and mountains are attractions, all within easy reach by automobile.

The future of Phoenix appears bright. With the high-tech boom, corporate relocations and lifestyle, this metropolis with its futuristic architecture merging with the wide southwestern sky, becomes infinitely attractive.

Guadalupe

South of Baseline Road, on the left side of the road, is the Yaqui Indian community of Guadalupe. These Indians have been called the "fighting farmers of Mexico" and have a history that parallels that of the Apache Indians of the Southwest. They fought a long, bitter war against the Spaniards, and later against the Mexicans, who coveted their fertile farm lands along the Yaqui River. Like the Apaches, many were rounded up and exiled to an alien climate. During the nineteenth century, Washington moved the Apaches to Florida, and during the same period Mexico City sent the Yaquis to the jungles of Yucatan. During the Mexican Revolution the Yaquis sided with General Francisco "Pancho" Villa, and when Villa's army was defeated, many Yaquis sought refuge in the United States. The Mexican government tried to have them extradited, but because of fear of their extermination, the United States refused. A large number of Yaquis then moved to the Salt River Valley, hiring out as laborers on canal-building projects and settling in Scottsdale and Guadalupe.

During their turbulent time in Mexico, the Yaquis were befriended and staunchly defended by the Catholic padres against Spanish oppression and land-grabbing. The Catholics left a deep impression on the native religion, resulting in an interesting blend of the two religions.

The Pima Villages

Exit 175—The Gila River Arts & Crafts Center provides an excellent introduction to the history and culture of this area.

Moving south along Interstate 10 a few miles south of Guadalupe, the freeway crosses out of the Salt River Valley and into the Gila River Valley. Here, on the sprawling Gila River Indian Reservation, live the Ackimoel O'Odham—the People of the River, better known as the Pima.

Organized in 1859, the Gila River Indian Reservation is the oldest in Arizona. Its residents, according to many anthropologists, trace their ancestry to the Hohokam Indians, who arrived in this area as early as 300 B.C. The name Pima is a misnomer. Early Spanish explorers who encountered the natives farming the fertile river valleys applied the name. The first native response to Spanish conversation was *Pi-nyi-match*, a phrase that meant "I don't understand you." The word rolled off the Spanish tongue and came out sounding like Pima. During the Spanish period, the area of Arizona between the Yuma Crossing and the San Pedro River and south of the Gila River was called *Pimeria Alta* or Land of the Upper Pima. The Pima are closely related to the Desert People, or Tono O'Odham, better known as the Papago, also a misnomer, as Papago meant "Bean eaters" and was applied by the Spanish at the same time they misnamed the Pima. Since the Gila River was on the extreme northern frontier of the Pimeria Alta and too close to Apacheria for safety, no missions were built in this region. Thus, the Pima remained relatively free from Spanish and, later, from Mexican influence. The Spaniards did make an important contribution to Pima agriculture with the introduction of winter wheat and barley. Up to then the natives grew summer crops like melons, squash, maize, and cotton. Now they could farm year around. The introduction of livestock by the Spanish led the Pima to expand their agriculture.

Of all the tribal lands traversed in the great westward movement during the mid-nineteenth century, the Pima Indians are remembered as the most hospitable and helpful to immigrants and military alike. They lived on the eastern edge of the most tortuous part of the southern route to California. Here travelers could rest and recoup among the friendly Pimas prior to or upon completion of the long desert trip.

The first contact of Pimas with Anglo-Americans came in the 1820s when fur trappers like Pauline Weaver, Bill Williams, Joe Walker, Ewing Young, and James O. Pattie trapped beaver on the Gila River. Relations between the two groups seem to have been cordial. Pattie claimed that the Robideaux party, of which he was a member, was massacred by "Papagoes," but most historians believe the party was attacked by Mojaves, Yavapais, or Tonto Apaches, since aggressive warfare against the whites was contrary to Pima/Papago nature.

The next major contact with Anglo-Americans came in 1846 when General Stephen Kearny's hardriding dragoons and their guide Kit Carson passed through on their way to California. Traveling with Kearny was Lieutenant William Emory of the Army Corps of Topographical Engineers. Emory was making the first scientific study of the land and its people, and his notes are significant because they paint a vivid picture of the natives living along the Gila before they had been influenced by other cultures.

The first meeting took place on November 10, 1846: "Where we encamped, eight or nine miles from the Pimos village we met a Maricopo Indian, looking for his cattle. The frank, confident manner in which he approached us was in strange contrast with that of the suspicious Apache." A few minutes later a small party of Pimas approached the soldiers. They had been cautioned at outposts to be on the lookout for Apache war parties. Therefore, there was much relief among the natives upon meeting friendly white soldiers rather than an Apache war party.

The following day the interpreter for Juan Antonio Llunas, the Pima headman, led the expedition into the main villages near today's Sacaton. Emory continues:

We came in at the back of the settlement of Pimos Indians, and found our troops encamped in a corn field, from which the grain had been gathered. We were at once impressed with the beauty, order, and disposition of the arrangements for irrigating and draining the land. Corn, wheat, and cotton are the crops of this peaceful and intelligent race of people. All the crops have been gathered in, and the stubbles show they have been luxuriant. The cotton has been picked, and stacked for drying on the tops of sheds. The fields are sub-divided, by ridges of earth, into rectangles of about 200 x 100 feet for the convenience of irrigating. The fences are of sticks, wattled with willow and mezquite, and in this particular, set an example of economy in agriculture worthy to be followed by the Mexicans, who never use fences at all. The houses of the people are mere sheds, thatched with willow and corn stalks.

With the exception of the chief, Antonio Llunas, who was clad in cast off Mexican toggery, the dress of the men consisted of a cotton serape of domestic manufacture, and a breech cloth. Their hair was very long, and clubbed up. The women wore nothing but the serape pinned about the loins, after the fashion of Persico's Indian woman on the east side of the Capitol, though not quite so low.

Then a ritual as old as mankind was begun, one to be played out many times over the next thirty years along the Gila Trail:

> The camp was soon filled with men, women, and children, each with a basket of corn, frijoles, or meal, for traffic. Many had jars of the molasses expressed from the fruit of the Cereus Giganteus. Beads, red cloth, white domestic, and blankets, were the articles demanded in exchange. Major Swords, who had charge of the trading duty, pitched a temporary awning, under which to conduct the business, which had scarcely commenced before this place formed a perfect menagerie, into which crowded, with eager eyes, Pimos, Maricopas, Mexicans, French, Dutch, English, and Americans. As I passed on to take a peep at the scene, naked arms, hands and legs protruded from the awning. Inside there was no room for bodies, but many heads had clustered into a very small space, filled with different tongues and nations. The trade went merrily on, and the conclusion of each bargain was announced by a grunt and a joke, sometimes at the expense of the quartermaster, but oftener at that of the Pimos. . . .

The rich culture of the Pima made a deep impression on the soldier-scientist:

> To us it was a rare sight to be thrown in the midst of a large nation of what is termed wild Indians, surpassing many of the Christian nations in agriculture, little behind them in the useful arts, and immeasurably before them in honesty and virtue. During the whole of yesterday, our camp was full of men, women, and children, who sauntered amongst our packs, unwatched, and not a single instance of theft was reported.

Captain Philip St. George Cooke, who passed this way a few weeks later, was equally impressed by the honesty and integrity of the Pima, not to mention their cheerful nature and sunny dispositions:

> Several miles short of the village, groups of men, women, and girls were met, coming to welcome the battalion; these last, naked generally above the hips, were of every age and pretty, walking often by twos with encircling arms; it was a gladdening sight, so much cheerfulness and happiness. . . . There must be two thousand in camp, all enjoying themselves very much; they stroll about, their arms around each other, graceful and admirable in form; . . . their honesty is perfect. . . . At the chief's house I stopped a few minutes; I told him I had seen many tribes, and that the Pimos were the happiest and most prosperous I had ever seen.

Although the Pima were friendly and hospitable, in time of war they were brave warriors, fearing neither the Mexican nomadic bands, or the Americans. The principal chief, Juan Antonio, told Cooke they always resisted encroachments with force. "He said I could see," Cooke wrote, "they were poor and naked but they were content to live here by hard work on the spot which God had given them; and they did not like others to rob or steal; that they did not fear us, and run like the Apaches, because they made it a rule to injure no one in any way, and therefore never expected any one to molest them. In fact the Apaches do not molest them; but it is owing to the experience of their prowess."

Cooke also had good words for the Maricopa Indians, neighbors and allies of the Pima: "The hospitality and generosity of these allied tribes is noted: they feed and assist in every way travelers who are in need."

The Pima had fought a long and sometimes bloody war against the various Apache and Yavapai bands on the east and north and against the Yuma and Mojaves to the west. During the 1860s and '70s, rugged Pima warriors rode with American troops against some of these warrior tribes.

Unfortunately, their gracious hospitality and military assistance was forgotten after the subjugation of the Yavapais and Apaches. White settlers poured into the Gila River area above the Pima villages and cut off the vital water that had made Indian crops flourish for hundreds of years. Despite pleas from both the Pima and friendly whites, the bureaucracy in Washington was incredibly slow in responding to the needs of the Pima. For a time the federal government planned to move the tribe to Oklahoma, a plan which met stubborn resistance in the Pima villages. During the 1860s to '70s some moved to the Salt River Valley, where there was more water. They are the ancestors of the people of the Salt River Indian Reservation, east of Scottsdale.

Although the tribal organization of the Pima was strong, the villages, similar to the city-states of ancient Greece, held much political power. Each village had a chief, and one chief presided over all the villages. Each village, usually had a war chief, or "hardman," to lead them in battle.

Like all peoples, the O'Odham, or Pima, have their own creation story. It was generally told by one of the elders to the youngsters in the wintertime: In the beginning, Earthmaker danced on a huge ball of dirt until it took its present shape. From this mass, Itoi (Eetoy), or Elder Brother, jumped out, followed by Coyote. The three worked to get the place organized prior to the coming of the human beings. But the first people turned out to be bad, so Itoi, Earthmaker, and Coyote decided to flood the world. (Coyote, wily, mischievous, cunning, and sometimes foolhardy, appears regularly in Pima mythology.) Each agreed that the first to emerge after the great flood would be Elder Brother. Itoi came first and gained the title. Earthmaker was angry and sank into the earth. Then Itoi created more people from clay, but these people (the Hohokam) were also bad, so Itoi went into the earth to find allies. Deep underground he found the O'Odham. He organized and led them to the earth's surface where they drove away the people who had mistreated Itoi. All that remains of these people are the ruins that are seen today (such as the Casa Grande). Itoi named the people O'Odham and told them all they needed to know—then he left, promising to return at some future time.

Historically, the clans were patriarchal; the women belonged to the father's family until marriage. Since most of the people in the village were related, young people had to go outside to find a spouse. Generally, marriage was a simple matter: the prospective groom came to the home of the girl, stayed four nights and then she went to live with his clan. Divorce was easy. If the two weren't getting along, they just separated. If children were involved, it wasn't uncommon for the boys to remain with their father and the girls with their mother. Family support was shared equally, so in case of divorce the woman was capable of supporting herself. Polygamy was practiced, so a woman usually had little trouble finding another spouse, especially if she was industrious. In case of death, it was common for the survivor to become the spouse of one of the in-laws, or of some member of the deceased's extended family, such as a cousin.

The O'Odham were not warlike, but they fiercely defended their lands against other tribes. Raids by neighboring tribes occurred once or twice a month. Pima warriors would try to lure the raiders into a trap by building fires in empty shelters and then setting an ambush when the enemy took the bait. Also, the Pima kept a number of dogs to sound the alarm in case of attack. The Pima retaliated against raiding war parties—after an attack the war chief ("hardman") went through the village enlisting warriors. When he had raised a sizable army, the punitive expedition hit the trail. Women often accompanied these groups to help carry supplies. Usually they were relatives of slain Pima warriors. Unlike their Papago cousins, who campaigned against their enemies in small search and destroy groups, the Pima usually organized a large army. A battle commenced with the two war chiefs squaring off and calling each other bad names. The warriors gradually followed suit, until the event turned into a big shouting match. This was followed by the usual donnybrook. When an Apache was slain, the Pima warrior immediately withdrew from the fighting and blackened his face. Afterwards, they and their wives were required to spend sixteen days in isolation and fasting for

Ira Hays, US Marine hero. This Pima Indian was one of those who raised the American flag at Iwo Jima on February 23, 1945. The photograph brought both fame and misfortune to Hays.
Courtesy
Southwest Studies

purification. Meanwhile the weapons used in the killings were also given a purification ceremony. After the purification rituals, the warriors received great honor and respect for their heroic efforts.

Arizona's first national guard units were formed from Pima and Maricopa warriors. In 1865 at the old Butterfield station at Maricopa Wells, Company C, under Lieutenant Antonio Azul, a Pima chief, and Company D, under Lieutenant Juan Chivaria, were enlisted to campaign against Apaches and Yavapais.

There are a number of modern-day Pimas worth mentioning, such as Mathew Juan and Ira Hays. Mathew Juan, of Sacaton, was the first Arizonan killed in World War I and the first Native American to give his life for his country in that war. Ira Hays, of Bapchule, was one of the most famous fighting men of World War II. After enlisting in the United States Marines in 1942, he participated in the landings at Vella La Vella, New Caledonia, Bougainville, and Iwo Jima. Hays gained immortality at the latter on February 23, 1945, when he and four other Marines were photographed raising the flag atop Mt. Suribachi. The picture captured the imagination of Americans and would become one of the most celebrated wartime photographs ever taken. Ira Hays came home to a hero's welcome. Unfortunately life in postwar Arizona offered a difficult adjustment for the state's most famous war hero, as his personal battles with alcohol were overblown in the newspapers. His tragic death in 1955 was reminiscent of the words of F. Scott Fitzgerald: "You show me a hero and I'll write you a tragedy."

Exit 185—Arizona 93 to Casa Grande

Regarding monuments, Will Rogers used to say: "You don't need much monument if the cause is good. It's only these monuments that are for no reason at all that have to be big."

On the outskirts of Casa Grande, along what used to be the main highway between Tucson and Phoenix, stands a simple concrete monument surrounded by weeds and showing the ravages of time. It was erected at an 1846 campsite to honor the Mormon Battalion. Monuments like this one are scattered along the old Gila Trail, some erected by Boy Scout troops, others by interested civic groups, or by the descendants of the Mormon Battalion. Some members of this famed group of trailblazers returned to Arizona by way of Utah more than thirty years after the Civil War to take root in the land and build a new life. The real beauty of these simple, concrete monuments is that they honor people who came to this area not to destroy or take, but to build.

The 397 men and five women who left Santa Fe on October 19, 1846 to mark an overland road to California were embarking on the second half of a two-thousand-mile journey, the longest infantry march in American history, and the roughest, requiring great stamina and rugged determination. Their commanding officer, Captain Philip St. George Cooke, and guides Antoine Leroux, Pauline Weaver, and Baptiste Charbonneau, were trail-toughened veterans used to the forbidding mountains and waterless wastes filled with impenetrable, boulder-choked canyons. But the Mormons, recruited by church leaders, were unprepared for the trials that lay ahead. They were in the army as volunteers, to show patriotism and receive government-paid transportation to California, where they hoped to locate a new home for their displaced church. But they rose to the occasion, and their heroic achievement won the respect of Captain Cooke, the no-nonsense professional soldier who was charged with building a wagon road to California.

Mormon Battalion at the Gila River in December 1846
Courtesy
Southwest Studies

Captain Cooke, disappointed at not receiving a combat command, would never know that his achievements and those of his Mormon volunteers would have greater significance than any glorious charge he might have led on the field of battle.

The task of building a wagon road would have been demanding enough for these citizen-soldiers, but the hardships endured along the desert trail north of Tucson, as recorded in the journals of Captain Cooke and Sergeant Daniel Tyler, paint a vivid picture of their desert ordeal.

The Mormon Battalion left Tucson on the morning of December 18, following the Santa Cruz River northwest toward the Gila River. Seven miles north of Tucson the river disappeared in the sand. The mules were watered, and the expedition set out across the desert, cutting its way on a twenty-four-mile path through dense mesquite thickets. At about 9:00 P.M. they made dry camp. Sergent Tyler of Company C and a stake patriarch in the Church, recorded the ordeal of that first night after leaving Tucson: "Straggling, worn out, famishing men came into camp at all hours of the night, and the rear guard did not reach camp until near daylight."

Resuming the march the next morning at sunrise, they traveled fourteen miles to a place where there was supposed to be water, but when they arrived, the hole was dry. "There was nothing to do," Cooke wrote, "but march on; there was the same baked-clay surface, with a little sand. At sundown a very small pool was come to; too shallow for dipping with a cup, but enough for most of the men to get a drink by lying down. . . . [This was the only method of drinking allowed.] Dipping was forbidden, in order that as many as possible might have a chance to drink. The main portion of the army, however, had no water during the entire day, save a few drops which the men managed to suck from the mud in small puddle holes found by the wayside."

Later that evening the pack mules were turned loose. Their keen instincts drove them to a small pool and they plunged headlong into the water. By the time the thirsty soldiers arrived, it was either consumed or undrinkable. Knowing that the only chance for survival was to press on, Cooke urged the men to move forward. By this time the battalion was strung out across the desert for several miles. Lieutenant George Rosecrans, of C Company, rode into the hills and located a small spring where a few were able to fill their canteens.

The soldiers continued on, crossing rocky arroyos and dense mesquite thickets. Finally Cooke called a halt to the march: "The battalion had then marched twenty-six hours of the last thirty-six; they were almost barefooted, carried their muskets and knapsacks; the mules had worked forty-seven miles without water. A little wheat was now given to them."

On the morning of December 20, the scouts left long before sun-up and were several miles down the trail by the time the battalion resumed its march. Before noon water was found and canteens were filled and loaded on pack mules and rushed back down the trail to assist stragglers, many of whom were now lying along the trail unable to continue. Cooke described the scene:

> The road was very bad; after three or four hours Leroux was met with information of some pools three or four miles on; he was sent on again to search further. At 11 o'clock, part of the battalion arrived there; sentinels were posted to prevent dipping, and one pool was reserved for the beeves. (When they reached it, they rushed in headlong, spoiling all.)
>
> Weaver, a guide, had reason to believe it was eighteen miles further to the river; the temperature was almost hot;—but soon, Leroux came again, to illume the gloomy prospect by the happy announcement of a sufficiency of rain ponds a mile or two on; and there, soon after noon, the battalion arrived and camped; and there was mezquit for the animals to browse. The guides were sent on.
>
> This great plain of clay, sand and gravel, with artemisias and mezquit, seems unbounded to the west. I am told it extends a hundred miles; with no water or animals; but in the dim distance unconnected fantastically shaped mountains appear. It is a gold district, and reported to be of the very richest; but never yet worked, on account of its utter barrenness, and the fear of Indians.
>
> I have been mounted thirty-two of the last fifty-two hours; and what with midnight conferences, alarms and marches, have had little rest for five days.
>
> The battalion have marched sixty-two miles from Tucson, in about fifty-one hours; no ration of meat was issued yesterday.

It was through the heroic efforts of these men and women, not to mention the pack mules, that the Mormon Battalion reached the little site north of Casa Grande on the evening of December 20, 1846. The monument at the site honors more than a campsite—it is a testament to courage, perseverance, and determination.

The small farming community that sprang up along the new railroad line in 1880 was called Casa Grande because at the time it was the nearest town to the ancient Hohokam ruins twenty miles to the northeast.

Originally the Southern Pacific called the place Bluewater but later chose Casa Grande. By the time the railroad reached this point, some of the company's moguls were uncertain whether to pour any more money into laying track until finances improved. In May 1879 work was suspended at Casa Grande, sixty-five miles from Tucson. Casa Grande, like Maricopa, became a transfer point for trains, stage coaches, and freight wagons. While Maricopa served Prescott and

Phoenix, Casa Grande did the same for Florence and Tucson. At the time, one could purchase a ticket and leave Casa Grande on Monday at 5:30 A.M., and arrive in San Francisco, 913 miles away, on Wednesday at 12:35 P.M. The cost of a first class ticket was $62.50. For twenty dollars less one could travel economy, or "Third Class."

When the big silver strike at Tombstone began to look like more than a "flash in the pan," the Southern Pacific decided to finish the railroad to Tucson, arriving there by March of 1880.

To Picacho (near the junction with Interstate 8)

Southwest of Casa Grande, along the Casa Grande Canal and just north of the Casa Grande Mountains is Arizola, established as a rail station in 1892. During the 1880s it was headquarters for one of the most controversial figures in Arizona history—James Addison Reavis, the Baron of Arizona.

Picacho, Arizona, during a recent re-enactment of the Civil War battle of 1862
Marshall Trimble photo

*James Addison Reavis, Baron of
Arizona*
Courtesy
Southwest Studies

Sofia, The Baroness of Arizona
Courtesy
Southwest Studies

Reavis was a former horse-car conductor from Missouri, who learned in the Confederate Army the dubious art of forgery by writing phony liberty passes. When his work improved, the homesick soldier put himself on permanent leave. The ability to forge documents made Reavis rich selling real estate in Missouri and planted the seeds for a grand scheme—to create a phony Spanish land grant in Arizona.

The Treaty of Guadalupe Hidalgo in 1858 stipulated that land grants awarded by the Spanish and Mexican governments in the territory taken in the war must be recognized as legal by the United States. All the claimants had to do was present proof of ownership. During the next sixty years, these claims would be validated by the courts, offering a glorious opportunity for a bold gambler like Reavis with a fertile mind to put his forgery skills to work. He left no stone unturned, or so he thought, as he traveled to the achives in Mexico and Spain, removing documents and inserting forgeries to substantiate his claims.

In 1885 he filed a claim on nearly twelve million acres of land that extended from west of Phoenix across rich agricultural and mineral lands to Silver City, New Mexico—a tract 236 miles long and 78 miles wide in the center of Arizona. Of course, the settlers and farmers on these lands were outraged, and there was even talk of lynching Mr. Reavis. Reavis further solidified his claim by taking an obscure peasant girl and convincing her she was a direct descendant of Don Miguel de Peralta de Cordoba, the mythical baron of the Colorados. His arguments didn't convince the settlers and farmers, but mining companies and the Southern Pacific Railroad weren't taking any chances. If the claim were real, they wanted to be on the good side of the baron, but it might not be, so they covered both options and paid the baron handsomely for use of his land. A few others followed suit, and soon Reavis and his family were touring Europe in a courtly manner. When Senator Roscoe Conkling, a stalwart in the Republican Party, and Robert Ingersoll, one of the nation's foremost attorneys, pronounced the documents authentic, it began to look as though a large number of Arizonans were going to become vassals, or tenants, on land they had formerly owned. While government agents tried to prove the claim fraudulent, the real heroes were Tom Weedin, editor of the Florence newspaper and his printer, William "Stammering Bill" Truman. Weedin's stinging edtorials were a veritable thorn in the baron's side. At one point it was suggested that some of the baron's hardbitten enforcers and bagmen might harm Weedin's family, but the editor was relentless. Then one day Bill Truman, whose hobby was calligraphy, noted that the ancient print used on some of the documents had been developed only a few years earlier. That was the beginning of the baron's undoing.

In a bold move, almost as if he had begun to believe his own phony claim, Reavis sued the United States government for millions. At one time, the government had considered buying Reavis out for a few million, but now that the baron had filed suit and had lawyers Conkling and Ingersoll backing him, the government ordered a full-fledged investigation to protect its interests. Agents like Pete Brady, ex-Texas Ranger and prominent Arizona pioneer, worked tirelessly to disprove the Reavis claims.

The case went to trial in Santa Fe in 1893, and as the government revealed its case, the baron's influential friends vanished like desert mirages. The baron's claim was ruled invalid, and now it was the government's turn to take the offensive. Reavis, all his wealth squandered on opulent living and legal fees, was a broken man. Found guilty, he was sentenced to two years in the New Mexico Penitentiary. After serving his sentence, he abandoned his wife and two sons in Colorado and became a drifter, occasionally appearing on the streets of Phoenix to promote some new scheme. When he died in 1914, he was buried in a pauper's grave in Denver.

His wife Sofia remained convinced, until her death in the 1930s, that she was truly a baroness. Reavis was a visionary, promoting irrigaton projects in his "barony" long before such projects became reality; but his obsession with gaining wealth through illegal schemes brought about his downfall and ruined his reputation. The good name of the Reavis family was restored, however, by the baron's two sons, both heroes in the First World War.

Picacho Pass

Picacho is a huge pile of volcanic remnants rising several hundred feet about fifty miles northwest of Tucson. To emigrants on the Gila Trail, the towering peak acts as a beacon in much the same way Chimney Rock and Independence Rock did for the wagon trains bound for California and Oregon.

Prehistoric Hohokam travelers stopped off here on their way to and from commerce dealings further south. Their modern-day descendants, the Pima and Papago, did the same; and Spanish missionaries on their way to Christianize natives along the rivers to the west and north, quenched their thirst at one of several springs near the base of volcanic mountains. When the Mormon Battalion built the first wagon road across the Southwest in 1846, they, too, stopped to rest at Picacho, its name coming from a Spanish word meaning "peak." *Anglos*, in their eagerness to apply easily understood descriptive place names to the lands they traversed, gave it the redundant name

CIVIL WAR MONUMENT

BATTLE OF PICACHO
APRIL 15, 1862
WESTERNMOST ACTION
BETWEEN CONFEDERATE & UNION FORCES
IN THE WAR BETWEEN THE STATES-DEDICATED
TO CAPT. SHEROD HUNTER'S "ARIZONA (RANGERS)
ARIZONA VOLUNTEERS" CSA.
ERECTED BY CAPT. HUNTER'S ARIZONA
RANGERS CAMP NO 1202 SONS OF
CONFEDERATE VETERANS

of Picacho Peak—or simply "Peak Peak." In the 1850s the Butterfield Overland Stage Line had a station in the pass. Today Interstate 10 and the Southern Pacific Railroad run through the pass, connecting Phoenix and Tucson with the outside world. Lengthy winter rains transform the harsh grey-buff desert in the foothills near Picacho into a tapestry of variegated color—as galaxies of wild flowers carpet the earth and herald spring.

In the spring of 1862 two American military units clashed briefly at the foot of the ancient *picacho* in a skirmish that is generally referred to as the westernmost battle of the Civil War. Monuments dedicated to this Civil War battle and to the Mormon Battalion are located on the south side of Interstate 10 at Picacho State Park.

Red Rock

The Southern Pacific Railroad located a station at Red Rock in the 1880s and established a spur line to the smelter for the mine at Silver Bell twenty miles to the south. The place was named for a red butte nearby.

One of Arizona's greatest ranching families, the Aguirres, descendants of Don Pedro Aguirre, still run cattle in the Avra Valley, south of Red Rock. This family traces back to the days of the *conquistadores*. Don Pedro was a prosperous freighter and *ranchero* in Chihuahua until 1852. At that time some United States troops crossed the border and stayed overnight at his ranch. Don Pedro was a good host and saw nothing wrong since the soldiers were in pursuit of hostile Apaches. A Mexican officer in the area had a different perception, accusing him of being a traitor. Don Pedro was given the choice of being shot or of moving to the United States—he chose the latter, of course.

Don Pedro Aguirre moved to New Mexico and started a prosperous freighting business on the old Santa Fe Trail. Later he established the Buenos Aires Ranch, one of southern Arizona's most famous early ranches. The Aguirres represented a wide gamut of frontier society, including merchants, ranchers, miners, and army officers. During the 1880s one of Don Pedro's sons, Don Yjinio Aguirre, began a successful freighting operation around Willcox. In 1892 he moved his freight business and cattle operation to Red Rock, where he established the *El Rancho de San Francisco*. In those days the Avra Valley was covered with lush native grasses that grew "stirrup-high," the area watered by overflow from the Santa Cruz River.

During the prosperous days of the Aguirre Cattle Company, Don Yjinio and his son Higinio ran thousands of head of cattle in southern Arizona. At the same time, the Aguirre freight wagons hauled ore from the Silver Bell Mine to the railroad spur at Red Rock. Later, a second ranch, the *El Rancho Grande*, which boasted a beautiful, Spanish-style adobe house, was built eight miles north of the *San Francisco*.

The life of the Aguirres and other Spanish ranch families like the Pachecos, Elias, Roblés, Redondos, Otes, Amados, Aroses, and Samaniagos of southern Arizona revolved around time-honored customs and traditions. The families socialized, intermarried, ran their cattle, and built a lifestyle that is today only a romantic memory of "the good old days."

Today, Yjinio and Enrique, grandsons of Don Yjinio Aguirre, are retired, but several younger generations of Aguirres still carry on the proud family tradition. Yjinio is a well-respected author and expert on the history and culture of early-day ranching in Arizona.

Marana

In the days before this area became farmland, thick groves of mesquite and catclaw inspired the Hispanics to call it "Marana," or tangle. When a flag station was established in the 1890s, it was called Marana. During the 1920s a small community was located nearby called Postvale after a Mr. Post, who drilled some irrigation wells. In the mid-1920s citizens had the good sense to go back to the original name of Marana.

During World War II, the Marana Army Air Field was established northwest of town. It was a Western Flying Training Command Base and was used as an air transport basic training school for multi-engine transports and bombers. The base was de-activated in 1945 but was reopened during the Korean War as a primary flying school. Most recently the old air field is used as a storage center for civilian airplanes.

Rillito Creek

Rillito is Spanish for "little river"; however, when heavy rains fall in the lofty Santa Catalina Mountains to the east, the Rillito becomes a raging torrent. Rillito Creek is another of those Arizona place names that should be listed in a redundancy file along with Table Mesa and Picacho Peak. The name first appeared on a military map in 1875, but it had been in use much earlier in the Tucson area.

In 1872 Fort Lowell was moved from its original site in downtown Tucson to the banks of the Rillito, where there was water and where alfalfa could be harvested for the cavalry mounts. Officers sought to get out of downtown Tucson to protect their soldiers from civilians and vice versa. Fort Lowell was one of Arizona's major military posts during the Apache wars but became less important after the surrender of Geronimo in 1886. It was abandoned in early 1891 and quickly took on a ghost-town appearance as the stately rows of trees died and the buildings deteriorated. Eventually, the city of Tucson expanded out into the desert and enveloped the ruins of old Fort Lowell. A few years ago civic-minded Tucsonians restored the old post and built a museum at the site.

Cañada del Oro

Cañada del Oro ran along the military road from Tucson to old Camp Grant, at the junction of Aravaipa Creek and the San Pedro River. Because of the rough terrain, it was a favorite base of Apache war parties. The twisting canyon was ideally suited for ambush. The most famous Apache attack occurred on May 10, 1869, when an estimated three hundred warriors swarmed down on a group of freight-wagons belonging to the Tucson firm of Tully and Ochoa. The train consisted of nine wagons before the Apaches closed in. A seven-man cavalry escort from Camp Grant arrived and fought their way through the surrounding warriors to the wagons. The freighters and soldiers made a gallant stand, suffering a loss of three killed and two wounded. When ammunition ran low, the men made a running fight to safety, but some $20,000 worth of wagons, livestock, and supplies were lost. Later, evidence indicated that the Apaches had stopped long enough to celebrate their victory by butchering several mules and roasting the meat.

Because placer gold had been found here before the occupation of the 1850s, this area came to be called Cañada del Oro, or Gold Canyon.

Watering horses at the well, circa 1900 Courtesy Arizona Historical Society

Interstate 17
Phoenix to Flagstaff

Paradise Valley

The land lying east of Interstate 17 north of Phoenix was referred to as "unclaimed desert land" a few years ago. Like all cactus-strewn lands north of the Arizona Canal, it was "unwatered and unused" except for grazing land. After World War II, creeping suburbia jumped the canal and spread across the desert like molasses.

This transition might have been different if the Rio Verde Canal Company had had its way in the 1890s. Canal promoters planned to dig a canal west from the Verde River, along the base of the McDowell Mountains, all the way to Union Hills; Paradise Valley seemed like an appropriate name for the area.

The scheme of the Rio Verde Canal Company was grandiose: "Eventually, they planned to extend the canal over seventy miles westward to the Hassayampa River and irrigate about 400,000 acres, an area one and one-half times the acreage of the Salt River Valley Water Users Association. The company drilled a tunnel at Horseshoe Dam and dug about twenty miles of canals before they stopped around 1901. That year another company, the Verde Water and Power Company, was organized but never put anything into operation. Fifteen years later, James A. Shea and Harvey Bell (Shea Boulevard and Bell Road), two farmers subsisting on irrigation wells, formed the Paradise Verde Irrigation District and took on the Salt Water Users Association in a tug-of-war competition that lasted nearly twenty years.

River Valley Water Users Association in a tug-of-war competition that lasted nearly twenty years.

In 1934 the Secretary of Interior ruled in favor of the Salt River Water Users and the grand scheme to irrigate Paradise Valley literally evaporated along with the dreams of the homesteaders who had hoped to turn it into a paradise. The land, which old-timers say could have been purchased for $2.50 an acre, remained virtually uninhabited until after World War II.

The natural evolution of most of the land in the Salt River Valley has gone from desert to agriculture to urban development. Paradise Valley skipped the middle part.

New River

A military road ran west from Fort McDowell through the McDowell Mountains, northeast past Cave Creek, and then north to Fort Whipple. No one seems to know how this area came to be called New River. In 1868 a stage station was situated on the banks of New River on the Prescott-Phoenix road. The proprietor at one time was "Lord" Darrell Duppa, a member of the first group of settlers in the Salt River Valley.

Captain John G. Bourke, in his classic *On the Border with Crook*, wrote a colorful account of his visit to New River in the early 1870s:

> Darrel Duppa was one of the queerest specimens of humanity, as his ranch was one of the queerest examples to be found in Arizona, and I might add in New Mexico and Sonora as well. There was nothing superfluous about Duppa in the way of flesh, neither was there anything about the "station" that could be regarded as superfluous, either in furniture or ornament. Duppa was credited with being the wild, harum-scarum son of an English family of respectability, his father having occupied a position in the diplomatic or consular service of Great Britain, and the son having been born in Marseilles. Rumor had it that Duppa spoke several languages—French, Spanish, Italian, German—that he understood the classics, and that, when sober, he used faultless English. I can certify to his employment of excellent French and Spanish, and what had to my ears the sound of pretty good Italian, and I know too that he was hospitable to a fault, and not afraid of man or devil. Three bullet wounds, received in three different fights with the Apaches, attested his grit, although they might not be accepted as equally conclusive evidence of good judgment. The site of his "location" was in the midst of the most uncompromising piece of desert in a region which boasts of possessing more desert land than any other territory in the Union. The surrounding hills and mesas yielded a perennial crop of cactus, and little of anything else.

The dwelling itself was nothing but a *ramada*, a term which has already been defined as a roof of branches; the walls were of rough, unplastered wattle work, of the thorny branches of the ironwood, no thicker than a man's finger, which were lashed by thongs of raw-hide to horizontal slats of cottonwood; the floor of the bare earth, of course— that almost went without saying in those days—and the furniture rather too simple and meagre even for Cathusians. As I recall the place in mind, there appears the long, unpainted table of pine, which served for meals or gambling, or the rare occasions when any one took into his head the notion to write a letter. This room constituted the ranch in its entirety. Along the sides were scattered piles of blankets, which about midnight were spread out as couches for tired laborers or travellers. At one extremity, a meagre array of Dutch ovens, flat-irons, and frying-pans revealed the "kitchen," presided over by a hirsute, husky-voiced gnome, half Vulcan, half Centaur, who, immersed for most of the day in the mysteries of the larder, at stated intervals broke the stillness with the hoarse command: "Hash pile! Come a' runnin'!" There is hardly any use to describe the rifles, pistols, belts of ammunition, saddles, spurs, and whips, which lined the walls, and covered the joists and cross-beams; they were just as much part and parcel of the establishment as the dogs and ponies were. To keep out the sand-laden wind, which blew fiercely down from the north when it wasn't blowing down with equal fierceness from the south, or the west, or the east, strips of canvas or gunny-sacking were tacked on the inner side of the cactus branches.

My first visit to this Elysium was made about midnight, and I remember that the meal served up was unique if not absolutely paralyzing on the score of originality. There was a plenty of Mexican figs in raw-hide sacks, fairly good tea, which had the one great merit of hotness, and lots and lots of whiskey; but there was no bread, as the supply of flour had run short, and, on account of the appearance of Apaches during the past few days, it had not been considered wise to send a party over to Phoenix for a replenishment. A wounded Mexican, lying down in one corner, was proof that the story was well founded. All the light in the ranch was afforded by a single table lantern, by the flickering flames from the cook's fire, and the glinting stars. In our saddle-bags we had several slices of bacon and some biscuits, so we did not fare half so badly as we might have done. What caused me most wonder was why Duppa had ever concluded to live in such a forlorn spot; the best answer I could get to my queries was that the Apaches had attacked him at the moment he was appoaching the banks of the Agua Fria at this point, and after he had repulsed them he thought he would stay there merely to let them know he could do it. This explanation was satisfactory to every one else, and I had to accept it.

As late as 1947 New River marked the end of the old paved Black Canyon Highway, which turned into a winding dirt road continuing on to Prescott.

Gillett

Gillett is one of a number of ghost towns in the Bradshaw Mountains on the west side of Interstate 17. At one time it was a thriving mill town for the silver mine at Tip Top. Like most mill towns, Gillett was located near a stream—on the left bank of Agua Fria. It was named for Daniel B. Gillett, superintendent of the Tip Top Mine at the height of its prosperity in the late 1870s. At one time the town boasted a fine hotel and several saloons. Judge Charles T. Hayden, father of Senator Carl Hayden, ran a store there for a brief time.

Like all boom towns, Gillett had its share of violence. In 1878 an enraged crowd of miners swarmed around the jail and demanded that a deputy named Colonel Taylor turn a murderer over to them for a dose of vigilante justice. The deputy, armed with a double-barrel shotgun, tried to dissuade the mob and was shot to death; the prisoner was taken out of jail and hung from the limb of the nearest tree.

Gillett's blacksmith was earning extra money by robbing stagecoaches on the road through Squaw Creek Canyon, cleverly caching the stolen coins at the muddy bottom of his quenching tub. The smitty was an avid gambler, but was a born loser; however, his cache of coins provided an inexhaustible source of gaming money, which caught the suspicious eye of a Wells Fargo detective sent to investigate the robberies. After some persuasion, the blacksmith confessed his extracurricular activities, and there was one less stage robber on the Black Canyon Highway. By the late 1880s Gillett's prosperous days were over and deterioration had set in.

Rock Springs

In the late 1920s a spring emerging from some rocks provided the inspiration for the name of Rock Springs, so designated when a post office was established in 1938.

Black Canyon and Black Canyon City

A few years ago Black Canyon City was considered the halfway point on the dusty highway between Phoenix and Prescott. The town goes back at least to 1875, when a stage station called Black Canyon was located where the Agua Fria River crosses the road.

A post office was located here in 1894, and the settlement was called Cañon. Charles Goddard was postmaster, so it was sometimes referred to as Goddard. The post office closed in 1906, and for a time local people received their mail at Rock Springs. Later a new post office opened and was given the name Black Canyon.

The town takes its name from the canyon through which Interstate 17 now passes. The new highway, opened in the mid-1950s, slices through the east side of the canyon to reach the top of Black Mesa. The old road, dating back to the 1860s, stayed closer to the bottom of the canyon that straddles the Agua Fria River. During the 1880s the Arizona Stage Company made the 140-mile run from Prescott to Phoenix every Monday, Wednesday, and Friday. The coach left Prescott at 8:00 A.M., and arrived in Phoenix the following day at noon. Some of this road is in use today and can be seen from the modern highway. In the early days it was used by freighters, stagelines, and the military. The steepest grade and the sharpest curves were on Antelope Hill. Stagecoach drivers used to announce their arrival at a hairpin turn with a shrill blast of a tin horn. A driver coming from the other direction replied with two blasts. If the two rigs met in a place too narrow to pass, it was the custom for the driver on the downside to unhitch his team and ease the wagon by and downhill to the first wide spot in the road. The rough country and steep grades made it an ideal place for ambushes by both outlaws and Indians.

Many historians believe the legends behind mythical Peralta Mine in the Superstition Mountains actually had their origin in Black Canyon. A Peralta did have mining claims in the area, and he was supposed to have sold them to an accomplice of James Addison Reavis, the "Baron of Arizona," providing the basis for Reavis's fictional tale about a Peralta who was heir to a vast land grant in central Arizona. Storytellers and seekers of lost treasure later moved Peralta's mine from Black Canyon to the Superstition Mountains.

Somewhere in these mountains lies another lost bonanza, the fabled Lost Pick Mine. The story begins in the 1870s in the small community of Phoenix, when two itinerant prospectors known as Brown and Davies, hanging around a general store, noticed an Indian paying for supplies with gold nuggets. They learned from the proprietor that the Indian lived in a canyon about fifty miles north of town. They also learned he was a Yavapai, who came into town once a year, always with enough gold to purchase whatever he needed. The two prospectors decided to follow the Indian to discover his source of gold. The Yavapai made no attempt to evade the pair of trackers, the trail leading deeper into the Malpais (bad lands) north of town. They crossed three streams—Skunk Creek, New River, and the Agua Fria—going deeper into the steep-sided recesses of Black Canyon. The Indian entered a side canyon and seemed to vanish into thin air. While trying to pick up the trail, Brown and Davies stumbled into a boulder-strewn arroyo that was a tributary to the Agua Fria. Before their eyes was the unmistakable glitter of gold! Every chunk of rock seemed to be laced with the yellow metal. They worked tirelessly for the next several days mining high-grade ore. An educated guess is that the pair had amassed a fortune of nearly $80,000, however, Brown and Davies, in their single-minded effort to dig the gold, had forgotten the ever-present danger of Indians. When a band of warriors attacked, Davies was killed in the first volley of gunfire. Brown hit the ground and rolled into the brush, waiting for the warriors to come after him; however, they turned and rode away. Brown quickly cached the ore, marking the site with his pick. He took a good look around to make sure of his bearings and headed west toward the Colorado River. Brown didn't return to reclaim his treasure until many years later. He was sure he could relocate it, but a fading memory and the desert terrain played tricks with his mind. On his deathbed, the old man told the story of a fabulous gold strike somewhere in Black Canyon. Years later someone claimed to have seen a rusty prospector's pick buried in rock outcropping, but he had ignored it. To this day the Lost Pick is supposed to be one of Arizona's richest lost mines.

Bumble Bee

Bumble Bee, perched on the west bank of Bumble Bee Creek, is one of the more easily accessible ghost towns along Interstate 17. There is a question about the unusual name: some say hostile Indians in the area were "thick as bumble bees"; another version has it that soldiers overheard a band of Indians holding a conference which sounded "like a swarm of bumble bees"; most likely, the name developed when early prospectors found a nest of bumble bees along the creek. Bumble Bee was never a boom town in the true sense of the word, although there was some placer mining there. It was better known as a way station and general store which sold groceries, hardware, and gasoline, at night turning into a dance hall and saloon. A one-room school was located east of the road.

In 1949 the town was sold, and during the 1960s entrepreneur Ed Chilleen from Phoenix tried to turn it into a tourist attraction, complete with a frontier-style false front, but the venture failed to materialize.

Bradshaw Mountains

The rugged, sprawling mountains west of Interstate 17 are among the richest of all the mineral-laden ranges in Arizona. They were

Bumble Bee in the 1930s
Courtesy Arizona Historical Foundation

originally called the Silver Range because of rich silver lodes, but the name was changed to honor Bill Bradshaw. Bill and his brother Ike ran a freighting business from San Bernadino to Ehrenberg-La Paz in the early 1860s, when gold was discovered nearby. Ike built a ferry and hauled freight and passengers across the Colorado River at Olive City. In 1863 Bill found gold in the mountains that were later named for him. The Bradshaw Mining District was created, and in 1871 Bradshaw City sprang up along the road to Prescott. At its peak, the town boasted about five thousand residents. Soon after the town was laid out, prosperity began to fade, and by the 1880s Bradshaw City was a ghost town.

At the height of mining in the Bradshaws, mines and towns with picturesque names like Tip Top, Columbia, Oro Belle, Big Bug, Senator, Bueno and Crown King produced millions of dollars in gold and silver, leaving an indelible mark on the colorful history of Arizona.

In 1899 the vast riches in the Bradshaws prompted Frank Murphy to take on what seemed to be a mission impossible, building a railroad from Mayer to the source of the minerals at Poland, on the north side of the mountains, and another line to Crown King, on the south side. Building railroads over rough terrain was nothing new to Murphy— he'd already completed a line from Ash Fork to Prescott to Phoenix and another from Prescott to Mayer.

Murphy advertised in eastern newspapers for strong-armed tracklayers willing to work for a dollar a day, which was twice the usual pay of that time. By October 1901 350 men were ready to tackle what was being described as an impossible railroad project. The determined crew of tracklayers and gandy dancers sliced their way into the Bradshaws, across rough arroyos and along steep barrancas.

When a dynamite blast exposed a rich body of ore, Murphy lost most of his workers to gold fever; however, he had no difficulty replacing his crew from eastern labor markets at a dollar a day. On April 21, 1902 the first locomotive steamed into Poland on shining narrow-gauge rails.

Poland, named for Davis R. Poland of Tennessee, had begun its ascent to prominence around 1900. Poland, who had arrived in Arizona in 1864 and discovered gold at the site named for him in 1872, died in 1882, twenty years before the arrival of the railroad. Frank Murphy was part owner of the rich Poland Mine when he began work on his visionary railroad.

In 1902 miners, following a vein of gold, cut through the mountain separating Poland from Walker. This turned out to spark an economic boom for Walker, named for famed trailblazer Joe

Walker—up to then ore had been hauled over precipitous mountain trails for several miles; now it could be hauled through the tunnel to the railroad at Poland.

The other part of Frank Murphy's "impossible" railroad headed southwest of Mayer to Crown King, clinging tenaciously to the sides of the lofty Bradshaws, with more kinks than a cheap lariat. Twelve switchbacks had turns so tight passengers in the caboose could look across and see the engine going the other way. The mine was finally completed in 1904 after exceeding its projected cost by about three hundred percent. It was worth every penny—by 1907 the mines at Tiger, Big Bug, Turkey Creek, Pine Grove, and Crown King were producing over a million dollars in gold and silver.

The boom times lasted until the end of World War I. By this time old age was catching up with the narrow-gauge line; furthermore, the price of metals was down, freight costs were up, and the mines were starting to play out. The days of glory were almost over, and by 1920 both the Poland and Crown King lines were abandoned.

Cordes

Before the arrival of Frank Murphy's railroad in the early 1900s, Cordes was called Antelope Station. The small community was situated on a plain above notorious Antelope Hill, a nemesis for drivers from the stagecoach era of the 1870s to that of the automobile of the 1940s. It was a regular stop for weary travelers prior to the construction of the new Black Canyon Highway (Arizona 69, later Interstate 17). The town takes its name from John Cordes, who came to the area with his family in the 1880s.

When the new highway opened in the mid-1950s, Cordes, like Bumble Bee, was left off the beaten path. The stillness of the place is broken only by the occasional passing of an auto headed down the dusty road to Mayer. Descendants of the Cordes family still live quietly in the town that progress has passed by.

Dugas (seven miles east of Interstate 17)

In 1879 Fred Dugas built a ranch on the spot he believed to be the exact center of Arizona. He missed his mark by a few miles but still selected a picturesque setting for his ranch. It's said that out of consideration for his cows, he noted their favorite places for bedding down, planting shade trees and setting up water troughs accordingly. A post office, located at the Dugas house in 1925 so neighboring ranchers could receive mail, was discontinued in 1938. Dugas could possibly become the future wine-growing center of Arizona if plans to establish vineyards prove successful.

Cherry (ten miles west of Interstate 17 off Arizona 169)

Cherry has an unusual twist to the origin of its name: Norville Cherry and his family moved there from Texas in the 1880s; however, the place was named for the wild cherry trees found growing along a nearby creek. In 1864 Lieutenant Colonel Francisco Chavez traveled through this area over what became known as the Chavez Trail—he was returning to Santa Fe after escorting the first territorial officials to Arizona.

Interstate 17 Junction
Camp Verde to Strawberry

The Crook Military Road

In 1870 the Military Department of Arizona was created and General George Stoneman was placed in command. Upon taking charge, he began upgrading military posts and building better roads. Another important mission was to establish feeding stations throughout Apacheria until permanent reservations could be created. Meanwhile the Indian attacks contiued, and Arizona's white citizens complained bitterly over the government's lack of punitive action. The appeasement policy, along with the citizens' understanding that General Stoneman wanted residents to handle their own problems, resulted in a large vigilante force in Tucson. In April 1871 this force attacked a group of Aravaipa Apaches living under army protection at Camp Grant. The vigilantes were welcomed in Tucson as conquering heroes; however, the massacre caused a furor in Washington. As a result, peace emissaries, including Vincent Colyer and General Oliver Howard, were sent out to negotiate peace treaties with the various tribes. On the military front, General Stoneman was removed, and General George Crook was sent out to deal with the tribes who refused to give up the old ways and move to reservations.

While Crook was waiting for emissaries from Washington to work out a peace treaty with the Apaches and Yavapais in the central mountains, he rode nearly seven hundred miles muleback across this unexplored area to gain valuable first-hand knowledge just in case a punitive campaign was necessary.

During these reconnaissance missions, Crook decided to construct a military road from Camp Verde up to and along the Mogollon Rim to Camp Apache. The two hundred-mile road along the precipitous escarpment provided a critical supply and communication link during his successful campaign in 1872-73 and helped bring an end to the long war.

Today the wagon ruts of General Crook's old mule trail are still visible. Milepost blazers on tree trunks and strands of telegraph wire can still be seen, and there are a few sandstone grave markers along the trail. Although the Crook Trail continued to be used well into the twentieth century, it was replaced as a main route when the railroad reached Holbrook in 1881.

Camp Verde

An old trail led west from the Zuni pueblo of New Mexico across to the Little Colorado River, thence on to the springs at the foot of the San Francisco Mountains. From there the trail went southwest of Bill Williams Mountains and drifted southwesterly into Chino Valley, ending at the territorial capital of Prescott. Some parts of that old road are still visible today. This was the trail Lieutenant Colonel Francisco Chavez followed in 1863-64, when he escorted the first territorial officers to Arizona. At the time, there was a plan to locate the permanent capital, which they planned to call Azatlan, at the mouth of the Verde River. However, when Chavez tried to follow the river, he found his path blocked by boulder-choked canyons. On his way back to Santa Fe, Chavez left the temporary capital at Del Rio Springs in Chino Valley and headed toward the area of Cherry; he then went down into Copper Canyon and past today's Camp Verde. Crossing the Verde River, Chavez proceeded north past McGuireville, and at the top of the grade turned east toward Stoneman Lake, passing through what is called Chavez Pass today, in the rugged range south of treacherous Canyon Diablo. Next Chavez angled northeast to Sunset Crossing (Winslow), then east to the Zuni pueblos. Dr. Jim Byrkit, geography professor at Northern Arizona University, has recently completed some painstaking research that pieces together the mysterious puzzle of this trail, which has been used for hundreds of years by the Hopi Indians. They call it the Palatkwapi Trail, and their legends tell of several clans that lived among the beautiful red rocks in the Verde Valley. Their name for the place was Palatkwapi—"warm valley among the rocks." According to the Hopi, life was so easy the people became degenerate, and the gods grew angry and drove them out. Eventually they wound up at Walpi, on the Hopi mesas about sixty miles north of Sunset Crossing.

Spanish explorers Antonio de Espejo, Marcos Farfan, and Juan de Oñate, followed this same route in the late 1500s and early 1600s while searching for rich Indian mines and the fabled Northwest Passage.

Camp Verde rests on the banks of the picturesque river from which it takes its name. It is the oldest white settlement in the Verde Valley. In June 1865 James Swetnam led a party of nine from Prescott into the valley to explore farming possibilties. The reliable Verde River had made this area one of the richest agricultural parts of Arizona since prehistoric times, when the Sinagua, Hohokam, and other Indian tribes occupied the region. These Indians prospered for hundreds of years before abandoning their villages about 1400. After they left, the area became the home of the Yavapai and Tonto Apache peoples. The Yavapai were of Yuman stock, while the Tontos were an Athabascan-speaking group. Ecological and environmental conditions dictated the similar lifestyles of these two groups, a development that was to confuse early anthropologists. Despite the fact that the Yavapai were a separate tribe and spoke a different language, writers often referred to them as Apaches.

These tribes fiercely resisted white encroachments in the valley so new settlers built a small fortress at the Verde—Clear Creek junction, indicating that they'd come to stay. The post was named Camp Lincoln, and by January 1866, a company of 126 Arizona volunteers was raised to battle increasing resistance from Apaches and Yavapai warriors.

Camp Verde became the supply base for patrols and punitive expeditions into the Tonto Basin. The post took on added importance during General George Crook's famous winter campaign of 1872-73. Crook, a tough campaigner who shunned politics and loved the outdoors, was both a friend and dreaded foe of the Indians of Arizona. He firmly believed the nomadic Indians' only chance for survival was to be subdued, by force if necessary, and then located on reservations and taught to be self-supporting through farming and ranching. Some bands heeded the call and gave up their war-like ways; others, however, scoffed at the idea of becoming farmers and ranchers and continued their traditional way of life.

Crook's general orders stated that all those bands who refused to come in by November 21, 1871 would be designated as "hostiles" and would be pursued relentlessly until they surrendered. On November 16, 1872 he sent his troops into the field. It was a tough campaign that ranged from the cactus-strewn deserts around Superstition Mountain to the waist-deep snows above the Mogollon Rim. "A dirtier, greasier, more uncouth looking set of officers and men it would be hard to encounter anywhere," one officer recalled. "Dust, soot, rain, and grime had made their impress upon the canvas suits which each had donned, and with hair uncut for months and beards growing with straggling growth all over the face, there was not one of the party who would venture to pose as an Adonis: but all were happy . . . we were now to see the reward of our hard work."

After a long winter spent dodging Crook's persistent soldiers and Indian scouts, Cha-Lipun (Charley-Pan), leader of some 2,300 natives, rode into Camp Verde and surrendered. A reservation was created near the fort, and soon, under the guidance of army officers, the natives had dug a ditch five miles long and were busy irrigating crops. Crook was convinced the nomadic Indians would become productive farmers if given a chance, and his plan seemed to be working. However, in the spring of 1875 General Crook was transferred out of Arizona, and political presssure led to the Indians' removal to the San Carlos Reservation (Hell's forty acres).

Living conditions on early military posts varied. In military pecking order, Fort Whipple, near Prescott, was the most "opulent," while Camp Apache, in the White Mountains, was one of the most primitive. In 1875 Martha Summerhayes, who had just returned from several momths at Camp Apache, had high praise for Camp Verde. "Here were lace curtain windows, well-dressed women, smart uniforms, and in fact, civilization, compared with what we had left."

In 1879 the post's name was changed to Fort Verde. By this time most of the hard campaigning was over, and the Indian situation at Fort Verde was quiet until July 6, 1882, when a renegade band under the leadership of Na-ti-o-tish murdered four men at San Carlos and bolted into the Tonto Basin. Army units converged on the band near East Clear Creek, in the Mogollon Rim country, on July 17, 1882. The Battle of Big Dry Wash was the last major confrontation between the army and Apache-Yavapai warriors.

Fort Verde in the early 1890s Courtesy Arizona State Library

With the surrender of Geronimo in 1886 it was only a matter of time before the military post on the Verde would be abandoned. Orders to close the post came on April 10, 1890, and a year later it was officially abandoned.

The civilian settlement at Camp Verde predated those at both Phoenix and Flagstaff. Five streams that flowed all year long—the Verde, Clear Creek, Beaver Creek, Oak Creek, and Sycamore Creek, along with part-timers Cherry and Fossil creeks—made the Verde Valley one of the most suitable agricultural areas in this water-scarce area. Before long, farmers were digging wells and irrigation ditches, clearing farmland, and planting their crops. At first the only market for cash crops was at the military posts at Verde. Soon, however, the industrious settlers were hauling harvested crops to the mining town of Prescott and to the military post at Fort Whipple.

Old timers used to say the native grasses in the Verde Valley grew "belly-high to a tall horse." Cattlemen were running thousands of beeves on the ranges by the 1870s, but a drought during the following decade and overstocking of the ranges brought disaster. The grasses were eaten down "pretty near to bedrock," and the ranchers were cutting "anything green," including trees growing along the river banks to keep their hungry cattle from starving. The drought was finally broken, but the steady rains fell on barren ground, washing tons of precious topsoil into the river. Some of the ranges never recovered, as chaparral replaced the nutritious native grasses. The 1880s marked the end of an era—the open range cattle industry in the valley was over.

The rediscovery of rich minerals in the Black Hills in the 1870s opened vast new markets for the settlers in the Verde Valley. The Jerome mines began to boom in the 1890s, providing a source of revenue for farmers and ranchers well into the twentieth century. By the time those mines closed in 1953, the new Black Canyon Highway reached the valley, providing the once-remote area a direct route to Phoenix.

Montezuma Castle

Montezuma Castle, a misnomer (the Aztec leader never came near the place), was the prehistoric rendition of a frontier town. Archaeological evidence indicates the existence of several cultures in this region, and items found around Montezuma Castle suggest that the area was a major trade center for prehistoric peoples of the Southwest.

The first inhabitants were the "master farmers" of the Southwest, the Hohokam, who came up from the south about 300 B.C. They lived

in clusters of pit houses—one-room structures made of mud, brush, and pole. Spring-fed Beaver Creek provided a reliable source of water, allowing the natives to divert it into their life-supporting irrigation ditches for crops of maize, beans, squash, and cotton.

About 350 years later, some Hohokam moved to the San Francisco Mountains. The eruption of Sunset Crater in 1064 A.D. had left a layer of rich ash-mulch, making the region around Wupatki ideal for farming.

The Sinagua (Spanish for "without water") were dry farmers, who arrived about 1100 A.D. from the Flagstaff area. They were pueblo, or apartment dwellers, living a communal lifestyle. About 1250 they embarked on a grandiose dwelling of stone known today as Montezuma Castle. The twenty-room apartment house, nestled beneath a limestone overhang above Beaver Creek, was occupied between 1100 A.D. and 1400 A.D. It was home for about twelve families, or about fifty people. Like other cliff dwellings found in the Southwest, Montezuma Castle, with its exposure to the winter sun, took advantage of solar heating, while the overhang protected it from rain and snow and provided shelter from the blistering summer sun. Another pueblo located about a hundred yards west was even larger, with more than forty-five rooms. The total population of this pueblo might have been about two hundred. Apparently the Hohokam and Sinagua lived harmoniously, sharing customs, practices, and arts.

The Sinagua, like all prehistoric peoples, left no written records. To learn more about their lifestyle, archaeologists have been working since the latter part of the nineteenth century trying to piece the mysterious Sinagua puzzle together. Not all the ruins at Montezuma Castle have been excavated. Since dating techniques have improved dramatically over the last thirty years, some sites are being left for future archaeologists, when new techniques may provide the key that unlocks the past.

Overcrowding might have eventually caused the abandonment of these pueblos. A long drought between the years 1276 A.D. and 1299 A.D. certainly had an impact on the valley. Too much competition for the spring-fed streams probably caused friction between the two cultures or perhaps there was increased pressure from nomadic, war-like tribes; in any case, the Hohokam eventually returned to the Gila Valley.

It is believed that the Sinagua who inhabited these pueblos, along with those eleven miles north at Montezuma Well, eventually traveled up the Palatwkapi Trail to join the Hopi Indians. By 1450 the entire area was deserted.

The first white man to visit Montezuma Castle was the great scout Antoine Leroux in 1854. The site was badly vandalized and in a state of near-collapse by the last of the 1890s. In 1906 President Theodore Roosevelt proclaimed Montezuma Castle and Montezuma Well national monuments.

McGuireville

McGuireville, originally the homestead of Eugene McGuire, was a community off the beaten path until the coming of Interstate 17 along a trail used hundreds of years ago by Hopi Indians, and during Spanish times by Espejo, Farfan, and Oñate, who explored along this ancient road. Later, in 1864 Lieutenant Colonel Francisco Chavez reopened the trail, and General George Crook's troopers used it in the 1870s. Martha Summerhayes writes of a harrowing ride along the steep mountain road in her memorable book *Vanished Arizona*.

Montezuma Well (McGuireville Exit)

Montezuma Well is actually a huge, natural sinkhole, the remains of an ancient cavern created by water percolating through limestone. A warm (75 degrees) underground spring provides nearly 1½ million gallons of water a day. During prehistoric times, limestone-coated irrigation ditches carried water to the thirsty crops of the Sinagua and Hohokam farmers. The sink is slightly less than five hundred feet in diameter, and the waterline is seventy feet below the rim. The well is about fifty-five feet deep. Many Native American tribes today consider the well a sacred place.

About eight hundred years ago at least two limestone pueblos existed at Montezuma Well. The smaller one had twenty rooms, while the larger, a two- or three-story structure, had over fifty. Usually the bottom floor of these taller pueblos had no openings. Residents climbed notched poles or wooden ladders, which were then pulled up out of reach to thwart enemies' easy entry. Doorways were built small not only to keep out the elements but to make it difficult for enemy warriors to overwhelm the defenders. Building under an overhang not only protected them from the elements, but also kept enemies from attacking from the rear.

About 1864 a tiny white settlement called Montezuma City developed around a small adobe fort. Rocks from the prehistoric pueblos were used in the construction of the community.

Stoneman Lake (fourteen miles east of Interstate 17)

Some writers claim Stoneman Lake, which is in the crater of an ancient volcano, was the only natural lake in Arizona prior to the coming of the Europeans. The name was given by Prescott editor John Marion to honor General George Stoneman. Stoneman first came to Arizona as a young lieutenant with the Mormon Battalion in 1846 and is best remembered for his unsuccessful attempts to haul supplies down the Gila River on a raft. The craft sank in the mighty Gila, and the young officer went down with his ship, but then walked ashore. Stoneman achieved fame in the Civil War and some degree of immortality in folk music of the 1960s, when his name was used in a song called "The Night They Drove Old Dixie Down."

A few years after the Civil War (1869), Stoneman was given command of the Military Department of California, of which Arizona was a part. He was a tough taskmaster but didn't achieve any great success defeating the Apache, Mojave, and Yavapai warriors. Two years after assuming command, he was relieved by General George Crook.

Apparently Stoneman was a cantankerous individual and had few friends. A story is told that at his funeral a large crowd showed up to pay last respects. When a young officer expressed surprise at the huge audience for someone so universally disliked, a fellow officer replied drily, "It just goes to show, you give the people something they want and they'll show up every time."

Earlier, Stoneman Lake was called Chavez Lake after Lieutenant Colonel Francisco Chavez of the New Mexico Volunteers and member of an illustrious New Mexico family. Chavez commanded the military escort for Governor John Goodwin and his governmental party in 1863-64 on their trek from Santa Fe to establish the first government in the new territory of Arizona. Chavez also gave his name to a road that ran from the Verde Valley to Sunset Crossing (Winslow). The road ran from Fort Verde up past Stoneman Lake (Chavez Lake), then through a break in the rugged canyons above the Mogollon Rim, still called Chavez Pass, and on to the Little Colorado River.

Martha Summerhayes camped at Stoneman Lake in the spring of 1875 on a journey from Camp Apache, across the Colorado Plateau and down to Fort Verde. After passing "evidences of hard travel, exhausted cattle, anxious teamsters, hunger and thirst, despair, starvation, and death," she proclaimed Stoneman Lake "a joy in the memory, and far and away the most beautiful spot I ever saw in Arizona." She went on to comment sagely, "But unless the approaches to it are made easier, tourists will never gaze upon it." Later she wondered if the lake really existed or was simply "an illusion, a dream, or the mirage which appears to the desert traveler, to satisfy him and lure him on. . . ."

The long, bumpy grade that led off the plateau at Stoneman Lake down to Fort Verde in the valley below rocked and jerked the army ambulance so much that Martha and her child had to get out and walk part of the way. After getting back on board, they reached another precipitous hill. The teamster tried to ease the wagon along while the six-mule team was forced into a gallop to keep from being overrun by the ambulance, which was by now swerving so close to the edge that rocks and gravel were being pushed down the steep precipice. Finally the ambulance reached the bottom in a cloud of dust. "Beaver Springs," the driver announced cheerfully.

As her husband lifted her out of the ambulance, Martha asked, "Why didn't you tell me?"

"Oh," he calmly replied, "I thought it was better for you not to know; people get scared about such things, when they know about them beforehand."

Then Martha turned to the driver and asked, "Smith, how could you drive down that place at such a rate and frighten me so?"

"Had to, ma'am," he calmly replied, "or we'd a'gone over the edge."

Martha admitted to being a flatlander with little understanding of driving six-mule teams along hazardous mountain roads. That night, while camped at Beaver Springs, sixteen miles north of Fort Verde, she reluctantly admitted "life (in Arizona) was beginning to interest me."

Schnebly Road

Schnebly Road was named for Theodore C. Schnebly, one of the early settlers in the community that came to be called Sedona.

190

Schnebly arrived in Oak Creek Canyon in 1901 and built a road out of the canyon and over Schnebly Hill to link the area with Flagstaff. When a post office was established in 1902, Ellsworth Schnebly suggested the name Sedona after his sister-in-law, Sedona Schnebly.

Back in the days before a road was constructed through Oak Creek Canyon, twisting and turning its way up and out of the north end, settlers around Indian Gardens followed a trail that led up the east side of the canyon. Wagons and mules were kept on top. Clara Thompson Purtyman, who was born in Indian Gardens in 1890, described how, as a young wife, she had carried her sick baby up the "Thompson Ladder" trail. At the top, she hitched a team and drove into Flagstaff, arriving in time to save the infant's life. That trail into Flagstaff roughly follows today's Interstate 17.

Munds Park and Canyon

Both Munds Park and Canyon were named for early settler James Munds, who homesteaded in this area in 1883. A "park" in the vernacular of the old West meant a large clearing in the forest. The high country meadows were ideal for cattle grazing in the summer but were grim in the winter because this "park" lay in a heavy snow belt; therefore, the cattleman opened a trail to the milder Verde Valley for winter grazing.

ASU's first football team, 1896
Courtesy
Southwest Studies

US 60
Tempe to Globe

They say British ex-patriot "Lord" Darrell Duppa gazed out across the desolate desert, spotted with greasewood and groves of grizzled mesquite, and thought the place reminded him of the Vale of Tempe in Greece. Thus came the inspiration for the naming of Tempe. We know "Lord" Duppa was strongly addicted to alcohol, so he may have been afflicted with a moment of grandeur. Whatever the reason, Tempe it became and Tempe it is.

In 1870 Charles Trumbull Hayden was operating a ferry on the Salt River. Hayden had first come to Santa Fe in an ox cart during the late 1840s. He became a merchant and later moved his enterprise to Tucson, arriving on the first Butterfield Overland Stage in 1858. A dozen years later he moved north to the south bank of the Salt River and established a ferry landing, flour mill, and store at the site of today's "Monti's La Casa Vieja" (the old house). The community was called Hayden's Ferry, although some referred to it as either San Pablo or Butte City. By 1879 everyone had agreed on Tempe, and a post office was established under that name.

Prior to the 1900s Tempe developed as a cattle shipping point, railroad junction, and important agricultural area. In 1885 the Territorial Assembly at Prescott created a normal school, which led to Tempe's emergence as an educational center. That year the population of Tempe consisted of eight hundred sunbaked citizens, and the main industry was a ferry business and a grain mill. The normal

192

school opened in February 1886, with thirty-three students (thirteen men and twenty women) and a two-year operating budget of $3,500. One of the first graduates was James McClintock, who later gained fame as historian, newspaperman, and captain of B Company of the Arizona contingent of Teddy Roosevelt's Roughriders during the Spanish American War. During the next quarter century, growth of the normal school was slow as it increased an average of only twelve students a year.

After the completion of Roosevelt Dam in 1911, irrigation created a man-made oasis, and Tempe began to prosper. The school became a four-year teachers' college in 1929 and four years later was renamed Arizona State Teachers College. In 1945, with the enrollment of 533 students, the name of the college was changed again, this time to Arizona State College. The last name change, to Arizona State University, came in 1958 after a hard-fought battle with Pima County and with die-hard University of Arizona students and fans who didn't want to share their university status. When the state legislature was unwilling to make the change, although the institution was well qualified, it was put to the people of Arizona, who voted overwhelmingly in favor of A.S.U., which at that time had about ten thousand students.

Back in 1885, the legislature stipulated that land for a normal school in Tempe had to be donated within sixty days or the "creation" bill would be null and void. George and Martha Wilson, a generous, civic-minded couple, endowed fifteen acres of the original twenty-acre parcel and sold the rest for $500. The Wilsons (Wilson Hall) impoverished themselves by making the donation in what is undoubtedly one of the most unselfish, public-spirited acts in Tempe history. Martha Wilson died soon after, but her husband George remained a caretaker on the campus until his death in 1916.

Arizona has a proud tradition in sports, but it was a rocky road to success in the early days. The first baseball field was located at the site of the Hayden Library. The team played its first game on February 14, 1891, against Stringtown, a "suburb" of Mesa. Stringtown had only six players but managed to build a 17-to-5 lead before the game was halted by a dust storm in the fifth inning.

Tempe Bridge in 1913. On bridge (right center) is Governor George W.P. Hunt, who served seven terms as Arizona chief executive.
Courtesy
Southwest Studies

A football team under the leadership of Fred "Cap" Irish (Irish Hall) was organized in 1896. Sixty-one male students were enrolled and none had ever played football. Cap's teams preferred to use the old flying wedge in a game that more closely resembled a mass collision of bodies than organized football. Players didn't have helmets or pads, and substitutions were allowed only when a player was too groggy to stand under his own power. Prior to each game, the field was plowed to cushion the falls.

In 1899 Tempe won the Arizona championship by whipping the University of Arizona 11 to 2. It would be a long dry spell of thirty-two years before the normal school would beat Tucson again. Tempe was known as the Bulldogs until 1946, when the name was changed to Sun Devils. The popular, devilish-looking mascot was designed by a cartoonist working for Walt Disney Productions.

Tempe, with a population of three thousand, was still a quiet college town in 1941, but post-World War II brought dramatic changes: young men home from the war headed for college on the G. I. Bill; and with the advent of air conditioning and with a new, more mobile America, came unprecedented growth in the Salt River Valley. During the 1950s, Tempe's population went from 7,700 to 25,000. By 1965, it had grown to over 45,000, roughly about the size of the university in 1985. During the mid-1980s, Tempe's population has reached the neighborhood of 150,000.

Mesa and Lehi

In 1877 the first Mormon settlers to establish a community south of the Little Colorado River Valley, arrived in the Salt River Valley. The party numbered eighty-four and they came in on the old road from Fort McDowell. The Mormons forded the river at the crossing known at various times as the McDowell, Maryville, and Whitlow Crossing, located about three and a half miles west of the Lehi School.

Maryville was located on the north side of the river near the junction of Arizona 87 (Beeline Highway) and McDowell Road. A small settlement boasting a store, hotel, and blacksmith shop, Maryville was also a junction for the road leading into the new settlement of Phoenix.

The earliest settlers, called the Lehi Pioneers, organized work parties and began digging irrigation ditches and planting crops. They erected an adobe enclosure near North Mesa Drive and Lehi Road, calling it Fort Utah. It would later be called Utahville and Jonesville before residents would settle on Lehi.

The following year another group of settlers from Utah arrived,

known as the Mesa Pioneers. A townsite was selected on the table-
land south of Lehi and called Mesa. The mail was still being delivered
at Hayden's Ferry or Tempe, but when the Mesa residents petitioned
for a post office, the name was rejected because of Mesaville in Pinal
County; therefore, in 1881, they called the town Hayden. By this time
Hayden's Ferry had been changed to Tempe, but this didn't stop the
postal service from getting the two places confused. In 1886, Hayden
was changed to Zenos for a prophet in the Book of Mormon. When the
post office at Mesaville closed in 1888, the settlers united on the name
Mesa.

The original homesites in Mesa were only four to a block, enough to
allow for a dwelling surrounded by a garden and orchard. Although
that expansive plan was modified later, the Mormon community was
farsighted when it came to designing streets. They were the only
settlers to plan thoroughfares wide enough for modern-day driving
and parking.

The phenomenal growth that characterized the rest of the Salt
River Valley was also true of Mesa. In 1940, with a population a little
over seven thousand, Mesa was still the state's third largest city. By
1950, it had more than doubled to just under seventeen thousand,
doubling again during the 1950s and again by 1970. By the mid-
1980s, Mesa's population had grown to about two hundred thousand,
with no end in sight. The agrarian society that characterized early
Mesa has been replaced by high-tech industry. Suburbia creeps over
what was once lush farmland, jumps the canals, and sprawls across
the desert.

Apache Junction

In 1944 Apache Junction consisted of one gas station. Every Sunday a three-piece hillbilly band played music in the lobby. Out back
was a crude zoo made of boards and chicken wire, the most interesting
part being the rattlesnake pens. The area around Apache Junction
has always had a good supply of rattlesnakes. In the 1960s a big
diamondback crawled into the dugout at a major league spring training game, sending the players scrambling to get out.

Superstition Mountains

The Superstitions, that awesome range of jagged mountains north
of US 80, are America's most storied mountains. Here, supposedly,
lies the fabled Lost Dutchman Mine. They are also the home of the
Apaches' Thunder Gods. A white streak of limestone, according to
legend, is the high water mark of a great flood that covered most of
the earth. It was said that people who ventured into these mysterious

mountains with their twisting, steep-sided canyons, never returned.

The most enduring legend is that of the Lost Dutchman, Jacob Waltz. Jake was supposed to have found an old Spanish mine in the Superstitions, killing anyone foolish enough to try to learn his secret. After his death in the early 1890s, the legend of the lost mine created some local interest for a time, then was mostly forgotten for some thirty years. During the 1930s, Dr. Adolph Ruth arrived at Apache Junction, claiming to have a map of the mine. An elderly man in poor health, Dr. Ruth ventured into the mountains one hot summer day and was never seen alive again. Several months later his skull was found with what looked like a bullet hole in it.

The newspapers around the country had a field day with the story as goldseekers, soothsayers, and would-be millionaires came out of the woodwork to search for the fabulous lode. Phoenix-area residents had a big advantage—they could go in search of the treasure every weekend.

During the 1950s a feud broke out between a grizzled, but friendly old cuss named Ed Piper and a black woman who claimed to be an ex-opera singer named Celeste Marie Jones. Each recruited a band of rogues and set up camp at the south side of Weaver's Needle. As expected, violence broke out between the two armed camps, and three people died before a tenuous truce was arranged. The feud ended when Piper died of natural causes and Ms. Jones abandoned her claim.

The rugged Superstitions are among the most spectacular mountains to be found anywhere in America. The chronicler of the great Coronado expedition in 1540, Pedro de Casteneda, might well have been thinking of this range when he recorded, "Granted they did not find the gold, at least they found a place in which to search." During the early spring, nearly every canyon stream flows with sparkling clear water, and the grass is emerald, with lupine and poppies everywhere. There is a treasure to be found in these mountains—it's called "being there."

Silver King

In 1873 sometime after the establishment of the Camp Picket Post by the army, a party of soldiers was building a road up what was called Stoneman Grade. On the way back to camp one day, a soldier named Sullivan picked up a curious chunk of black rock and stuck it in his pocket. Later he showed it to a friend, Charles Mason, who lived along the Salt River. Mason examined the rock and declared it was nearly pure silver. Sullivan's enlistment was about up, and soon he disappeared without saying much about where he had found the ore except that it was near the foot of Stoneman Grade. Mason believed he'd been killed by Apaches, so plans to locate the lode were delayed for a while. However, Mason and Isaac Copeland, Bill Long, and Ben Reagan, three Florence-area farmers, soon decided to go prospecting. Not far from Stoneman Grade a war party of Apaches jumped them, and during the fight one of the burros wandered away. Afterwards they found the animal standing directly on top of a rich outcropping of chloride of silver, characterized by the same "black rock" that Sullivan had found. It looked like the king of all silver mines, so they called it the Silver King, and named the district Pioneer. Not being savvy prospectors, they unwisely tossed the high grade ore onto a tailing dump, hauling low grade ore to San Francisco. The freight bill alone was $12,000. Discouraged, the four hapless farmers tried unsuccessfully to unload the property on a Florence storekeeper in payment for grubstaking their trip. The farmers-turned-prospectors were saved from a life of poverty by some mining men who offered to work the Silver King for half the profits. The first shipment netted the outfit $50,000. Jim Barney, a merchant from Yuma, bought out two of the partners for $130,000 and eventually gained control of the company. The Silver King was incorporated in 1877, and by the time the boom ended eleven years later, the mine had produced more than six million dollars in silver, making it the richest silver mine in Arizona history.

The Silver King story ends on an interesting human interest note: during the prosperity of the Silver King, an old down-on-his-luck itinerant wandered into Pinal and identified himself as Sullivan, the ex-soldier who'd been the original discoverer. In California he'd heard of the fabulous Silver King and wanted to take a look at it before he died. The sympathetic owners were convinced that his story was true and offered him a job and pension for life.

Pinal City

Pinal City, three miles southwest of Superior, was a mill town for the fabulous Silver King Mine. The post office was established in 1878 as Picket Post but was changed to Pinal a year later. Pinal was located on the ranch of L. DeArnett, who sold the owners of the Silver King a mill site, five miles from the mine. For ten years the town boomed, boasting such amenities as a brewery, two churches (Protestant and Catholic), several lodges, and the sundry businesses usually found in a mining town.

Several years earlier, General George Stoneman ordered Camp Pinal, about ten miles northeast, to be relocated to the foot of Picket

Post Butte, where a new post was laid out. It's not certain when it was abandoned, but Camp Picket Post was absorbed by the bustling town of Pinal. When the bottom fell out of the silver market in the early 1890s, the population of Pinal, which had reached two thousand, dwindled to ten.

Highgraders around Silver King devised a clever scheme for stealing the rich ore that came from the mine. Muleskinners made a habit of tossing chunks of ore from the wagon, ostensibly at the stubborn mules. Not surprisingly, a partner-in-crime was always on hand to pick up the throwaways and stick them in his pocket.

Superior

The towering, red-streaked cliff that hovers above the town of Superior is known as Apache Leap. The story is told that one day a picket spotted an Apache war party heading up a precipitous mountain trail to a secret hideout. An expedition of soldiers from Camp Pinal was sent in pursuit, cornering the Indians on the edge of the cliff. Rather than face an humiliating surrender, the warriors plunged over the edge and were crushed on the rocks below.

During the 1870s, a rich lode was found and lost by a man named Sullivan. The lode was later relocated and became the fabulous Silver King. Prospectors flocked to the area in search of the lost lode and during the search, found another silver outcropping, where Superior is today. The ore wasn't as rich as the Lost Silver King's, so they named the mine the Silver Queen. In 1880, the Silver Queen Mining Company was organized in New York. The lode was inconsistent, so the Queen never reached the expectations of its developers.

A 1900 map shows the town at the site as Hastings. That same year the name was changed to honor the Lake Superior and Arizona Mine located near the Silver Queen and the source of much of the area's economy. Ten years later the Magma Copper Company was organized to take over the Silver Queen properties. Beneath that silver capping was an incredibly rich deposit of copper, the old Queen coming up a winner after all. The Magma, founded by W. Boyce Thompson, went on to become one of Arizona's greatest copper bonanzas.

Top of the World

Nine miles south of Miami, US 60 tops out and begins a long descent toward the mining town. The old highway used to wind its way further east past the Top of the World guest ranch, popular during the 1950s. The outside of this ranch was ordinary, but the interior was paneled with white pine, and the lobby had a coke machine and a juke box that lit up like a Las Vegas casino. However, the main attractions were the "working girls," who were among the prettiest in Gila County and noted far beyond county and state borders.

Camp Pinal

Six miles south of Miami is an old wagon road leading off to the west of the highway. On November 28, 1870, General George Stoneman, Department Commander, established a military post near the headwaters of Mineral and Pinto creeks in Mason Valley. The original name was Infantry Camp, named for the foot soldiers who first located there. By the following year, about four hundred cavalrymen were stationed at Camp Pinal, their purpose to protect miners and prospectors from Apaches. In 1871 the troops were moved a few miles west to Queen Creek, and at the foot of Picket Post Butte they established a new camp.

In 1878 Robert A. "Old Man" Irion came here from Colorado and located a ranch on the site of Camp Pinal. It became a favorite resting place for travelers on the old Florence-Globe road. In the late 1930s the furnishings at Irion's Ranch, now called Pinal Ranch, still bore bullet and arrow marks, testimony to a more violent time.

Miami

Miami sits in a small valley at the foot of the Pinal Mountains. The business district is laid out on the valley floor, while most of the residences are perched on the slopes of the foothills that surround the town. Bloody Tanks Wash runs through the middle of the valley known as Miami Flat. The old Miami Copper Company and Inspiration Mines, along with company offices and dwellings, were located on the north side of town near where a massive man-made mesa of bleached-out dirt lies today.

Bloody Tanks Wash was named for a fight that took place in 1864 between King Woolsey's expedition and a party of Apaches. The fight occurred during a "peaceful parley" between the two groups. Both sides were carrying concealed weapons, each hoping to get the drop on the other. Gifts of tobacco and pinole (ground corn mixed with sugar) were offered to the natives; then at a pre-arranged signal by Woolsey, the militiamen pulled their guns and opened fire. It was said the water in the creek turned red from the blood and inspired the grim name. The late Gila County historian Clara Woody believed that the battle between Woolsey and the Apaches occurred at Fish Creek and that the Bloody Tanks name came as a result of a fight between Lieutenant Howard Cushing's troops and a band of Pinal Apaches about 1870.

Black Jack Newman, a Polish immigrant, located a rich prospect in Big Johnny Gulch, which he named the Mima, for his girlfriend, Mima Tune. At about the same time, a group from Miami, Ohio, staked a claim near Bloody Tanks Wash. Black Jack wanted to name the fledgling community Mima, but the others insisted on calling it Miami. A compromise was finally reached when both sides agreed to spell it "Miami" but pronounce it "Mima."

Black Jack Newman was a smart Polish miner—he sold his mine to the Lewisohn brothers of New York, but struck a deal whereby he received a commission on every pound of copper sold by Lewisohns' Miami Copper Company. With Lewisohns and Inspiration, Miami, founded in 1907, faced the prosperous future with enthusiastic optimism.

The community of Miami had a rather shaky beginning, however. The Miami Copper Company and Inspiration wanted a company town so they could control housing and businesses. Also, whenever an unhappy employee quit the company, it was unlikely that he could hang around to cause trouble. The businessmen in Globe weren't enthusiastic about a company town, as it meant an economic loss to them. The original owners of the property at Miami Flat finally abandoned the futile project. Then along came a developer named Cleve Van Dyke. He tossed in $25,000 and bought the townsite. Then he acquired a newspaper, the *Silver Belt*, and began promoting Miami. It was too much for opponents in Globe, and the community of Miami Flat was on its way.

Inspiration began construction of a reduction plant in 1909, and by the end of World War I, the "Concentrator City," as Miami was sometimes called, had a larger population than Globe.

Like most of the old copper towns, Miami has fallen on hard times recently, when the market has been glutted with foreign imports; also, outdated equipment has failed to meet environmental standards, and companies have deemed it unprofitable to re-equip. Thus, the pendulum has swung back to Globe's advantage.

Globe

Set against the majestic backdrop of the Pinal Mountains on one side and the Apache range on the other, is the rough-and-tumble mining town of Globe. Perched on the banks of Pinal Creek, its old buildings huddled on steep slopes, Globe was one of the great mining camps of old Arizona. Its intrepid citizens braved everything from isolation to frequent, but unwelcome, visits by Apache war parties, to carve out a community in the rugged mineral-laden mountains.

The first reports of mineral riches came in 1864. That year, King

Woolsey, a rancher on the upper Agua Fria River east of Prescott, led three punitive expeditions into the area. Their reports inspired prospectors to defy the always-dangerous Pinal and Tonto Apache bands and to stake claims. The establishment of Camp Pinal, in 1870, thirteen miles west, provided some security. Still,those lonely mountain roads leading out of Globe were not meant to be traveled by the weakhearted.

The first mine of importance near Globe was established by a party of prospectors in 1873. Two years later the Globe Mining District was formed. The origin of the name Globe is up for speculation. Three colorful legends regarding the name would find support in the adage attributed to Mark Twain: "If it didn't happen this way, it *could* have happened this way." The first explanation comes from a large, round chunk of silver with lines resembling the land continents of the earth. The second, a similar claim, states that prospectors found a large, circular silver boulder. And the third says that Pinal Apaches were using silver bullets and a closer investigation led to the discovery at Globe.

In 1878, the settlers moved a short distance to the banks of Pinal Creek to be closer to a source of water and called their town Globe City. Later the "City" was dropped. In 1880 Globe incorporated, but city fathers either had short memories or liked celebrations, for they incorporated again in 1905, then dropped incorporation a year later because it was too expensive, but re-incorporated in 1907. The main street was Broad Street, which meandered along Pinal Creek with more kinks than an alley cat's tail. Old timers attribute this to the fact that miners and prospectors stubbornly refused to move their shanties so the surveyors could lay out a straight road.

Globe has an early history of isolation. During the first twenty-two years of existence, the nearest railroad was 120 miles away. In the 1870s supplies were hauled in by wagon from Silver City, New Mexico, 150 miles to the east. By 1878 supplies were brought from the new town of Florence, only sixty miles away, but the trip took five days. In 1898, the Gila Valley, Globe, and Northern Railroad was stretched along the San Simon and Gila valleys to Globe, thus allowing the mining companies to get down to serious business. The first highway to Globe was the Apache Trail (Arizona 88), built during construction of the Theodore Roosevelt Dam in the early 1900s. By 1811, a trip from Globe to Phoenix took only two days. Finally, in 1922, US 60 linked Globe with Phoenix, and the trip took only a day.

The granddaddy of all the mines in the Globe district was the Old Dominion, on the north side of town. It had a few lean years in the early days. Then, in 1895, the Lewisohn brothers of New York bought control of the company, built a new smelter, and ran a railroad in from the Southern Pacific main line at Bowie. However, the mine was plagued by a persistent water problem, and pumps proved ineffective. Eventually the New Yorkers gave up on the Old Dominion and sold out. In 1903, Phelps-Dodge acquired the property on the sage advice of Dr. James Douglas. Douglas put Dr. L. D. Ricketts in charge, and after a thorough overhaul of equipment, the mine started turning a profit—for the next twenty years the Old Dominion was one of the greatest copper mines in the world. The Old Dominion shut down its smelter in 1924 and closed its mine during the Great Depression. By that time it had produced $134,000,000 in gold, silver, and copper.

Globe's spunky citizens could always be counted on to display a spirit of independence characteristic of frontier society in the face of bureaucracy. Maggie Wilson, author and Globe native, tells a story about the time when work on the new Central School was completed before residents realized it was located near a house of ill repute. The law required that parlor houses not be located within four hundred feet of a school. Citizens formally requested the sheriff to close the house. Another group of concerned citizens immediately petitioned the sheriff to "move the school." The sheriff obligingly measured the distance between the two structures and found that the four-hundred-foot limit extended four feet into the parlor. The matter was settled in a typical frontier problem-solving manner when the sheriff told the madam to confine all activities to the back rooms, which were within the legal limit.

Maggie also has claim to a story of a French immigrant, Andre Maurel, "the only man who ever shut down a mining company single-handed and lived to tell about it." Mr. Maurel had a peach orchard near the mine, and the miners were helping themselves to his peaches without paying. The resourceful Frenchman got even with the peach thieves one night by injecting each peach with a dose of croton oil. The company had to shut down for three days because all the workers were at home in the outhouse.

The Globe-Miami area has produced its share of successful people in all walks of life. Included among these is Rose Perica Mofford, present Secretary of State and one of Arizona's most popular and colorful personalities. Rose is also a former women's amateur softball player, who starred for the Arizona Cantalope Queens at the height of women's softball. Another is longtime writer Maggie Wilson. Jack Elam, one of Hollywood's best-known character actors, hails from Globe, as did the Marine hero during the Iranian hostage crisis of 1980, Sergeant James Lopez. High school sports improved relations among ethnic groups. Each community had its Mexican, Italian,

Globe in 1903
Courtesy
Southwest Studies

Irish, and Slavic sections, and it was said nobody dared venture into another ethnic area after sundown, but the situation was different on the playing fields and in gymnasiums. It wasn't unusual for an athletic team to have a Martinez, O'Leary, Ivanovich and Battina in the starting lineup. Outstanding ballplayers from the Globe-Miami area include Lupe Acevedo and Fito Trujillo, who later starred at Northern Arizona University; Teddy Lazovich and Ken Giovando at the University of Arizona; and Ed Anderson, the Vucichevich brothers, Rad and Johnny, at Arizona State University. All have gone on to successful careers in other fields after their playing days were over.

The silver boom in Globe lasted only four years, but before it played out, copper was coming into great demand, and the silver camp slid right into a prosperous copper mining town. By 1886, the town was boasting that all U.S. copper coins had been minted from Globe copper.

Globe began to fade as a mining town in 1909, when richer deposits of low-grade copper ore were located seven miles west and the new upstart town of Miami was born. Local merchants led the exodus, as they rushed to establish stores in the new community. Ironically, today the situation is reversing itself, as the former silver camp is making a comeback.

*Scottsdale, 1936,
looking west. Street
in foreground is
Brown Avenue.
Scottsdale Road
runs across the
center. At top is
Indian School Road.*
Courtesy Scottsdale
Historical Society

Arizona 87
Scottsdale to Winslow

Scottsdale

Phoenix was a city of three thousand and just one year away from becoming the permanent Capital of Arizona on a February day in 1888 when army chaplain Winfield Scott arrived to look at some real estate. Scott's reputation as a colonizer with integrity inspired local promoters to invite him to see the Salt River Valley. He crisscrossed the valley on horseback for about a week before finding his utopia in the east valley. William J. Murphy had just completed construction of the Arizona Canal, opening vast new areas for irrigation. Five months later Scott purchased a section of land for $2.50 an acre under the Desert Land Act. Scott's original homestead encompassed the area bounded by Hayden Road on the east and Scottsdale Road on the west; Chaparral and Indian School roads marked the north and south boundaries.

Since the Desert Land Act required that the land be irrigated within three years, the army chaplain brought his brother, George Washington Scott, out to clear the acreage, build fences, and dig irrigation ditches. Afterwards, he planted barley, citrus, and grapes. George W. Scott also erected a tent on the northeast corner of today's Scottsdale and Indian School roads, the present site of a modern financial center. Scott, therefore, is considered Scottsdale's first citizen in residency.

Winfield Scott, still in the army, continued to promote the area. In 1889, he was transferred to Fort Huachuca and spent much of his free time preaching sermons at churches in Phoenix, Tempe, and Mesa.

He retired from the army in 1893 after a distinguished career and moved to his homestead. He brought along another retiree, an army mule named Old Maud. The mule was a veteran of the Apache wars and, like Scott, came to spend last years in the tranquil community east of Phoenix. A painting of Old Maud by noted artist Marjorie Thomas hangs in the mayor's office at city hall.

Albert J. Utley, a Rhode Island banker, bought a section of land south of Scott's and subdivided forty acres into a townsite in 1894. He hoped to create a resort community that would include a hotel, tuberculosis sanitarium, and streetcar line to Phoenix. Utley asked Scott to take charge of the townsite. Giving the town a name headed the list of priorities. Suggested names included Murphyville for the canal builder and Utleyville for the developer. Utley, to his credit, preferred Orangedale, and for a brief time the town used that name. However, before the lots were offered for sale, the townsite name was changed to Scottsdale to honor the man primarily responsible for its success.

In the fall of 1896, the first Scottsdale school opened with seventeen pupils and Mrs. Alza Blount as teacher. Years later, as the town slowly grew, the historic Little Red Schoolhouse, sitting proudly in the Civic Center Plaza today, was built. In 1910 the school cost forty-five hundred dollars to build and furnish. In 1911, Scottsdale had its first post office; that same year the citizens voted for prohibition.

Scottsdale was founded by church-minded people, and the community leaders were determined to keep the "vices and moral decadence of Phoenix" out of their town. It wasn't easy—"bad boy" Johnny Rose ran a pool hall on Brown and Main streets and made regular runs into Phoenix to buy tanglefoot whiskey for local imbibers. The town later billed itself as the "West's Most Western Town," but was in reality a quiet farm village, a haven for healthseekers, and a refuge for artists.

The town did get "Western" for a brief spell each year when ranchers gathered their cattle in Paradise Valley and drove them down Scottsdale Road to the stockyards at Tempe. It also had several shooting frays, but not the kind glorified on the silver screen. In 1900 "Popcorn John" Rubenstein, a mail carrier from Phoenix, shot and killed two men in an argument resulting from a wagon allegedly blocking his path.

During the 1930s, town constable Al Frederick shot and killed a winter visitor's chauffeur after the latter attacked him with a cue stick in Guy Roberts's pool hall.

Scottsdale farmers grew everything from peanuts and olives to citrus and barley, but the big moneymaker was cotton. During World War I, when Pima long staple was in great demand for uniforms and balloon tires, a farmer could pay off his mortgage in one year.

In those days, Phoenix didn't allow people with lung disease to take up residence, so many convalescents came to live in Scottsdale. Minnie Elliott, afflicted with tuberculosis, was given only six months to live. She came to Scottsdale to bask in the sun, and in six months her lungs healed, and she lived to the age of eighty-six. She became friendly with the local Pima Indians, and they took it upon themselves to cure her. Each day they gave Minnie a bitter tea brewed from the leaves of the creosote bush and buried her up to her neck in desert sand. Some believe the treatment cured Minnie; others believe she made herself well to escape the treatment.

Most of the houses were built of orange crates and canvas. Phoenix residents snobbishly referred to the town as "White City" because of all the white tent dwellings.

An interesting contrast in Scottsdale's history was its collection of resident artists. Most people believe the community became "arty" after World War II. Noted artist Lew Davis told Scottsdale historian Dick Lynch that the reason many artists came to Scottsdale in the early days was that residents treated them like regular people rather than "Bohemians." Like farmers, artists needed credit until their works sold. As for the merchants, waiting for art to sell was like waiting for crops to come in. Noted among Scottsdale's art colony were artists Jesse Benton Evans, Lew Davis, Oscar Strobel, Jr., Marjorie Thomas, Lon Megargae, and poet Rose Trumbull.

The first of a long history of zoning fights occurred in 1910, when city fathers made George Cavalliere build his "smelly, fly-attractin' blacksmith shop at the city limits"—way out on 2nd Street and Brown Road. It still does business at that location and is one of Scottsdale's richest historical treasures. Another is the venerable Our Lady of Perpetual Help Catholic Church, which sits next door. The adobe building was erected by Mexican residents who came as farm workers and wanted a church of their own.

Among the early arrivals in Scottsdale was the Tomás Corral family. Tomás worked in the mines in Cananea, Sonora, but his wife Cecilia didn't want her six sons to spend their lives in the mines or get caught in the bloody revoluton that had engulfed the Mexican Republic since 1910. In 1919, the family migrated to Scottsdale. Their sponsor was E. O. Brown, a prosperous merchant and rancher for whom Brown Road is named. Brown gave them jobs as farm workers. In the early 1930s, the Corral family built an adobe pool hall on 2nd Street just east of Brown Road. The building was also used as a

Corral family portrait taken in 1919. They emigrated to Arizona to escape the revolution in Mexico and eventually found prominence and prosperity in Scottsdale. Courtesy Corral family

classroom for the Catholic Church. During World War II, Tomás Corral's sons, like a lot of other young men in Scottsdale, went off to join the military. They came home from the war expecting the civil liberties they had fought to preserve, but which were sometimes denied in their own country. After being refused service in a local restaurant, they converted the old pool hall to a restaurant. Corral's *Los Olivos* restaurant continues to be one of Scottsdale's finest, its classic Mexican design a lasting tribute to the artistic talent of the Corral brothers.

During World War II, a large prisoner-of-war camp was located near 64th Street and Oak at Papago Park. For reasons understood only by a bureaucratic army, the most incorrigible (and apparently resourceful) prisoners were assigned to Papago. Many were naval personnel—the idea being to get them as far way from the sea as possible. The prisoners, noting the Arizona river system, schemed to tunnel out, then float down the Salt River to the Gila, then to the Colorado and on to Mexico, where they could eventually arrange a safe return to Germany. The tireless Germans, using spoons for shovels, dug a 178-foot tunnel through the clay-like caliche, emerging at 66th Street and Wilshire. On December 23, 1944 twenty-five Germans escaped. They waded down the Cross-cut Canal carrying a prefabricated boat and headed for the Salt River. The river was dry, as it usually is, so the prisoners tossed the boat away and separated after spending Christmas Eve huddled in the basement of Phoenix Union High School. Within about six weeks all had been rounded up and put back behind barbed wire ending the largest prisoner-of-war escape in the United States during the Second World War.

Prior to World War II, Scottsdale grew at a snail's pace. In 1920, the same year the first electric wires were strung out from the falls of the Arizona Canal (56th Street and Indian School Road), the population was only eight hundred. Thirty years later the town had a population of two thousand. In 1960 the town had grown to over ten thousand. Five years later, a special census put the figure at fifty-five thousand,

and by the mid-1980s, the city had grown to well over a hundred thousand, with no end in sight.

Scottsdale's tough zoning restrictions and world-wide reputation as a culture-oriented tourist city, have skyrocketed the price of available real estate, a far cry from the early days of a quiet farm community.

Fort McDowell

On September 7, 1865 Fort McDowell was established at the confluence of Sycamore Creek and the Verde River by five companies of California Volunteers. Named for General Irvin McDowell, military commander in the area, the post was located about seven miles above the junction of the Salt and Verde rivers. This site was selected because of its strategic importance for scouting and punitive expeditions against the Yavapai and Tonto Apache bands. These nomadic natives raided Pima Indians and whites alike and then retreated to the sanctuary of the Superstition, Sierra Ancha, and Mazatzal ranges, and of Salt River Canyon.

The original post, made of adobe, washed away in a thunderstorm. Undaunted, the troopers built another. By 1870, the new department commandant, General George Stoneman, was calling Fort McDowell one of the finest forts in the territory.

Martha Summerhayes and her soldier-husband, Jack, were stationed here in the mid-1870s. Her account paints a good picture of the old fort:

> The officers' quarters were a long, low line of adobe buildings with no space between them; the houses were separated only by thick walls. In front, the windows looked out over the parade ground. In the rear, they opened out on a road which ran along the whole length, and on the other side of which lay another row of long, low buildings which were the kitchens, each set of quarters having its own.
>
> We occupied the quarters at the end of the row, and a large bay window looked out over a rather desolate plain, and across to the large and well-kept hospital. . . .
>
> There were interminable scouts, which took both cavalry and infantry out of the post. We heard a great deal about "chasing Injuns" in the Superstition Mountains, and once a lieutenant of infantry went out to chase an escaping Indian Agent. . . .
>
> It was cool enough (in the winter) to wear white cotton dresses, but nothing heavier. It never rained, and the climate was superb, although it was always hot in the sun.
>
> We had heard that it was very hot here; in fact, people called MacDowell by very bad names. As the spring came on, we began to realize that the epithets applied to it might be quite appropriate. . . .

208

In front of our quarters was a *ramada*, supported by rude poles of the cottonwood tree. Then came the sidewalk, and then the parade ground. Through the *acequia* ran the clear water that supplied the post, and under the shade of the *ramadas*, hung the large *ollas* from which we dipped the drinking water, for as yet, of course, ice was not even dreamed of in the farm plains of MacDowell. The heat became intense, as the summer approached. To sleep inside the house was impossible, and we soon followed the example of the cavalry, who had their beds out on the parade ground.

Two iron cots, therefore, were brought from the hospital, and placed side by side in front of our quarters, beyond the *acequia* and the cottonwood trees, in fact, out in the open space of the parade ground. Upon these were laid some mattresses and sheets, and after "taps" had sounded, and lights were out, we retired to rest. Near the cots stood Harry's crib. We had not thought about the ants, however, and they swarmed over our beds, driving us into the house. The next morning Bowen placed a tin can of water under each point of contact; and as each cot had eight legs, and the crib had four, twenty cans were necessary. He had not taken the trouble to remove the labels, and the pictures of red tomatoes glared at us in the hot sun through the day; they did not look poetic, but our old enemies, the ants, were outwitted.

. . . the sun rose incredibly early in that southern country, and by the crack of dawn sheeted figures were to be seen darting back into the quarters, to try for another nap. The nap rarely came to any of us, for the heat of the houses never passed off, day or night, at that season. After an early breakfast, the long day began again. . . .

. . . Hammocks were swung under the *ramadas*, and after luncheon everybody tried a siesta. Then, near sundown, an ambulance came and took us over to the Verde River, about a mile away, where we bathed in water almost as thick as that of the Great Colorado. We taught Mrs. Kendall to swim, but Mr. Kendall, being an inland man, did not take to the water. Now the Verde River was not a very good substitute for the sea, and the thick water filled our ears, and mouths, but it gave us a little half hour in the day when we could experience a feeling of being cool, and we found it worthwhile to take the trouble. Thick clumps of mesquite trees furnished us with dressing rooms. We were all young, and youth requires so little with which to make merry.

Military duty in Arizona was monotonous and tiresome. Captain Corliss of C Company said to Martha one day: "Four years I have sat here and looked at the Four Peaks and I'm getting almighty tired of it."

On April 10, 1890, Fort McDowell was turned over to the Yavapai Indians, when 25,000 acres were set aside as a reservation. The Yavapai Indians are related linguistically to the Yuma language group, and their name translates to "People of the Sun." A nomadic people, they traveled in small family groups or bands similar to the Apaches, with whom they are often confused. Like the Apaches, with whom they were intermarried and allied, they are recognized and admired for their fine basketry. During General George Crook's famous winter campaign of 1872-73, the Yavapai and Apache bands were defeated and moved to reservations at Date Creek and Fort Verde, despite protests from a few military officers who recognized the Yavapai as a people separate from the Apaches. In 1875 they were rounded up and herded like cattle (the Yavapai call this humiliation the "March of Tears") to the San Carlos Apache Reservation. In the 1890s, they were allowed to return to Fort McDowell. Most of today's residents of Fort McDowell are descendants of those who survived the March of Tears.

Sycamore Creek

On October 11, 1867, construction began on a military road between Fort McDowell and Camp Reno, in the Tonto Basin. The construction was handled by two companies of infantry under the command of Lieutenant R. C. DuBois. The project moved rapidly along the flatlands above Fort McDowell, but slowed when it hit the mountains. The road headed east from Fort McDowell, along the west side of Sugarloaf Mountain and along Sycamore Creek to where Arizona 87 crosses today. Camp Carroll was established on the flat ground east of the highway and just north of the bridge. From Sycamore Creek the road climbed up the ridge to the present site of Sunflower, then headed east through Reno Pass to the new military post.

In February 1868, Lieutenant George Chilson replaced DuBois on the project, and three months later the road was completed. After the adobe buildings at Camp Reno were completed, about sixty soldiers remained to garrison the post, the rest of the two-hundred-man work force returning to Fort McDowell.

Sunflower

Sunflower was located on the old military road from Fort McDowell to Camp Reno at the foot of Mt. Ord. During construction, a temporary post, named Camp O'Connell, was established on the east side of Sycamore Creek. Later, Sunflower served as a water station for the camp.

The lofty Mazatzal (pronounced by natives as "Matazals") Mountains present a formidable barrier to the Tonto Basin on the east. Mazatzal in Apache means "bleak or barren." The old military road went by the south side of Mt. Ord, named for General E. O. C. Ord, department commander for this area in the 1860s, when Camp Reno was established. Ord is best remembered for his hardbitten attitude toward the Indians he was supposed to control. At one point he ordered a subordinate to withhold water and food from Indian prisoners. Camp Reno, located in an exposed area at the east entrance to Reno Pass was an easy target for Apache sharpshooters and raiding parties, especially during the late 1860s, when the post was too ill-equipped and undermanned to retaliate.

Rye

Rye took its name from the wild rye growing along Rye Creek. Ranching in this area goes back to the 1870s. A post office was established in 1884 at the Rye Creek Crossing, but was discontinued in 1907.

Tonto Basin

In the old days, the Tonto Basin ran south from the Mogollon Rim to the Salt River and was bordered on the east and west by the Sierra Anchas and Mazatzal ranges. It was rough country, and it bred a tough, formidable people. They used to say that if you could hold a job cowboying in the Tonto Basin, you could work anywhere. The families who ranched this rugged land were a close-knit community, and their life centered on the old Packard Store on Tonto Creek, now known as Punkin Center. Here, ranch families picked up their mail, held dance socials, and bought supplies. Time has brought little change as descendants of pioneer families with names like Haught, Conway, Armer, and Cline still congregate at the store to catch up on the latest happenings in the basin.

The area takes its name from the ferocious bands of Tonto Apaches who used to live there. *Tonto*, a Spanish word that means "fool," is said to have been bestowed on those Indians by their relatives, the White Mountain Apaches, for refusing to renounce the warpath for reservation life. The war with the United States Army reached its inevitable conclusion in the 1870s, after General Crook's spectacular winter campaign of 1872-73.

Tonto Creek was named in 1864 by pioneer rancher and Indian fighter King Woolsey, during a punitive expedition against the Apaches. A few years later, Captain William Hancock, the man who would survey the original townsite for Phoenix, was leading a campaign against the Tontos in the eastern part of the basin when he found a hundred dollar bill. Apparently Apaches had taken it during a raid, but since they had no use for paper money, had tossed it into the brush. Hancock named the place Greenback Valley, and that's what it's still called.

In 1867 Camp Reno was established in the basin a mile west of Tonto Creek. Until it was abandoned in 1870, Reno, located at the entrance to strategic Reno Pass, would play a major role in subduing the Apache bands that roamed the region. Reno was named for General Jesse Reno, a Union hero who died during the Civil War at Turners Gap.

Gold prospectors tried their luck in the basin during those years but didn't find enough to make wages. Soldiers from Camp Reno did some panning in their spare time and found a little gold in Reno Creek. The famous scout Al Sieber was one of many who filed claims. Tonto Basin was destined to make its name in the cattle business rather than by gold mining. The first cattle herds in the basin were driven in by the army to feed the soldiers at Camp Reno. It wasn't until about five years after the post had closed and the Apaches had been relocated that the ranchers arrived, the first being David Harer of California.

In 1872, following Captain Hancock's suggestion, Harer took a look at the Tonto Basin and decided to settle there. Three years later he moved in with his family, including son-in-law Florence Packard. They fattened their cattle and hogs on the nutritious range grasses, then drove them over to Globe to feed the hungry miners.

Tonto Basin has produced its share of champion rodeo performers. Two of the best were Joe Bassett and Asbury Schell. Both were descendants of pioneer families, and both won world championships. Bassett won the Team Roping title in 1942, and he and his partner and longtime friend, Schell, teamed up to win the title again a decade later.

The best-known name in the basin is Cline. Six generations of this family have ranched in the basin since Christian Cline arrived in 1876 and started a prolific ranching dynasty. He turned the outfit over to his son John in 1892. George Cline, John's oldest son, was the stuff of which legends are made. Stories about the exploits of this colorful cowboy are still told whenever cattlemen gather to reminisce. Standing tall with George was his wife Roxie. George and Roxie rode horseback into Payson in 1911 to tie the knot. After the wedding, they rode sixty miles back to the basin and started a ranch with $200 George had borrowed from a storekeeper at Roosevelt.

George Cline was one of several top hands who succeeded on the professional rodeo circuit. In 1923 he won top money in the calf roping contest at Yankee Stadium. Later, he competed in the then-new Madison Square Garden and was the first man to rope a steer in that arena. During those years he won events at Denver and at the "granddaddy of 'em all," Cheyenne.

George and Roxie ranched and bred fine horses when he wasn't rodeoing. She rode roundup, branded, and cooked for the cowboys. Old timers say she was one of the best cowboys and cooks in the whole

Tonto Basin. George Cline died in 1976 at the age of 90. He'd lived all but eleven years of the history of white settlement in the Tonto Basin area.

A post office was established at both Tonto Basin and Punkin Center, a small community, which has grown up around Florence Packard's store. Citizens used to have an annual pumpkin growing contest, and the Packard Store was the official weighing station. In 1929, the post office at Punkin Center was discontinued.

Payson

The storied Mogollon Rim serves as a panoramic backdrop for Payson. This huge escarpment, called the "backbone of Arizona," is most prominent above Payson. The rim, pronounced "muggy-own," is named for Juan Ignacio Flores Mogollon, governor of New Mexico from 1712 to 1715.

Payson was for years one of the most isolated and remote communities in Arizona. Prior to 1890 it was in Yavapai County, but when Payson later became part of Gila County, its isolation didn't change. Globe, the county seat, was about ninety miles in the opposite direction, and the two best roads, if they can be labeled in such dignified terms, were to Flagstaff and Globe. Both were five tough days of travel, by wagon.

Tuffy Peach, a Verde Valley cowboy, carried the mail on horseback from Camp Verde to Payson. Tuffy started delivering the mail when he was only fifteen and continued through every weather condition until the government discontinued the service in 1914. He was a cowboy all his life and made roundups until he was eighty. Tuffy Peach, the last of America's horseback mailcarriers, died in 1984.

Payson began its existence in 1876 when Bill Burch built a cabin on the site of what is today the fifth green of the local golf course. The community began in 1882, when John and Frank Hise (father and son) opened a store. Local people called the place Union Park, and

Payson in 1900
Courtesy Arizona
State Library

soon the population reached forty. Two years later, Senator Louis Payson, chairman of the committee on post offices, secured a post office for the town, and they named it Payson in his honor. Prior to this, Payson seems to have had several whimsical but descriptive names including Big Valley, Green Valley, and Long Valley. The Pioneer Saloon was the social gathering place at the time. Other amenities included another saloon, two stores, two cafes, and "one street." By 1975 Payson had a population of six thousand.

Payson was on the fringes of the notorious Pleasant Valley War (1887-1892) further east. The primary families involved in the feud were the Grahams and Tewksburys, but most of the other families in Pleasant Valley were compelled to take sides or get out.

Like most frontier towns, Payson had brief spells of "Western" trouble, usually on Saturday night, when the cowboys had too much to drink and one would mistake "shut up" for "stand up!" The town marshal usually chained the men to a tree until they sobered up enough to ride back to the ranch. Once in a while the situation was more serious, like the time when Jake Lane, a new arrival from Texas, tried to hurrah the town. The drunken cowboy rode up and down the main street firing his six-shooter. Then he broke up a ladies' croquet game by riding through the middle of the court. The final straw came when he pointed his pistol at Bill Colcord and Sam Stewart, two no-nonsense cattlemen. Colcord drew his gun and plugged the Texan. He was given a vote of thanks by the local citizens for preserving law and order.

In 1959, Arizona 87 was finally paved, and Payson was, at last, linked up with the "outside world." Phoenix is only two hours away on the Beeline Highway, and Payson has never been the same.

Following the completion of the Beeline Highway, tourism has become the number one income-producing industry. Payson's mild climate has made it a favorite home away from home for residents of the greater Phoenix area. It is also the gateway to the state's spectacular high country. Summer months are filled with activities designed to attract tourists. Each September the Old Time Fiddlers Contest draws entrants from all over the country. Since 1975, Payson has been officially recognized as the "Old Time Music Capital of the West." Each summer some five thousand country music fans gather to enjoy the show in the cool pines "under the Tonto Rim."

Few people in Arizona realize the importance of the logging industry in Arizona history. Fewer still realize that a few miles north of Payson is the world's largest stand of Ponderosa pine. During the late 1960s, a local businessman, J. W. Floyd, conceived the idea of a "Loggers Jamboree." The contest, now headed by public-spirited

Walt and Elaine Drorbaugh, has grown in size and stature down through the years. Today, lumberjacks compete in some twenty-six fun and competitive events that include a log toss, pulp throw, and ax throw. Following the contest a "Logger of the Year" and "Lady Logger of the Year" are chosen, who are then eligible to attend a national "Tournament of the Kings" in North Carolina.

Back in 1884, when Payson was still called Union Park, citizens began celebrating "August Doin's." After a huge town picnic, local cowboys would compete in a contest of skills that included riding and roping in the town's main street. Today, the Payson rodeo confines its ropers and bronc peelers to an arena and bills itself as the "World's Longest Continuous Rodeo."

Some of the interesting place names around Payson include the following: Ox-Bow Hill, four miles south of town, and named for an ox yoke left behind by an Apache war party after they had slaughtered the team for meat; Hardscramble Mesa (between Fossil Creek and Strawberry), a rocky flat that was so "pore yuh couldn't even raise hell on it," and Lousy Gulch, located a mile and a half southeast of town—during the 1880s, Ben Cole and his sons, Elmer and Pink, were working some claims in the area and all they got for their trouble were lice.

Tonto Natural Bridge

Located on Pine Creek, a few miles south of the community of Pine, is Tonto Natural Bridge. The first white men to see this great natural arch were army troops from General Crook's command. They were watering their horses in the creek when one noticed the huge natural bridge a hundred yards away.

In 1882, Davy Gowan filed a claim, built a cabin, and planted corn and fruit trees on the flats near the bridge. Gowan later turned the place over to a Scotsman, David Goodfellow, who built a house and six tourist cabins. The buildings were at the bottom of a precipitous three-mile grade. The road took six years to complete, aweing the tourists as much as the natural bridge did. A lodge was completed in 1927, and as many as sixty tourists at a time visited the site. Fruit trees planted by Davy Gowan in the 1880s still thrive on the property.

Pine

In July 1876 a few weeks after Mormon colonists settled along the Little Colorado River at St. Joseph (Joseph City), William Allen, John Bushman, Pleasant Bradford, and Peter Hansen made the first Mormon exploration of the Tonto Basin. They found it unsuitable for colonization, but a year later another party that included Rial Allen and Price Nelson settled near the east fork of the Verde River. The following year Allen established the settlement of Pine. By the late 1880s the population reached nearly two hundred. Allen turned his home into a small fort for protection against Apaches, but there was no serious trouble with Indians.

Strawberry

When the first white settlers arrived here in 1886, they called the site Strawberry because they found wild strawberries growing in profusion. During King Woolsey's historic Apache campaign of 1864, Henry Clifton called the place Wah-Poo-eta for a notorious Tonto Apache war chief, better known to settlers as Big Rump.

A school made from hand hewn logs was established in Strawberry in 1887. The arrival of the Peach family (eleven children) increased the size of the school dramatically. Alfred and Frances Peach named their offspring in rhymes to keep them straight: "Kate, Ede, Ide and Ell—Mick, Hank, Gus, Bob, and Bill—Tuff and Tom, the baby—he's the last—well maybe." The school building still stands, and the school is considered the oldest in Arizona.

The old Strawberry School House. Built in 1895, it is the oldest school building in Arizona. Pencil drawing by Bill Ahrendt

Arizona 87

Plans were made in the late 1930s for a north-south highway that would run parallel to the Verde River. Prior to 1940, all paved roads in Arizona except one went east and west, the exception being Arizona 89 through Wickenburg to Prescott, then north to Route 66.

Efforts began in 1938 to build the new north-south highway. That same year the Northern Gila County Chamber of Commerce was created. Some residents felt the proposed road was too close to the Black Canyon Highway (Interstate 17), so a movement was begun to promote a highway from Mesa to Payson and eventually up over the Mogollon Rim to Winslow.

In the early 1940s the State Highway Commission agreed to take the kinks out of the Bush Highway (for road promotor Harvey G. Bush) and build a direct road to northern Arizona.

Arizona 87 follows an 1880s wagon road that crosses the old Crook Military Trail above the rim. A few miles further north, the road joins part of the Chavaz Trail and Sunset Pass, continuing into Winslow. This is also the ancient Palatkwapi Trail, recently rediscovered by Northern Arizona geographer Jim Byrkit.

Jack's Canyon, just west of the highway, was named for a settler in the area named Jack DeSchradt—settlers felt compelled to anglicize Jack's name to "Jack Dishrag."

Early Roosevelt
Courtesy
Southwest Studies

*Road construction
on the Apache Trail*
Courtesy Salt
River Project

Arizona 88
The Apache Trail

Since 1906 tourists have wound along the Apache Trail. This stretch of country is blessed with some of the most spectacular desert scenery in Arizona. The Apache Trail begins at Apache Junction and travels some forty-five miles to Roosevelt Dam.

Long before the white man came, the prehistoric Salado Indians inhabited this area. Later, nomadic Tonto Apaches and Yavapai bands used these twisting canyons as sanctuaries from punitive expeditions by Pima Indians living along the Gila River. During the Apache wars United States troops, led by Apache and Yavapai scouts, scoured these uncharted regions in search of their cunning and illusive adversaries.

Perhaps the most notorious character to inhabit these parts was a reprobate known only as Hacksaw Tom. According to local legend, he used to rob stages and wagons in the vicinity of Fish Creek Hill, then hightail it into the rugged mountains. Hacksaw Tom knew his way around this area so well, and was so mean, that none of his victims dared organize a pursuit.

According to legend the noted Lost Dutchman, Jacob Waltz, found riches in the fabled Superstition Mountains just east of Apache Junction. Whether or not one chooses to believe in the Lost Dutchman Mine—and most historians are skeptical of its existence, a vast amount of gold was found just west of Superstition Mountains, and the fabulously rich Silver King Mine was located a few miles east.

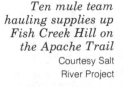

*Ten mule team
hauling supplies up
Fish Creek Hill on
the Apache Trail*
Courtesy Salt
River Project

Gold mine or not, this marvelous piece of real estate is a treasure in itself. All one has to do is climb on a horse or don a pair of hiking shoes and go out and experience it.

During the 1890s residents of the Salt River Valley, led by far-sighted individuals like Ben Fowler, Dwight Heard, John Orme and Joe Kibbey, became the driving force in what was later to become the Salt River Project. The central mountain range was a vast watershed containing about 13,000 square miles. These men realized that if the capricious river could be harnessed, the Salt River Valley would become one of the nation's richest agricultural regions.

The Arizona Canal began carrying water to the thirsty desert in 1887, yet the citizens were at the mercy of the fickle Salt River. Some years the river went on a flooding rampage; other times she ran dry, turning productive farms into dust bowls. Since the valley already had farms, canals and ditches, the federal government was seriously considering the area as a site for the first major reclamation project in the West. Billy Breakenridge, an ex-Cochise county deputy sheriff, Jim McClintock, future Rough Rider, and John Norton were commissioned to find a site for a future dam. The place they chose, at the confluence of Tonto Creek and the Salt, eventually became Tonto Dam, later changed to Theodore Roosevelt Dam, named for the hard-charging, ex-Rough Rider who had promoted establishment of the Bureau of Reclamation. Funds for the dam were approved in 1903 and road construction on the old path known as the Tonto or Yavapai Trail began. By the following year over 400 roadbuilders were on the job. Early in 1905 the Apache Trail was completed. And before the year was out more than a million and a half pounds of freight had been hauled up the trail to the dam site. The sixty-two miles of road through rough terrain was completed at a cost of just over a half million dollars. In 1986 plans were being made to make the Apache Trail an Arizona Historic Highway.

Goldfield

Perhaps no one will ever find the fabled Lost Dutchman's gold in the Superstitions, but nobody can deny there was gold in "them thar hills nearby." A few miles east of the Superstition Mountains was the legendary Silver King Mine, and the boom town of Goldfield was located just west of the mountains. Some sources claim gold mines around Goldfield produced at least three million dollars worth of the yellow metal. The first claim filed in the area was in 1886. In 1918, one mine, the Buckhorn-Boulder, a rich pocket of high grade ore, assayed out at nearly nine hundred ounces to the ton.

Goldfield, nestled between the Goldfield Mountains and the Superstitions, became a busy place, crowded with would-be millionaires in the 1890s. It was founded by George U. Young in 1893 and was, for a time, called Youngsberg.

Several months earlier, a claim was filed on a rich outcropping of gold that became the Black Queen Mine. The Mammoth and Mormon Stope were located not far from the Black Queen. The Mormon Stope alone produced a million dollars in gold. These mines were discovered within a year or two of the Dutchman's death, and one of them might have been the legendary Lost Dutchman lode.

Tortilla Flat

The flat-top mountains of this area were appropriately named the Tortillas, or pancakes, by boundary commissioner Major William Emory in 1853. While surveying the new territory acquired in the war with Mexico, Emory applied the name. A member of the Wheeler Survey in 1873, Arch Mavine, called the most prominent tortilla Tortilla Butte. The small community that takes its name from these "flat tortllas that resemble mountains" established a post office in 1927.

*Fish Creek Hill on
the Apache Trail*
Courtesy Salt
River Project

Fish Creek

Some historians believe the 1864 battle between King Woolsey's punitive expedition and a band of Apaches occurred in Fish Creek Canyon rather than at Bloody Tanks (see US 60—Miami). The battle took place on January 24, 1864, when Woolsey's party of forty met an Apache war party numbering about 250 warriors "painted and feathered up" for battle. The two sides agreed to hold a parley, but during the conference, Woolsey touched his hat, a pre-arranged signal. Woolsey's men jerked out their weapons, getting the drop on the Indians. When the smoke cleared, at least nineteen Apaches were dead. Woolsey's casualties were understandably light—one killed and another, a man named Tonto Jack, receiving an arrow wound in the neck.

The Bloody Tanks fight might have been between Lieutenant Howard B. Cushing's troops and Apaches several years later. Cushing, a dashing hero of the Apache wars, was killed in 1870 near Babocomari Creek, along the Cochise-Santa Cruz county line.

Roosevelt Dam

The dedication of Roosevelt Dam in 1911 is still, without a doubt, the most significant historical event in the history of central Arizona. Without this dam and other dams to follow, Phoenix would still be a small desert community relying on the fickle waters of the Salt River to supply its needs.

The dam was the first major project of the Reclamation Act of 1902. Construction began in 1905 at the site selected and surveyed by former Tombstone deputy Billy Breakenridge. A road was constructed from Mesa, as each piece of machinery and all supplies had to

*President Theodore
Roosevelt on Apache
Trail to dedicate
Roosevelt Dam in
1911*
Courtesy
Southwest Studies

be hauled in from the nearest railroad, sixty miles away.

Italian stonemasons were imported to quarry huge granite blocks that eventually ridged a canyon 680 feet wide at the top. The dam, rising 284 feet from bedrock, formed a reservoir with a capacity of 1.3 million acre feet of water.

On March 18, 1911, former President Theodore Roosevelt, led an automobile entourage up the Apache Trail for the dedication ceremony. Up to this time, the site had been called Tonto Dam, but henceforth it would carry the name of the old "Roughrider."

The full cost of the project, about eleven million dollars, was repaid in full in 1955. It was the first major irrigation project funded by the federal government and most certainly one of the best investments Washington ever made.

During the 1920s Horse Mesa, Mormon Flat, and Stewart Mountain dams would finally tame (most of the time) the mighty Salt.

Arizona 288
Young and Pleasant Valley

Among the earliest settlers in Pleasant Valley were John Tewksbury, Sr., and his sons, Ed, John, Jr., Jim, and Frank. They arrived about 1880. Two years later, the Graham brothers, Tom and John, moved into the valley and it wasn't long before there was bad blood between the two families. Nobody knows for certain what started the feud. The nearest law in those days was at Prescott, 150 miles away over rough mountain trails. Whenever the situation got out of hand, "Winchester litigation" took over. Over the next several years close to thirty men would die with their boots on, ironically in Pleasant Valley.

According to reliable sources, the Grahams had been increasing their herds by a process that defied the natural laws of biology. It was called running a "maverick factory," or more commonly, rustling cows. Soon the Grahams and Tewksburys were accusing each other of rustling cattle, and the residents of Pleasant Valley started taking sides. In 1884 Mart "Old Man" Blevins and his sons, one of whom was the notorious Andy "Cooper" Blevins, turned up in Pleasant Valley. Soon they were riding with the Grahams. Jim Roberts, who later became a noted peace officer, moved into the valley and took sides with the Tewksburys.

Tom Graham, leader of the Graham faction in the Pleasant Valley War. He was shot and killed in Tempe in 1892.*
Courtesy
Southwest Studies

In February 1887 the Daggs brothers, a sheep outfit from Flagstaff, hired Bill Jacobs, a Tewksbury partisan, to drive a herd of sheep into Pleasant Valley. Hollywood and the pulp writers tried for years to create a sheepmen-cattlemen war out of this feud, but in reality sheep played a minor role in the drama. The sheep were quickly removed after a sheepherder was killed and beheaded.

The following July "Old Man" Blevins rode off into the hills and was never seen again. It was presumed someone from the Tewksbury clan had plugged him. Two weeks later a group of Graham supporters, including Hamp Blevins, picked a fight with the Tewksbury brothers and Jim Roberts. When the smoke cleared, Blevins and one of his pals lay dead. A few days later Jim Houck (see Houck Interstate 40) shot and killed eighteen-year-old Billy Graham. Clearly, up to this point the Grahams were getting the worst of it.

On September 2, 1887 the Grahams and Andy "Cooper" Blevins got revenge. The gang surrounded Tewksbury's ranch house before sunrise and waited. Bill Jacobs and John Tewksbury stepped outside and walked some distance from the house, unaware that several rifles were trained on them. The sound of gunfire broke the stillness of the morning, and both men fell, their bodies riddled with bullets. During the ensuing gunfight, a herd of hogs began devouring the bodies of the slain men. One version of the story has it that John Tewksbury's wife, Eva, was inside the cabin with her infant. When she saw the grisly act taking place, she braved the gunfire to drive off the hogs and dig shallow graves for her husband and Jacobs. Further bloodshed was averted when a posse from Prescott arrived and drove off the Graham-Blevins clan.

Two weeks later the Grahams tried another early morning attack. This time Jim Roberts arose early and saw the men setting up the ambush. Roberts and the Tewksburys, all expert marksmen, opened fire, killing one and wounding several others.

Meanwhile, John Graham and Charlie Blevins were killed when they tried to outrun a posse that was sent out to arrest and bring them in.

Later, prominent members of both groups were arrested and charged in Prescott. Charges were dropped when witnesses failed to appear. For all practical purposes, the Graham-Tewksbury war was over. However, the killing didn't stop. With many of the notorious gunslingers out of the fight, brazen vigilantes, determined to rid the area of rustlers, went on a campaign of terror. Any outsider was suspect, and the exact number of men given "suspended sentences," or simply gunned down, will never be known.

Tom Graham, the "last man" on his side, moved to Tempe, got married, and settled down, but feuds die hard—in 1892 Ed Tewksbury shot and killed Graham near Double Buttes, a short distance east of today's Interstate 10 and Broadway. Ed Tewksbury, with the help of some clever attorneys, was released on a legal technicality. He then moved to Globe, where he spent his last days as a peace officer.

Jim Roberts, one of Arizona's premier lawmen. Earlier, he was a participant in the Pleasant Valley War.
Photo Bill Roberts

III Colorado Plateau

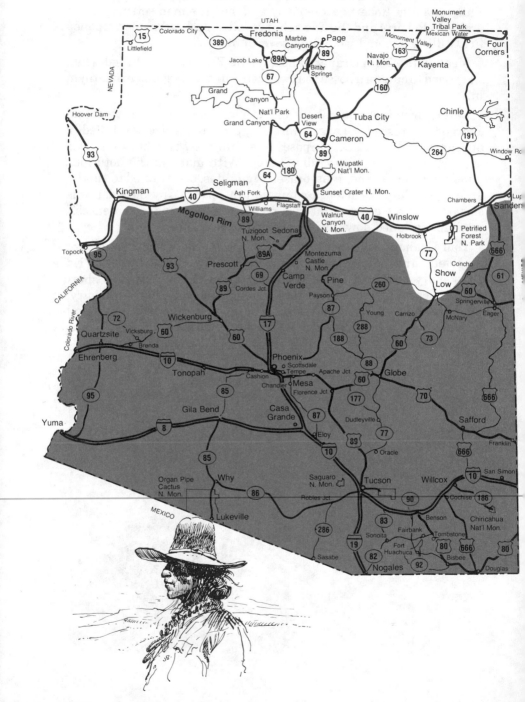

General Amiel W. Whipple during Civil War; he was killed at Chancellorsville in 1863.
Courtesy
Southwest Studies

Route 66 and Interstate 40

The National Old Trail Highway

In 1853 Secretary of War Jefferson Davis was authorized to make four railroad surveys from the Mississippi River to the Pacific coast. A fifth route, the Oregon Trail, wasn't included since it was already well known as a possible railroad route. The task was assigned to the Army Corps of Topographical Engineers, and testimony to a job well done is the fact that all four routes eventually became transcontinental railroads. Two of these routes were to cross Arizona: one along the thirty-second parallel near the Gila Trail, and the other along the thirty-fifth parallel. Lieutenant Amiel W. Whipple, a reliable and experienced veteran of earlier boundary surveys, was chosen to survey the thirty-fifth parallel route, running from Fort Smith, Arkansas, across the plains to Albuquerque, then west through *terra incognita* to Los Angeles. Accompanying Whipple were Lieutenant Joseph C. Ives, who would later survey the Colorado River and be the first white man to set foot in the Grand Canyon; and artist Heinrich Baldwin Möllhausen. The latter's writings about his experiences in the American West would earn him the title of the "German Fenimore Cooper." Möllhausen's portfolio included about one hundred thirty watercolor sketches made on the Whipple expedition plus one made on the trip with Ives in 1857-58 along the Colorado River. Unfortunately, all but six sketches were destroyed by fire in Berlin during the last days of World War II.

Northern Arizona was not unknown to the topographical engineers. Two years before Whipple's expedition, Captain Lorenzo Sitgreaves made a reconnaissance of the thirty-fifth parallel. Sitgreaves had been provided with information by Francois X. Aubry, a trader who had made the crossing between Alburquerque and Los Angeles many times. Sitgreaves and his men, guided by Antoine Leroux, completed their work in November 1851 but not before undergoing severe hardships and near annihilation at the hands of Yuma Indians.

On November 29, 1853 with the ubiquitous Antoine Leroux leading the way, Whipple left Zuni, New Mexico, and headed west to the Rio Puerco, following that stream to where it joins the Little Colorado River, just east of today's Holbrook. The expedition followed that river to Sunset Crossing, near today's Winslow, and headed west to the San Francisco Mountains, where they spent a chilly Christmas camped at the foot of those majestic peaks. The "German Fenimore Cooper," Baldwin Möllhausen, was also a member of the expedition. In 1858 he published an outstanding two-volume work based on his experiences, *Journey to the Pacific*.

By the time the party reached the San Francisco peaks, slogging through heavy snows had left the pack animals exhausted. Whipple decided to call a halt to allow the stock to recoup and to give the men a chance to celebrate Christmas. While opening up the packs, the men uncovered "some well preserved bottles of what makes glad the heart of the traveling man." The wine and food were turned over to the cooks "for the glorification of our Christmas dinner in the Wilderness."

One pack included eggs that by some miracle had survived the journey. While the cooks were preparing venison, wild turkey, and other tasty delights, Lieutenant John, a resourceful young officer in the party, took the eggs and liquor and conjured up a punch that would grow hair on a gila monster. Möllhausen describes the celebration:

"All gentlemen are requested to assemble after supper before Lieutenant John's tent, and to bring with them their tin drinking mugs."

No one had a previous engagement, nor was it at all tempting to decline, and as soon as the night set in and the stars began to flitter in the deep blue firmament, and to look down upon us between the snowy branches, the company began to assemble at the appointed spot. . . .

Lieutenant John was busy with his brewage and that fragrant steaming pail, with the inviting froth at the top, was a most agreeable sight to men who had been so long limited to water. Lieutenant John made a speech, as nearly as I can remember to this effect:

"Let us now forget for a few hours our hardships and privations, the object of our journey, and the labours still before us; and here, under a roof of boughs, and on the spotless white carpet that God Almighty has spread for us, for as we are far from our homes, let us think of our friends, who, very likely, are thinking of us as they sit around their firesides; and drowning our cares in a social glass of toddy, drink to their health, and to our own happy return."

We sat in a circle, smoked, drank, toasted and told jokes—hearts became lighter, blood ran more swiftly in veins, and all joined in a hearty songfest that echoed through ravines and mountains and must have sadly interfered with the night's rest of the sleeping turkeys.

The Mexicans made their contribution to the festival by throwing firebrands into the cedar thickets: "The pointed leaves, or needles, rich in resin, caught fire immediately; the flames blazed over the tops of the trees and sent millions of sparks up to the sky. It was a most beautiful spectacle!

"Snow glittered with magic splendor. All objects were suffused in a red glow. Most exquisite effects of light and shade were produced among the neighboring rocks and mountains. The splendour of the sight served to enhance the gaiety of the company till it reached an almost perilous pitch."

The evening festivities were climaxed by joyous singing. The Americans sang Negro spirituals, and the Mexicans shared their traditional Christmas songs. This multi-cultural event, certainly symbolic of Christmas in Arizona a century later, was given an added dimension when two men, former prisoners of the Navajo, performed native dances.

Antoine Leroux was the only one who remained vigilant during the festivities. The old scout had lived in the mountains by his wits too long to let his guard down for a Christmas party. He was heard to mutter between sips, "What a splendid opportunity it would be for the Indians to surprise us tonight."

To old Antoine's relief, no attacks came that night. Möllhausen mentions that December 25 was spent in quiet observance and with a sense of nostalgia: "We looked up at the sublime summits of the San Francisco Mountains and needed no temple made with hands within to worship our Creator." This occasion marked the first recorded Christmas in Arizona north of the Gila River.

Traveling west from the base of the San Francisco peaks, an elevation of seven thousand feet, Whipple sought a gradual downward grade to the Colorado River, less than two hundred miles to the west. He took a route south of Sitgreaves's route, following the stream he named the Bill Williams Fork (part of which today is called the Big

Sandy) to the Colorado. (Later, the railroad ignored this part of Whipple's survey and steered on a more westerly course, crossing the river at Needles, California.)

In the vicinity of Big Sandy River, Whipple's party met a group of Yampai Indians, the same tribe that had ambushed Sitgreaves's party three years earlier and inflicted three arrow wounds in Leroux. Möllhausen described the scruffy-looking Yampais: "More repulsive-looking physiognomies and figures than those ... could hardly be imagined." Whipple's words were underlined when one surly warrior grabbed a white towel used as a flag of truce and unceremoniously converted it into a breechclout, while another grabbed a hat belonging to a Mexican muleteer and put it on his own head. After some discussion, Whipple presented the Yampais with an assortment of gifts, and the natives in turn pointed the way to the nearest water hole.

The expedition eventually reached the Mojave villages near the mouth of the Bill Williams Fork. A meeting with the villagers was cordial, although the six-months' growth of whiskers of the explorers provided laughter among the Mojave women. After this pleasant interlude, Whipple's party continued on to California and the completion of their historic survey.

The next major survey of the thirty-fifth parallel was the famous Beale Camel Experiment in 1857. Jefferson Davis, an ex-cavalry officer, was Secretary of War from 1853 to 1857 and was the Washington official primarily responsible for the camel project. The use of camels in America was not a new idea; someone had suggested the idea as early as 1701, but it wasn't until the opening of the arid lands west of the ninety-eighth meridian in the 1840s that the idea of using camels as pack animals was taken seriously. In 1855 Congress appropriated $30,000 for "the purchase and importation of camels and dromedaries to be used for military purposes."

The U.S. Camel Corps on the march Courtesy Southwest Studies

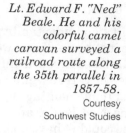

Lt. Edward F. "Ned" Beale. He and his colorful camel caravan surveyed a railroad route along the 35th parallel in 1857-58.
Courtesy
Southwest Studies

Davis placed Major Henry Wayne in charge of the experiment, to be assisted by navy officer David Porter and ex-navy officer Edward F. "Ned" Beale. Porter later rose to be ranking admiral in the Union navy during the Civil War. Beale's life story reads more like an adventure novel. He was with General Stephen Watts Kearny at the siege of San Pasqual. During the seige, he, Kit Carson, and a Delaware Indian sneaked through the Mexican lines, reaching San Diego in time to bring back a rescue party. When gold was discovered in California, Beale was chosen to carry the news to President Millard Fillmore. Dressed in miner's clothes and wearing a Mexican sombrero, Beale filled a poke sack with nuggets and made an epic dash across the continent. He went by ship to San Blas, on the west coast of Mexico then overland to the Atlantic coast. During the trip, Beale shot his way out of several attempted holdups, outriding his pursuers. Once he rode down a steep mountainside with such reckless abandon that none of the *banditos* dared follow.

Upon reaching the nation's capital, he spilled his nuggets on the President's desk, dispelling the stories going around that the discovery of gold in California was a hoax and triggering what became known as the California Gold Rush.

Porter and Wayne traveled extensively in the Middle East during the next few months on the ship *Supply* to make their selection of animals. Wayne turned the ship into a camel stud farm, certainly a first for the United States Navy, and although several of the beasts died on the rough ocean voyage, the navy made a net gain of one.

231

Stalls were located below deck, but one camel was so large Wayne had to cut a hole in the deck to make room for its hump. Realizing correctly that a personality clash between American muleskinners and camels was inevitable, Major Wayne hired several Arabs, Greeks, and Turks to tend the animals. The ship, carrying thirty-four camels, arrived on the Texas coast in May 1856. Less than a year later another shipload increased the herd size by forty-one.

The camels passed all tests for durability and adaptability with flying colors, including winning a race against horse-drawn wagons. The camels carried a heavier load yet still finished first. During rainy weather they plodded right through the slick Texas gumbo that mules couldn't manage. In 1857 the task of implementing the camel experiment fell on the shoulders of young Ned Beale, after Major Wayne was recalled to Washington. Wayne couldn't have had a more worthy or enthusiastic successor. Beale was ordered to survey a wagon road from Fort Defiance (near today's Window Rock) to the Colorado River along the thirty-fifth parallel.

Beale's camel caravan, accompanied by Arab, Greek, and Turk "camel conductors" in their traditional garb, presented a colorful spectacle as it passed through the villages of New Mexico.

Beale looked and played the part of circus ringmaster, riding on a wagon painted bright red. One curious New Mexican asked:

"Dis show wagon, no?"

Beale replied, "Yes."

"Ah,ha! You be dee showmans, no?"

"Yes, sir."

"What you gottee more on camelos? Gottee any dogs?"

"Yes, monkeys too, and more."

"Whatee more?"

"Horse more."

"Whatee can do horse?"

"Stand on his head, and drink a glass of wine."

"Valgarne Dios! What a people these are to have a horse stand on his head, and drink a glass of wine."

By the middle of August, they were following Lieutenant Amiel Whipple's railroad survey along the thirty-fifth parallel. The camels were hauling even hundred pounds each, or about twice what a mule could carry. Beale generally rode a mule, but once when he needed to pay a social call to a military outpost, he climbed on top of a white dromedary named "Seid." No doubt the appearance of this dashing young officer sitting high on a white camel had the desired effect.

Beale couldn't have been more pleased with his camels. While camped at the foot of the San Francisco peaks in mid-September, he wrote:

> The camels are so quiet and give so little trouble that sometimes we forget they are with us. Certainly there never was anything so patient and enduring and so little troublesome as this noble animal. They pack their heavy load of corn, of which they never taste a grain; put up with any good food offered them without complaint, and are always up with the wagons, and, withal, so perfectly docile and quiet that they are the admiration of the whole camp. . . . They are better today than they were when we left Camp Verde (Texas) with them; especially since our men have learned, by experience, the best mode of packing them.

The camels endured the arid lands between Flagstaff and the Colorado River unusually well. During a stretch of thirty-six hours without water, the horses and mules suffered, but the camels took all the hardships stoically. ". . . one of the most painful sights I ever witnessed," Beale wrote, "was a group of them (horses and mules) standing over a small barrel of water and trying to drink from the bung hole, and seemingly frantic with distress and eagerness to get at it. The camels appeared to view this proceeding with great contempt, and kept quietly browsing on the grass and bushes."

Not only were the camels durable, they could subsist on the natural desert flora. In fact, according to Beale, they seemed to thrive on it. "With all this work they are perfectly content to eat anything, from the driest greasewood bush to a thorny prickly pear, and, what is better, keep fat on it."

After the expedition, Beale took his camels to his ranch at Fort Tejon, California. He made another trip along the thirty-fifth parallel the following year, but the experiment, although highly successful, was doomed. The outbreak of the Civil War ended all plans for a southern railroad to the Pacific in the near future. When the railroad did come across northern Arizona in the 1880s, it closely followed the trail blazed by Ned Beale and his camels nearly a quarter of a century earlier. (For more on the camels and their famous driver see Interstate 10, Quartzsite.)

Most of the towns and cities along Interstate 40 trace their ancestry to the Santa Fe Railroad or its forerunner, the Atlantic and Pacific. Many of these settlements were named for railroad officials or those closely associated with the company. Much has been written of this era, which marked the closing of the American frontier—the "great and glowing West." About the time the history of the West was fading into the realm of romantic nostalgia and false-front saloons were disappearing and trail dust had settled for good, Americans had begun an enduring love affair with the horseless carriage. Henry

Ford had figured out a way to mass-produce his product and soon nearly everybody could afford a car. America had become, in one generation, a mobile society. A national clamor arose for decent highways, and by the 1920s the nation was embarked on an unparalleled roadbuilding program. And of all America's great highways, none possessed a greater piece of Americana than The National Old Trail Highway, commonly known as Route 66. Stretching from Chicago, it rambled hundreds of miles through the Midwest, across Oklahoma and out to California. It was the twentieth century's rendition of the golden road to the promised land—the Gila, Beale's Camel Road, and the Oregon Trail all rolled into one.

In Arizona, old Route 66 began its 376-mile journey across Arizona at Lupton on the New Mexico line, then angled southwest to the former frontier town of Holbrook. The narrow, two-lane dirt road then headed west across the windswept high desert, past Winslow and on to Flagstaff, snaking its way through tall pine forests and grassy meadows to Williams before beginning its long descent down treacherous Ash Fork Hill. Beyond Ash Fork, a high windswept plateau with countless islands of cedar-studded mesas and rolling hills and mountains spread for miles in all directions. At five thousand feet the plateau was carpeted with native grasses and spotted with piñon and juniper. Herds of antelope broke the monotony of the journey, racing across the plain at the speed of an automobile. A few miles past Kingman, the highway approached Oatman Hill, the last great obstacle before Route 66 ended its Arizona odyssey. Twisting and winding its way through the rugged Black Mountains, the Oatman Hill section of the highway was the standard by which drivers measured other treacherous hills. When a driver entered California, Oatman Hill offered an ominous greeting for the westbound traveler, providing enough anxious moments to make the experience unforgettable.

Route 66 was many things to many people. To refugees of the Oklahoma dust bowl, it was the yellow brick road to the promised land of California. The trials and tribulations of the Joad family in John Steinbeck's *The Grapes of Wrath* paint a vivid picture of hard times during the Great Depression. During the post-World War II years, others came "to get something or someplace or to get away from something or someplace" or, as Bret Harte said a century earlier, they were "looking for a fresh deal all around." They too found their champion in the lyrics of Bobby Troup's "Git Your Kicks on Route 66." The television generation learned all about Route 66 from behind the wheel of a shiny Corvette following the weekly adventures of two idealistic young men who were traveling from Chicago to Los Angeles each week, saving that part of the world just off Route 66.

Entire town of Flagstaff; 1882 along Santa Fe Avenue
Courtesy
Southwest Studies

Interstate 40/Interstate 17
Flagstaff

Flagstaff
"The Clearest Air in North America"

In 1911 Jesse Laskey and Cecil B. DeMille decided to pack up their New York motion picture company and head west. They kept traveling on the Santa Fe Railroad until the train halted at Flagstaff, a small community nestled at the foot of the spectacular San Francisco Mountains. It looked like an ideal place to shoot outdoor movies, so they unloaded the equipment and prepared to make Flagstaff the movie capital of the world. Then suddenly a bone-chilling wind swept scythe-like down off the towering peaks followed by icy drizzle; and a heavy snowfall blanketed the ground. Laskey and DeMille quietly packed their gear and boarded the next westbound train, not stopping until they reached sunny southern California.

Flagstaff, located in one of the most picturesque settings in America, seemed marked by destiny to be an important city. The location of two springs, Leroux and San Francisco, at the foot of the loftiest mountains in Arizona, along with being near the thirty-fifth parallel made it a natural campsite. During the 1850s Secretary of War Jefferson Davis had commissioned the Army Corps of Topographical Engineers to survey a possible transcontinental railroad route along the thirty-fifth parallel. During a campaign against the Navajo Indians in 1849, Lieutenant James Simpson and Francois X. Aubry, a reknowned trailblazer, discussed a possible wagon road across northern Arizona. Aubry had made the trek many times and knew the country like the back of his hand. Simpson relayed the information to Washington, and in 1851 Captain Lorenzo Sitgreaves made the first reconnaissance expedition along the thirty-fifth parallel. During their harrowing journey, Sitgreaves and Simpson traveled over 650 miles of some of the West's most forbidding land. Along the way they battled a party of Yavapai warriors. Antoine Leroux, the legendary scout, was hit by three Indians arrows. The doctor on the expedition, Samuel W. Woodhouse, who had been bitten by a rattlesnake was forced to operate on Leroux with one hand. It was said Leroux suffered more from the humiliation of being shot than from the actual pain of the arrow wounds. After suffering many hardships, the expedition finally reached the Colorado River. Heading south, Sitgreaves hoped to reach Fort Yuma but first had to pass through the warrior tribes along the Colorado—the Mojave and Yuma. They passed through the Mojave territory unscathed but were attacked by a large band of Yumas. One soldier lagged behind and was caught and beaten to death. The warriors took his rifle but didn't know how to use it. In a running gunfight, four warriors were killed and the attacks ceased. The party was on the verge of starvation, reduced to eating their mules, by the time they straggled into Fort Yuma in November 1851.

The next group of engineers to survey the thirty-fifth parallel was led by Lieutenant Amiel W. Whipple in 1853. Whipple's party spent a snowy Christmas day camped where Flagstaff is now located. Whipple's survey turned south in the vicnity of the west fork of the Verde River, then went west to the headwaters of the Big Sandy River and followed it to the Bill Williams River and down that stream to the Colorado. He then continued on to the California coast along the thirty-fifth parallel.

Another expedition, this one eastbound and led by Lieutenant Joseph Christmas Ives in 1858, went up the Colorado by steamboat to study the navigability of that river. On the way downriver, Ives divided his group, sending one back to Fort Yuma, while he led another overland to Santa Fe. Along the way, he made several side trips to gaze in wonder at the Grand Canyon. With the help of some Indian guides, Ives snaked his way down, thus becoming the first white man to reach the bottom of the canyon.

During these same years Lieutenant Edward F. Beale made his legendary survey using camels as beasts of burden, part of the army's experiment to find an animal more naturally suited to cross the arid, waterless deserts prior to the building of the railroads. The experiment was beset with problems. Muleskinners, known for being able to swear in paragraphs, found their oaths falling on deaf ears. The independent camels simply refused to learn English and looked upon their American handlers with contempt. The Americans, for their part, couldn't speak Arabic. It was said the breath of a camel could wilt the Yellow Rose of Texas, but nobody bothered to ask the camels what they thought of a muleskinner's breath. Finally the stalemate was broken—camel drivers were imported from the Middle East, and the survey proceeded on schedule.

All these military surveys along the thirty-fifth parallel during the 1850s would prove invaluable later on when the Atlantic and Pacific Railroad, later the Santa Fe, would build a transcontinental line. The timetable was delayed, however, for several years by the outbreak of the Civil War. Since Arizona was too far south, it would not have a line along the thirty-fifth parallel until 1883.

Although the area was well traveled by adventurers, the next recorded activity of note near the future site of Flagstaff came in the spring of 1876 with the arrival of the first party of colonists from Boston. During the 1860s Samuel Cozzens came to southern Arizona and lived a brief, but adventuresome life, getting to meet the great Apache leaders Cochise and Mangas Coloradas. During his travels, he visited the Zuni pueblos and had the chance to view in the distance the vast, sprawling rangeland. "Somewhere out there" he visualized rich fertile farmland, cool mountain streams—in short, a land crying out for settlers. The well-meaning but uninformed Mr. Cozzens returned to New England and wrote an enthusiastic book about Arizona called *Marvellous Country*, going on the lecture circuit to promote colonization of this rich breadbasket. It mattered little that Cozzens had never set eyes on northern Arizona. A party of fifty colonists, all men, was quickly organized. Some were convinced the San Francisco Mountains were laced with veins of gold.

This first Boston group expected to settle along the Little Colorado, but a colony of Mormons from Utah arrived ahead of them, so they headed west to the San Francisco Mountains. A town was laid out near Leroux Springs, in Fort Valley (a few miles northwest of downtown Flagstaff). The Boston colonists quickly became discouraged. It wasn't the kind of farmland they'd envisioned from Cozzens's descriptions, and they found no gold. Within a short time, nearly all had left for other places or returned home to Boston.

Around July 4, 1876 a second party of Boston colonists arrived at the foot of the San Francisco Mountains. According to legend, they skinned the branches off a tall pine tree and raised the American flag. The second group of Boston colonists didn't stay any longer than the first. However, the old flag pole remained a landmark for many years afterward and inspired the name Flagstaff. One might say "Flagstaff had three flagstaffs" because three trimmed pine trees claim to have produced the name.

The first was erected by the second party of colonists from Boston in

1876 near today's Flagstaff Junior High School and China Canyon on what was known as the McMillan Ranch. The second was at Old Town, or Antelope Spring, and the third was located to the east, along the railroad tracks near Switzer Mesa. It is said that in 1888 some irreverent saloonkeeper chopped down "flagstaff number 3" and used it for firewood. Noted Flagstaff historian Platt Cline suggests in his definitive history of the town that the strongest evidence indicates that the Boston colonists deserve credit and most historians agree. On July 4, 1985 a ceremony was held at this site and a tall pine flagpole and monument was dedicated.

Flagstaff's first permanent settler was Thomas F. McMillan. In the spring of 1876 he built a cabin and corral at Antelope Spring, at the foot of Mars Hill. When the railroad arrived in 1881, a station was built further west of the spring. (The site of Old Town Spring is just west of today's Milton Road underpass.) The settlement grew up around the railroad depot, and the spring and McMillan's place became known as Old Town (Old Town Spring was sometimes called Flagpole Spring). McMillan, a native of Tennessee, had led a venturesome life prospecting for gold in California and Australia before settling at Flagstaff. In the mid-1880s he homesteaded on the land where the Museum of Northern Arizona is now located. His two-story log house stands on the property today and is still used by the museum staff. McMillan remained active in political and community affairs and was one of the town's leading citizens until his death in 1906.

Significantly, McMillan's homestead was referred to as Flagstaff Ranch on a survey taken in 1878. This seems to be the first official use of the name, and it is possible that Tom McMillan was responsible for naming the town.

By 1880 the ranges in northern Arizona lay virtually undiscovered. Most of the cattle were dairy cows brought in by Mormon colonists from Utah. Since the area south of Flagstaff boasted the largest stand of Ponderosa pine in the world, in a few years, cattle and timber became the stalwarts of northern Arizona's economy. What was needed was a railroad to transport cattle and timber to markets outside the territory.

Large land grants by the federal government were made to railroad companies in the 1860s to entice them into building railroad lines in western territories at almost no cost to taxpayers. In northern Arizona twenty-mile sections were awarded the Atlantic & Pacific (Santa Fe) line along each side of the track, giving deed to the odd-numbered sections in each township. At first without great value, land values soared for vast, isolated regions when the railroad

*Railroad
construction in
Northern Arizona in
the 1880s*
Courtesy
Southwest Studies

was actually built. Selling this land back to ranchers and settlers, the railroad earned back costs of building the line. The east and west coasts were now linked together.

The coming of the railroad in 1881 was the primary reason for the great change that was about to take place. That year John W. Young, a son of Brigham Young and a pioneer settler in the area, was contracted to deliver fifty thousand ties for the new line. He built a camp for his tie-cutters in what is today Fort Valley, nine miles north of Flagstaff. The threat of raids by bands of Apache and Navajo warriors caused Young to turn the camp into a fortress, which he called Moroni, after the Mormon angel. A log cabin about seventy-five feet long acted as one side of the bastion. The other three sides of the square consisted of railroad ties set in the ground on end. A tent city was established inside the stockade to shelter the tie-cutters. The Indian raids, however, never materialized, and the fortress walls were torn down and used for firewood. The arrival of iron-bellied locomotives the next year marked the real beginning of the cattle business in northern Arizona. Young and several companions organized the Mormon Cattle Company that same year, stocking the ranges around Flagstaff for the first time on a large scale. By 1883 the price of beef was $50 a head, up from $15 a head just two years earlier.

In Flagstaff, newspaper accounts of the time tell of citizens' outrage when cowboys periodically drove several hundred range cows down the town's main street or when law-abiding folks were sent scurrying for safety as drunken cowpunchers rode hell-for-leather through town, waving their revolvers in the air and "shootin' holes in the sky."

The local *Chronicle* expressed its displeasure at the behavior of Flagstaff-area cowboys in an article on September 20, 1883 which read:

They are bragging, whiskey-drinking bummers who delight in six-shooters, fine horses, saddles, and fast women. Their aim in life seems to be to have a good time. They delight in disconcerting the eastern tenderfoot. Nearly all die with their boots on and no one mourns their death.

For all its reputation as a frontier Sodom and Gomorrah, Flagstaff was no worse than most of the other western boom towns, and better than most. As in any developing community, the more numerous law-abiding citizens, merchants, churches, and schools soon prevailed. The town bragged about its healthful climate and opportunities for a "fresh deal," as Bret Harte said, for those who would give up Eastern security to settle in a new community nestled at the foot of the grandiose San Francisco Mountains.

In what could pass for a Department of Tourism commercial, newspaperman George Tinker wrote in 1887: "The climate of northern Arizona is moderately dry, the days warm and the nights cold . . . the air is dry, the soil porous, the water pure, scenery cheerful and sunlight brilliant . . . the value of the climate as a remedial agent is demonstrated daily . . . around Flagstaff the sun shines nearly every day, and but few are cloudy. Even during the rainy season which begins in July and lasts about six weeks, the daily showers are followed by the brightest sunshine."

The first permanent settlement at Flagstaff developed in 1880 when work crews building the transcontinental line for the Atlantic & Pacific Railroad established a camp at the springs where Old Town is today.

By 1886 Flagstaff was the largest city on the main line of the Atlantic & Pacific between Albuquerque and the Pacific coast. It was also slated to be the northern terminus of the Mineral Belt Railroad, an ambitous but ill-fated line, whose backers attempted to bore a hole through the Mogollon Rim and lay tracks to the prosperous mining camp of Globe. The 160-mile line had to be built through some rough terrain, the most notable engineering feat a 3,100-foot tunnel through the rim. This precipitous raw edge of rock and faulted displacement, which separates Arizona's high country from the lowlands, would require a grade rise of two thousand feet in just a few miles. The visionary scheme might have worked; however, after they had laid forty miles of track and tunneled seventy feet into the rim, the promoters ran out of funds.

Large cattle ranching had its beginning in 1883 when John Young teamed up with a group of Eastern captalists that included Colonel Jake Rupert, the man who owned the New York Yankees during the days of Babe Ruth and who founded the Arizona Cattle Company, with headquarters at Fort Moroni. Young, a polygamist, didn't stay in the business long. In 1885 a warrant was issued for his arrest, and he was forced to sell his share and make a hasty exit.

After Young left, the outfit built several new buildings at Fort Moroni and renamed it Fort Rickerson, in honor of C. L. Rickerson, an officer in a New York-based firm. At its peak, the Arizona Cattle Company grazed about sixteen thousand head of cattle on some of the finest cattle country in Arizona, which ran from south of Flagstaff near Lake Mary, north to the Grand Canyon, and from Ash Fork on the west to the Little Colorado River on the east. This huge acreage (132,000 acres) had been purchased from the railroad for fifty cents an acre.

The town of Flagstaff was still rough around the edges on a chilly March morning of 1886 when two aspiring cattlemen named Dave and Billy Babbitt arrived. A fire had destroyed the town's small business district a short time earlier, and the familiar sound of sawing and hammering heralded the building of a new town over the smoldering ashes of the old. The wind that swept down from the towering San Francisco Mountains was bone-chilling cold. The nearest source of supplies and merchandise was Albuquerque, more than three hundred miles away, and most of the residents in the rough-hewn community were aptly described as "unchurched, unmarried and unwashed." Raw, untamed Flagstaff didn't seem a likely place to invest one's life savings, but the Babbitts were visionaries aspiring to fulfill the dream held by so many nineteenth century adventurers—to come West and become cattlemen.

The Babbitt story began a few years earlier in Cincinnati, Ohio, where Dave and Billy, along with brothers Charlie and George, ran a grocery store. This crackerbarrel cornucopia was a favorite hangout for traveling drummers, and the Babbitt brothers sat in wide-eyed amazement as a salesman colorfully described the awe-inspiring beauty of Arizona and the unlimited opportunities for young adventurers who dared to take up the challenge of starting a cow ranch in the "great and glowing West." The irresistible urge to go out and see for themselves prompted Dave to board a westbound train in 1884. His travels took him from Wyoming to southern Arizona in search of

The five Babbitt brothers in 1908. From left: George, Charles "C.J.," Edward, William, and David
Courtesy
Southwest Studies

Mars Hill view of Flagstaff, September, 1895
Courtesy Northern Arizona University Library

the right place, and he soon returned to Cincinnati to affirm the salesman's report. The young brothers then combined their cash resources, coming up with $20,000, hardly enough to buy a big cattle outfit in the developed lands. Their only hope, therefore, was to find something in the areas opened in 1883, so in 1886 they headed west to look over the Atlantic & Pacific cattle country.

Although Dave and Billy might have been apprehensive as they gazed at the barren, desolate land west of Albuquerque, their spirits lifted when they reached the junction of the Rio Puerco and the Little Colorado River, where a bustling community originally referred to as Horsehead Crossing was now called Holbrook, and where the newly formed Aztec Land and Cattle Company, or the Hashknife (after its brand), was running sixty thousand cows over two million acres of grassland.

By the time the train pulled up the long grade into Flagstaff at the foot of the majestic San Francisco peaks, the two brothers were convinced they had found a perfect place to start a cattle ranch. A few weeks later they sank most of the family savings into a small outfit between Flagstaff and Winslow. The perceptive seller threw his foreman in on the deal, and the amateur cattlemen were in business. As a tribute to their hometown of Cincinnati, they stamped a CO with a bar underneath on the hides of their "hairy banknotes." A few months later they gathered and shipped their first herd—seventeen carloads—to California, and the storied dynasty was in the making. Charles, or C. J., and George sold the family business in Ohio, tying up the loose ends and joining Dave and Billy in Arizona. A younger brother, Edward, participated in the enterprise on a limited basis but preferred to remain in the East.

Across the street from the Babbitt grocery store in Cincinnati was a wealthy Dutch merchant named Gerald Vercamp. Vercamp had several daughters and was not at all displeased when Dave, C. J., and Edward courted them and eventually married into his family. The old Dutchman respected and admired the ambitious and hard-working young businessmen. However, when they decided to become cattlemen, he strongly urged them to diversify, and fortunately they heeded his advice. Dave opened a mercantile store, George got involved in real estate, while C. J. and Billy ran the cattle operation. In 1889 they formed the Babbitt Brothers Trading Company. Drought and bad markets would have bankrupt the cattle operation several times had it not been for the other enterprises to carry the brothers through hard times.

The golden age of the CO Bar Ranch was 1909 to 1919, when the Babbitts ran thousands of sheep and cattle on ranges that extended from Ash Fork on the west to the New Mexico line on the east; from the Grand Canyon on the north to the Mogollon Rim on the south. They also owned large ranches in Kansas and California.

During these years, Flagstaff became the cultural and mercantile center of northern Arizona, and the industrious brothers from Ohio were involved in most of the enterprises. There is no doubt they were a powerful influence in northern Arizona, but they did not wield a heavy hand in controlling politics and business in the region. Rather than constructing opulent mansions as testament to their wealth, they chose instead to live in unpretentious homes, setting an example for benevolent power that is rare in the annals of dynasty.

Through the years the Babbitts diversified their holdings far more than Gerald Vercamp could have imagined, in this way avoiding bankruptcy during rough economic times. They operated a vast network of trading posts on the Hopi and Navajo reservations; owned Flagstaff's first automotive garage, a bank, an ice plant, livery stable, beef slaughter house, an opera house, and a mortuary. It's been said

The C O Bar wagon in early 1900s. On horseback is Lewis Lee.
Courtesy Museum of Northern Arizona

that the Babbitts "fed, clothed, equipped, transported, entertained, and buried Arizonans, doing it more efficiently and more profitably than anyone else."

Today the CO Bar ranch is still one of the state's largest cow outfits, and it's still a family business ably managed by John Babbitt, a son of the legendary C. J. The enterprise isn't nearly as large as it once was, but the company still maintains a strong presence in northern Arizona. The Babbitt brothers' trading posts and mercantile stores still extend far into northern Arizona. The Babbitt Ford dealership is one of the oldest in the western states, and one of C. J.'s grandsons, Bruce, served two terms (1978-1986) as governor of the state.

The Babbitts weren't the only brothers to find business success in Flagstaff. Timothy and Michael Riordan came to the area in 1886 on the advice of a third brother, Dennis. In 1887 they organized the Arizona Lumber Company, one of northern Arizona's leading enterprises. The original lumber company had begun operations in 1882 by Edward Ayers. When the construction of the Atlantic and Pacific Railroad had been delayed while a bridge was built across Canyon Diablo, Ayers got off the train at Winslow and rode by wagon to Flagstaff. He saw the vast forest of ponderosa and quickly founded the Ayers Lumber Company, Arizona's first major manufacturing industry. Dennis Riordan was hired as manager. A few years later Ayers sold out to the Riordans. In 1903 Tim built a dam at the end of a long *cienega* south of town and named it Lake Mary in honor of his oldest daughter. The lake later became Flagstaff's main source of water. The town's first electric plant was also built by the innovative Riordan brothers.

CO Bar building located in Fort Valley, north of Flagstaff. This site was originally called Fort Moroni for the Mormon Angel. It was later ranch headquarters, called Fort Rickerson.

Courtesy
Southwest Studies

The Riordans were a close-knit family. In 1904 Mike and Tim built an impressive log mansion and named it Kinlichi, Navajo for "red house." The house, now managed by the state parks department and

The Riordan brothers' Arizona Lumber Company, the first major manufacturing industry in Arizona.
Courtesy Northern Arizona University

located next to the campus of Northern Arizona University, had separate living quarters at each end for the two families and a common area in the center which was shared. Since the Riordans were among the most prosperous citizens, the home was the center of social activity in the Flagstaff area.

In 1927 tragedy struck both families on the same day. Timothy's twenty-six-year-old daughter Anna contracted the dreaded disease polio. Members of both families took turns over the next few days administering artificial respiration to the stricken young woman. The house was placed under quarantine and nobody was allowed to leave. An iron lung was ordered by rail but failed to arrive in time to save her life. That same night, Mike's thirty-year-old son Arthur passed away. The bodies of Anna and Arthur were placed in the center of the Riordan family mansion to lie in state as mourners from all over northern Arizona came to pay last respects.

A few years ago, the mansion was scheduled to be torn down to allow for expansion on the campus of Northern Arizona University. The site avoided condemnation proceedings when descendants of Flagstaff's lumbering dynasty allowed it to become a state park. Today park staff and volunteers provide guided tours through this unique and interesting legacy of Flagstaff's historic past.

Another trio of brothers, the Camerons—Ralph, Niles, and Burton—also came to Flagstaff in the 1880s. Ralph was the best known, serving as territorial delegate and a leader in the struggle for statehood. He was elected to the United States Senate in 1920.

Dr. Dennis J. Brannen and his cousin Patrick B. Brannen were the town's first doctor and merchant, respectively. Dr. Brannen was not only a dedicated physician, who had turned down several opportunities in large cities to practice in the mountain community of Flagstaff, but he also found time to serve in Arizona's thirteenth

Timothy Riordan's family lived at one end of the mansion and Michael Riordan's at the other. The central area was used as a social center by both families
Courtesy
Southwest Studies

legislature. In addition, he was an enterprising businessman, accumulating a sizable fortune, but his true vocation was medicine. Patrick Brannen and his nephew Peter J. Brannen arrived in Flagstaff before the railroad. They had been operating a mercantile store in Prescott in 1880, but realizing the railroad would open a vast new market, they hauled in a wagonload of merchandise to Flagstaff and went into business there. Their first store, soon to be replaced by a log cabin, was located in a tent near Antelope Spring. Like most towns made up of clustered wooden structures, one careless act with a wood stove, or a coal oil lamp, would cause the community to go up in smoke. When Old Town had a fire, Brannen's Store was a total loss. P. J. was instrumental in moving the community a half-mile east, near where the railroad had placed a boxcar as the town's first depot.

In 1883 Brannen invested $10,000 in the construction of a stone building across the street from the train depot. This historic building still stands on the corner of Santa Fe Avenue and San Francisco Street. Because of his community involvement, P. J. Brannen was the town's "unofficial mayor" for several years before incorporation in 1894.

As in most communities of the "real West," most Flagstaff citizens were caught up in everyday pursuits. Schools, fraternal organizations, and churches needed to be built. In 1883 money to buy land to build the first Protestant church was raised by a preacher who passed the hat in local saloons and raised twenty-five dollars. A Jesuit padre came to administer the needs of Roman Catholics, and a chapter of the Women's Christian Temperance Union was organized.

The Babbitts built an opera house and a theater that showed real moving pictures. A story is told about a cowboy coming into town and

246

Babbitt Brothers Corner – Aspen Avenue in Flagstaff in 1917
Courtesy
Southwest Studies

seeing his first moving picture. In one scene, several young ladies were disrobing before taking a dip in the local swimming hole. Just as they were getting down to their undergarments, a freight train went roaring by. When the tracks were clear again, the ladies were safely submerged in water up to their necks. After the film, the cowboy went to the ticket window and bought five more tickets. When the salesgirl asked why he wanted to watch the same show five more times, the cowboy replied matter-of-factly, "Ma'am, I don't know much about moving pictures, but I do know somethin' about trains and I'm bettin' that out of the next five that goes by, one is bound to be late and I'm goin' to be there when it happens."

By 1891 the population of Flagstaff had grown to about fifteen hundred. That same year Coconino County was carved out of a piece of old Yavapai (one of the four original counties in the Arizona Territory, the other three being Pima, Yuma, and Mohave). With lumber, commerce, ranching, farming, and of course, the Santa Fe Railroad, Flagstaff, in a short decade, became Arizona's most important city north of Prescott.

Tourism in the twentieth century became the new major industry of Flagstaff, as large numbers of tourists came to visit the Grand Canyon, and the building of Route 66 in the 1920s would make the tourist industry one of Flagstaff's most important sources of income.

Lowell Observatory sits on top of Mars Hill, at the west end of Flagstaff. From inside the great observatory one can look up to man's newest frontier and at the same time be a stone's throw distance from Old Town and Antelope Spring, the historic genesis of Flagstaff. In 1893 Dr. Percival Lowell had selected the observatory site, expecting to chart the path of Mars, which was to come closer to Earth than ever

247

before observed. Lowell selected Flagstaff because the clear mountain air made it the best available site in the United States; he believed intelligent life had constructed irrigation canals on the red planet, a revolutionary theory at the time. Before his death in 1916 Lowell predicted the discovery of an unknown planet. In 1930 Clyde W. Tombaugh, of the Lowell Observatory, discovered Pluto in the exact position indicated by Dr. Lowell.

Northern Arizona University has come a long way since 1901 when four young ladies stepped forward to receive their degrees. Destined to become teachers, they were the normal school's first graduating class. The school had opened its doors September 11, 1899 with a faculty of two and a handful of students.

After years of haggling about funds and purpose and name, in 1925 the legislature approved the creation of Northern Arizona State Teachers College. Three years later the name was changed to Arizona State Teachers College, and in 1945 the "Teachers" was dropped. Since several years earlier the school had been granted approval to offer a Master of Arts degree in Education, Flagstaff was becoming known as an ideal place for teachers to go for summer school. Then, on November 28, 1964 the regents changed the name to Northern Arizona University, and on May 1, 1966 the university status became official.

Earle Forrest worked as a cowboy for the CO Bar ranch. He carried a camera on horseback and recorded a rich part of Northern Arizona's cattle industry. Later he wrote an important book on the Pleasant Valley War.
Courtesy Museum of Northern Arizona

Interstate 40
Flagstaff to Lupton

Walnut Canyon National Monument (Exit 204)

Sinagua Indians arrived and made their home under the natural overhangs of steep-sided Walnut Canyon over 850 years ago. A permanent stream flowing at the bottom of the four-hundred-foot deep chasm allowed native farmers to grow abundant crops of corn, beans, and squash. The growing season in this part of Arizona is brief, which may be one reason why the cliff dwellers remained only a little over a century. Another reason may have been drought. Although the normal rainfall is about twenty inches, the natives had to rely on summer showers to sustain their crops. Whatever the reason, about 1250 A.D., the Sinagua, who at one time occupied about 120 sites and about four hundred rooms in the canyon, left.

The cliff dwellings at Walnut Canyon are among the most unusual in the Southwest. Over a period of two hundred million years, Walnut Creek sliced its way through soft limestone, creating ledges on which the Sinagua built their homes.

To get down to these ledges today one must make a steep descent of nearly two hundred feet. A trail follows a ledge around a peninsula-shaped mountain about two hundred feet above the canyon floor. Here, beneath these natural overhangs, are the Sinagua homesites. The overhangs made construction of houses a simple task. The natives merely closed in the front and made partitions with rocks. Clay was used as mortar and plaster as a floor covering. Although the average height of the Sinagua was only 5'6", the doorways were much smaller, probably to minimize the loss of warm air. Animal skins were used as door coverings. A small opening above the door allowed campfire smoke to escape. Although the Sinagua built small dams in Walnut Creek, they didn't irrigate their crops like their relatives in the Verde Valley.

Lieutenant "Ned" Beale mentions that on February 6, 1858 he spent the day exploring the ruins. Lieutenant Whipple referred to the site as Pueblo Creek because of the abandoned ruins. James Stevenson, of the Smithsonian Institution, visited the site in 1883 and in 1912 Dr. Harold S. Colton, founder of the Museum of Northern Arizona made a survey. Unfortunately Walnut Canyon was plagued by vandals and pot hunters, and the ruins were almost completely destroyed before the area was declared a national monument in 1915.

Winona
"Flagstaff, Arizona, don't forget Winona"

There's no doubt that Bobby Troup's lyrics gave tiny Winona notoriety that far exceeds its importance in the mainstream of American history. It would be impossible to estimate the number of times tourists had a fleeting glance at the town's name as they passed by and then recalled the catchy Troup lyrics. It's also impossible to guess the number of people who have stopped just out of curiosity and contributed to the local economy. If royalty commissions were paid for this sort of thing, Bobby Troup would have collected a fortune far beyond the dreams of Arizona's most incurable jackass prospector.

Located a mile east of Walnut Creek, Winona was originally called Walnut by the railroad. There are at least thirty-two place names in Arizona using "walnut" and one was a railroad station, so in 1886 Walnut was changed to Winona. A post office was located here in 1924, but there had been a small community along the railroad since 1912. About 1920 Billy Adams is believed to have opened the nation's first camp for tourists at Winona. The new highway in the mid-1920s was moved further south of the railroad, and the original community dried up.

Two Guns

Two Guns sounds like a Wild West name conjured up for the benefit of the tourist trade, and perhaps this is partly true; however, Two Guns does have a brief, voilent history that befits its name. The original inhabitant of the site was an ornery individual who called himself "Two Gun" Miller and claimed to be an Apache. He killed a neighbor in a fight, but the jury ruled it was self-defense, and "Two Gun" was acquitted. Some of the victim's friends marked the headboard of the grave "Killed by Indian Miller." This angered Miller, so he painted out the uncomplimentary epitaph and was jailed temporarily for defacing a grave. The eccentric "Two Gun" Miller lived in a cave in Canyon Diablo and was reported to be hostile to visitors.

Just west of modern-day Two Guns is an interesting collection of "Indians pueblos," probably erected during the heyday of Route 66. Some of the old tourist-attracting signs are still hanging from the crumbling rock walls. A short hike along an old rock ridge used by early-day automobiles leads one on an interesting trek into the not-too-distant past—the walls of Canyon Diablo are literally covered with remnants of old rock dwellings, all within sight of Interstate 40.

Canyon Diablo. The A&P (later Santa Fe) crossing the canyon in the 1880s
Courtesy
Southwest Studies

Canyon Diablo

Because Canyon Diablo presented the greatest natural obstacle to Lieutenant Whipple on his historic thirty-fifth parallel survey in 1853, he gave the canyon its name of Canyon Diablo, which means Devil's Canyon. On December 14, Whipple's party reached the edge of the deep gorge. Apparently he wasn't expecting a canyon of such magnitude, writing in his journal as follows: ". . . we were all surprised to find at our feet, in magnesian limestone, a chasm probably one hundred feet in depth, the sides precipitous, and about three hundred feet across at top." (Whipple underestimated the depth. The railroad bridge over Canyon Diablo is 250 feet above the canyon floor.) "A thread-like rill of water could be seen below, but descent was impossible. . . . For a railroad it could be bridged and the banks would furnish plenty of stone for the purpose."

Whipple had to travel north about twenty-five miles to the junction with the Little Colorado River before he could find a suitable crossing for his mules and wagons. Lieutenant "Ned" Beale reached the canyon on September 8, 1857 and reported the canyon as impassable. Like Whipple, he had to go several miles out of his way to cross.

There may have been plenty of stone for a bridge, but a comic-opera event occurred in 1881 when the railroad tried to span the canyon. Timber parts of the bridge were pre-assembled elsewhere, and someone misread the plans; the bridge came up several feet short.

A settlement sprang up east of the bridge and was called Canyon Diablo. For a time it was reputed to be one of the roughest towns in the territory. A story is told that when an outlaw robbed the payroll intended for the construction crew, a posse of workers was quickly formed and went in hot pursuit. They caught up with the bandit, but sometime during the chase he had lost his saddlebags, which contained the loot. A search of the area failed to locate the money, so the posse decided to have a hanging. They put a noose around the outlaw's neck and draped the other end of the rope around the limb of a huge pine tree. About the time they were going to administer the "suspended" sentence, a bolt of lightning struck the tree. Nobody was hurt, but the posse, suspecting some kind of divine intervention, decided to commute the sentence and turn the condemned man over to the proper authorities. He was given a term in the Yuma Territorial Prison, and the incident was nearly forgotten, until several years later when a cowboy out herding cattle happened to glance down and see a pair of weatherbeaten old saddlebags with the payroll still inside.

Another spectacular train robbery took place in the spring of 1889 when four men robbed the Santa Fe express car at Canyon Diablo. At 11:00 P.M., on the night of March 20, the Eastbound Number 2 stopped to fill its wood box. Suddenly four men, all cowboys working for the Hashknife outfit, climbed on board; they held the crew at gunpoint, broke open the safe, and took seven thousand dollars in cash and some jewelry. The robbers were pursued by a posse led by Buckey O'Neill, the legendary sheiff of Yavapai County (Canyon Diablo was part of Yavapai County at the time). O'Neill and his three-man posse chased the outlaws for three weeks and six hundred miles before catching them at Wahweap Canyon on the Utah border. In a running gunfight, O'Neill and his men captured the bandits and brought them to justice.

Today Canyon Diablo is a quiet place three miles north of Interstate 40 on a rough dirt road. The name is still partly visible on the white stucco adobe building on the north side of the tracks. Nearby are the melted mounds of adobe ruins, all that remains of the old town. The stillness of the old place is broken only by the occasional passing of a Santa Fe train.

Canyon Diablo as it looks today
Marshall Trimble photo

Meteor Crater (milepost 233)

Meteor Crater is said to be the best preserved crater in the world. It was formed about twenty-two thousand years ago when a giant nickel-iron ball weighing several million tons and traveling at a speed of 133,000 miles per hour slammed into the earth and exploded with such force that scientists tell us it destroyed all life within a hundred-mile radius. One scientist estimated the meteorite to be only eighty-one feet in diameter. Today the crater is nearly six hundred feet deep, has a lip about one hundred fifty feet, and is nearly a mile in diameter. Apparently some prehistoric peoples found the crater a suitable place to settle, as ruins have been found inside the rim. The place has had several names over the years, including Barringer Crater, Great Arizona Crater, Coon Butte, Meteor Mountains, Sunshine Crater, and Franklin's Hole.

The white men first noted the crater in 1871, but it wasn't considered to have been caused by a meteorite until 1886 when sheepherders found pieces of meteorites near Canyon Diablo. In 1891 a leading geologist, G. K. Gilbert, declared that the crater had not been made by a meteor. In 1903 Dr. Daniel Barringer, a mining engineer, began drilling at the site. Barringer was convinced a large metallic meteorite had caused the crater, but attempts to mine the mineral proved unsuccessful. Most people accepted Barringer's claim that it was a meteor crater, but attempts to locate the main mass of the meteorite proved futile. Since the hole was round, it was assumed that the meteorite hit the earth head on and would be in the center of the crater.

One day Dr. Barringer fired a rifle at a mud hole from a flat angle and discovered the resulting crater was still a round hole. Exploration was begun on the southeastern slope of the crater, but after drilling to a depth of nearly fourteen hundred feet, the bit jammed and the cable broke; the project was abandoned in 1929. Modern technology reveals that about 80% of the meteorite had been vaporized on impact and that only about 10% still lies beneath the south rim.

Prior to their moon landings during the late 1960s the Apollo astronauts trained at Meteor Crater.

Early Mormon Missions on the Little Colorado River

It is probable that the first Mormon *entrada* into Arizona from Utah came as early as 1854, but the Navajos were on the warpath at that time, and by 1855 the Mormons had been driven out. Between 1858 and the early 1870s Jacob Hamblin, the Mormon's greatest trailblazer, made several reconnaissance missions in Arizona, locating river crossings, water holes, and suitable trails. By this time the Navajos were at peace, thus making attempts at colonization safer, the greatest enemy being the harsh land itself.

The primary mission of the church during these years was expansion. Under the dynamic leadership of Brigham Young, the Mormons were determined to establish a far-flung empire from their base in Utah west to California and south to the Salt River Valley and eventually to Sonora, Mexico. Mormon settlements at Kanab (Utah), Pipe Spring, and Lee's Ferry would serve as bases from which to launch new settlements in Arizona.

A reconnaissance expedition was sent to the Little Colorado River Valley in 1873 to make a feasibility study for colonization. The scouts reported the area unsuitable. A Norwegian missionary, Andrew Amundsen, summed up the bleak land—his spelling left something to be desired, but the meaning was clear: "From the first we struck the little Collorado . . . it is the seam thing all the way, no plase fit for a human being to dwell upon." Amundsen concluded his report succinctly, calling the area "the moste desert lukking plase that I ever saw, Amen."

In spite of adverse scouting reports, an expedition of a hundred colonists arrived on the Little Colorado in late May 1873 after a miserable, windblown journey from Moenkopi Wash. By this time, the river was drying up. One journal entry referred to the Little Colorado as "a loathesome little stream . . . as disgusting a stream as there is on the continent."

Strong willed as they had been at the outset, the dispirited colonists soon packed their gear and returned to Utah. Undaunted, Brigham Young was determined to establish colonies in the valley of the Little Colorado River, and three years later he was successful.

A major figure in the Mormon colonization along the Little Colorado River was a fiery red-headed frontiersman named Lot Smith. Smith is best remembered for his daring guerilla attacks on United States Army supply trains during the Mormon War in 1857. In 1876 a mission was established at the ancient Hopi community at Moencopi. Over the next two years Smith and other church leaders, like William C. Allen, George Lake, and Jesse O. Ballinger, led parties of colonists to the lower Little Colorado River Valley near today's Joseph City, Sunset Crossing (Winslow), and Holbrook. Townsites were marked, irrigation ditches dug, dams erected, and crops planted. The Mormons had finally taken permanent root in Arizona.

Four colonizing parties, each numbering about fifty, established camps and named them for their respective captains. Later, Lake's Camp became Obed; Smith's Camp was changed to Sunset, for the river crossing nearby; Ballinger's Camp became Brigham City; and Allen's Camp became St. Joseph. (Since St. Joseph, Missouri, was also on the Santa Fe line, St. Joseph, Arizona, was changed to Joseph City in 1923.)

Sunset and Brigham City were located on opposite sides of the Little Colorado near the site of present-day Winslow. As a precaution against Indian attack, all four communities constructed forts of cottonwood logs and sandstone. The forts were self-contained units including communal mess halls and housing. The average size was about two hundred feet square with walls reaching seven to nine feet. Elevated guardhouses stood at the corners. Each community had shops, cellars, storehouses, and wells in case of prolonged siege.

St. Joseph was the only one of the four communities to survive and is considered the oldest Mormon colony in Arizona. Despite numerous crop failures and dams destroyed by the rampaging Little Colorado, the gritty colonists won their battle against the elements. In 1939 the river was tamed by the construction of a durable dam. On the other hand, Obed, Sunset, and Brigham City all succumbed to the capricious river and to possible dissension and lack of cooperation among the colonists—by the early 1880s the Mormons had abandoned these sites. The sturdy sandstone fort at Obed was later used as a corral by the Hashknife outfit.

Earlier, the Little Colorado, or Rio Chiquito Colorado, was known by the Navajo as *Tol-Chaco*, meaning red or bloody. Coronado named it *Rio de Lino*, or Flax River, because of the wild flax along the river's banks. In 1604 explorer Don Juan Oñate named it the *Rio Colorado*, or Red River. This muddy brown river of many moods has its headwaters near 11,470-foot Mount Baldy and empties into the Grand Canyon after cutting a two hundred fifty-mile gorge south across the Colorado Plateau. Although the Little Colorado isn't as well known as some of Arizona's more illustrious rivers, this tempestuous little river has been loved, feared, and respected by all who have come to know it.

Sunset Crossing and Winslow

Sunset Crossing, near the present site of Winslow, was important as one of the few places to cross the treacherous, sandy-bottomed Little Colorado River. Because it was located on a rocky ledge, Chavez, Whipple, Beale, Leroux, and all the others who marked trails along the thirty-fifth parallel used it as a crossing. It was named for Sunset Gap, a pass through the mountains twenty miles southwest of Winslow on a trail blazed by Francisco Chavez but used hundreds of years earlier by Hopi Indians.

Martha Summerhayes described a harrowing river crossing here in 1875 on a journey from Fort Apache to Camp Verde, when the wagons bogged down in some quicksand and the luggage went floating down the river. "All our worldly goods were in those chests," she wrote, "and I knew they were soaked wet and probably ruined; but, after all, what did it matter, in the face of the serious problem which confronted us?"

The trunks were rescued by the soldiers, and a heavy rope was stretched across the river. The wagons were turned into "ferryboats," and all hands were escorted safely across the river. The river crossing ordeal took all day, causing Martha to write: "The unpleasant reality destroyed any poetic associations which might otherwise have clung to the name of Sunset Crossing in my ever vivid imagination."

In 1876 Mormon settlers under the leadership of Lot Smith arrived and established the community of Sunset, three miles north of Winslow. Sunset had a brief existence—after building a small fort and digging a few irrigation ditches, the Mormons abandoned the project.

In 1881 two desperados, Bill Campbell and "Thick-lipped Joe" Waters, murdered a storekeeper named Bill Blanchard. The two were captured and jailed at St. Johns, but a band of vigilantes took the pair out of jail and lynched them before justice could prevail.

Sunset Crossing began to fade when the new community of Winslow sprang up around the new train station. Winslow was probably named for General Edward Winslow, a railroad executive, although a prospector near Mayer named Tom Winslow later claimed the honor. Winslow has remained an important division terminal of the railroad. The Winslow Harvey House, the La Posada, with its classic Spanish architecture, was one of several legendary eating establishments located along the Santa Fe line by Fred Harvey.

Before the days of railroad dining cars, passengers were forced to eat in the local hash houses wherever the train happened to stop. The food was terrible, and the service was even worse. The passengers would rush in, place an order, and just about the time the food arrived, the conductor would shout, "All aboard." Meal tickets were sold to the passengers by the trainmen, and it is not unlikely that they received a kickback on meal tickets if a meal were not eaten.

Not only were conditions deplorable for train passengers, they were even worse for single men in the cities and towns. Travelers were at the mercy of the local restaurants and hotels, while residents cooked their food under primitive conditions at home. The basic tool was the frying pan, and it was cause for much dyspepsia among Southwesterners.

It took a gentleman from England named Fred Harvey to bring top quality cuisine to the American Southwest. After experiencing deplorable eating conditions along the rail lines, Harvey approached the Santa Fe Railroad in the early 1870s with a visionary plan that would provide passengers with attractive surroundings, superior service, and above all, good food. The railroad company accepted his proposals enthusiastically, for food services had been one of the most serious problems plaguing all the railroads at this time. The Santa Fe agreed to supply buildings, food transportation, and restaurant furnishings and personnel free of charge. In addition, Harvey was to receive all the profits from this venture.

The first Harvey House opened for business in Topeka, Kansas in the spring of 1876 and was an immediate success. French chefs were hired away from prominent restaurants in the East and paid handsome salaries. In at least one instance, the Harvey House chef was making more money than the president of a local bank. Foods were purchased from local farmers.

During the next twenty years, Harvey opened his Spanish-style restaurant-hotels at hundred-mile intervals throughout the Southwest. It was said that they were spaced that distance so they would keep "western traffic from settling in one place where Harvey served his meals." Eventually, Arizona had five Harvey Houses along the main line, and due to popular demand they were spaced at close intervals.

It wasn't just the excellent food that attracted Southwesterners to Harvey's establishments. Harvey added one more ingredient, the feminine touch. In a land where women were scarce, Harvey provided the Southwest with as wholesome a group of young women as had yet been seen in that region. The old adage about there being "no ladies west of Dodge City and no women west of Albuquerque" no longer held true.

The Harvey Girls were recruited in the eastern part of the country through newspaper advertisements which read: "Young women 18 to 30 years of age, of good character, attractive and intelligent, as waitresses in Harvey Eating Houses in the West. Good wages with room and meals furnished."

Ash Fork's grand Harvey House, the Escalante
Courtesy
Southwest Studies

For a young woman hoping to escape from hometown doldrums or one with hopes of acting out some romantic role of adventure, the ad sounded like a dream come true. For many it was, for they were a welcome sight to the lonely cattlemen, miners, and railroaders, and few of the Harvey Girls stayed single long. Cowboy humorist Will Rogers once said, "Fred Harvey kept the West in food and wives." The turnover of help was never a problem as there was always a long list of applicants anxious to go west to work as Harvey Girls.

The pay was only $17.50 a month, and the girls were required to live in dormitories similar to those of a conservative college sorority house. The girls had to be in by 10:30 P.M., on weekdays and 11:30 P.M., on Saturdays. A matronly housemother, or *duena*, saw to it that the ladies always obeyed Mr. Harvey's strict rules of moral conduct— theoretically, at least.

Not all of Harvey's Girls were comely. One old-timer noted dryly that "though rapid and efficient, neatly dressed, and in good health, there were no beauties among them." It was said that Harvey made a practice of hiring the more common-looking girls because the pretty ones always got themselves married shortly after arriving. "The plain ones seemed to get in less trouble," another old-timer observed. Whatever the case, the wholesome Harvey Girls, affectionately called "biscuit shooters," represented the finest type of young American womanhood.

The Harvey system was the amalgamation of efficiency, cuisine, service, and feminine charm. Prior to reaching a station, the brakeman would take orders and then wire the information ahead. When the train was a mile away from the meal stop, it would blow its whistle. Upon hearing the whistle an employee would ring a gong which signaled the waitresses to set up the first course. By the time the train arrived and the hungry passengers were ushered in, the meal was ready to serve. Waitresses were not allowed to serve men without a coat; however, any man who didn't have one was given a "loaner" by the establishment, compliments of Fred Harvey.

Everything on the table had to be set in a prescribed manner. The water glasses, silverware, salt and pepper shakers all had their proper place. Conversation with and between the girls was forbidden while the train was in the station. They communicated through the use of signals and codes. The "drink girl" knew that if the customer's cup was turned upside down, it meant he had ordered tea. When the cup was upright in the saucer, coffee was desired, and if the cup was taken away, the customer wanted milk. Usually the girls learned to talk to each other through the sides of their mouths to escape detection from the watchful eyes of the company inspectors who were constantly passing through, a frequent inspector being Fred Harvey himself. The boss loved surprise visits to his establishments and was known to fire a manager on the spot if all wasn't up to Fred Harvey standards.

About the turn of the century one could be served a breakfast consisting of cereal or fruit, eggs on a steak, hash browns, and a stack of six large hotcakes with butter and maple syrup, topped off with apple pie and coffee, all for only 50 cents. Dinners went for a quarter more and always included a gourmet dish of wild game.

Leroux Wash (milepost 285)

Heroes of the old West gained public recognition in a variety of ways. Some reputations, like "Buffalo Bill" Cody, grew by self-promotion. Jim Bridger was glorified in the dime novels of Ned Buntline and in the prolific journals of "Pathfinder" John C. Fremont and in the florid writing of his talented wife, Jessie, who made Kit Carson a legend in his lifetime. Others, like Pauline Weaver, Tom Fitzpatrick, and Ewing Young never received the recognition they so richly deserved. Perhaps the most deserving of all the Western heroes, yet the least known in Arizona, is Antoine Leroux.

Unlike many who were recruited from the grog shops of St. Louis, Leroux was a member of an affluent French merchant family and educated in the finest St. Louis academies. But there was a sense of adventure in his blood, and in 1822 he joined the storied Ashley-Henry Expedition, which left St. Louis in 1822 to explore to the headwaters of the Missouri River. The members of that expedition read like a "Who's Who" in the frontier hall of fame and include Jim Bridger, Dave Jackson, Jed Smith, Tom Fitzpatrick, Hugh Glass, Jim Kirker, "Frenchy" Sublette, and Jim Clyman. Most of these adventurers were young, in their early twenties at the time.

Two years later Leroux was trapping in the Gila watershed of Arizona and New Mexico. By the time the Americans took over the region after the Mexican War ended in 1848, Leroux was considered the most experienced, competent, and celebrated scout in New Mexico. Among his assistants on many expeditions during the interim years between 1830 and 1848 was Kit Carson.

Antoine Leroux's achievements in the opening of the Southwest are impressive. In 1846 he was a guide for the Mormon Battalion on their historic roadbuilding trek from Santa Fe to California. In 1851 he led the first of several expeditions by the Army Corps of Topographical Engineers charged with locating proposed railroad routes. Of the four proposed routes (all are still used today), Leroux was a guide on three, including the thirty-second, thirty-fifth and thirty-eighth parallels.

During the 1851 expedition, under the leadership of Captain Lorenzo Sitgreaves, Leroux walked into an ambush near the Big Sandy River and received three arrow wounds from Hualapai warriors. It was said the humiliation of getting ambushed hurt the tough veteran of frontier warfare more than the painful Hualapai arrows.

After guiding the Sitgreaves reconnaissance party to San Diego, Leroux was hired to lead United States Boundary Commissioner John R. Bartlett and Lieutenant Amiel Whipple east across the desert to Yuma, thence along the Gila River and across New Mexico to El Paso.

In early 1853 Leroux was hired by Captain John W. Gunnison to guide his ill-fated surveying expedition across central Colorado along the thirty-eighth parallel. Since Leroux had a prior commitment to guide Lieutenant Whipple across northern Arizona, he had to leave Gunnison in Utah. Later Gunnison was murdered by the Ute Indians. Most historians believe the experienced Leroux could have avoided the massacre had he been present. In the meantime Leroux did brief service for Lieutenant Edward F. "Ned" Beale of camel exploration fame before joining Whipple in Albuquerque in November 1853.

The Whipple party mapped a railroad route along the thirty-fifth parallel, spending Christmas camped at the foot of the San Francisco Mountains. A spring nearby, Leroux Springs, was named in honor of the great scout. A festive party was held that Christmas Eve. One of the resourceful officers had conjured up a large crock of high octane egg nog. The ever-vigilant old scout's only recorded comment that night was, "What a splendid opportunity it would be for the Indians to surprise us tonight!"

Perhaps the most interesting part of the Antoine Leroux story goes back to fifty years before his birth. Ironically it began in New Mexico, where he later gained his reputation. About 1750 a Comanche chief named Onacama visited Taos during a trade fair and was smitten by the beautiful four-year-old granddaughter of Don Pablo Villapando, the biggest *ranchero* in the valley. Onacama wanted to purchase the little girl and raise her to become one of his wives. But Don Pablo saw an opportunity to protect his ranch from frequent Comanche raids, so he struck a secret bargain. "If the Comanche will cease raiding my ranch, I will let you take her for a wife when she is old enough," he told the chief.

The Comanche chief stuck by his agreement for ten years. Each year the youngster grew more beautiful. Finally in 1760 Onacama claimed the fourteen-year-old girl to be ready for marriage. Fearing for his granddaughter's safety, Don Pablo took her and fled. Enraged, the chief gathered his warriors and began one of the bloodiest massacres in New Mexico history. Onacama's warriors hit Don Pablo's ranch and killed all the men and any women who took up arms, including the patron's wife, Anna Maria. During the attack, she bravely grabbed a lance and charged a party of warriors, who beat her to death. Among the fifty-six women and children taken prisoner was thirty-four-year-old Maria Rasalia, the little girl's mother. Later sold to the Pawnees, she met and fell in love with a French trader named Jean Baptiste Lajoie. He took her to St. Louis, where they were married and raised two daughters. One, Helene, married a French merchant named Will Leroux. They had four children; the youngest, born about 1801, was named Antoine, and was to become the famous Western scout.

Holbrook

Horsehead Crossing was a small community located at the junction of the Rio Puerco and the Little Colorado River. Juan Padilla was the first settler in the area, arriving in 1878 with an ox team. He hired a man named Berado to run a saloon. Berado's enterprising wife opened a store and restaurant in one part of the tavern. The saloon became a favorite watering hole for travelers along the thirty-fifth parallel, and apparently Berado's spirited wife became a favorite of a lonesome fellow from Showlow named Henry Hurning. The story goes that Hurning arranged to get Berado drunk on his own whiskey, then had the lady kidnapped and delivered to his house in Showlow. History doesn't record how this caveman-style courtship culminated, but Berado eventually returned to Albuquerque without his *esposa*.

Prior to the building of the railroad in 1881 John W. Young, a son of Brigham Young, was contracted to provide ties for the new line. A year after the arrival of the railroad, a new town developed a few miles west of Horsehead Crossing. Young named it Holbrook for H. R. Holbrook, first engineer on the Atlantic and Pacific Railroad. Holbrook became the county seat for Navajo County in 1895 and until 1914 was said to be the only county seat in the United States that didn't have a church.

Holbrook was the setting of one of the West's most spectacular gunfights. In September 1887 the Pleasant Valley War, or Graham-Tewksbury feud, was just getting started. On September 2, Andy Cooper, whose real name was Blevins, and members of the Graham faction had ambushed some of the Tewksburys and murdered two men. After the fight, Andy, a tough cattle rustler from Texas, headed for the Blevins family home in Holbrook, thus setting the stage for the epic shootout.

Commodore Perry Owens, sheriff of Apache County during the Pleasant Valley War
Courtesy
Southwest Studies

When the new sheriff of Apache County first rode into Holbrook, he immediately found himself the subject of restrained amusement on the part of the local citizenry, for he was a most unusual sight for those parts. Lawman Commodore Perry Owens, a handsome man with his hair reaching past his shoulders, wore his pistol with the butt forward. This ostentatious style might have been popular in towns such as Dodge city or in the dime novels of Ned Buntline, but Holbrook's residents considered Owens a dandy. His arrival coincided with the arrival of the Cooper-Blevins gang, and citizens anxiously awaited the inevitable meeting.

When he arrived in Holbrook, Owens was probably unaware of the shootings in Pleasant Valley, but he was carrying a warrant for the arrest of Andy Cooper, or as he was sometimes called, Andy Blevins. The warrant was for horse-stealing rather than murder.

Meanwhile, Cooper was visiting the Blevins family home on Center Street, next to the railroad tracks. Witnesses later said he had been boasting in the saloons about killing two men in Pleasant Valley two days earlier. He was at the Blevins house later that day when Sheriff Owens stepped onto the front porch and attempted to serve a warrant on him for horse stealing. Andy cracked open the door and raised his revolver, but before he could fire, Owens, armed with a Winchester, put a round through the door and into Andy's midsection, mortally wounding the outlaw. From the opposite side of the room, John Blevins pushed open a door and fired at Owens, who cranked another shell into his rifle, turned and fired from the hip, wounding Blevins. A relative, Mose Roberts, leaped out a side window at the same time the sheriff moved out into the street. Before Roberts could get a shot off, the Winchester cracked once more, killing him. Meanwhile, fourteen-year-old Sam Houston Blevins wrestled Andy Cooper's pistol away from his mother and ran out the front door to join the fight. Before he could take aim and fire, Owens shot the youth through the heart.

Controversy over the gunfight continues. To most, C. P. Owens is a celebrated legendary hero. Others consider him a hired assassin brought in by county officials to rid the area of desperados—instead, he gunned down the Blevins boys and Mose Roberts without giving them a fighting chance. Whichever side one chooses to believe, none can doubt the courage of Owens that day, and few outside the family were sad to see Andy Cooper die with his boots on.

Holbrook received more dubious notoriety in 1899 when Sheriff Frank Wattron received a reprimand from President William McKinley for sending out an ornate invitation to a hanging. The guest of honor was George Smiley, and the card read as follows:

George Smiley, Murderer
His soul will be swung into eternity on Dec. 8, 1899 at 2 o'clock P.M., sharp.

The latest improved methods of scientific strangulation will be employed and everything possible will be done to make the surroundings cheerful and the execution a success.

Although stock raising was one of the territory's largest industries, the ranges in northern Arizona remained empty of range cattle. Most of the cattle were dairy cows brought in from Utah by Mormon settlers. In 1881 the railroad brought new life to the sleepy little settlements along the old Beale Camel Road, when the Santa Fe linked northern Arizona with the rest of the civilized world. Horsehead Crossing, on the Little Colorado River, was now being called Holbrook.

During the 1860s the federal government devised a clever scheme to finance building railroad lines in the western territories at virtually no cost to taxpayers. Since the nation was too poor to finance the enormous building costs, the railroads were given large land grants along the right of way as incentives. The grants awarded the Atlantic & Pacific (Santa Fe) in northern Arizona were in twenty-mile sections along each side of the track. The railroad was given deed to the odd numbered sections in each township. These vast, isolated regions weren't worth much until the railroad stretched its ribbons of steel across the country. Then, by selling the land back to ranchers and settlers, the railroad earned back the cost of building the line. In this manner, the western lands were opened for settlement, and the east was linked up with the Pacific coast.

Holbrook, with about two hundred fifty inhabitants, became an important shipping center for cattle, wool, hides, and merchandise for the army, Indians, cattlemen, and settlers. This bibulous Babylon on the Little Colorado also attracted a full complement of social outcasts who could usually be found bellied up to the bar in the saloons along both sides of the tracks. Lawlessness and violence were prevalent among this wide gamut of frontier society, where voluminous consumption of snakehead whiskey and the slightest provocation or a misdeal of cards were apt to bring the hammer down on forty grains of black powder.

Hell-raising, devil-may-care cowboys in from the open range took delight in the challenge of trying to "down a shot of whiskey before it touched the bottom of the glass" in saloons with sanguinary names like "Bucket of Blood," before heading over to pay a visit to the "ladies on the line."

Bucket of Blood
Saloon in Holbrook
Courtesy
Southwest Studies

Arizona's most spectacular ranching enterprise began in the spring of 1884 when a stockholder of the Atlantic & Pacific Railroad named Edward Kinsley went west to inspect the new main line across northern Arizona. Unusually heavy winter rains had provided an abundance of lush, nutritious grasses on the rangelands and water along the Little Colorado River Valley. Kinsley was sure he had found one of America's great feeding grounds, where one could turn a $4 yearling into a $40 steer. He returned to New York and persuaded a group of business associates to invest more than $1.3 million in a cattle ranch, and thus was born the fabled Aztec Land & Cattle Company. Other investors included Henry Kinsley, Frank Ames, James McCreery, and the Seligman brothers, all stockholders in the Atlantic & Pacific. The following year the railroad offered twenty million acres of grazing land for sale at prices ranging from forty cents an acre to $1.50, selling a million acres to the Aztec Land & Cattle Company for fifty cents an acre. The fledgling cattle barons then brought in a large herd of Texas cattle to stock their new range, using the Hashknife brand, which resembled a cooking tool used by chuckwagon cooks. The company also imported a large number of Texas cowboys, who brought along all their vices and virtues. It was said that many of these punchers left Texas to seek greener pastures because they were not wanted in Texas and that a good many others left because they *were* wanted in Texas. The Texas range country had

Holbrook circa 1884
Courtesy
Southwest Studies

been suffering through a long drought, and the cattle were too undernourished to be driven, so they were loaded on the Atlantic & Pacific and shipped to Holbrook.

The Aztec Land and Cattle Company, better known as the Hashknife, ran as many as sixty thousand cows and two thousand horses on two million acres of private- and government-owned land north of the Mogollon Rim, between Holbrook and Flagstaff, with nothing but a brand burned into their hides to prove ownership. Until the company sold out in 1902, the Hashknife was considered the second largest cattle ranch in the United States; only the legendary XIT in Texas was larger.

From that day on, Horsehead Crossing, or Holbrook, would never be the same. The local newspaper reported: "Since the construction of

265

*Hashknife cowboys
in Holbrook*
Courtesy
Southwest Studies

the Atlantic & Pacific Railroad, the whole northern portion of the territory seems to be undergoing a great change. Our plains are stocked with thousands of cattle, horses, and sheep, and still there is room for more. We are astonished at the immense number of ranches that have been located during the last sixteen months in this country alone."

Rustlers and small ranchers bent on "stealing a start" in the cattle business hung around the fringes of the big outfits like a pack of timber wolves. The eastern-owned ranches like the Hashknife suffered the most because public sympathy was usually against them, and a small rancher caught rustling cows could usually get off easily by getting several friends on the jury. The community attitude was that the big outfits had been grazing their cows free on government land, so the citizens had the right to rustle a few beeves now and then. The Hashknife went fourteen years without getting a single conviction.

Finally, in desperation, the company hired Burt Mossman, a rawhide-tough cowboy from New Mexico, to run the outfit. Mossman's life story reads like something out of a Louis L'Amour western. He had a stocky build on a 5'8" frame and weighed 180 pounds. Of Scots-Irish ancestry, he was born in Illinois in 1867, the son of a Civil War hero, and by 1882 he was working as a cowboy in New Mexico.

As a young cowboy, Mossman earned a reputation in New Mexico of being a wild and restless youth with a hot temper who would fight at the drop of a hat. In spite of these dubious virtues, the youngster was known as dependable and honest. He once walked a hundred ten miles in forty-seven hours across a desert too dry for a horse, to deliver an important letter for his employer.

When he was twenty-one, Mossman was made foreman of a ranch in New Mexico that ran eight thousand head of cattle. At twenty-seven, he was manager of a big outfit in Arizona's Bloody Basin. By the time he was thirty, Mossman was superintendent of one of the

266

*Burt Mossman,
Superintendent of
Hashknife Ranch
and first Captain of
the Arizona Rangers*
Courtesy
Southwest Studies

biggest outfits in the West, the fabled Hashknife of northern Arizona.

It was at the Hashknife where Mossman gained his greatest early notoriety. Gangs of rustlers, both in the employ of the company and those who had set up maverick factories on the fringe of the ranch, had been shipping out trainloads of cattle stolen from the ranch. Up to that time, the rustlers had always been able to control jury verdicts in their favor.

Mossman didn't waste any time settling into his new role. His first day on the job, he captured three cattle thieves and tweaked the nose of Winslow's town bully. Next he fired fifty-two of eighty-four Hashknife cowboys and installed trusted cowmen as wagon bosses. In a brief time, he had the Hashknife turning a profit. A prolonged drought followed by a great blizzard finished off the outfit in 1901 when the absentee owners decided to sell out. Despite the failure of the Hashknife, Mossman earned a reputation as a formidable foe of outlaws as well as that of a smart businessman who had carved a niche for himself in Arizona history as the "man who tamed the Hashknife." However, Mossman's career in Arizona was far from over. When the Arizona Rangers were organized in 1901 to resist the rustler element that was running rampant in the territory, he was named its first captain. Many years later Burt Mossman was elected to the National Cowboy Hall of Fame in recognition of his career as a cattleman and peace officer.

The ranges of northern Arizona had filled with cattle by the mid-1880s, some estimates running as high as one and a half million head by 1891. But cattlemen, who saw no end to prosperity, crowded the ranges with more cattle than the native grasses could sustain.

In the 1890s constant enemies of all cowmen—the elements and hard times—combined to cripple the industry. Heavy rainfall in the winter of 1888-89 produced high hopes for the new decade, but then came the national depression of 1893 and with it a severe drought. Wells and natural water sources went dry. Ranchers who had been holding on to steers during the depression in the hope of getting a better price, found there was not enough feed to fatten their cattle for market. Creditors called in their notes, and cattlemen had to sell their stock at low prices in order to pay off their debts, a large number of ranchers going bankrupt.

The free-wheeling days of the great open range in northern Arizona drew to a close with the dawn of a new century. Gone were the days when large ranches enjoyed free use of government land to graze their vast herds of cattle. Newcomers moved in with legal claim to small plots under the Homestead Law, and Joseph Glidden's new-fangled contraption "unraveled the Devil's hat band," mass producing miles of barbed wire, which the settlers used to fence off their *ranchitas*; soon there were enough newcomers to gain control of county politics.

A more serious blow, however, was dealt by Mother Nature—cattlemen had overstocked the ranges for years, leaving the land in poor condition, and prolonged droughts in the 1890s brought a day of reckoning.

Although the old days of the open range have passed, big outfits have remained in northern Arizona. The introduction of purebred cattle and better range management has insured the continuation of ranching on a large scale in spite of cycles of bad weather and markets.

*Hashknife cowboys
in Holbrook*
Courtesy
Southwest Studies

Adamana (south of Interstate 40, milepost 306)

Adamana was a rail station for passengers visiting what was to become the Petrified Forest National Park during the peak of passenger trains. A small post office was established in 1896 at the ranch headquarters of Jim Cart and Adam Hanna, the latter giving the settlement its name.

Near Adamana is Flattop Site, a seasonally-occupied agricultural village that was a point of contact between Anasazi, Hohokam, and Mogollon cultures about 600 A.D. The petroglyphs, some of which were used to mark the solstice and equinox by use of sunlight passing through a crevice onto drawings, are among the best preserved in Arizona. Another prehistoric site, dating back to the thirteenth century, is Puerco Ruin. This one-story, rectangular compound had more than a hundred rooms, including three *kivas* or ceremonial chambers. The Twin Buttes Archaeological District (500-900 A.D.) was an Anasazi cluster of slab-lined, subterranean homesteads. All these sites are within the confines of the Petrified Forest National Park.

Petrified Forest National Park

Lieutenant Amiel Whipple visited this area on December 2, 1853 and wrote: "Quite a forest of petrified trees was discovered today, prostrate and partly buried in deposits of red marl. They are converted into beautiful specimens of variegated jasper. One trunk was measured ten feet in diameter, and more than a hundred feet in length."

This ancient forest that "turned to stone" after being inundated for millions of years beneath a prehistoric sea was early depleted by pilferers. Before it was made a national monument in 1906, people gathered the stones and shipped them out by carload to be polished and sold to tourists. In the 1890s a mill was erected to crush the stones into industrial grinding powder.

In 1962 the Petrified Forest was designated a national park. According to Indian legend, a trail-weary goddess cursed the area. Hungry and exhausted when she came upon the logs, she killed a rabbit and tried to make a fire, but the logs were wet and wouldn't burn. In anger she turned the logs to stone.

The "petrified forest" was formed about 170 million years ago when the area was part of a large valley that also included Utah, New Mexico, and west Texas. The Sierra Nevada range hadn't risen yet, so the valley sloped all the way to the Pacific. Giant amphibians and reptiles roamed the area. Eventually the valley filled with sediment until the large Schilderia, Woodworthia, and Araucaria trees floated into the lowlands and were buried beneath three thousand feet of soil. Mineral-laden water seeped into the trees before they decayed, the wood cells of the trees being replaced by silica, iron, manganese, copper and other minerals. During the Cretaceous period, an ocean covered this region, and during the mountain-building period, beginning about sixty million years ago, the Rocky Mountains uplifted, this area eventually rising to its present five-thousand-foot elevation. Over eons of time, wind and water erosion once again exposed the "petrified forest." Giant logs are still being exposed by erosion— some have been found in deep arroyos 250 feet beneath the earth's surface.

In 1985 the fossil remains of one of the earliest known dinosaurs was found in the Petrified Forest. At present these are the world's oldest known fossil remains.

The Painted Desert was included in the Petrified Forest National Park in 1932. The Spanish explorers with Coronado referred to the area as *El Desierto Pintado*. Dr. J. S. Newbery, with the Lieutenant Joseph C. Ives expedition crossing eastbound to explore the Colorado River in 1858, also named the area the Painted Desert.

The historic Painted Desert Inn, with its classic pueblo-style decor that includes murals by noted Hopi artist Fred Kabotie, is located at Kachina Point. It was built in 1924 and is on the National Register of Historic Places.

This stretch of brilliant multi-hued land north of the Rio Puerco and the Little Colorado River is the most spectacular in the three hundred square miles of the Painted Desert. Despite the beauty of vividly banded purple, scarlet, and pink tints, whose colors vary with changing temperature, sunlight, and air purity, cowboys refer to the place as *malpais*, or badlands. As any cow-minded person would declare, "It'd be a helluva place to try to graze cattle."

Navajo

Navajo Springs, located three miles southeast of Navajo, was a favorite watering place for those traveling between the Zuni pueblo and Horsehead Crossing (Holbrook).

Lieutenant Amiel Whipple camped here in 1853, noting that the Navajo Indians frequented the area. The "springs" were more like seeps, but the water was pure and lay in the middle of an open meadow that provided good grazing for the animals. On September 1, 1857 Lieutenant "Ned" Beale and his camel caravan came to the area and reported finding evidence of Whipple's earlier expedition.

In October 1863 Major Edward B. Willis and a party of soldiers left

Santa Fe and followed this trail to the San Francisco peaks, then on to Chino Valley, where they established the original Fort Whipple. In December Willis negotiated a treaty with three hundred Yavapai and Tonto Apaches living nearby. The treaty was soon broken, when the military escort for the gubernatorial party opened fire on the natives, killing twenty. Warfare raged between the two groups for many years.

On December 29, 1863 the first territorial gubernatorial party camped on the site in a raging snowstorm. There had been some question as to where the new line dividing Arizona and New Mexico was located, and the officials wanted to be sure they were standing on Arizona soil before holding the first ceremony. Lieutenant Colonel Francisco Chavez, who provided military escort for the group, assured them that Navajo Springs was in Arizona.

Historian Will Barnes wrote of the event in 1937, saying, "The writer knew three members of the expedition, Colonel Chavez, Louis St. James, and James D. Houck. James D. Houck was an acquaintance of over thirty-five years and often spoke of the matter.

"The day was raw and cold. Six or eight inches of snow covered the ground, the camp was muddy and uncomfortable. They were out of fresh meat and Colonel Chavez sent Houck and two or three soldiers out to kill some of the many antelope near the camp.

"They brought several back with them and after the flag raising the entire company feasted on antelope steak and drank a few rounds of champagne, provided especially for such occasions, in celebration of the establishment of the new territory of Arizona." After the ceremonies were held, Governor John C. Goodwin took the oath of office, and the territory of Arizona was formally established.

The railroad station at Navajo Springs was shortened to Navajo in 1883 when the post office was established. Five miles west of Navajo, Whipple crossed into the Rio Puerco Valley. Baldwin Möllhausen mentions Zuni Indians wearing precious stones, especially large garnets, as jewelery for their ears. In this village, the men kept a sharp eye out for precious stones, finding small rubies, emeralds, and garnets in large, cone-shaped ant hills. The stones were pea-sized or smaller because of the ants' inability to move anything larger.

Chambers

The railroad named a station Chambers in honor of Charles Chambers, who had opened a trading post several years earlier at the site. A post office opened in 1907. The name was changed to Halloysite in 1926, which came from a halloysite (bentonite clay used in the maufacture of fine china) mine located nearby, but four years later the name was changed back to Chambers. Near Chambers is Kin Tiel, a Hopi-affiliated pueblo that dates back to 1226-1276 A.D. The site is characterized by high-quality masonry and includes *kivas*, a walled spring, a plaza, and burial grounds.

Sanders

Sanders was named either for C. W. Sanders, office engineer for the Santa Fe Railroad, or for Art Saunders, proprietor of the trading post at the site. The name Sanders was already in use by the Santa Fe line, so the rail station was called Cheto, which is a Navajo word meaning "movement" and refers to the trains hauling goods and people.

Houck

According to cowboy-historian Will C. Barnes, James D. Houck was a member of the military escort traveling with the first gubernatorial party in 1863-64. However, Houck's biographer, Fran Carleson, says he didn't arrive in the Southwest until the 1870s. In 1874 Houck was employed as a mail carrier between Prescott and Fort Wingate, New Mexico. Three years later he established a trading post on the lonely road between Fort Wingate and Horsehead Crossing. At first the Navajo resented the intrusion of this white man but Houck was stubborn and tough enough to make a stand. Eventually the Indians began to come into the trading post to swap sheep and wool for the white man's merchandise, Houck accumulating a large flock of sheep in the exchange. Houck was always careful to avoid a direct confrontation with the Navajo. On one occasion, when his horses were missing, the trader locked the doors to the store and waited. A few days later some Navajo leaders appeared and wanted to know what was wrong. Houck told them the store would be reopened when his horses were returned. They went away silently, and the next day Houck's horses were back in the corral. The community grew up around Houck's trading post after the railroad arrived in 1881. A small station was built along with a water tank for the steam-driven locomotives.

During the 1880s Houck went into politics, representing Apache County in the Thirteenth Territorial Legislature, and during the late 1880s Houck was a deputy for Apache County sheriff Commodore Perry Owens. During that time he also became a major figure in the notorious Graham-Tewksbury feud in Pleasant Valley. Houck was friendly with the Tewksburys, but what really turned him against the Grahams was the murder of his brother-in-law by the Graham partisans. On August 17, 1887 Houck rode into Pleasant Valley carrying a warrant for the arrest of John Graham. Later that evening he met a lone rider whom he took to be the wanted man. As the two

272

came closer Houck discovered the other rider was John's younger brother Billy. He tried to wave the young man by, but Billy jerked out his six-shooter. In an exchange of gunfire, Billy was mortally wounded, but was able to ride home, where he died the next day. Houck later gave a terse account of the fight, telling Barnes, "We both drew at sight of one another, but I shot first and got him."

Years later Houck moved to the Salt River Valley. The large sheep outfits around Flagstaff had begun wintering their flocks in Paradise Valley, and Houck settled at Cave Creek, where he opened a shearing station and saloon. He became known during those years as the prosperous "Sheep King of Cave Creek."

A long drought in the early 1900s brought hard times to the sheep ranchers of Paradise Valley, and sheepmen began taking their flocks elsewhere. In April 1921 Houck, despondent over financial losses and old age, calmly swallowed poison, lay down, had his boots removed, and died.

Lupton

Lupton has historically been a community supported by livestock and tourism. It was named for G. W. Lupton, trainmaster at Winslow in the early 1900s. Nearby is the old Zuni-Hopi trading trail. Colonel John Washington and his troops passed this way during the Navajo Campaign in 1864. The original settlement was located at the mouth of Helena Cayon, probably named by construction crews for the railroad about 1879.

Early tourists
Courtesy Arizona
Historical Foundation

In 1951 this all-star baseball team of players from Williams, Ash Fork, and Seligman competed in the state's first Little League tournament. these northern Arizona all-stars lost the title game to Prescott, 2-0. Author Trimble, middle rou left end, played right field.

Interstate 40
Flagstaff to Topock
(westbound)

Bellemont

Bellemont was named in September 1882 in honor of Belle Smith, daughter of F. W. Smith, general superintendent of the Atlantic & Pacific Railroad. Before that it was called Volunteer, apparently because a company of volunteer militia camped at the site sometime about 1863.

In 1876 a New Englander named Walter J. Hill drove a small flock of sheep into Volunteer Spring, and in ten years he was reputed to have the biggest sheep outfit in Arizona. Hill was later wounded in a gunfight near the Colorado River while pursuing a gang of outlaws, and after his recovery, he moved to California.

Volunteer Spring was also a way stop for the first territorial officials in 1864 on their way to establish the first Capital of Arizona. Apparently the spring at Volunteer was a bonanza for the railroad as two large water tanks were built there to supply trains, saving an eighty-mile trip to the Little Colorado River for refills.

During World War II the Navajo Ordinance Depot (now the Navajo Army Depot) at Bellemont was one of the nation's largest munitions storage sites for the Pacific Theater.

Parks

Parks, at the foot of Sitgreaves Mountain, has had several names. The first was Rhoades, when a post office was established on March 28, 1898. The name didn't last long for that same day someone crossed out Rhoades and scribbled in "Maine," honoring the famous battleship sunk in Havana Harbor a month earlier.

The original site of Parks, Maine, or Rhoades was next to the railroad tracks. Typically, a boxcar was used as the first depot and post office. The settlement's main industry was a sawmill. When the highway came through, the town was moved two miles east, and the store at the original site kept the name "Old Maine." A man named Parks opened a store at the new site and began handling the mail.

In 1907 the postal department finally realized that local citizens had opted for Maine over Rhoades and officially changed the name. No sooner had this occurred than it was discovered that another town was already using the name "Maine," so this time it was the postal department's turn to cross out the proposed name and insert their choice of Parks, in honor of the storekeeper.

Williams

The picturesque town of Williams takes its name from Bill Williams Mountain, which towers above the town and provides as beautiful a setting for a community as can be found in America. It's fitting for this place name to honor old Bill Williams, the "greatest fur trapper of 'em all."

Old Bill was as colorful a man as any who ever forked a horse or mule and headed toward the setting sun. To those who knew the tireless old mountainman, he'd always seemed old and eccentric. His drunken sprees around Taos set a standard others tried to match but never could. He rode alone into forbidding hostile Indian country where no white man had dared venture and always returned, his pack mules laden with "hairy bank-notes."

Bill was a tall, skinny redhead, with a high-pitched voice, his body battle-scarred and worn. He had amazing durability even in his later

Bill Williams Street in Williams, 1917
Courtesy
Southwest Studies

years. He was known to run all day with six traps on his back and never break into a sweat. He had a peculiar way of walking—it has been described as closely resembling a stagger, and he never walked in a straight line. He fired his long-barreled "Kicking Betsy" with unerring accuracy in what was described as a "double wobble." Since he couldn't hold the gun steady for long, Bill just let it wobble or sway back and forth past his target until the sights crossed the mark—then he squeezed the trigger and never missed! He used to bet on himself in shooting matches, at $100 a shot. On horseback he wore his stirrups so short his knees bobbed just beneath his chin. He leaned forward in the saddle resembling a hunchback on horseback. All these eccentricities enhanced his reputation as the Old West's most unforgettable character.

George Frederick Ruxton, an English adventurer who toured the West in the 1840s wrote this colorful description of Old Bill:

> Williams always rode ahead, his body bent over his saddlehorn, across which rested a long, heavy rifle, his keen gray eyes peering from under the slouched brim of a flexible felt-hat, black and shining with grease. His buckskin hunting shirt, bedaubed until it had the appearance of polished leather, hung in folds over his bony carcass; his nether extremities being clothed in pantaloons of the same material. . . . The old coon's face was sharp and thin, a long nose and chin hob-nobbing each other; and his head was always bent forward giving him the appearance of being hump-backed. He appeared to look neither to the right nor left, but, in fact, his little twinkling eye was everywhere. He looked at no one he was addressing, always seeming to be thinking of something else than the subject of his discourse, speaking in a whining, thin, cracked voice. . . . His character was well-known. Acquainted with every inch of the Far West, and with all the Indian tribes who inhabited it, he never failed to outwit his Red enemies, and generally made his appearance at the rendezvous, from his solitary expeditions, with galore of beaver when numerous bands of trappers dropped in on foot, having been despoiled of their packs and animals by the very Indians through the midst of whom old Williams had contrived to pass unseen and unmolested. On occasions when he had been in company with others and attacked by Indians, Bill invariably fought manfully—but always "on his own hook."

They called him "Old Solitaire" for his lonesome ways (Bill wasn't that lonesome—he always seemed to have an Indian woman waiting somewhere). He spoke several Indian dialects and was more at home among the friendly tribes than he was with his own people. It was said he came west as a missionary to the Osage Indians, but they converted him. He married an Osage wife, who died after bearing two daughters, so Bill headed for the mountains and became a trapper.

Bill had more lives than a cat, surviving one hair-raising adventure after another. His luck finally ran out after thirty years in the wilds, when on March 14, 1849 a war party of Utes killed him and Dr. Ben Kern near the headwaters of the Rio Grande in southern Colorado.

Two years later, Richard Kern, a brother of Dr. Kern, was traveling with the Sitgreaves expedition in northern Arizona. Kern took copious notes of everything he saw and heard on the journey. During the trip, Kern and guide Antoine Leroux applied the name "Bill Williams" to the 9,200-foot mountain range that provides the picturesque setting for the town of Williams. Later the pair honored Bill again by giving his name to the river that has its headwaters near Hackberry. Later the river was changed to Big Sandy, and today becomes the Bill Williams River after it joins the Santa Maria River near Alamo Lake, on its journey to the Colorado River.

Like the Indians, with whom they sometimes lived and sometimes fought, mountainmen like Old Bill were "Nature's Children." They loved the outdoors, hated fences and restrictions, respected grizzlies and rivers, and rode anything that "wore hair."

Storing the knowledge of this vast *terra incognita* in their heads, the mountainmen guided the storied Army Corps of Topographical Engineers on their historic surveys along the thirty-second and thirty-fifth parallels during the 1850s. These trails, or paths of least resistance, later became the trails that led immigrants to the promised land in what has been called the greatest mass migration of greenhorns since the children of Israel set out in search of Caanan.

In the late 1870s the Southern Pacific and Santa Fe railroads began stretching their rails along these same trails. In the twentieth century, thanks to Henry Ford's Model T, US 80 and Route 66 introduced millions of Americans to the natural beauty and rich Hispanic and native cultures of Arizona. Today, those nostalgic highways have been replaced by modern freeways. The ghosts of Antoine Leroux, Pauline Weaver, Tom Fitzpatrick, Ewing Young, Joe Walker, Bill Williams, and others must gape in amazement when they look out across a land that has changed so much in such a short time. It is ironic that those who sought sanctuary from the civilization they generally despised would be the ones who opened trails that brought that same society to what has been described as the most remote and unharnessed sanctuary of freedom man has ever known.

The first settlers arrived in Williams in 1876, about the same time as Flagstaff was settled. Like most communities in this area, nothing much happened until the railroad arrived in 1881.

Good help was hard to find in those new towns. In 1881 the Prescott *Miner* reported: "Geo. Rich, Deputy Sheriff of Williams, has resigned his position. He is supposed to have had a hand in the robbery lately committed upon the wholesale liquor firm of W. E. Talbott & Co., of Williams."

After the railroad arrived on September 1, 1882 the most important industries in the mountain settlement were cattle and lumber. That same month the *Miner* reported: "Williams, on the A. & P. R. R., 56 miles from Prescott, has 100 houses, and over 500 population. Flagstaff has about the same number."

The Santa Fe laid track from Williams to the Grand Canyon and began hauling tourists to the South Rim in 1901, giving Williams a legitimate claim to being the "Gateway to the Grand Canyon." Every so often, some Johnny-come-lately tour promoter moves into Flagstaff and tries to borrow the slogan but the residents of Williams are quick to set the record straight.

The opening of Route 66 in the mid-1920s turned Williams into a first-class tourist town, as millions of cars passed through annually. The Federal Highway Act, passed in 1944, called for the building of a national system of highways; included were Route 66 along the thirty-fifth parallel and US 80 along the old Gila Trail on the thirty-second parallel. In 1956 Congress approved the Interstate Defense System, which required the federal government to pay 90% of the construction costs of multiple-lane freeways.

Doomsdayers claimed that the completion of these freeways would sound the death knoll of towns like Williams, the last town on Route 66 (from Chicago to Los Angeles) to be bypassed by the Interstate; however, Williams continues to prosper. The re-opening of passenger service to the Grand Canyon and the absence of eighteen-wheelers barreling through town should restore tourism to the peak days of Route 66 and the time when the Atchison, Topeka, and Santa Fe passenger trains made regular stops at Williams.

Pine Springs

In the halcyon days of Route 66, Pine Springs gave eastbound travelers their first glimpse of Arizona's spectacular high country. The whole town consisted of a gas station and some cabins. Nestled at the foot of Bill Williams Mountain and surrounded by stately pine trees, Pine Springs was a welcome sight to those who had just crossed wind-swept plateaus and the searing desert west of Needles, California.

Mormon colonists from Utah arrived here in 1876, building a sawmill and calling the settlement Millville. Six years later they sold out and moved their lumber operation to Pinedale, along the Mogollon Rim near Showlow.

278

Just west of Pine Springs is Ash Fork Hill. The freeway, built in the mid-1950s, cuts its way down the long grade toward Ash Fork. It is not much of a hill any more, but old timers can recall when Route 66 was a two-lane road that hugged the east side of the canyon and made a hairpin turn at the bottom. It was a motorist's nightmare during heavy snow but provided teenagers a thrill a minute when the pavement was dry.

A few miles west of Pine Springs, and a mile or so north of the freeway, is the world's largest steel dam. Appropriately named Steel Dam, it was built by the Santa Fe as a water storage dam for the steam locomotives at the Ash Fork "filling station."

Ash Fork

The town of Ash Fork lies slumbering on gentle, juniper-studded slopes fifteen miles west of Bill Williams Mountain. People have passed through here since prehistoric times, and evidence of primitive civilizations is scattered throughout the region. In the late 1500s Spanish conquistadores found rich minerals in the mountains a few miles to the south. When this area was part of the Republic of Mexico, traders and fur trappers like Ewing Young, Antoine Leroux, Bill Williams, and Kit Carson went through today's Ash Fork on their way from Santa Fe to Los Angeles. A few years later Captain Lorenzo Sitgreaves and Lieutenant Amiel W. Whipple, of the United States Army Corps of Topographical Engineers, surveyed routes along the thirty-fifth parallel for a proposed railroad. About that same time, the area witnessed one of the Old West's most unusual events as camels trudged across northern Arizona on their way to California. The trail became known as the Beale Camel Road, named in honor of the man who headed the project, Lieutenant Edward F. Beale, and the beasts of burden that made the experiment a success.

The Civil War delayed the proposed transcontinental railroad line across northern Arizona for several years, but when laying track across the region began in 1881, northern Arizona was never the

Ash Fork in the 1920s. Note approaching locomotive. Bill Williams Mountain is in the background.
Courtesy
Southwest Studies

Ash Fork in the mid-1920s in the heyday of Route 66, before bypassing by Interstate 40. Main Street, or Lewis Avenue is a quiet avenue once again.
Courtesy
Southwest Studies

same again. Towns mushroomed and industries flourished along the Atlantic & Pacific (later Santa Fe) line, linking cultural groups as well as geographic regions.

Constructing a railroad across the rugged Southwest was no easy task. The builders were warned when they started that they would be stopped by perpendicular grades, rugged canyons, and gorges, where mountain goats closed their eyes and walked sideways. The right of way, it was said, ran from nothing, through nowhere, to no place.

In spite of dire predictions, the line was built—with switchbacks and lazy loops offering more kinks than a cheap lariat. The lines doubled back on themselves so much that it took thirty miles of track to go ten. "It's the world's crookedest railroad," someone deadpanned.

Pioneer railroaders built lines that couldn't be built right up the backs of forbidding mountains that couldn't be climbed, cutting and gouging all the way; and when the tracks were finally laid and the first steam engines puffed into town belching smoke and steam, people began an enduring love affair with the iron horse. These iron-bellied locomotives pulling their freight and passenger cars quickly replaced the durable burro and the mule-driven freight wagons as the most efficient and economic way of transporting ore, merchandise, and people. The trains were dubbed affectionately "peanut roasters" and "coffee pots," and it was said a reasonably sober fat lady could outdistance one in a downhill race.

For the most part, the raw, raucous towns that sprang up along the railroad were peopled at first by boisterous, devil-may-care reprobates. It was said there were three hundred fifty saloons along two hundred miles of track. In time reputable citizens arrived, set up businesses, and insisted on some semblance of law and order. Ash Fork, during one turbulent period, organized a vigilante committee to rid the town of unwanted miscreants. This committee, with a mythical "Judge Lynch" presiding and threatening to administer suspended sentences (from the limb of an ash tree), was usually warning enough to cause even the most incorrigible rascal to leave town in a hurry.

The coming of the railroad opened up the cattle business in northern Arizona. Big outfits like the Ash Fork Livestock Company ran thousands of head on the vast, grass-carpeted ranges south and west of Ash Fork. Stockyards were built on the outskirts of town, and cattle were shipped off to market from the new railroad.

In 1907 an elegant Harvey House named the Escalante (after a Franciscan friar-explorer) was built in Ash Fork. Fred Harvey's restaurants and hotels along the Santa Fe line brought a touch of elegance and a cuisine never before seen or tasted in the Southwest. Citizens of Prescott thought nothing of driving fifty miles over a rough dirt road to dine at the Escalante. Cowboys rode forty miles just to sample the hot biscuits and catch a friendly smile from a young Harvey Girl. Since women were scarce in these parts, single men hoped for more than just a smile from these young and refined ladies hired by Fred Harvey to work as waitresses. Few of them remained single for long.

Although most of the towns along the Santa Fe line took their names from people associated with the railroad, Ash Fork is an exception. In the early days freighters hauling ore from Jerome traveled along Ash Creek. In 1882 when the railroad reached the site of Ash Fork, freighting companies pressured the railroad for a more convenient location than the one at Williams. In October 1882 the railroad established a new siding eighteen miles west of Williams. The original townsite and stage depot was located near Ash Canyon, where three southerly flowing forks of Ash Creek joined. Soon both passengers and freight were being unloaded at what was then being called Ash Fork.

On April 21, 1883 a post office was established in the town, and two years later Wells Fargo opened a station. Thomas Cooper Lewis came to Ash Fork in 1882 and opened a grocery store next to the railroad tracks. Five generations later, some of Lewis's descendants still call Ash Fork home, something rare in the annals of Arizona's history. The original townsite, located on the north side of the tracks, burned in 1893 and the present town was rebuilt on the south side.

A line running south to Prescott was finished in 1893. Because of its many curves and switchbacks, it was quickly dubbed the "Peavine." Two years later the line reached Phoenix—no easy task. Since the company couldn't afford to move the mountains, it decided to go around them. "It may take all day to get to Phoenix," someone said, "but you could see the country two or three times on one trip."

This linking of Phoenix to Ash Fork in 1895 is regarded by most historians as marking the closing of the frontier period of Arizona's history.

Water, the arid Southwest's most precious commodity, was always scarce in Ash Fork. The porous lava that lies just beneath the surface in that region does not hold water. During the 1960s drillers finally hit water and a small well was able to provide an adequate supply. In the past, water had been hauled by train from Del Rio Springs in Chino Valley, thirty miles to the south.

When Henry Ford's Model T coughed and sputtered into Arizona, the demand for better roads increased. During the 1920s horse-drawn scrapers, gravel lorries, and steamrollers, cut, gouged, leveled, and packed their way across northern Arizona to construct what was to become known as Route 66. During the Great Depression of the 1930s thousands of displaced midwestern families loaded their belongings in the family jalopy and headed for California. These tin-lizzie travelers took with them little more than hope and memories of places they would never see again. On top of their Model T's were a few sticks of furniture tied down with cotton rope, and flapping on the door handles was a desert water bag. They were the twentieth century's version of gold-seeking argonauts bound for the Promised Land.

The advent of the automobile added a new dimension to the economy of towns like Ash Fork. Motels, cafes, and gas stations sprang up to accommodate a restless America; and during the 1940s a booming wartime economy dealt an end to the Great Depression. Troop trains made regular stops in Ash Fork, adding to the community's prosperity.

Fading prosperity came in the 1950s when the Santa Fe moved its main line ten miles north of town. Ironically this new line closely followed the old Beale camel survey of a hundred years earlier. Furthermore, a tragic fire swept through the old business district in the mid-1970s, wiping out historic buildings. What many considered the fatal blow, however, came in 1979 when the new Interstate 40 bypassed the town.

Towns like Ash Fork don't die easily, and the freeway bypass may be a blessing in disguise—eighteen-wheel trucks and out-of-state cars no longer come speeding through town at full throttle. The town's few businessmen now believe the worst is over and that the outlook is bright—travelers on Interstate 40 still have to stop for gas, food, and lodging.

Ash Fork has become a quiet community again, reminiscent of bygone days when people weren't in such a hurry. The mountain setting is a refreshing change from the crowded streets of Phoenix.

Here the spirit can soar, free from the confusion and noise of city life.

The heart of a community, however, lies not in its beautiful scenery or historic and picturesque buildings, but in its people. The citizens of Ash Fork display a sense of public spiritedness that seems lost in today's urban sprawl. As in many small communities, there is a grassroots warmth and hospitality that is more reminiscent of an earlier lifestyle. One gets the feeling that in places like Ash Fork lies the real heart of America.

Seligman

Seligman was established a few years later than the other communities stretched out along the Santa Fe line. It takes its name from a pair of New York bankers. The Seligman brothers had helped bankroll and were part owners of the spectacular Aztec Land and Cattle Company (the Hashknife outfit). They were also large stockholders in the Atlantic & Pacific Railroad.

In 1886 a fast-talking promoter named Tom Bullock convinced Prescottonians to raise $300,000 to construct a seventy-five-mile line connecting Prescott with the main line at Seligman, which was known in those days as Prescott Junction. The spur had to reach Prescott no later than midnight, December 31, or Bullock would face a stiff $1,000-a-mile penalty. No sooner had construction begun than beer was being shipped to mobile tent saloons set up along the way. Cattlemen, angry over the railroad right of way across their grazing lands, had their cowboys stampede cattle through the construction sites.

Meanwhile, in Prescott the betting was heavy as to whether Bullock would meet his deadline. Some residents tried to hedge their bets by vandalizing the line: some tried to blow up a caboose; another group of reprobates set fire to a trestle, but a rain storm doused the flames; other vandals tried to derail a work train by removing a section of track—the plot failed when the engine ran aground before reaching the damaged area.

Working feverishly against the clock, tracklayers reached Granite Dells with a day to go, and by the evening of the final day, they were only two miles from Prescott. At one point odds against the Bullock line reaching Prescott on time had gone as high as twenty to one, and some who had taken those odds tried to insure their bets by putting on work clothes and joining the construction gang as volunteers. The Bullock line reached Prescott with five minutes to spare. Throngs cheered as the territorial governor, Conrad Zulick, drove a gilded spike into a tie painted red, white, and blue. Prescott, at last, was linked by rail to the outside world.

The Prescott and Central Arizona Railroad was the epitome of inefficiency. During the first months of operation, the line had only two small sixteen-ton steam engines, the "F. A. Tritle" and the "Hassayampa." Since the turntable at Prescott was not ready, the trains had to make the trip to Seligman (Prescott Junction) in reverse. Incidentally, the entire railroad consisted of those two engines, four boxcars, and one passenger car, all "pre-owned." The fare was ten cents a mile, but customers could usually get a better deal buying a ticket from one of the crew. Trains made unscheduled stops along the way such as for a "beer call" at Del Rio Springs and hunting trips in Chino Valley.

By 1891 local people were beginning to call Bullock's line the "Mudball Express." After a heavy rain, the rails would sag, tossing the little locomotives into mud holes. The poor old "Hassayampa" once lay on its side for three weeks before someone got around to hauling it out.

After the Prescott and Central Arizona Railroad went out of business, Bullock promptly tore up the track and moved his railroad to California. Taxpayers and investors had lost several million dollars, thanks to this smooth-talking huckster.

A new line, called the Peavine because of its numerous curves, began construction at Ash Fork, twenty-four miles east, in January 1892. The Peavine was built on higher ground, thus avoiding the costly and frequent washouts of Bullock's railroad; furthermore, it was run more efficiently. The Peavine reached Prescott in 1893, and two years later the first locomotive steamed into Phoenix. With the completion of the line, Prescott Junction became Seligman and the Arizona & Pacific Railroad moved its western terminus and its roundhouse from Williams to Seligman. In May 1897 the Arizona & Pacific reorganized and two months later officially became the Santa Fe Railroad.

The railroad and tourist traffic along Route 66 were Seligman's main sources of economic security for the next three-quarters of a century. In the late 1970s the new Interstate 40 bypassed the town, but the most serious blow to the local economy came in February 1985 when the Santa Fe closed its operations. Seligman had been a terminal point on the line between Winslow and Needles, and dozens of railroaders had rented rooms, eaten in local cafes, and patronized other businesses in town during their layover.

Today, express trains flash through Seligman without stopping, marking the end of an era in the illustrious railroad history of the town.

Old Route 66

West of Seligman, Interstate 40 makes its first major break from old Route 66 and heads west through the Juniper Mountains toward Kingman. The old route follows "Ned" Beale's 1857 survey across Aubry Valley (Aubry is usually misspelled on maps as Aubrey Cliffs, Aubrey Valley, and Aubrey City. All three are named for the great "Skimmer of the Plains," Francois Xavier Aubry.)

Yampai

The Yampai Indians were a wandering, ragamuffin people probably related to the Hualapai tribes, but not much is known of them. They are mentioned in the reports of Sitgreaves, Whipple, and Beale, and none of the remarks concerning those Indians are complimentary. Still, they have a section house on the railroad named in their honor. Some historians believe Yampai was a misspelling of the word Yavapai by early explorers.

Peach Springs

Recorded history of Peach Springs goes all the way back to the days of that tireless Franciscan explorer Father Garcés. On June 15, 1775 he named this spring Pozos de San Basilio (St. Basil's Wells). Lieutenant "Ned" Beale and his camel entourage were the next recorded visitors, on September 17, 1858. He called it Indian Spring. There were peach trees in this area, apparently growing from pits planted by Mormons, since no mention of peach trees is made before the arrival of the Mormons.

The springs in Peach Springs Canyon provided water for the steam locomotives and a water tank and station were built at this site, and a community grew up around the station. In 1883 the town was reported to have ten saloons, but no mention is made of the number of churches or schools.

The tribal headquarters of the Hualapai Indians is located here, and is near the road leading to a village of the Havasupai Indians in the Grand Canyon.

Both of these tribes are related linguistically to the Yuman or Quechan peoples. Hualapai means "Pine Tree People," while Havasupai signifies "People of the Blue-green Water." Traditionally the Hualapai were hunters and gatherers. Their close relatives, the Havasupai, took up residence in fertile Cataract Canyon, and from the Hopi Indians, living further east, they learned to irrigate and farm crops of corn, beans, and squash. Early accounts refer to the Havasupai as Cosninos, a name given them by the Hopi and providing the place-name for Coconino County.

The original home base of the Hualapai was along the Colorado River above the Mojave villages, near the Cebat and Acquarius Mountains and the Hualapai, Sacramento, and Yavapai valleys. The Hualapais waged a brief but furious war with the United States Army in the 1860s under their great chief Wauba-Yuba. During the peace that followed, they were moved to a reservation in the malaria-infested tules along the Colorado River. After a few years they were allowed to return to their beloved home surroundings which had inspired the name "Pine Tree People."

Truxton

Lieutenant "Ned" Beale camped at a spring in this area on October 8, 1857. It was typical of early-day surveyors to apply place names along their routes. Beale, an ex-navy man, named several sites along the thirty-fifth parallel in honor of old navy friends, but most of these names were lost in time. Truxton, however, was named either for his brother Truxton or for his mother, Emily Truxton Beale.

Beale described the spring as "a beautiful one; the water pouring over rock is received in a basin of some 20 feet diameter and 8 or 10 feet deep." The party clashed with Yampai Indians, who resented the intrusion and being forced to share water with the newcomers.

In 1775 Father Garcés named today's Truxton Canyon "Arroyo de San Bernabe." In 1851 Captain Lorenzo Sitgreaves called the stream that runs through the canyon Yampai, for the local inhabitants. Later it was changed to Truxton Wash.

The Atlantic & Pacific Railroad made use of the abundant water for its steam locomotives, erecting a large pump and water tank on the site in 1883, an action that caused the Hualapai Indians to file suit in the 1920s. Today's diesel engines have eliminated the need for water, and all that remains from earlier towns are a section house and a railroad siding called Truxton. Relatively new, the present community of Truxton developed in 1951 from a gas station and cafe.

Valentine

Valentine, located about a mile from the Truxton railroad siding, is today a sub-agency for the Hualapai Indians. In 1900 six hundred sixty acres were set aside for the Hualapai, and an Indian school was built on the site. The Indian agent also served as postmaster, and the community was officially called Truxton Canyon. When the school was closed, the post office was discontinued and, according to rules, when it was re-established in 1910, a new name had to be designated—it was named Valentine, for Robert G. Valentine, Commissioner of Indians Affairs, 1908-10.

Hackberry

The spring near Hackberry is probably the same site Lieutenant Beale called Gardiner. In the 1870s prospectors found a rich vein of ore a mile and a half west of the spring. A large hackberry tree near the spring inspired the name.

A newspaper at the time mentions that the mine and settlement were named for "this tree which in summer bears an abundance of fruit . . . (and) they have named the beautiful mine with the hope that it may prove as prolific of bullion as the tree of edible berries. . . ." For a time Hackberry prospered with a population of over a hundred. The hackberry tree continued to bear fruit, but the mine eventually played out.

The Big Sandy River rises near Hackberry. In 1854 Lieutenant Amiel Whipple turned south and led his survey down the Big Sandy, which he called the Bill Williams River, following it to where it joins the Santa Maria. From there Whipple turned west and followed the Bill Williams River to where it flows into the Colorado near Parker Dam.

Interstate 40

Fort Rock

This new stretch of freeway takes a more direct route to Kingman, running close to the old Hardyville-Prescott road. William Hardy established a port on the Colorado in 1864 and grew prosperous freighting goods over a road he built to the territorial capital at Prescott. Before the arrival of the railroad, most of the freight, both military and civilian, came to Arizona by steamboat. For a time Hardyville, now buried beneath Lake Mohave, was at the head of navigation on the Colorado.

Fort Rock, a stage station (now just south of Interstate 40 near milepost 95) on Hardy's road, received its name in an unusual way. One day in 1866 stationmaster J. J. Buckman's son Thad was building a stone playhouse when a large party of Hualapai warriors attacked. Buckman and a soldier were caught outside the station when the shooting started. They jumped behind Thad's rock playhouse for protection. The defenders, both inside the station and behind the low-slung rock wall, held off more than fifty warriors for an entire day before finally driving them off. In honor of the occasion the station's name was changed to Fort Rock.

Kingman

Kingman was established as a railroad stop in 1883, on the last leg along the thirty-fifth parallel line. The locating engineer, Lewis Kingman, named the stop for himself. There is evidence to prove that Kingman was originally called "Shenfield Railroad Camp," for Conrad Shenfield, a railroad contractor who created the original townsite. Kingman, however, was the name agreed upon, and because of the railroad, it became Mohave County's most important city, being selected as county seat in 1887.

Beale Springs is located in the rugged foothills a short distance northwest of town. Lieutenant "Ned" Beale camped here during his historic camel survey in 1857 but apparently did not give his name to the site. A decade later several skirmishes with Hualapai Indians took place here, and military reports referred to the site as "Beale Station," or Beale's Springs. A military post called Camp Beale Springs was established in 1871 to deal with the warring Hualapais. When peace was restored three years later, the post was abandoned.

Trivia buffs may be happy to know that Clark Gable and Carole Lombard were married in the little Methodist church in Kingman. Although actor Andy Devine was born in Flagstaff, he was raised in Kingman and always referred to it as his hometown. The town's main street is named for Andy, considered to be one of Hollywood's greatest character actors.

As was the case with many Arizona cities, World War II had a great impact on Kingman's growth. An air force base was located at the site of today's Mohave County Airport. After the war, it became a huge storage place for surplus warplanes.

Prior to its importance as an air base, Kingman was a regular stop for early mail and passenger airlines. In 1928 Charles A. Lindbergh, the first pilot to solo the Atlantic, selected Kingman as a stop between Los Angeles and Winslow. Lindbergh was greeted by more than fifteen hundred Arizonans when he arrived on July 8, 1828 to inaugurate the new forty-eight-hour air mail service between Los Angeles and New York.

The construction of dams along the Colorado River during the first half of the twentieth century and the mining of the mineral-rich mountains of Mohave County have played a major economic role in the history of Kingman. Also, because of its strategic highway location, Kingman became an important stopover for fishermen and other water enthusiasts headed for recreational lakes such as Mohave and Mead.

Kingman has been an important motel-cafe-service station for travelers since the opening of Route 66 in the 1920s. The town also provides a stopover for residents of the greater Phoenix area on their way to and from the Las Vegas gaming tables.

The spectacular growth of Kingman since World War II illustrates the importance of being located at a strategic highway junction: to the north on US 93 are Hoover Dam and Las Vegas, and US 93 southbound goes to Phoenix; westbound Interstate 40 leads to Los Angeles; and eastbound Interstate 40 connects with every major highway system in the eastern United States.

*Oatman in the early
1900s*
Courtesy
Southwest Studies

Old Route 66
Kingman to Oatman

Since the early 1950s Route 66 (and later Interstate 40) has swung south of Kingman for twenty-five miles, skirting the south end of the Black Mountains and bending its way along Sacramento Wash, then heading west to the Colorado River at Topock, about ten miles southeast of Needles, California. The old highway went in a southwesterly direction, cutting and twisting its way through the Black Mountains and passing through the picturesque towns of Goldroad and Oatman. The old highway has a few potholes here and there, but the trip is worth the extra time and wear.

Goldroad's high point came in the early 1900s. A party of prospectors led by John Moss had first discovered gold deposits in this area in the 1860s; however, the discovery of gold in the Cerbat Mountains, twenty-five miles to the northeast, in the 1880s, created a temporary exodus as prospectors stampeded to the new-found riches. At this time Arizona experienced another gold rush in the early 1900s, when the price of gold increased dramatically.

A big strike occurred near Goldroad in 1902 when prospector Joe Jenerez's pick struck paydirt. Jenerez and the man who grubstaked him, Henry Lovin, eventually sold their claim for twenty-five thousand dollars. Lovin opened a store in what became the community of Goldroad. When a post office was established in 1903, the place was known as Acme but was changed to Goldroad three years later. By 1907 the high grade ore was starting to play out, and the mine closed soon after. The town, however, held out for several more years. The post office closed in 1925 but re-opened a dozen years later before

290

closing again in the early days of World War II. The buildings were torn down in 1949 for tax purposes. By Arizona law, property owners have to pay taxes on structures whether they are doing business or not. Unfortunately this law has caused the destruction of many important historical sites in Arizona, including the famous old Harvey House in Ash Fork in the 1970s.

Today all that remains of the once-thriving community west of Goldroad Pass are a few crumbling rock walls that used to house the miners and their families.

Oatman, a few miles west of Goldroad, had its rise to prominence about the same time as Goldroad. In 1902 Ben Taddock was riding along a trail when he saw the unmistakable glitter of yellow metal. A year later Taddock sold out to several speculators who sold the property the following year to the Vivian Mining Company. The next three years were boom times, the mine producing more than three million dollars in gold. It was during this period that Oatman came into existence. At first it was called Vivian, but in 1909 the name was changed to Oatman.

There has been some speculation that the town was named for Olive Oatman, the girl kidnapped by a war party in 1851 near Gila Bend and later traded to Mojave Indians. In 1857 Henry Grinnell was able to secure Olive's release. According to local legend, Olive was found near the site of present-day Oatman. Another account says the town was named for a half-breed Mojave Indian named John Oatman, who claimed to be the son of Olive. The town might have been named for John Oatman, but he was not related to Olive. Olive Oatman was not married nor did she have any children during her captivity.

In 1910 another rich discovery, called the Tom Reed Mine, brought new life to Oatman's economy just as the Vivian Mine was beginning to play out. In 1916 the Tom Reed Mine and the Gold Road Mine were combined into the Oatman district. Oatman remained a prosperous mining community into the 1930s before hard times came once again. The entire Oatman district is considered by mining historians to be the richest gold mining area in Arizona.

Hollywood discovered the town in the late 1930s when Clark Gable and Carole Lombard honeymooned in the old hotel in downtown Oatman. During the early 1960s a major segment of the epic movie "How the West Was Won" was filmed in Oatman. Some of the false front buildings from the movie set are still standing. Modern-day descendants of the ubiquitous desert canary, or burro, still stalk the streets of Oatman, adding to the colorful character of the town.

Interstate 40
Kingman to Topock

This stretch of highway opened in the 1950s to by-pass treacherous Oatman Pass in the Black Mountains; the road hugs the old 1883 railroad line.

The town of Yucca has been here since 1905 when a post office was established, the town taking its name from the prolific growth of yucca in the area. The yucca is not a cactus but is a member of the lily family. The particular species growing in these parts is commonly called the Joshua tree. It grows to a height of fifteen to thirty-five feet and has a spread of up to twenty feet. The Joshua tree differs from the many species of yucca plants because of its short, pointed leaves growing in dense clusters and with a definite trunk crowned by numerous "hairy" branches. The plants thrive in the high desert of this area, where the annual rainfall is eight to ten inches. The Joshua tree was named by the Mormons because it appeared to be raising its arms in supplication to heaven, resembling the Biblical Joshua. At the height of gold mining in the mountains nearby, the thick trunks of the Joshua trees were used for fuel.

Broad-leaf yuccas, a different species, are frequently seen along the state's highways and are commonly referred to as soapweed, Spanish bayonet, or amole; newcomers often confuse the broad-leaf yucca with agave or century plant, and with sotol and beargrass. The yucca was one of the most important plants for prehistoric people and Native Americans. The tough fibers of the leaf were used for making rope, matting, sandals, basketry, and coarse cloth. The buds, flowers, and flower stalks were used for food; the fruits were eaten raw or roasted; and the seeds were ground into meal. The roots of the plant were (and still are) used as soap, especially as a hair shampoo.

Topock

The original name for Topock was Needles, after the pointed mountains on the California side of the Colorado River. Lieutenant Amiel W. Whipple applied the name Needles after noting the three peaks rising prominently from a large range of rocky hills.

When the railroad reached this point in 1883 a post office was established on the Arizona side and called Needles. At the same time a settlement developed on the California side of the river and was also named Needles; therefore, late in 1883 Needles, Arizona, changed its name to Powell. A post office was established under that name but was discontinued three years later. Other names used at the site were Red Rock and Red Crossing. By 1891 a new community was established and was being called Mellon, honoring the legendary Colorado steamboat skipper, Captain Jack Mellon.

In 1903 a post office was opened at Mellon but was closed six years later due to dwindling population. By 1915 the community had enough citizens to re-apply for a post office. Residents preferred Needles, but by this time the Californians had a prior claim. Since the railroad was calling the place Topock, the postal authorities followed suit. Nobody seems to know the origin of the name Topock, although it could be a corruption of a Mojave word.

Interstate 15 to Littlefield

Littlefield

Daniel Bonelli was a native of Switzerland and one of those who made the first ox-train trip to Utah with Brigham Young. In 1864, he was asked by the church to build a ferry crossing on the Colorado River near the mouth of the Virgin River. The industrious entrepreneur also established a prosperous freighting business, salt mine, and farm, building a sturdy stone house for his family. After his death, Bonelli was buried on a mesa overlooking the ferry. During the 1930s as the waters of Lake Mead began to innundate the river crossing, his body was taken to Kingman for reburial.

A year before moving to the river crossing, Bonelli settled at Littlefield, giving this community bragging rights as the first in Arizona of Anglo-American origin. That same year floods washed out his place, forcing him to move on. Other floods along the Virgin River in later years forced new arrivals to move elsewhere. During the mid-1870s a group of Mormons arrived and established small farms which, of course, had "little fields."

There have been several explanations of how Virgin River, Basin, and Canyon were named, a logical one being that the first explorers considered this area to be virgin country. During his search for a road to California in 1776, Franciscan padre Silvestre Escalante called it the Rio Virgin. A half century later famed explorer Jedediah Smith passed along this river valley in search of a route to California. In this small party was a man named Thomas Virgen. Virgen was later killed by Mojaves near Needles, and it is said the place is named for him and Virgin is an incorrect spelling. The Paiute Indians, who lived there for centuries and knew the river better than anyone, called it *Pah-Roose*, meaning "very muddy stream."

US Alternate 89
Fredonia to Bitter Springs
Arizona Strip County (see also Arizona 389)

Jacob Lake

Jacob Lake is named for the legendary Mormon explorer Jacob Hamblin. Hamblin, known as the "Buckskin Missionary," explored much of northern Arizona from the 1850s to the 1870s, searching for sites for prospective Mormon colonies. He was also the first American missionary to go among the Hopis and Navajos. During the 1850s he crossed the Colorado River at the Crossing of the Fathers, now buried beneath Lake Powell, on his way to the Hopi mesas. Hamblin was the first white to follow this route since Fathers Escalante and Dominguez in 1776.

In 1869 Hamblin helped guide the famous John Wesley Powell expedition in the area north of the Grand Canyon. He also helped Powell negotiate a treaty with the local Shivwits Indians who earlier had killed three members of the expedition. In 1871 Powell and Hamblin went to Fort Defiance and worked out a treaty with the Navajo over the rustling of Mormon cattle in southern Utah. In 1871 Hamblin moved his family to the Springerville area. He died in 1886 and was buried at Alpine.

House Rock

While seeking shelter from a storm, a party of Mormon travelers found several large slabs of sandstone butted together to create an alpine-like roof. Some clever person had scratched "House Rock Hotel" on the side with a piece of charcoal, and the name stuck. A few miles south of House Rock, a herd of buffalo roams. Back in 1905 Uncle Jim Owen, a long-time warden of the Kaibab National Forest, brought eight buffalo (bison) to this area. The herd multiplied rapidly on the grassy plateau, and twenty-six years later he sold it to the government for $10,000. Owen was also a celebrated hunter and guide, earning as much as $500 a day leading parties in this region.

In the early 1900s Arizona's native elk (wapiti) became extinct. During Teddy Roosevelt's administration a small herd was imported and, like the bison, continue to thrive on the vast, remote ranges of

Cliff Dweller Springs

Located along the Hamblin Road, Cliff Dweller Springs takes its name from the prehistoric sites found nearby.

Vermillion Cliffs

Byrd H. Granger, in her informative book *X Marks the Place*, credits this name to John Wesley Powell, who wrote poetically:

> I look back and see the morning sun shining in splendor on their painted faces; the solient angles are on fire and the retreating angles are buried in shade, and I gaze on them until my vision dreams and the cliffs appear on a long bank of purple cliffs plowed from the horizon high into the heavens.

Marble Canyon

John Wesley Powell, the Grand Canyon explorer, is responsible for many place names in this region. As the tiny boats were passing through the deep chasm, Powell looked up at the titanic cliffs and, believing them to be marble, applied the name Marble Canyon. The river along this stretch is fraught with whirling rapids and swift currents, giving river runners, then and now, a thrill a minute.

In 1925 the United States Geological Survey officially named this canyon Marble Gorge. The name was changed to Marble Canyon in 1961 and eight years later was made a national monument.

Lee's Ferry

A few miles north of Marble Canyon is Lee's Ferry, the noted river crossing on the Hamblin Road to Utah. In 1864 Jacob Hamblin made his crossing at the confluence of the Paria and the Colorado rivers.

John Doyle Lee arrived here in 1871. He was a fugitive from justice and figured this area was about as good a place to hide as any. Major John Wesley Powell passed through on his second Grand Canyon expedition with an extra boat, which he gave to Lee, who converted it into a ferryboat.

John Lee was an early convert to the Mormon Church, joining in 1838. During the Mexican War, Brigham Young sent him to collect, on behalf of the Church, wages due members of the Mormon Battalion. A few years later, Lee, who had risen to prominence in the Church, was living in southern Utah near one of the immigrant trails to California. Some of the travelers passing through were old adversaries from Missouri, where much bloodshed had taken place a de-

Lee's Ferry
Courtesy
Southwest Studies

cade or so earlier. One thing led to another, and on September 11, 1857 Lee and some other Mormons organized a Paiute Indian attack on a wagon train. The seige lasted four days before the Mormons offered the immigrants refuge if they would lay down their arms. As soon as the immigrants had placed themselves in custody, a signal was given, and a hundred forty immigrants were slaughtered in cold blood. The only survivors were seventeen children, too young to bear witness against the perpetrators.

When word of the massacre became known, there was a vindictive uproar against the Mormons and a demand to bring those responsible to justice. The Church hierarchy determined that John Lee should be the one to answer charges. Lee claimed he had taken orders from Salt Lake City, then headed for the hills as a fugitive.

United States marshals finally caught up with him at Lee's Ferry in 1874. At his trial Lee insisted he was being made a scapegoat, a defense many historians still believe. He was found guilty and sentenced to die by a firing squad at Mountain Meadows, the site of the massacre. On March 2, 1877 Lee sat patiently on his coffin while a marshal read his death warrant. Several of his sons were present but were kept at a safe distance as lawmen feared they might attempt a daring rescue. Then Lee stood in his coffin and faced the five riflemen. "I am ready to die," he said, "I trust in God. I have no fear. Death has no terror." Five shots rang out, and a dark chapter in Mormon history was thought to have ended; for seventy-three years the Church denied any involvement. In 1950, Juanita Brooks, a Mormon, wrote a controversial book about the incident called *The Mountain Meadows Massacre*. Largely because of her book and pressure from Lee's many descendants (he had nineteen wives), the Church in 1961 reinstated him to full membership.

Lee's old ferry operation continued until 1928 when a bridge was built across the Colorado River.

US 89
Flagstaff to Page

Sunset Crater

Sunset Crater was the last volcano to erupt in Arizona. In the fall of 1064 the mountain blew its top, sending billowing smoke and ashes into the atmosphere and a molasses-like lava flow toward the Little Colorado River to the north. A heavy layer of ash was left on the land around the volcano, a condition that created an ideal situation for dry farming. Soon Indians we call the Sinagua were raising crops; however, about 1300 A.D. a long drought, coupled with dry winds that blew the ash-mulch and top soil away, caused the natives to abandon their farms.

The crater was named by John Wesley Powell, who led an expedition through the Grand Canyon in 1869. The cone rises a thousand feet above the plain and has a crater four hundred feet deep. The ice caves located near the cinder cone provide bone-chilling cold air and ice year round. During the 1880s saloonkeepers in Flagstaff used to haul blocks of ice into town to keep the customers' drinks cold in the summer.

The site was made a national monument in 1930.

Deadman Wash and Deadman Flat

Place names like Deadman Wash and Deadman Flat are usually self-explanatory, but in this case there is an interesting twist: when a trapper heading across the plains lost his horse he chased the animal until he was too weary to go further, finally shooting the horse in desperation. Despondent over what he had done, he sat down next to the animal and shot himself. This story was pieced together by trackers who later discovered the two bodies.

Wupatki National Monument

Wupatki National Monument, created in 1924, is not just a city standing alone. Some eight hundred sites have been located here. Wupatki, the largest, is a Hopi word meaning "tall house." Here on the windswept plains with the towering San Francisco peaks for a backdrop, the prehistoric Sinagua people farmed for about a century. During its cultural peak in the twelfth century, Wupatki had a population of about three hundred people occupying more than a hundred rooms. A large "amphitheater," unique in the Southwest, is a circular depression that may have been an adaptation of the kiva, a ceremonial chamber used by the cliff-dwelling Anasazi in the Four Corners area. Although prehistoric ball courts are common in Mexico, few have been found this far north. The oval-shaped depression was used by the Sinagua for a game played with a rubber ball and a small hoop.

The San Francisco peaks are of religious importance to both the Hopi and Navajo today. They are home to the Hopi Kachinas and mark the sacred southwest boundary of Dinetah, or Navajoland.

Not far away is Sipapu Canyon, where a pair of caverns three hundred feet deep run along a fault. The Sipapu is the wondrous opening through which the Hopi believe their ancestors arrived into this world from the underworld.

Babbitt's C O Bar chuck wagon
Courtesy
Southwest Studies

Spider Web

Spider Web Ranch, nearly hidden by the rolling hills, is winter headquarters for the historic Babbitt brothers' CO Bar Ranch. Here, each February, cowpunchers start the slow process of gathering the mahogany-coated Herefords for the drive toward summer ranges located north and west of the San Francisco peaks. During the summer months, the punchers and their families take up residence at one of a number of houses on the ranch and keep an eye on the cows until fall, when they are headed back to the Spider Web.

Cameron

In 1911 Hubert Richardson named Cameron for Senator Ralph Cameron. Cameron came to Flagstaff from Boston in 1882, working as a lumberman and sawmill employee. An ambitious man, he later was a cattle and sheepman, co-owned a general store, and was involved in mining. Around the turn of the century, Cameron ran the Bright Angel Camp at the South Rim of the Grand Canyon.

In 1891 he became the first sheriff of the newly-created Coconino County. He was the last territorial delegate to Washington prior to statehood in 1912. In 1920, he ran for the United States Senate and was elected for one term. The first bridge across the Little Colorado River was erected in 1911, and at the same time a trading post was established and run by a Navajo named Scott Preston. A small community grew up around the store; in 1917 a post office was established and named for the pioneer northern Arizonan.

Moenave

The ubiquitous Father Francisco Tomás Garcés visited the natives in this area in 1776. In 1871 Jacob Hamblin, the Mormon "Buckskin missionary," established a colony in the spring-fed area at the foot of the Moenave cliffs. The remains of the buildings erected by Mormon colonists are still in evidence.

During the 1870s Hamblin blazed a trail through here from Utah to the Little Colorado River Valley, opening the Mormon colonial period in Arizona. Since Arizona did not have a temple until 1926, young Mormon couples desiring to solemnize their wedding vows had to travel back up this trail to St. George, Utah. The exhausting journey took weeks and covered several hundred miles. Despite the hardships, most couples, in later years, considered the experience among their most cherished memories. This road was affectionately referred to by Mormons as the Honeymoon Trail.

Pioneers had an unresistible urge to stop at places along their way and carve their names as a lasting testament to *paso por aquí*. The travelers on the Oregon Trail climbed on top of Independence Rock in Wyoming and scribbled their names. Westward bound wagons reached this site around July 4, which inspired the place name. Spanish conquistadores dating back to the 1500s scratched their names on the sedimentary stone cliff at El Morro, near Zuni, New Mexico. Arizona pioneers had their inscription rock in Moenave Wash—dozens of names and dates going back to the 1870s are carved in the reddish-hued sandstone along the wash.

Page

Page was a planned community developed in the 1960s by the Bureau of Reclamation to provide headquarters and to house workers for the building of Glen Canyon Dam. The town was destined for success as a gateway to the Glen Canyon and Lake Powell national recreation areas. Page was named for John C. Page, who spent many years planning and developing the proposed dam site while serving as Commissioner of Reclamation. Page died in 1955, several years before the actual construction of the dam was begun.

Glen Canyon was named by Major John Wesley Powell in 1869. Powell, awestruck by the beautiful red rock chasm, noted the "carved walls, royal arches, glens, alcove gulches, mounts and monuments; from which of these features shall we select a name? We decide to call it Glen Canyon." During the late 1900s prospectors looked for gold in Glen Canyon. Before the waters of Lake Powell filled it, the canyon was one of America's most beautiful and primitive areas.

A short distance east of Page was the *Vados de los Padres*, or Crossing of the Fathers. The historic crossing, now buried beneath the azure waters of Lake Powell, was made by Fathers Escalante and Dominguez in 1776. The padres were trying to locate a route from Santa Fe to San Gabriel (Los Angeles). Their journey took them from Santa Fe, across the Four Corners area, and northwest to the area around Salt Lake before they decided to turn back. Discouraged and disappointed, they headed south, crossing the Colorado River at this site. They went to the Hopi mesas, where the outfit was resupplied and then returned to Santa Fe. The route to Los Angeles, called the Old Spanish Trail, would not be set for a half century after the brave padres made their futile attempt.

Navajo Indians
Courtesy Northern Arizona Pioneers' Historical Society

US 160
Tuba City to Four Corners

Tuba City

In 1878 the Mormon apostle Erastus Snow established a town two miles north of the village of Moenkopi. He named the town Tuba, or Toova, for the Hopi headman at Oraibi of the third mesa. Tuba had re-established the farm community of Moenkopi several years earlier as a colony for Oraibi. When the Navajo reservation was enlarged, the Mormon settlers, finding themselves on land set aside for the Indians, were forced to sell out to the federal government.

For years the Babbitt Brothers Trading Company ran a store in Tuba City. For religious reasons, the Navajos will not enter a place where someone has died. If a death occurs in a hogan, the dwelling will be abandoned. One day an elderly Navajo man suddenly went into death throes inside the Babbitt Trading Post. Realizing the business would go into an immediate depression if the man were to die on the premises, the quick-thinking manager gently assisted the man outside and placed him under a shade tree to die. Several years ago, a trading post near Leupp was finally abandoned after a Navajo died—other Indians simply refused to go into the place.

Tonalea and Red Lake

Tonalea is a two-part Navajo word meaning "water—where it sinks in," and it is a well deserved name. There used to be a dry pond here, and when it did rain enough to fill the pond, the water just "drifted on down, out of sight." Today a storage dam provides a more reliable source of water.

The Anasazi

This is the land of the Anasazi, perhaps the best known of all prehistoric cultures. They ranged throughout this part of the Southwest and had an advanced culture by any standards. They built cities in the canyons throughout the Four Corners area. Some of the most interesting sites in Arizona are at Navajo National Monument (junction of Arizona 564 and US 160). Betatakin Ruin, perched under an impervious dome at the bottom of an eight hundred-foot canyon, exemplifies the ingenius Anasazi method of using solar energy. Cities in these cliffs were always located with a southern exposure so that during the cold winters the pueblos would face sunlight most of the day. During the summer, the sun would be directly overhead, and the residents would have plenty of shade. Great ceremonial kivas, or undergrond ceremonial centers, have been found at these sites, indicating a rich and advanced culture. This people's mastery of agriculture allowed them to store great amounts of surplus food in large baskets or pottery containers. The Anasazi ruins at Chaco Canyon also demonstrate the Indians' ability to construct multi-storied buildings of masonry without the benefit of mortar.

The Anasazi culture was prehistoric, but can be traced back two thousand years. Modern man has given them the name Anasazi, a Navajo word meaning "ancient ones."

The earliest Anasazi were called "basketmakers"; they lived in this area from about 100 A.D. to 700 A.D. Unlike the familiar cliff dwellers, these people lived in caves. Physically they were slender and short with long, narrow faces. Since hair was used to make ropes, the women were called upon to sacrifice their hair; the men also plucked out most of their hair but left enough for a long braid down the back.

About 700 A.D. the Anasazi settled down at one location. They left the caves and moved into pit houses, adapting to the arid high plateau and learning to cultivate corn, beans, and squash. Living at a permanent site, they discarded the baskets, which are more indigenous to a nomadic people, and began creating durable pottery for household and ceremonial use. Three kinds of pottery have been found at this site: black and white, polychrome, and corrugated. Some time during this period, the bow and arrow replaced the *atlatl* (a device used like an extended throwing arm for adding velocity to a spear).

About 1150 A.D. the Anasazi began moving into their dwellings in the cliffs. It has been speculated that this was a defensive measure as protection from nomadic tribes. Agriculture flourished with the building of small diversion dams. Betatakin and Keet Seel are the prominent sites in this area. The former had two hundred rooms while the latter had three hundred fifty and is the largest and best preserved cliff dwelling in Arizona.

About 1400 A.D. the Anasazi culture went into a decline. Villages were gradually abandoned, and by the time the Spanish arrived in the sixteenth century, the Anasazi appeared to have mysteriously vanished. Archeologists generally believe the Anasazi in this part of Arizona moved to the south end of Black Mesa and settled in what is today Hopiland.

Kayenta

John and Louisa Wetherill established a trading post here in 1910. A nearby spring surrounded by a glue-like clay soil caused livestock

Navajo marines saved thousands of American lives during World War II. They developed a code for transmitting battle plans that kept English-speaking Japanese intelligence officers in a constant state of confusion.
Courtesy USMC

to bog down in the mire. The Navajo word "kayenta" means "a natural game pit," and like most Indian place names, it is aptly descriptive. John Wetherill was a member of the famed family that discovered the Mesa Verde cliff dwellings in southwest Colorado.

Mexican Water

At some past time, the Navajos observed wells dug by Mexicans, naming the wells "Mexicans dug shallow-wells." The translation from Navajo to English proved too difficult for Americans, so they took the Navajo meaning and altered it to Mexican Water.

The Mormons, passing this way as early as 1879, forded Walker Creek at this point. The creek was not named for famed mountain man Joe Walker, but for Captain John G. Walker, who crossed it in 1859 while on an expedition across the Colorado Plateau. The bridge nearby was built in 1939.

Teec Nos Pos

The trading post at Teec Nos Pos has been the community gathering place since about 1910.

Four Corners

Four Corners aptly fits the old description of going from "no place through nothing to no where." Its real significance lies in the fact that it is the only place in the United States where four states come together.

Babbitt Brothers wagons were a major part of Reservation life. Courtesy Southwest Studies

US 163
Monument Valley

Monument Valley

The limited amount of historical information about this area is more than offset by the massive stone monuments shaped by the hand of nature. The date of the Navajos' arrival in Monument Valley is uncertain. It is known that during Kit Carson's Navajo Campaign in the early 1860s, many Navajos escaped the "long walk" to the Bosque Redondo Reservation in New Mexico and found refuge among these majestic sandstone skyscrapers.

In 1923 Harry and Mike Goulding opened a trading post on the Arizona-Utah border, taking an active interest in helping the Navajo make the sometimes painful adjustment to the twentieth century. They not only purchased wool blankets and the arts and crafts created by Navajo artists but settled disputes among the people and acted as a liaison between the Indians and the federal government.

During the Great Depression, times were hard and unemployment was high. Harry took it on himself to entice the movie industry to come to Monument Valley to film westerns, which had been filmed in the hills around Hollywood. Harry knew that if he could convince director John Ford to take a first-hand look at the remote, but spectacular sandstone monoliths that could serve as a backdrop for the westerns, Monument Valley would sell itself, and he also knew the movies would employ large numbers of Indians at good pay. Harry then headed for Hollywood with spectacular pictures of Monument Valley. When it became difficult to get an appointment with the famed director, the persistent trader hauled his bedroll into the receptionist's office and spread it out on the floor, saying firmly that he would camp there until Mr. Ford was available. This tactic proved successful: Ford looked at the photos, made a trip to Monument Valley, and the rest is history. The setting was perfect for *Stagecoach*, the epic western Ford was planning. A young actor named Marion Morrison, also known as John Wayne, would play the Ringo Kid—his first starring role in a major motion picture which became an American classic, partly because of Monument Valley.

At last the world knew about Monument Valley. Hundreds of Navajos were cast as Apache, Cheyenne, Comanche, and other Indians, but they always spoke Navajo. Noted for their keen sense of humor, some of the lines would never have made it past a Navajo-speaking censor. When the film played theaters in Flagstaff and Winslow, whites were bewildered by the conduct of Navajos in the audience who snickered during some of the more serious dialogue between natives and hardriding heroes.

Harry Goulding died in 1981, but area residents will never forget him and Mike and all they did for the Navajo of Monument Valley.

US 180 and Arizona 64
Flagstaff and Williams
to the Grand Canyon

The Grand Canyon

Despite its grandeur, the canyon was a well kept secret until 1903, when the Santa Fe Railroad built a line right to the south rim. Up to then, a few entrepreneurs in the Flagstaff and Williams area hauled tourists over a rough wagon road to the Bright Angel Trail, but only the most durable of visitors dared make the trek.

Several mining ventures by prominent Arizonans including Buckey O'Neill took place before the canyon became a national park in 1918. Until 1902 the village of Grand Canyon was known as Hance's Tank, for Captain John Hance, noted trailblazer and yarnspinner in the area.

The first white men to view the canyon were those of Coronado's expedition in 1540. Hopi Indians told one of Coronado's officers, Pedro de Tovar, about a great river, possibly the fabled Northwest Passage, several days' journey west of their villages. Soon after Garcia Lopez de Cardenas led an exploring party to the canyon's edge. They attempted, in vain, to climb down. Certain that it was not the passage to India, they returned to the main group at Zuni. Others came to the canyon over the next three hundred years but were not particularly impressed.

In 1776 Father Garcés descended into the canyon and visited the Havasupi Indians. Trapper James Ohio Pattie saw it in 1826, but was not overawed by its majestic beauty. Pattie described the ". . . horrible mountains, which cage it up, as to deprive all human beings of the ability to descend its banks and make use of its waters."

In 1854 Lieutenant Amiel Whipple explored the Little Colorado down to where it empties into the Colorado. In 1857 Lieutenant Joseph C. Ives, after his journey up the Colorado on the tiny steamer *Explorer*, headed overland for New Mexico. On the way he viewed the big canyon from the south rim and appraised it as altogether valueless. "It can be approached only from the south and after entering it there is nothing to do but leave. Ours has been the first and will doubtless be the last party of whites to visit this profitless locality." Dr. John S. Newberry, traveling with Ives, would be the first of many scientists to study first-hand this wonder of wonders.

The first to actually explore the Grand Canyon was the courageous, one-armed Civil War veteran John Wesley Powell. He made another attempt in 1871-72 and provided the aptly descriptive name.

Ellsworth and Emory Kolb, a pair of daring, enterprising brothers from Pennsylvania, came to Ralph Cameron's Bright Angel Camp in 1902 and took jobs. A year later they set up a photography studio to take pictures of tourists. Emory later estimated that they took one

El Tovar at the turn of the century
Courtesy Grand Canyon National Park

and a half million pictures of tourists, and in 1911 they took the first motion pictures of the canyon.

The El Tovar, perched precariously on the south rim is truly Arizona's "grandest hotel." The long, rambling inn, built with massive Kaibab limestone blocks and durable split logs from Oregon, was originally a playground for the rich during those days when only the affluent could afford to travel. The hotel opened in 1905, with Fred Harvey as concessionaire for the National Park Service. The station and hotel were located on ten acres of land granted to the railroad by the federal government. The architectural design was a blend of a Swiss chalet and a Scandinavian hunting lodge.

The construction work was done by Hopi Indians, and the hotel cost a quarter of a million dollars to build. (A recent renovation cost five million dollars.) Its spacious lobby was a social gathering place for kings, queens, and presidents. Despite the presence of high society, the prices were reasonable. A room with bath went for from six to eight dollars. One without a bath could be had for four dollars, including the "million dollar view." Breakfast and lunch cost a dollar, and a full course dinner served by one of the famous Harvey Girls cost a dollar and a half. The hotel, in all aspects, epitomized the Fred Harvey elegance.

Arizona's and the world's grandest natural architectural masterpiece is the Grand Canyon. Words alone cannot describe it, although many writers have tried. Viewers have gone to extremes in their descriptions. The first missionary to come on the great abyss noted that such a wonder of wonders could only have been created by the Almighty. A cynical voyager remarked that it was nothing but a bad case of soil erosion. A humble cowboy who lived in and loved the outdoors and enjoyed a unique kinship with nature described it another way, noting ruefully, "It'd be a helluva place to lose a cow."

One of the reasons Arizona's storytellers tend to exaggerate so much when waxing eloquent about our wonders is that they have trouble finding enough words to describe the grandeur, so they keep on adding superlatives until they believe they have said enough.

For years, jokers have debated whether or not the thirsty climate, relentless heat, and uninterrupted sunshine have anything to do with the dry humor and penchant for exaggeration of Arizona's storytellers.

The Grand Canyon's first promoter was Captain John Hance, a lean, weather-beaten man, with a long, angular face, wirey whiskers, and deep blue, mirthful eyes that crinkled up into a permanent squint from years of gazing into the far distance. Hance built the first trail down into the canyon from Bright Angel and promoted and led the

*John Hance,
everyday
yarnspinner and
trailguide at Grand
Canyon*
Courtesy
Northern Arizona Pioneers'
Historical Society

first tourist excursions down. He was also the first to provide accommodations for tourists on the south rim in 1886. His debut as a windjammer began one day when he was pointing out the sights to a group of tourists at the canyon's edge.

"Mr. Hance," a lady from the East interrupted, "how did you lose your finger?"

Hance stopped talking for a moment and looked down at his hand, pretending to notice the missing finger for the first time. "Why, Ma'am," he replied, straight-faced, "I musta plumb wore that thing plumb off pointin' at all the beautiful scenery around here."

The crowd loved it, and a legend was born. From that time on, until his death in 1919, John Hance provided lying and lodging, pulling the legs of thousands of tenderfeet. Since his proteges came from all parts of the globe, Hance's fame spread far and wide. You had not really been to the canyon unless you had heard a Captain Hance whopper.

Hance's windy style was geared to lead the listener down the paths of plausibility—the stories always began logically enough—until suddenly listeners found they had reached conclusions that were obviously impossible; however, many visitors went away convinced that the Captain's tales were entirely within the realm of possibility, such as his story of warriors near the south rim.

Hance was riding his trusty old white horse, Darby, along the south rim one bright day, when he noticed a band of hostile Indians riding towards him. He turned and started to go back but noticed another band coming from that direction. He turned toward the south and spotted yet another party riding hard. There was only one way left— across the canyon. He gave old Darby a running start, putting the spurs to him, and the great white horse gave a mighty leap. They had nearly reached the other side when Darby began to lose altitude. Down, down they fell, thousands of feet into the canyon. At the last moment they were saved when Darby pulled up short at his master's call of "Whoa," just three feet above the canyon floor.

Hance's windies didn't always fall on appreciative ears. One day a stranger asked him how the deer hunting was around the south rim. "Why, it's jest fine," Hance replied; "I went out and killed three all by myself jest this morning."

"That's wonderful!" the stranger exclaimed. "Do you know who I am?"

"No, I don't," Hance admitted.

"Why, I'm the game warden, and it looks like you've been breaking a few game laws."

"Do you know who I am?" snorted the old windjammer.

"No, I don't," the game warden replied.

"Well, I'm the biggest damned liar in these parts."

Captain Hance spent the last forty years of his life sharing whoppers with visitors to the canyon. Nobody knew for sure just how old he was. A newspaper listed his age as eighty-four when he died in 1919. Voting records showed him to be sixty-four in 1906 and only sixty in 1908, a net loss of four years in two years' time.

Arizona 67
Jacob Lake to North Rim

Explorer John Wesley Powell believed the Paiute Indians called this area Kai-vav-wi (pronounced Kaibab), or "Mountains lying down." Old maps refer to it as either Kaibab or "Bucksin," the latter a Paiute word for "deer." Later the spelling of Bucksin was changed to Buckskin and refers to the nearby mountains.

North Rim

The first tourist facility here was called Wylie Way Camp. In 1926 a post office opened and took the name Kaibab. In 1947 the National Park Service changed it to North Rim, the term referring to all the Grand Canyon country north of the Colorado River. Because of heavy snow, the roads are closed in the winter as of 1985.

*William J. Flake,
member of National
Cowboy Hall of
Fame, at the age of
93 and still able to
fork a horse*
Courtesy Arizona
State Library

Arizona 77
Showlow to Holbrook

Shumway

Charles Shumway, who settled here in 1881 and the man for whom the community is named, is said to have been the first Mormon to cross to the west side of the Mississippi River. During the 1840s he was one of the original one hundred forty-three colonists to travel west to the Great Salt Lake with Brigham Young.

Taylor

In 1878 after the five Mormon dams built along the Little Colorado River washed out, a number of colonists decided to relocate along the more gentle waters of Silver Creek. The first name chosen was Walker, but this was turned down because there was already a Walker in the Prescott area. They then named the settlement for John Taylor, an early Mormon leader who suffered a gunshot wound at the same time Joseph Smith was murdered by a mob at Nauvoo, Illinois, in 1844. Taylor later became a president of the Mormon church.

Snowflake

Martha Summerhayes passed through here with her infant son on an arduous wagon trip in 1875. In her book she mentions Jim Stinson as having a ranch at this site. In 1878 Stinson sold out to William J. Flake and moved to Pleasant Valley, where he would become a major figure in the feud between the Tewksburys and Grahams. Late that same year a Mormon apostle, Erastus Snow, arrived with a party of colonists from the Little Colorado River area—the river had gone on a rampage and wiped out their tiny community. A townsite was selected at Flake's ranch, and the name honored the two founders. The town was large enough to be the county seat for Apache County from 1879 to 1881. In 1895 the western half of the county seceded and created Navajo County.

US 191
Chambers to Mexican Water

This one hundred fifty-mile stretch of open highway passes through places with curious sounding descriptive names like Wide Ruins, Klagetoh, Beautiful Valley, Ventana Mesa, Chinle, Many Farms, and Rock Point.

Wide Ruins

The Navajo meaning for this area translates to either "Wide Rock" or "Pueblo House" and refers to a prehistoric pueblo dating back to the thirteenth century.

Klagetoh

A prehistoric ruin dating back to 1100 A.D. is located near here. Klagetoh is a Navajo word for "water going into the ground," which describes all the country of this area.

Beautiful Valley

The first whites passing through here named this area—a few good rains turn it into a beautiful valley.

Ventana Mesa

Ventana is a Spanish word for "window" and a number of "hole-in-the-rock foundations" gave the place its name.

Chinle

Chinle is best known as the gateway to the spectacular Canyon de Chelly. The name in Navajo means "the place where it flows from the canyon," a name that fits the community's setting at the mouth of the canyon.

In 1864 Colonel Kit Carson held a parley with the Navajos near here that ended a long war with the whites. Carson had been ordered to conduct a war of extermination against the Navajos, but he chose to starve them into submission. Following a relentless campaign in Canyons de Chelly and del Muerto, more than eight thousand Navajo surrendered and were taken on the famous "long walk" to the Pecos River Reservation in New Mexico.

The first trading post was established in a tent in 1882, and the government school opened in 1910.

Many Farms

One cannot find a more descriptive place name this side of Kansas. The first Americans arrived and saw the many Navajo farms that gave the community its name.

Henry Chee Dodge, last chief and first tribe Chairman of the Navajo Nation
Courtesy
Southwest Studies

Arizona 260
Payson to Eagar

Star Valley

The history of Star Valley goes back to 1878, when John Starr had a mine in the area. Andrew and Sam Johnson moved in that year and named it for him.

As Arizona 260 winds and climbs its way toward the top of precipitous Mogollon Rim, it passes other small towns like Kohls Ranch and Christopher Creek. Kohls Ranch, a relative newcomer, established a post office in 1939 for residents and summer refugees escaping the heat of the Phoenix area. Isadore Christopher started ranching here in the early 1880s. In July 1882 Apache renegades from Cibicue (see Fort Apache, Arizona 73) made a sweep through this area while Christopher was away and set fire to several log cabins. He had recently killed a bear and tacked the hide up on the wall to cure; when the soldiers arrived and saw the charred bearskin on a burned-out cabin wall, they thought poor, old Isadore had been skinned and hung out to dry. According to local legend, they held a brief but somber ceremony, then buried the rancher's "hide."

Farther up the rim is Woods Canyon, named for Jack Woods, a sheepman in the area during the 1880s. Western writer Zane Grey had a hunting lodge near here that was restored in recent years and today is a fine museum. It pays tribute to the area where Grey produced some of his best works, including *To The Last Man*, a fictionalized account of the Pleasant Valley War, and *Under The Tonto Rim*. Canyon Point, at the top of the rim, presents a panoramic birds-eye view of Pleasant Valley, scene of a bloody feud in the 1880s (see Young, Arizona 288).

Heber and Overgaard

Heber was settled in the early 1800s by Mormon colonists unhappy with the capricious Little Colorado River farther north. Here John Scarlett found a reliable source of water and named the place either for Heber C. Kimball or for Heber J. Grant—both were patriarchs in the Mormon Church. Overgaard, up the road about three miles from Heber, takes its name from a family living in the area during the late 1940s, when a post office was established.

Clay Springs and Pinedale

Clay Springs and Pinedale are quiet, rural communities on what used to be one of the backroads. The highway between Overgaard and Showlow was not paved until the mid-1970s. Up to then few tourists drove through here. Clay Springs is named for some springs that emerge from a clay bank. Pinedale goes back to 1879, when Niels Mortenson settled here. For a time it was named after him. Another name was Percheron in honor of Mortenson's breeding stallion, but when the post office was established in 1888, Pinedale was the name agreed on. A few miles south of Pinedale are the remains of a lumber camp and sawmill called Standard. From 1924 to 1938 the small community even had a post office. Further down Arizona 260 Linden takes its name from the species of tree known for its large cordate leaves. When the Mormons first arrived in 1878, they called the place Juniper, but five years later settled on the present name.

Lakeside and Pinetop

When the Mormons dammed Showlow Creek in the 1880s, a lake was created, and they changed their settlement's name from Fairview to Lakeside. Pinetop, a short distance down the road, was not named for the lofty trees that abound, but for a tall, bushy-headed saloonkeeper named Walt Rigney. The saloon was operated originally by Johnny Phipps, in the 1880s. It became a favorite watering hole for the black cavalry troopers stationed at Fort Apache. When Phipps died in 1890, Bill Penrod took over, and for a time the saloon

Martha Summerhayes, army bride who came to Arizona in 1874 by steamboat. Later she wrote a classic book, Vanished Arizona, *about her adventures.*
Courtesy
Southwest Studies

was called Penrod; however, the soldiers insisted on calling the place Pinetop for the lanky barkeeper, and in 1895 the post office officially named it Pinetop. Hon-Dah is located at the junction of Arizona 73 and 260 and is a gateway to the White Mountains, its name coming from the Apache word for "welcome."

The old Cooley Ranch was located just south of the junction at Hon-Dah. Corydon E. Cooley was a scout for General George Crook during the Apache Wars. He maintained a ranch that was a favorite resting place for soldiers traveling from Fort Apache along the Crook Military Road to Fort Verde. Cooley had several Apache wives and enough kids to start his own public school. Martha Summehayes stayed at the ranch briefly in 1874 and made these observations:

> Towards night we made camp at Cooley's ranch, and slept inside, on the floor. Cooley was interpreter and scout, and although he was a white man, he had married a young Indian girl, the daughter of one of the chiefs and was known as a squaw man. There seemed to be two Indian girls at his ranch; they were both tidy and good-looking, and they prepared us a most appetizing supper.
>
> The ranch had spaces for windows, covered with thin unbleached muslin (or *manta*, as it is always called out there), glass windows being then too great a luxury in that remote place. There were some partitions inside the ranch, but no doors; and, of course, no floors except adobe. Several half-breed children, nearly naked, stood and gazed at us as we prepared for rest. This was interesting and picturesque from many standpoints perhaps, but it did not tend to make me sleepy. I lay gazing into the fire which was smouldering in the corner, and finally I said, in a whisper, "Jack, which do you think is Cooley's wife?"
>
> "I don't know," answered this cross and tired man; and then added, "both of 'em, I guess."

Now this was too awful, but I knew he did not intend for me to ask any more questions. I had a difficult time, in those days, reconciling what I saw with what I had been taught was right, and I had to sort over my ideas and deep-rooted prejudices a good many times."

McNary

The McNary Lumber Company started operations here in 1924 and also started a sawmill town, naming it after the owner, James G. McNary. McNary, a company town, had a peak population of nearly 2,000 in 1950. When a fire destroyed the sawmill in 1979, Southwest Forest Industries didn't rebuild. The once-booming sawmill town decayed quickly. By 1980 the population dwindled to fewer than 500. Vandals have destroyed many of the old, wooden dwellings, and one of these days McNary will likely join that list of Arizona ghost towns.

Soon after James McNary and his partner William Cody started lumbering in this area, Cody transported 800 workers from his operation in Louisiana. Most of these employees were black and segregation between the races was strictly enforced. For many years McNary was separated along racial lines—the blacks lived in the "Quarters" near the sawmill and the whites on the "Hill."

Back in 1879 Oscar and Alfred Cluff harvested wild hay here and sold it to the government at Fort Apache. The place was known at the time as Cluff's Cienega. (*Cienega* is a Spanish word for "marsh" or "boggy area.") A post office was established in 1919 and named Cooley for noted scout Corydon E. Cooley, who had died two years earlier.

Big Cienega

A few miles west of the junction to Greer is a small, round-top mountain cluttered with a few scattered remnants of a ski area known as Big Cienega. Prior to the construction of the modern facility at Sunrise, Big Cienega's gentle slopes offered the only skiing in the White Mountains.

Junction of Arizona 260 and 373

A few miles south of Arizona 260, at Arizona 373, is Greer. This beautiful, lush valley near the headwaters of the Little Colorado River used to be called Lee Valley. Mormons from Utah, including Willard Lee, arrived here in 1879. Americus Vespucius Greer joined the community and provided its name. The naming of offspring after famous people seems to have run in the Greer family—his twin brother was named Christopher Columbus Greer.

Eagar

The Eagar brothers, John, Joe,, and William, homesteaded here in 1878. Although nine members of the Snider gang were killed near the Eagar cemetery, this Mormon community has had a tranquil history. Its residents were hard working people of the soil not given to the wilder pursuits of life, even though their community was close to the rough-and-tumble town of Springerville.

Moencopi, a Hopi farm village
Courtesy
Southwest Studies

Arizona 264
Tuba City to Window Rock

Moencopi

In 1870 Chief Tuba, or Toovi, village leader at Oraibi, established a farming settlement along Moencopi Wash so the people on Third Mesa would have a good place to irrigate their crops. Moencopi, a Hopi word that means "place of the running water," is the only Hopi pueblo with a reliable resource of water for farming. Hopi Indians, long known for their ability as distance runners, used to jog from Oraibi to Moenkopi, a distance of sixty-two miles, to tend their crops. The community has the dubious distinction of being located on the Navajo Reservation.

Moencopi is believed to have been occupied by Hopis during earlier times. Evidence indicates that Juan de Oñate was here in 1604 and Father Garcés in 1776. Also, a party of American mountain men under Joe Meek reputedly ransacked the place in the 1820s.

In 1879 the Hopi allowed John W. Young to establish a Mormon colony and woolen mill using native labor, but the enterprise had a short life. Believing the Native Americans to be descendants of the "lost tribes of Israel," the Mormons attempted to assist and maintain friendly relations with all Indian tribes. They were not always successful but on the whole their efforts stand as a record they can be proud of.

Old Oraibi sitting on top of Third Mesa has been occupied since about 1100 A.D. and is considered by many to be the oldest continuously inhabited village in America. It was the largest of the pueblos until 1906, when the so-called "hostiles" and "friendlies" had a falling out. The leaders of the two factions had the traditional shoving match, and the loser and his followers moved out, settling at Hotevilla. It was a hard year for the losers, and a few decided to return to Oraibi. The returnees were refused permission to re-enter, so in 1907 they established the community of Bacabi.

The correct name for Arizona's only Pueblo Indians is Hopitu, meaning the "peaceful people." A collection of many groups, they are believed to be descended from the prehistoric Anasazi culture. It is said that each new arrival had to demonstrate some contribution before being accepted into the tribe; thus, the Hopi are a "melting pot" of different peoples. Although they are generally peaceful, the Hopi fiercely resisted attempts by the Franciscan missionaries to Christianize them during the 1600s. The Spanish soldiers and priests at Hopiland were all murdered during the Great Pueblo Revolt of 1680. Since that time, Catholics have not been allowed to build churches on the mesas. Other church groups have found the going rough, but this has been due to their own lack of consideration. In 1901 a Mennonite church was built on the mesa near Oraibi without village consent. The church was struck by lightning not once, but twice!

The first whites to visit Hopiland were soldiers from Coronado's expedition in 1540 during his quest for the mythical Seven Cities of Gold. Zuni Indians told the Spaniards of "seven villages to the northwest." Hoping those villages might be the golden cities or Cibola, Coronado sent Pedro de Tovar to investigate. Tovar's mounted troops easily overran the Hopi footsoldiers, and a tenuous peace was established. He called the place Tusayan. In their pursuit of treasure other Spanish explorers, including Espejo, Farfan, and Oñate, all visited the mesas in the late 1500s. The Franciscans established the first mission in Hopiland in 1629. Hopi leaders resisted this intrusion, but it was not until the Great Revolt in 1680 that the Spanish were driven out. Four priests were killed and the church destroyed. Beams from the church were used to construct a new kiva at Oraibi, still in use today.

Left, Walpi on First Mesa Courtesy U.S. Department of Interior
Right, Old Oraibi on Third Mesa. Hopi men are emerging from an underground ceremonial kiva. Courtesy Southwest Studies

The Hopi villages have a complicated, interwoven social structure. Like the city-states of ancient Greece, each village is a separate power. Each individual has a particular responsibility, and each clan is designated for particular duties. The clan system is much stronger among the Hopi than among other Pueblo peoples. They are a matrilineal society, and although a man marries and lives with his wife near her clan, he still has responsibility to his own clan mother—or his "real home." Women own the home, gardens, and pueblo furnishings, while men take care of herding, farming, and activities away from the village.

Most of the villages in Hopiland are perched on top of three barren, limestone-colored mesas that extend out on the south end of Black Mesa. Whites number the mesas first, second and third, moving right to left, while the Hopi number left to right. Second Mesa is the only one that doesn't have to concern itself with numbering. Kivas, or underground ceremonial chambers, can be seen in all the villages and are characterized by long ladder-poles extending upward through a hole in the roof. Religion is a seven-day-a-week affair with the Hopi, and most of the ritual is concerned with crops. Corn is symbolic and the most important commodity. Ceremonies begin in January and last until the crops are harvested in the late summer. Today these celebrations are usually held on weekends to accommodate Hopi living off the reservation.

The well known masked kachinas are actually represented in three ways. The first is the doll that tourists are fond of collecting. The purpose of the dolls is to teach youngsters to become familiar with the Hopi religion. The second representation occurs when men dress as kachinas and perform ceremonial rites in the plazas and kivas. The third way represents the spiritual kachinas, who reside high in the San Francisco peaks but who visit the village periodically, bringing gifts to the people; however, not all kachinas are benevolent. Some are ogres who handle discipline. There is even a kachina called "Navajo girl" to provide comic relief at the expense of long-time Hopi adversaries.

Perhaps the most famous Hopi of all was Louis Tewanima, the "happy Hopi from Shongopovi." Tewanima was one of America's greatest distance runners. He received his early training chasing jackrabbits, and just for sport he used to run sixty-seven miles along what is today's Arizona 87 to Winslow to watch the trains; then he'd run back home again—all in the same day.

Tewanima attended school at the famous Carlisle Indian School in Pennsylvania with Jim Thorpe. In the 1908 Olympics at London, he finished ninth in the marathon. In 1912 he won the silver medal in the 10,000-meter run at Stockholm, a record not matched by an American until another Native American, Billy Mills, won the gold in 1964.

Tewanima died in a fall in 1969, at the age of ninety-two. Going home from a ceremony on a dark night, he took a wrong turn at Second Mesa and fell seventy feet to his death. It is worth noting that when the Arizona Sports Hall of Fame was created, the first athlete selected was Louis Tewanima.

Keams Canyon

Keams Canyon is named for Thomas V. Keams, an Englishman who established a trading post here in 1872. Keams rode with Colonel Kit Carson during the Navajo Campaign in 1864. A government school was located at Keams Canyon in 1886, as was a Hopi agency three years later. The canyon is the seat of tribal government for Hopiland.

Not far south of Keams Canyon, on the windswept Jeddito Mesa, are the ancient ruins of Awatovi. Franciscan padres came here and tried to re-establish a mission after the Pueblo Revolt of 1680. The people of Oraibi were so enraged they decided to destroy the pueblo. The attack caught the people of Awatovi by surprise. The men were trapped when the kiva was set afire. The surviving women and children were resettled with clans on the mesas, and Awatovi was never rebuilt.

Hopi-Navajo Land Dispute

Sometime during the late 1700s the Navajo began encroaching on the vast stretches of territory surrounding the mesas. These lands had been used for hundreds of years by the Hopi for hunting, sheep grazing, herding, and religious purposes. Because of pressure from Anglo and Mexican settlers demanding protection from the warlike Navajo, Colonel Kit Carson and his troops rounded up about eight thousand Navajo in 1864 and resettled them on a reservation in New Mexico. The attempt to relocate the Navajo was a failure, and four years later they were allowed to return to the Four Corners area, where a reservation was established. Once again, the aggressive Navajo began encroaching on Hopi lands. In 1882 the Hopi Reservation was vastly reduced to about 2.5 million acres. The Navajo tribes continued to grow, and soon they were moving onto Hopi lands again. In 1962 a federal panel took away another 1.8 million acres and declared the land to be owned jointly by the two tribes. The Hopi protested, and in 1977 the United States District Court divided the joint-use area equally. This decision called for the relocation of about sixty Hopi and three thousand Navajo. With a Navajo population in Arizona of close to eighty thousand as opposed to about seven thousand Hopi, the Navajo have historically carried more political clout, but they could only protest this latest turn of events, calling the verdict the "second long walk," while the Hopi insist it is long overdue justice.

Ganado-Hubbell Trading Post

Ganado was named by trader John Lorenzo Hubbell for his friend Ganado Mucho (many cattle), a local Navajo headman who had befriended the young man. This trading post was an important place to the Southwest tribes. Here they could have contact with the world outside. They could barter for essential items such as sugar, flour, coffee, canned goods, tobacco, and clothing. In exchange, they offered wool, sheep, silver work, and rugs. Neither side had much use for cash.

Walking into the Hubbell Trading Post is like taking a long step back in time. The long, flat-roofed building is constructed of large, salmon-hued sandstone rocks. Huge beams of ponderosa pine stretch across the ceiling and act as hangers for such former essentials as saddles and horse collars. The room is illuminated by stark light bulbs dangling at the end of an electrical cord. The inside walls are of thick plaster reminiscent of an old Spanish hacienda, and the floor is well worn hardwood.

Except for the 1920-vintage electric lights, the venerable trading post has not changed much since 1883, when it was built. During the

The immortal Jim Thorpe and Hopi legend Louis Tewanima were teammates at the famous Carlisle Indian School. Thorpe (front row, left) and Tewanima (front row, right) were both medal winners at the 1912 Olympics and combined to make Carlisle one of the top track teams in the country. The man in the suit is coach Glen "Pop" Warner, who later gained fame as a football coach.
Courtesy
Charlotte Thorpe

early days the Hubbell Trading Post was one of the most important in the Southwest, taking in a quarter of a million dollars in wool and hides alone.

Navajos still come in from time to time as they did during Don Lorenzo's day, carrying wool blankets or silver jewelry and bartering with a white trader in their native tongue. Hubbell was fluent in four languages—English, Spanish, Navajo, and Hopi. Trade goods used to be hauled in by wagon from Gallup, New Mexico, fifty-six miles away, a trip that took four days. Trucks took over the hauling chores about 1913, cutting travel time from Gallup to less than a day.

Hubbell homesteaded this piece of land before it became a part of the Navajo reservation but almost lost it when the reservation was enlarged. An Act of Congress and help from his friend Teddy Roosevelt allowed him to keep his land.

John Lorenzo Hubbell, the son of a Spanish mother and Anglo father, was born in Pajarito, New Mexico, in 1853. He came to Ganado at the age of twenty-three and remained until his death in 1930. Don Lorenzo, as he was called, was a remarkable man. He was always trying to improve the economic lot of the Indians through various ventures. One time he brought a silversmith from Mexico to teach silver working to the natives. Because he had been a victim of smallpox, he had developed an immunity to this dreaded disease that brought fear to the bravest warriors. During a smallpox epidemic, the trader awed the Navajo by treating the afflicted without contracting the disease himself.

Hubbell was never too busy to get involved in the political process. He was elected sheriff of Apache County in 1882. Later he was a member of the territorial legislature, and from 1912 to 1915 he was a state senator. He ran unsuccessfully for the United States Senate in 1914.

Hubbell was a friend of Presidents, but he was happiest at his remote trading post dealing with the people he had come to know and respect, and these feelings were reciprocated by the natives. Don Juan Lorenzo Hubbell represented the highest ideals of the Indian trader. Author Hamblin Garland called him "Lorenzo the Magnificent," and it would be difficult to find anyone who would disagree with Garland.

Window Rock, Tribal Capital of the Navajo Nation
The Athabascan Peoples, Diné

The Apache and Navajo are Arizona's only Athabascan-speaking Indians. Some anthropologists believe they came to North America about six thousand years ago, in the second of three great migrations from Asia. They arrived in the Southwest about 1350 A.D. after a long journey from Canada. It is believed that the Apaches came south by way of the Great Plains and that the Navajo came down through the Rocky Mountains on a trek that must have lasted at least four hundred years. Eventually, the Apaches broke up into separate bands. For example, the Jicarilla migrated to northern New Mexico, and the Mescalero migrated to the southern part. The Chiricahua occupied southeast Arizona, northern Mexico, and southwest New Mexico. Out on the southern plains the Lipan Apaches adopted customs and warfare techniques of Plains Indians. The Western Apaches included the Gila, Pinal, Aravaipa, Coyoteo, and Tonto.

The Navajos moved into the Four Corners area. Being more sedentary than their Apache cousins, they farmed some of the old areas previously occupied by the prehistoric Anasazi. They called themselves Diné, which meant "the People"; however, others had less kind names for these nomadic warriors. The Zuni called the more raucous ones *Apaches*, or "enemies." The rest were called *Apaches de Navahu*, or "enemies of the arroyo with the cultivated fields," shortened to Navajo. Navajoland is known in traditional Navajo as *Dinetah*, or "among the People."

According to their creation legends, the Navajo arrived on earth after passing through a progression of underworlds. The first was Black World, when the first man and woman were created. An angry god then set a fire that planted a seed, and the people climbed up the plant to the next layer or room, called Blue World. Once again a god became angry and set fire to Blue World. In the third, or Yellow World, existed two rivers, a male and a female. At this time, the four sacred mountain ranges, including Navajo Mountain and the San Francisco peaks were formed. (These mark the western boundary of Dinetah. The eastern boundaries are Mt. Taylor and the San Juans.) Spiritual forms and inner souls were also created at this time. The cunning but mischievous Coyote, a prevalent figure in native legends and lore, looked into the water and saw Water Monster's baby and took it. The monster grew angry and flooded Yellow World. The people then climbed into the fourth, or "Glittering World." Turkey was the last to escape the rising tide, the floodwaters of Third World touching his tailfeathers—that is why today the tip of a turkey's tail is white.

In Glittering World, Changing Woman was created, along with the Twins. It was their mission to make the world safe for the Navajo. They would get rid of all the monsters by turning them to stone. The massive rock monuments found throughout Navajoland today are the supposed result.

After the nomadic Navajo settled in the Four Corners area, they began to adopt such Pueblo customs as the matrilineal society, clans, origin myths, and lifestyle. Despite these adaptations, they preferred to live in a circular, dome-like hogan, a dwelling traced to their Asian heritage. For the most part, these changes and other Pueblo rituals such as sandpainting, weaving, and ceremonialism, distinguished the Navajo from the Apache, who had less contact with the Pueblo culture.

The Navajo fought a long series of wars with the Spanish, Mexicans, and finally the Americans. After their "long walk" home again in 1868, the Navajo gave up their warlike ways.

Navajo life today is changing rapidly. The desire for consumer goods is causing more people to seek wages for income. Although farming and sheep-raising are still symbolically important, fewer people are living in the traditional way. There is a wealth of coal, uranium, and gas on the reservation, and one of the greatest challenges facing the Navajo today is how to develop these resources while preserving time-honored values.

Arizona 389
Colorado City to Fredonia

Until 1958 Colorado City was called Short Creek for a stream nearby that did not run far. The town began in 1909, when a group of "unreconstructed" polygamists established a colony, calling it Millennial City. The Mormon Church had outlawed polygamy in the early 1890s as part of an agreement with the federal government to allow Utah's admittance into the Union. However, many patriarchs did not want to give up polygamy, so they moved to Short Creek, which straddled the Arizona-Utah border. It was said the living room was located in Utah and the bedroom in Arizona. Others claimed the houses were set on skids and could be dragged from Utah to Arizona or vice-versa, depending on where the heat was coming from.

Outsiders claimed that young girls were being taken into polygamous marriage against their will. Mohave County officials complained of an increasing number of women requesting welfare—many of these listed the same man as their husband. The community leaders protested these accusations and, in effect, notified all outsiders to mind their own business.

In the summer of 1953 a large force of the Arizona Highway Patrol made a surprise raid on Short Creek, rounded up the polygamists, and took them to Kingman. The women and children were taken to the Phoenix area in buses and placed in foster homes. The children moved from the nineteenth to the twentieth century overnight when they were enrolled in urban schools. Their rural customs and their clothes—the girls were still wearing long dresses—made them conspicuous. Several months later the state's case against the citizens of Short Creek fizzled, and they were allowed to go home.

Fredonia

Fredonia is another of those towns created by polygamists escaping federal prosecution in Utah. The settlement began in 1885 and was originally called Hardscramble. Noted Mormon apostle Erastus Snow suggested Fredonia—a clever combination of "free" and "donia" (Spanish for women).

Pipe Springs National Monument

Pipe Springs was a welcome sight to Jacob Hamblin and his fellow Mormons when they came here in 1852. It had the only water for sixty miles. While resting at the springs, "Gunlock Bill" Hamblin, known for his marksmanship with a rifle, wagered he could put a hole in a bandana at fifty yards. Those old rifles did not have the muzzle velocity to penetrate a limp piece of cloth at this distance, so each time he fired, the target blew aside, and the shot appeared to miss. Undaunted, Hamblin suggested that Dudley Leavitt allow him to shoot at his pipe—not while it was in Dudley's mouth of course. Leavitt placed the pipe on a rock, and "Gunlock Bill" shot the bottom out. In honor of this accomplishment, the place received its name.

The first settlers arrived in 1863 but were killed by Indians. A decade later, Mormon ranchers combined their efforts and formed the Windsor Castle Livestock Growers Association. A castle-like fort was built of huge stone blocks, in case of Indian attack. Over the years the fort, called Windsor Castle, acted as a sanctuary for polygamists escaping prosecution in Utah.

Arizona's first telegraph service was established here in 1871. Luella Stewart, a teenaged daughter of a local rancher was the first telegrapher. She later married David King Udall and moved to St. Johns. One of their sons, Levi, later became a state supreme court justice. Two grandsons, Stewart and Morris, distinguished themselves as United States Congressmen; the former was Secretary of Interior during John F. Kennedy's administration. Morris "Mo" Udall has been one of the nation's most prominent Democrats. In 1976 he made a strong bid for the party's nomination for president before losing out to Jimmy Carter.

In 1923 Pipe Springs National Monument was created.

The Arizona Strip

That part of Arizona north of the Grand Canyon and lying between the Nevada line on the west and the Colorado River on the east is considered to be some of the most remote "inhabitable" land in America. Cut off from the rest of Arizona, the Strip is more closely linked to Utah. Several times during the last century Utah tried to persuade the government in Washington to redraw the boundary lines and include the Strip as part of Utah. As an example of the distance involved, a citizen of Bundyville, located near Mount Trumbull, has to travel four hundred fourteen miles to reach the county seat at Kingman, passing through three states on the journey.

*Pipe Springs
National Monument*
Courtesy
Southwest Studies

IV Central Mountains

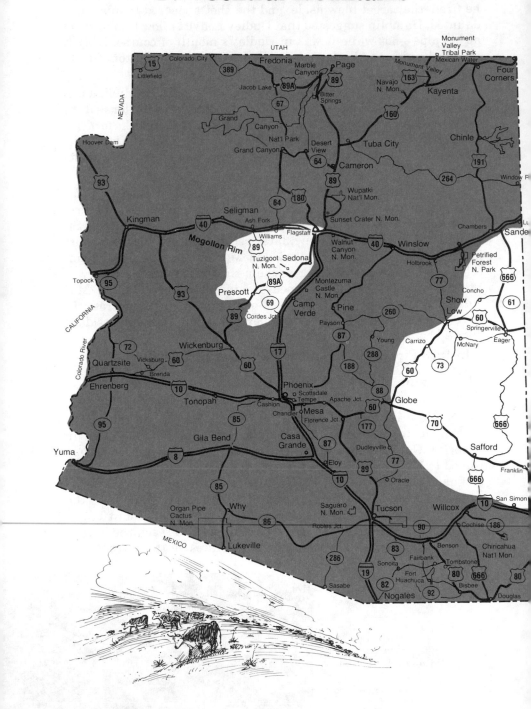

Pauline Weaver, Mountain Man, scout, gold prospector. He was one of Arizona's most prominant trailblazers and is called "Prescott's first citizen"
Courtesy
Southwest Studies

US 89
Prescott

Prescott

One of Joe Walker's last great adventures was the gold hunting expedition that led to the founding of a wilderness capital at Prescott. In early 1863 Captain Joe Walker led a party of prospectors up the Hassayampa River and discovered rich gold placers in the area where Prescott would be located. Walker, despite the fact that old age was slowing him down and his eyesight was failing, was one of the most indestructible frontiersmen in American history. He stood well over six feet and weighed two hundred pounds. During the 1830s he was one of the nation's foremost scouts and mountain men. In 1833 he led a winter expedition over the treacherous Sierra Nevada range, becoming the first to accomplish that feat and the first Anglo-American to see Yosemite National Park. In 1837 he was exploring Arizona in the Gila, Little Colorado River, and Mogollon Rim country. In 1851 Walker's explorations along the thirty-fifth parallel provided valuable information to the government about the feasibility of a transcontinental railroad across northern Arizona. A decade later he led a party of prospectors into northern Arizona, searching for gold around the San Francisco peaks. Finding no gold, the group headed for Santa Fe to spend the winter and while in that city, Walker met General James Carleton, military commander of New Mexico. Carleton suggested Walker explore the possibility of gold in the Bradshaw

Prescott in the 1870s
Courtesy Arizona
Historical Foundation

Mountains, and the rest is history. The highest tribute to Joe Walker came from another mountain man who, upon being asked which trail the old scout had followed, responded: "He don't follow trails, he makes 'em."

When President Abraham Lincoln proclaimed Arizona a territory on February 24, 1863, it was naturally assumed that the capital would be located at Tucson, "the hub of culture." The only communities north of the Gila River at the time were La Paz and Hardyville, port cities on the Colorado River. The gubernatorial party, headed by Governor John W. Goodwin, probably would have established the capital at the "old pueblo" had their minds not been changed at Santa Fe by General James Carleton. Carleton and his California Volunteers had driven the Confederates out of Arizona in 1862, and he had not forgotten that Tucson had been a hotbed of Secessionist activity. Perhaps even more important, Carleton had recently learned of the discovery of gold in the Bradshaw Mountains. He had already sent Major Edward B. Willis into the area to establish a military post to protect the prospectors. The officer was able to persuade Goodwin to locate the capital near the Fort Whipple military post. The post had been named in honor of General Amiel Whipple, who had explored and surveyed much of Arizona during the previous decade. Whipple was killed in the bloody battle of Chancellorsville in 1863. At the time Fort Whipple was located on the windswept plains at Del Rio Springs, on the north side of Chino Valley near the headwaters of the west fork of the Verde River. The governor's party arrived at Fort Whipple on a chilly January day in 1864. The resourceful Secretary of the Territory, Richard C. McCormick, had brought along a small printing press, and by March a newspaper, the Arizona *Miner*, northern Arizona's first paper, was in business. The following month Governor Goodwin selected a townsite on Goose Flats above Granite Creek, and on May 30 a meeting was held in a humble log-cabin mercantile store appropriately called Fort Misery. The miners had been calling the rustic settlement of a dozen or so shacks Granite City. Other names were suggested, such as Goodwin, Audubon, and Azatlan (for all the prehistoric ruins mistakenly thought to be Aztec). Someone even suggested Gimletville. But McCormick had in his possession William Hickling Prescott's classic work on the history of Mexico, and in honor of that great historian, wisely suggested the community be named Prescott, a name that suited everyone.

Soon after the townsite was selected, Fort Whipple was relocated to its present site a short distance northeast of town. Although Van Smith had established squatter's rights to most of the townsite, with a grand display of public-spirit characteristic of Prescottonians down through the years, he agreed to give up the land. Robert Groom surveyed the townsite, using an old prospector's skillet for a transit. The first buildings were wood structures (Virgil Earp, of Tombstone fame, operated a lumber mill in Prescott before moving to Cochise County), and the population was overwhelmingly Anglo-American, a rarity in the Southwest.

Prescott's first building was the previously mentioned Fort Misery. Manual Ysario built it as a store but when the supplies ran out, he left, and Caroline Ramos, better known as "Virgin Mary," turned it into a boarding house. Apparently the nickname came from her generosity and her tender care of sick and injured miners. Fort Misery was the most popular resort in town. A sign tacked outside stated: "room and board, $25 in gold, cash in advance." The menu didn't offer much variety, but the hungry miners didn't complain. Breakfast consisted of venison and chili, along with coffee, bread, and goat's milk; lunch provided roast venison, chili bread, coffee, and goat's milk; and supper offered venison, chili smeared over a tortilla, coffee, and goat's milk.

Fort Misery was converted into a church on Sunday, and Judge John "Blinkey" Howard dispensed justice or "misery" as the miners called it, during the week. Today Fort Misery sits on the grounds of the Sharlot Hall Museum at West Gurley.

Prescott's first saloon, called the Quartz Rock, was a rustic collection of timber with a plank for a bar. Tangleleg whiskey was dispensed by an army deserter who had lost his nose in an altercation. This establishment was perched on the banks of Granite Creek but was later moved over to Montezuma Street. Several reasons have been passed down as to why it was moved. One version says imbibers became sick at being so close to Granite Creek's pure water. Another says that sober citizens grew tired of pulling drunks out of the creek. Whatever the reason, by the early 1900s there were forty saloons situated on the west side of Montezuma Street. The district became known as Whiskey Row and began with the Kentucky Bar at the corner of Goodwin and Montezuma and stretched down to the Depot House Saloon near the Santa Fe Depot. Noted cowboy poet Gail Gardner, a Prescott native, immortalized Whiskey Row in his poem "Sierry Petes" or "Tyin' Knots in the Devil's Tail." Back before drinking and gambling were outlawed, Whiskey Row ran under a full head of steam twenty-four hours a day. The macho custom of thirsty cowboys in off the range was to start their binge, or "whizzer" as they called it, at the Kentucky Bar and take a drink in every bar all the way to the Depot House, thirty-nine saloons away. If one were really feeling his oats, he drank all the way back again. Gardner's poem, based on personal experience, tells about one of those whizzers. Later, on the way back to cow camp, he and his partner, Sandy Bob, had an encounter with the Devil, who wanted to "gather in their souls." The two punchers roped old Lucifer, cropped his ears, tipped his horns, branded his hide, and then tied knots in his tail. The poem, written in 1917, is one of the best-known pieces of Arizona cowboy culture. Many years later George Phippen, one of the founders of the Cowboy Artists of America, was commissioned to create a painting of this epic battle between two cowboys and the Devil. That painting is a classic in Arizona folklore.

By the summer of 1864 Prescott was taking on the appearance of becoming Arizona's newest boom town. Prospectors, freighters, cowboys, tin horn gamblers, merchants, shady ladies, and the rest of the wide gamut of frontier society were walking the wide streets that were named for historical figures who had played a role in settling the area. Gurley, for example, was named for John Gurley of Ohio. He was Lincoln's first choice for governor but died soon after his appointment. Other streets were named for American and Spanish explorers, including Coronado, Alarcon, Cortez, Leroux, Aubry, Walker, and Whipple. Freight wagons were kept busy hauling supplies over the treacherous roads between Prescott and the steamboat landings at Ehrenberg and Hardyville on the Colorado River.

Thanks to another famous scout, Pauline Weaver, peace prevailed during the first few months of the gold strike. Weaver was born in Tennessee around 1800, the son of a white father and a Cherokee mother. For a time he worked for the Hudson's Bay Company but preferred warmer climates, so he headed for the Southwest. He first arrived in Arizona in the late 1820s and over the next few years established a reputation as a first-rate mountain man, coming to know Arizona's mountains, deserts, and rivers like the back of his hand. Somebody scratched his name on the Casa Grande ruins in 1832, but since Weaver made his mark with an X until his dying day, the signature remains a mystery.

In 1846 General Stephen Watts Kearny hired Weaver to scout for the Mormon Battalion. During the 1850s he trapped beaver along Arizona's streams and grew to be friendly with most of the Indian tribes. In 1862 natives along the Colorado River in western Arizona showed him some rich gold placers. The strike that followed produced twelve million dollars in gold and led to the founding of La Paz, Weaver being credited as the discoverer. Not long after the Walker party found gold in the Bradshaws, he guided the Abraham H. Peeples party up the Hassayampa River in search of the yellow metal. A few miles north of Wickenburg they stumbled on a treasure trove of gold nuggets lying on top of a rocky knoll that became known as Rich Hill, the richest single placer strike in Arizona history.

Weaver worked tirelessly to negotiate a treaty between the native tribes and newcomers, and he succeeded for a spell. He gave the Indians the password "Paulino-Tobacco," which was to indicate to the whites that they were friendly Indians. As more whites poured in who were not aware of the arrangement, or didn't care about it, the treaty became meaningless. Too many cultural differences and mutual mistrust caused the inevitable outbreak of hostilities. In the mid-1860s Weaver was jumped by a war party and seriously wounded. The old scout, thinking he was about to die, went into his "death song," a custom he had adopted from the Plains Indians and felt perfectly natural using, but the suspicious warriors, not familiar with the ritual, believed he had gone crazy, and they quickly left. When Weaver saw he was not going to die, he arose and casually walked home; however, his wound continued to trouble him for the remainder of his days. It is said the natives were remorseful about shooting Weaver and during friendly parleys always asked how "Pawlino" was getting along.

When the first settlers moved into the Verde Valley, the army was called in to provide protection from a growing number of attacks. The officers wisely brought Weaver in to arrange a peace treaty. His service, according to military records, was invaluable. His health was deteriorating, and on June 21, 1867 Pauline Weaver died. He was buried at Camp Verde (Lincoln) with full military honors. Later, when the post was abandoned, his remains were taken to California. In 1929 poet-historian Sharlot Hall organized a campaign to have Weaver's remains returned to Prescott. Thanks to the Boy Scouts and Prescott school children, funds were raised, and Weaver was reburied on the grounds of the old territorial capital. Ms. Hall declared him to be "Prescott's first citizen." In 1863, when the Walker party arrived in the pristine wilderness, Pauline Weaver was already camped on Granite Creek, the future site of Prescott.

Melissa Ruffner Weiner, local historian, recounts three Prescott affairs of the heart that have all the ingredients of tragic Hollywood movies. In 1865 Richard C. McCormick was on his way east when he met and fell in love with a New Jersey woman named Margaret Hunt. After a brief courtship, they were married, and she joined him in Prescott, where her former husband was now territorial governor. Unaccustomed as she was to the hardships of the frontier, Margaret was determined to make the best of frontier life. In no time at all she was a favorite of the local citizenry. She had brought a rose bush all the way from New Jersey, planting it on the grounds of the capital. On April 30, 1867 just before her twenty-fourth birthday, she died during childbirth along with her baby. Margaret was placed in a coffin with her arms cradling the baby and buried in the forest close to the capital grounds. Prescottonians, from the most genteel to the rough-hewn miners, mourned the tragic death. Today the rose she planted still blooms on the grounds of the old capital.

One of the earliest arrivals in Prescott was a fiery newspaper editor named John Marion. Considered one of Arizona's greatest and most energetic newspapermen, Marion was either hated or loved by his readers. At one time or another, almost every other editor in Arizona fell victim to the vitriolic attacks of editor Marion. He was a staunch Democrat and was constantly at odds with the Republican appointees sent out to govern the territory. Marion also had a soft side, as demonstrated in the love for his wife of eleven years, Flora. Although she had borne him two children, Flora ran off with the local district attorney, Charles Rush. The fact that Rush was a family friend and a fellow Democrat kept Marion from saying much in public. Privately he pined over the loss for several years. Marion, hoping she would tire of her new lover, waited three years before filing for divorce. He died a few years later without ever seeing his beloved Flora again.

The third in this trilogy of broken hearts concerned the Miller family, for whom Miller Valley is named. Sam and his brother Jacob entered into a prosperous freight business; but Jake was lonesome for

Motoring near Prescott
Courtesy Arizona Historical Foundation

his wife, Jane, and his family in Illinois, whom he hadn't seen for several years. Since Sam didn't want to lose Jake, he forged some divorce papers and told his brother that Jane had left him. Then he wrote Jane, whom he did not get along with, telling her Jake had been ambushed and killed by Indians. Many years later one of Jake's children learned that Jake was alive in Prescott and wrote him about the family. Jake returned to Illinois only to find that his wife, believing Jake dead, had long since remarried. He returned to Prescott without seeing her, but his children did come to live with him in Arizona. Jake continued to grieve about the loss of his wife, and when he died on April 7, 1899, his last words were of Jane. Right after the funeral a telegram arrived informing his family that Jane had passed away one day later and that her dying words were of her lost husband Jake, whom she thought had died so many years ago on the remote Arizona frontier.

Affairs of the heart played a role in the lives of some of Arizona's most illustrious citizens. Morris Goldwater arrived in 1876 to work in the family mercantile business. He rented a room from a young widow, Sarah Fisher. After six months, the city council passed a proclamation suggesting that he should marry the lady. Goldwater and Mrs. Fisher were married, and later he was elected mayor of Prescott and served in the territorial legislature. He helped bring the Prescott and Arizona Central Railroad to Prescott and established a bank in the city. In 1910 Goldwater was selected vice president of the Constitutional Convention. He is considered the "Father of the Democratic Party" in Arizona, and in 1964 Prescott, celebrating its one hundredth anniversary, chose him as their "man of the century."

Sam Miller, who arrived with the Walker party, was out hunting one day and shot a lynx. But when he tried to pick up the animal it locked its teeth to Sam's wrist and held on. Sam pulled out his revolver and fired three times point blank, killing the cat before it had done much damage. Later that day Sam, bandaged hand and all, decided to pan for gold on the edge of the creek near where he had killed the lynx. To his pleasant surprise several small nuggets turned up in the first washing. By evening he had taken out $17 in nuggets. A gold rush followed, and they named the place Lynx Creek in honor of Sam's battle with the lynx. It was to become the richest streambed in Arizona history and is still a favorite spot for weekend prospectors.

Sharlot Hall, who arrived in February 1882, was another significant figure in Prescott and Arizona history. The Hall family emigrated to Arizona from Kansas. Sharlot rode the entire distance on horseback. She helped manage the family ranch east of Prescott and was as at home writing poetry as she was panning for gold in the rocky creeks of Yavapai County. In 1909 she became territorial

*Sharlot Hall at the
Governor's Mansion*
Courtesy Sharlot
Hall Museum

historian and the first woman in Arizona to hold a political office. In 1924 she was chosen to go back east and represent Arizona in the electoral college. Sharlot couldn't afford the proper clothes so she turned down the offer. At this point officials at the United Verde Mine at Jerome stepped in and bought her a blue silk dress with a fine copper mesh coat and accessories. Sharlot Hall's "copper dress" was a hit back east, and Arizona's copper industry benefitted from the publicity. During the trip, she visited numerous museums and vowed to create a museum in Arizona. She leased the old capitol grounds on West Gurley and began to restore the territorial capitol building. The clapboard sidings were stripped away, exposing the original logs. The work required a great deal of stamina, and although Sharlot was never in the best of health, somehow she persevered. After the restoration, she lived in the old "mansion" of the governor until her death in 1944. Today the Sharlot Hall Museum is one of the finest historical institutions in the entire state.

The first rodeos took place during the days of the open range, when cowboys from neighboring ranches began competing during roundup. Each ranch took pride in the riding and roping ability of its punchers, along with their ability to sit on the hurricane deck of an unbroken horse. From these early beginnings grew the sport of rodeo. In 1888 Prescott held the first paid-admittance rodeo, and for almost a century the Frontier Days Rodeo has been the highlight of the annual cowpuncher festivities around Prescott, attracting the nation's finest professional rodeo cowboys.

July 14, 1900 was like any other summer day in Prescott, until some careless miner jammed his pick candle into the wall of the Scopel Hotel, on the corner of Goodwin and Montezuma, and forgot about it. The hotel caught fire, which spread quickly through the business district. Volunteer fire companies with colorful-sounding names like Toughs, Dudes, O.K.'s, and Hook and Ladder arrived, but the town's water supply was low and all anybody could do was save a few furnishings. Customers in the Palace Bar grabbed the storied backbar with its contents, carrying them across the street to the plaza. Another group carried a piano to safety, and while someone played the popular tune "Hot Time in the Old Town Tonight," roulette wheels and faro tables were relocated at the plaza. A barber chair was carried over to the bandstand, where business resumed, as it did at the gaming tables and bar, open for business while flames licked the sky over Prescott. Sheriff George Ruffner led a group of powdermen into the area ahead of the holocaust and began dynamiting structures. By about three A.M. the fire had burned itself out.

The next morning Prescottonians took inventory: twenty-five saloons and five of the town's largest hotels were gone, as was the entire red light district. The area was still smouldering as shopkeepers sifted through the ruins hoping to find something worth salvaging. By mid-morning they had set up "business as usual" counters on the sidewalks in front of their burned out buildings.

One of Prescott's most famous landmarks is the old County Courthouse, built in 1916, with the equally well known majestic bronze statue of the Rough Rider in front. Thought by most to be the "Buckey" O'Neill statue created by Solon Borglum, it is actually a tribute to all Arizonans who served in the First Volunteer Cavalry, better known as the Rough Riders, in the Spanish-American War. William "Buckey" O'Neill was the only regimental officer killed in the war and next to Teddy Roosevelt was the most famous Rough Rider of them all. Buckey, who earned his nickname from his betting against the house in faro, or "bucking for tiger," was a popular political figure and newspaperman before he enlisted in the army. In the early 1890s he was county sheriff and is best remembered for his daring capture of four men who robbed the Santa Fe at Canyon Diablo, east of Flagstaff (see Canyon Diablo).

O'Neill was killed by a Spanish sniper shortly before the Battle of San Juan Hill. His death was deeply felt not only in Prescott but throughout Arizona, as his colorful personality, daring exploits, and strong stand for statehood had made him a bona fide folk hero.

*Rough Rider statue
in Prescott by
Solon Borglum,
considered one of the
best equestrian
sculptors in the
United States*
Courtesy
Southwest Studies

William O. "Buckey" O'Neill, popular mayor of Prescott, Sheriff of Yavapai County, newspaperman. He was the only Rough Rider officer from Arizona killed in the war with Spain in 1898.
Courtesy
Southwest Studies

Prescott was not as wild as Tombstone and Holbrook. Stalwart lawmen like Buckey O'Neill and George Ruffner kept a lid on the town most of the time; there were occasions, however, when violent crimes occurred, but justice was swift and severe.

One of the last men hung on Prescott's courthouse plaza was an obscure outlaw named Fleming Parker. His career as a badman was not spectacular; in fact, he might have escaped trouble with his old friend Yavapai County sheriff, George Ruffner, if the Atlantic & Pacific Railroad had treated him with more consideration. Fleming was an uncurried cowboy addicted to alcohol and the painted *filles de joie* of Whiskey Row. On the other side of the coin, he was well known over northern Arizona for his expertise with horses and his fondness for well bred animals. One day two of his string wandered onto the tracks and were killed by a passenger train. When the railroad offered a measly recompense, the indignant cowboy retaliated by robbing the train at Peach Springs. Sheriff Ruffner quickly picked up the trail, and a few days later Fleming was behind bars in the Prescott jail.

Parker and Ruffner had cowboyed together in their younger days but had taken separate trails. Ruffner had gone on to become a famous sheriff, and Fleming had done five years in San Quentin for burglary before coming back to northern Arizona, where he had saved enough money to buy a string of horses. Residents were sympathetic in his dispute with the railroad, and the sheriff was an old friend. It looked for a time as though Parker would get a light sentence, until he broke out of jail and killed Lee Norris, the deputy district attorney. Ruffner got word of the break while he was at Congress investigating another crime. He immediately commandeered a train for Prescott. Meanwhile, after killing Norris, Parker

336

and two accomplices headed for Ruffner's livery stable. Parker, who had an eye for good horseflesh, stole the sheriff's prize white gelding, Sureshot, and fled north. One of the escapees was caught at Chino Valley, and the other vanished and was never brought to justice. Ruffner, an expert tracker, quickly picked up Parker's trail. The outlaw knew his old companion would be following, so he reversed Sureshot's shoes to throw Ruffner off track. When the animal went lame, Parker turned him loose, continuing on foot. Ruffner finally caught up with Parker north of Flagstaff, and with Parker he boarded a Santa Fe train bound for Prescott. Public opinion had shifted after the murder of Norris, and there was talk of a lynching. Sensing trouble, Ruffner took his prisoner off the train outside Prescott and sneaked in the back way to the county jail. When the welcoming committee learned of the ruse, they gathered outside the jail and demanded that Parker be turned over to them. Ruffner, armed with a twin barreled shot gun, boldly faced the mob and ordered them to disperse. The lynch mob went home, and Parker was held for trial without further incident. He was sentenced to hang at 7:30 A.M. on the morning of June 3, 1898. On the evening before the scheduled hanging, Sheriff Ruffner visited Parker and asked if he had any last request. The condemned man was not hungry, but he wondered if Ruffner would mind if "Flossie," one of the girls over on Whiskey Row, paid him a visit. The obliging sheriff found Flossie and brought her over to the jail and then said adios for an hour or so. Parker's only other request was that Ruffner carry out the sentence because he wanted to be assured that the man given the honor of cashing him in be someone he respected.

The law required that a certain number of witnesses attend the hanging, and it was standard practice to send out invitations. Ruffner had forgotten to have the invitations made up, so on the morning of the hanging, he took a deck of cards and dealt one to each witness. Nobody was admitted to the gallows area without a card from the sheriff's personal deck of cards.

George Ruffner had a long and illustrious career as sheriff of Yavapai County. When he died in 1933 at the age of seventy-one, he

George Ruffner, longtime sheriff of Yavapai County. He was the first Arizonan admitted into the National Cowboy Hall of Fame at Oklahoma City.
Courtesy
Southwest Studies

was the oldest Arizona sheriff in seniority and age. Many years later the National Cowboy Hall of Fame in Oklahoma City chose him as the first Arizonan to be inducted into that select association of authentic Western heroes.

Old Sureshot never recovered completely from his ordeal with the reversed shoes so Sheriff Ruffner retired him to a farm in Phoenix at the site of what became the famous Biltmore Luxury Resort. According to the sheriff's colorful nephew, longtime Prescott historian "Budge" Ruffner, Sureshot was the only member of the family to ever reside in such opulent surroundings.

US 60
Globe to Springerville

McMillanville

Part of the naming of McMillanville may be shrouded in myth, but the story is told that Charlie McMillan and his partner, Dore Harris, went on a wild toot in Globe one spring evening in 1876. It was said Charlie got so drunk he could not hit the ground with his hat in five tries. The next day the pair went prospecting a few miles north of Globe. They had not traveled far before Charlie started complaining about his hangover, wanting to get off his mule for a siesta. While Charlie was snoozing, Dore started breaking off chunks of rock with his pick, uncovering a rich outcropping of almost pure silver. By now Charlie was wide awake, and the boys staked their claims. They named their mine the Stonewall Jackson, and the town that sprang up nearby was called McMillanville. A fabulous ledge of Stonewall Jackson silver ran ten miles. It was claimed the mine produced two million dollars before it played out.

McMillanville outgrew Globe for a time. By 1880 about fifteen hundred miners were living there, and the mine had a five-stamp mill. Actually, Charlie and Dore did not fare all that well with their prosperity—they took out about $60,000 worth of ore, then for $160,000 they sold the mine to a Californian who earned the two million. Charlie drank himself to death a few months later, and Dore lost his earnings playing the stock market.

By 1890 the population had shrunk to one man—old "Uncle Charlie" Newton, who sat on his porch chomping on a pipe and telling anyone who would listen that McMillanville would boom again.

Salt River Canyon

Back in the days before fast lanes and freeways, truckers hauling freight to and from eastern markets traveled US 60. The highway through Salt River canyon was the most treacherous part of the trip. If the brakes burned out coming down that long, steep grade, it was "Katy, bar the door."

This was the heart of Apache-Yavapai country and one of the last Indian refuges to be penetrated by the United States Army and their Indian scouts before General Crook's winter campaign of 1872-73 chased the Indians out of these twisting, steep-sided canyons. Until at least the mid-1880s the area remained a sanctuary for renegade Apaches who had bolted the reservations. Warriors claimed they used to sit in caves high above the canyon floor and casually watch the cavalry troops plodding along below in fruitless pursuit of their elusive foe. In December 1872 a Yavapai scout led the soldiers to a hostile camp in Salt River Canyon near today's Horse Mesa Dam; the natives were caught by surprise and retreated into a large opening in the canyon wall. The soldiers and scouts quickly blocked the entrance and ordered the warriors to surrender, a request met by defiant war cries. The braves then were told to send out their women and children. With *mucho bravado*, the Indians challenged the army to "come and get 'em."

The battle was one-sided—the soldiers fired into the walls causing bullets to ricochet down on the helpless Indians. Another party of soldiers managed to get above the rock fortress and start a rock slide. When the dust and smoke cleared, the band had been almost annihilated: seventy-six Yavapais were dead, most of them warriors; a few prisoners were taken to Fort McDowell. Because of other hostile bands in the canyon, the soldiers left the area as quickly as possible, the site remaining undisturbed for thirty-four years, until Jeff

Adams, a rancher in the area and later sheriff of Maricopa County, accidentally came across the battle ground. Inside the cave, skeletons from the almost-forgotten battle were scattered around, giving the site its name of Skeleton Cave.

The Salt River flows across Arizona's central mountains for two hundred miles before emptying into the Gila a few miles west of Phoenix. On its journey, the river passes through an area called Salt River Draw. Frontiersman King Woolsey operated a mine here in the mid-1870s. According to him, the brackish taste provided the river's name. In 1698 Father Kino dubbed it *Rio Salado*. In 1775 Father Garcés referred to it as the *Rio de la Asumpcion*. Army surveyor Lieutenant John Parke called it *Rio Salinas*.

Apache camp, circa 1880
Courtesy
Smithsonian Institute

Carrizo

Carrizo is Spanish for ditch reed, and the name refers to the growth of this reed along Carrizo Creek. A few miles west of here the Apache cult leader, Nock-ay-del-Klinne, and his followers lived (see Fort Apache, Arizona 73).

The medicine man was holding dances at Cibicue and developing a large group of disciples, including many Apache scouts. His teachings proposed a return of dead warriors and better times ahead after the whites were driven out. The agent at San Carlos sent the Apache police out to arrest Nock-ay-del-Klinne, but they came back empty handed, and after a second attempt failed, the army was called in. On August 30, 1881 soldiers from Fort Apache arrested the so-called prophet.

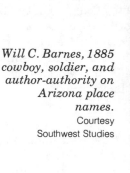

*Will C. Barnes, 1885
cowboy, soldier, and
author-authority on
Arizona place
names.*
Courtesy
Southwest Studies

As the troops were leaving Cibicue with their prisoner, several Apaches, stripped for battle, opened fire. They were joined by the Apache scouts. Eight soldiers were killed in the skirmish, and Nock-ay-del-Klinne was shot to death as he tried to make his escape. This was the only time in the history of Apache warfare that Apache scouts were disloyal.

The Apaches stalked the soldiers on the forty-mile return trip to Fort Apache. Two days later they attacked the garrison and killed several soldiers. A volunteer was sent to get help from Fort Thomas, ninety miles away, but his mutilated body was found a week later. Will C. Barnes then volunteered to go for help. Taking a more indirect route through the hills, he reached the rope ferry on Black River. Because a war party of Apaches were camped near the ferry, Barnes ripped his blanket roll into pieces which he tied around his horse's hooves to muffle the sound. While crossing the stream, the pads worked loose, and the Apaches heard the clatter of hooves on the rocky bottom. They arrived just in time to fire a few scattered rounds as the young soldier was climbing out the other side. Barnes completed his mission, and a relief force arrived from Fort Thomas to help disperse the Apache warriors. For this and other heroic action, Barnes was awarded the Congressional Medal of Honor. Barnes remained in Arizona after his enlistment and became a well-known cattleman. Years later he compiled thousands of Arizona place names.

Showlow

In 1875 Corydon E. Cooley, a scout for General Crook during the Apache campaigns of the early 1870s, lived here with his two Apache wives, Molly and Cora. Both were daughters of Pedro, a noted chief of the Carrizo Creek area. Cooley and his neighbor Marion Clark decided they were living too close together and that one had to move, so they decided to settle the issue by a game of cards. On the last hand, Cooley needed a low card to claim victory. "If you can show low, you win," Clark said. Cooley drew the deuce of clubs and replied, "Show low it is." That was how the town was named and the main street through Showlow, the "gateway to the White Mountains," is called "Deuce of Clubs" in honor of Cooley's lucky draw.

Springerville

The first Mexican settlers arrived in this area sometime prior to 1871 and named the place *Valle Redondo*, or Round Valley. Horse thieves used Round Valley as a refuge where they could alter the brands of livestock stolen in northern Arizona and sold later down south. Apparently they did not show partiality, for on the way back, they rustled a herd from a southern ranch to sell up north.

The Arizona Rangers swept through here in October 1901 in pursuit of the notorious Bill Smith gang of New Mexico. The lawmen caught up with the Smith crowd in Graham but lost the ensuing fight. Ranger Carlos Tafolla of St. Johns and Apache County deputy sheriff Will Maxwell were killed. Smith later said he was sorry he had killed Maxwell but was glad he had killed an Arizona Ranger. Earlier, in New Mexico, members of the Smith gang ambushed and killed famed Texas lawman George Scarborough. The gang left Arizona after killing Tafolla and Maxwell. It is believed they went to Mexico, but they were never apprehended.

Springerville was named for merchant Henry Springer, who unwittingly extended credit to most of the unsavory characters in Round Valley and eventually went broke. The townsite was originally called Omer by the Mormons who settled there. Eventually they relocated at Eagar, and the name was changed to Springerville. The two communities, Springerville and Eagar, are an interesting contrast—the former was settled primarily by Hispanics of the Catholic faith, the latter by Mormons of Anglo ancestry.

Springerville's most prominent merchants were Julius and Gustav Becker, who arrived in 1876 and opened a freighting business, hauling merchandise from the Rio Grande by ox trains. Julius W. Becker, a son of Gustav, played a major role in getting US 60 to come through Springerville. The first auto, appropriately named Pathfinder, passed through here in 1910 on the first transcontinental auto trip. Six years later the "ocean to ocean" journey brought a caravan of autos through town. Transcontinental caravans were important in stressing the need for a better highway system in the United States.

In 1928 the National Old Trails Association and the Daughters of the American Revolution dedicated twelve statues of the "Madonna of the Trail," depicting the hardy but largely unsung pioneer women who "Wested" in the nineteenth century. One of those statues is located at Springerville.

Showlow in the mid-1940s
Courtesy
Southwest Studies

US 70
Globe to Franklin

San Carlos

The San Carlos Reservation came to be known as Hell's Forty Acres soon after it was created in 1873. The reservation was located on the San Carlos River about a mile from its junction with the Gila. San Carlos Reservation was named by General Oliver Howard during his peace mission of 1872. At the same time, he abolished reservations at Fort McDowell, Date Creek, and Beale Springs, formally establishing the White Mountain and Fort Apache reserves. Over the next three years Indians from the closed reservations were taken to San Carlos. General George Crook opposed the plan, feeling that the gathering together of so many Indian bands hostile to each other was bound to cause trouble. The animosities among the Indians provided unreconstructed rebels like Geronimo the opportunity to recruit malcontents for his renegade forays off the reservation.

Apache agent John Clum was one of the best-known whites at San Carlos during those early years. He arrived in 1874, fresh from the East and full of ideas. Clum seems to have been on congenial terms with General Crook, but when the general was reassigned in 1875, Clum began quarreling with the military over who would govern the Apaches. He established an Indian police force and set up a self-government system for each tribe. In late 1875 he asked that the soldiers be withdrawn from the reservation. By this time four thousand Apaches, Mojaves, and Yavapais were crowded into San Carlos, and tensions grew, not only among the Indians, but with the soldiers.

In 1876 Geronimo broke from the reservation and cut a wide swath of terror and death across southern Arizona and Mexico. The following year Clum and his Apache police made a daring capture of both Geronimo and the notorious Victorio, successor to Mangas Colorados.

Clum's disagreements with the military and his frustrations led him to resign that year. Silver had recently been discovered in Tombstone, and Clum wryly suggested that every tombstone needed an epitaph, so he headed for Cochise County and started a newspaper. He later became mayor of Tombstone and was one of the best-known personalities in the Arizona Territory.

Living quarters at San Carlos were not any better for the soldiers than they were for the Apaches. One report mentions that the only bathing facility for an entire company was a small circular tub. However, bathing was not a problem, because there was not enough water available. The enlisted men's quarters offered little protection from the elements. During one summer it was reported that the temperature was 110 degrees inside, only two degrees lower than it was outside; that winter temperatures of 11 degrees were reported inside the barracks.

Camp San Carlos was closed in 1900. After the construction of Coolidge Dam in the late 1920s the waters of Lake San Carlos gradually backed up to the old cemetery, but before the area was inundated, concrete slabs were poured over the graves.

Calva

Calva was short for *calvario*, Spanish for cavalry. Not far from here in 1846 General Stephen Watts Kearny was forced to make a twenty-three mile detour around Box Canyon because the mules were unable to pull his two mountain howitzers through. The journey took several days and left the men and animals so exhausted they had

Freight wagons at the tent city of Geronimo in the 1880s
Courtesy
Southwest Studies

Dad Hardiman and Uncle Hal Young with the CCC horse herd on Apache Reservation, circa 1911
Courtesy
Southwest Studies

to rest for another two days.

Calva was, around the turn of the century, an important shipping point for the storied Chiricahua Cattle Company. Cowboy artist, Ross Santee, tells a story about a stampede at Calva in 1927:

> The cattle were penned for the night, and since the pens were plumb full we built a rope corral long side for the saddle horses. We turned in early and every thing went fine until a freight train came along about midnight. To make matters worse the engineer blowed his whistle when he was directly opposite the pens. The cattle was penned so tight they couldn't get a run at the fence, but the saddle horses went through that rope corral as if it was made of twine.
>
> We were camped at the lower end of the pens and when the ponies passed us they were goin' like a bat out of hell. Fact is some of the boys took to the brush for fear they'd get run over. But Otho Cox (brother of the noted Breezy) managed to get a mane holt and swing aboard one as they went by. When he did the pony went to buckin.' At that you can't blame the pony none. He probably thought a ghost had crawled him, for Otho didn't have nothin' on except his underwear. When they hit the river the pony was still abuckin' but Otho stuck. Riding with nothin' but a mane holt he finally got the ponies headed and drove them back to the pens. Breezy has won plenty of money in big-time rodeos but Breezy never made a better ride than his brother made that night.

Bylas

Bylas is an Apache word for "one who does all the talking" and refers to a peaceful Apache headman who, during an Apache revolt in 1882, attempted to alert the agency at San Carlos. His warning went unheeded, and a major outbreak ensued. The rebellious Indians cut the telegraph lines to thwart attempts to call out the troops.

The introduction of the white man's "talking wires," or telegraph, awed the Apaches at first, but they quickly overcame their awe and located its Achilles' tendon. A favorite tactic was to find an isolated place where the wire ran through a heavily wooded area. Then an Apache would climb up and cut the wire, tieing the loose ends together with rawhide and thus breaking the current but keeping the line intact. This cunning trickery frustrated repair crews sent out to find the severed telegraph wire.

Geronimo

This community, located on the Arizona Eastern Railroad from Globe to Bowie, was named for the notorious Chiricahua war chief several years after he left the territory for the last time.

Most of the buildings in Geronimo had flat roofs and were made of adobe. During the hot summer months outlaws found a sanctuary by climbing up on the roof and then pulling the ladder up. This way they could get a good night's rest without worrying about someone's sneaking up on them.

Today's disreputable land promoters selling lakeshore lots on the edges of mirages are mere amateurs compared to some of the wheeler-dealers of yesteryear. The lawless Arizona territory attracted a wide gamut of frontier con men ranging from tin horn gamblers to stock swindlers. Most Arizona history buffs are familiar with the notorious James Addison Reavis, the self-styled Baron of Arizona, who tried to steal about twelve million acres of prime Arizona territory by forging some old Spanish land grants. For a time he was successful, amassing a fortune, all of which was quickly squandered on an opulent lifestyle, and later, attorneys.

Another famed Geronimo con man was a "Doctor" Richard Flower, who made a living selling cure-all bottled medicine. His recipe, according to Flower, would cure everything from baldness to toothache. Although the nostrum had no redeeming medicinal value, it contained enough alcohol to mellow "Doc" Flower's patients so that they didn't feel cheated.

Doc Flower, who eventually grew weary of small time scheming, decided to play for higher stakes. Fortunes were being made in the Arizona mines, and since he did not have a bona fide mine to call his own, he decided to create one. Although he had never been to Arizona and would not have known a nugget from rolled oats, he rushed about with his phony scheme—he erected a fake movie set mine complete with headframe near Geronimo, bought a few samples of ore from a producing mine, and headed east to promote his strike.

He called his company the Spendazuma: "mazuma" was slang for money, so in effect he was promoting the "spend yer money" mine. Would-be millionaires were waiting in line to buy stock in Doc's mine.

The balloon burst when a reporter from the Arizona *Republican* (today's *Republic*) named George Smalley rode out to have look at the mine that was creating such a stir back east. The property was being guarded by one of Doc's hirelings, a character named Alkali Tom. Tom tried his best to keep the snoopy reporter from getting too close to Doc's imaginary gold mine, but Smalley was not to be denied. Because workers were about as scarce as horseflies in December, Smalley became suspicious. A closer examination revealed the whole setup as phony.

When Smalley's exposé made the papers, Doc's lawyer indignantly threatened to sue for a hundred thousand dollars, demanding a retraction. Smalley could hardly keep from laughing, so they offered him five thousand to rewrite the story and admit he had made a mistake. When the spunky reporter assumed a pugilist's pose, the lawyer retreated, and Doc Flower's blossoming Spendazuma scheme withered away.

Bret Harte spent enough time around mining camps to become an authority on the art of selling worthless claims to unsuspecting tenderfeet. He wrote rather poetically on the subject:

> The ways of a man with a maid may be strange
> yet simple and tame
> when compared to a man with a mine
> when buying or selling the same.

Fort Thomas

Fort Thomas was established along the Gila River in 1876 to replace Camp Goodwin several miles downstream. The abandonment of the latter was caused by a serious malaria problem. The new post on the Gila was named to honor Civil War hero General George Thomas. However, health problems were not solved—doctors reported severe cases of malaria, depression, lassitude, and typhoid fever. Fort Thomas had a total of twenty-seven adobe, shingle-roof buildings with water piped in but with no sewer system; it was considered by many to be the worst post in the whole United States Army and was closed on December 3, 1892.

Fort Thomas in the 1880s
Courtesy
Southwest Studies

On May 11, 1889 one of Arizona's more puzzling crimes occurred on the road between Forts Grant and Thomas. Major Joseph Wham, army paymaster, and his 10th Cavalry escort were ambushed and robbed of $26,000 in gold and silver by a gang numbering between eight and twenty. The outlaws fired down on the troops from a high, rocky ledge, forcing them to abandon the money wagon and run for cover. Seven of the eleven soldiers providing escort were wounded. Two black soldiers from the 10th Cavalry, Sergeant Ben Brown and Corporal Isaiah Mays, were later awarded the Congressional Medal of Honor for bravery. Several outlaws were captured, and it turned out they were members of prominent families in the area. The families hired a battery of high-powered attorneys, including Tombstone lawyer Marcus Smith, who, despite overwhelming evidence presented by the prosecution, convinced a jury their clients were innocent. The Wham Robbery case is considered one of the worst miscarriages of justice in Arizona history.

Ashurst

Ashurst was originally called Redlands because of its reddish soil. In 1918 residents wanted to name the new post office Pershing in honor of the famous World War I general. The postal department crossed out Pershing and selected Ash. Residents, not wanting Washington to have the last word, altered it to Ashurst.

Henry Fountain Ashurst came to Arizona from his birthplace in Nevada in 1877 at the age of three. In his younger years, he worked as a cowboy around Flagstaff and was elected to the territorial legislature in the late 1890s. He practiced law in Flagstaff and became well known for his knowledge of Shakespeare and his ability as an orator. When Arizona became a state in 1912, Ashurst went to Washington as a United States Senator. He served five terms and became nationally known in the senate as the "silver tongued orator of the Colorado."

Pima

When the first Mormon settlers arrived here in 1879, they laid out a townsite, planned an irrigation canal, and chose the name Smithville, for Mormon leader Jesse Smith. Despite the lawless reprobates that inhabited the area and an occasional Apache threat, the colonists planted their crops and raised their families.

*Pima, Arizona
Territory, 1884*
Courtesy
Southwest Studies

Thatcher

The first Mormon settlers arrived here in 1881 and named the place in honor of apostle Moses Thatcher. Thatcher, along with apostle Erastus Snow, paid a visit on Christmas 1882. A stage line operated out of here during the 1880s, and in 1892 Eastern Arizona Junior College was relocated at Thatcher. The college had started as St. Joseph State Academy and was controlled by the Mormon Church. In 1933 this institution became a county junior college.

Safford

In 1872 a group of farmers from Gila Bend relocated here after several devastating floods downstream and named the town for the third territorial governor, Anson P. K. Safford.

Safford, known as the "little governor" because of his diminutive size, was the only governor to be granted a divorce by an act of legislature. He promoted Arizona's mines to eastern investors and pushed hard for more schools in the territory. On one occasion the governor rode at the head of a punitive expedition in pursuit of raiding Apaches. In 1877 poor health kept him from accepting a second appointment as governor.

Solomonville

Isador E. Solomon came to America from Germany when he was sixteen. He settled here in 1876, ran a store, and was the town's most prominent citizen. The settlement was first called Munsonville for Bill Munson, who owned a house and store. Solomon bought the property and enlarged it. When the mines around Clifton began operations, he built ovens and produced charcoal from mesquite wood. Pioneer rancher William Kirkland was working as a mail carrier here in 1878 and suggested the name Solomonville. Renegade Apache bands bolting from San Carlos and making their way to the Mexican border were a threat to settlers here, and the Solomon family had several close calls. One time, when illness caused the

The hanging of Augustine Chacon at Solomanville
Courtesy
Southwest Studies

family to delay a planned trip, the stage they were supposed to be riding was attacked and all the passengers were slaughtered. Apaches raided his ranch on another occasion, killing twelve men, a woman, and child, then slaughtering five hundred sheep.

Solomon was a major figure in the founding of the Gila Valley Bank in 1899. From that humble beginning in Solomonville, the Gila Valley Bank evolved into the Valley National Bank, one of the state's most prominent financial institutions.

Augustine Chacon was a notorious Mexican outlaw, who boasted of having killed nearly thirty "gringos," not bothering to count his own countrymen he had killed. He was a tall, powerful man with a thick shock of hair and a handsome, rugged face. At times he wore a bushy beard, causing folks to call him *Peludo* or Hairy One.

Chacon and his gang came to Arizona periodically to rob and pillage. On one foray they robbed a casino in Jerome and killed four people, then robbed a stagecoach outside Phoenix. The crafty outlaw gave several posses the slip and returned to his hideout in Mexico's Sierra Madre. In 1896 he robbed a store in Morenci and in a rage hacked the owner to pieces with an ax. Later when a posse had him surrounded, a deputy named Pablo Salcido, an old friend of Chacon's tied a white handkerchief to his rifle barrel and called for a parley. Chacon asked him to step out into the open. After Chacon had spoken to his old friend from a concealed place, he shot the friend in cold blood.

The outraged posse eventually caught their man, and he was taken to Solomonville and sentenced to hang. Despite all his bad traits, Chacon had a way with women. A lady friend hid a hacksaw blade in the binding of a Bible and delivered it to his cell. The next night she sweet-talked the jailer into letting her into his office for some lovemaking. In another part of the jail, the inmates were singing *Corridos* with a guitar and concertina while Chacon sawed away on the bars. The jailer heard only sweet nothings and a background chorus of loud Mexican music. Less than twenty-four hours before Chacon was to hang, the jailer released himself from a fond embrace to check on his prisoner only to find the cell empty. Chacon had made his escape and headed for the Mexican border, remaining free until 1902, when Arizona Ranger Captain Burt Mossman slipped into Mexico and made a daring capture. Chacon was returned to Solomonville, and this time the hanging came off on schedule.

Duncan

When the Arizona and New Mexico Railroad connected Clifton with the main line in 1883, the rail stop was located on the property of

Duncan Smith. Black Jack Ketchum, notorious stagecoach robber, and his gang were among many desperadoes who stopped off at Duncan.

In 1880 Henry Clay Day arrived in this part of Arizona between the New Mexico line and the Peloncillo Mountains and homesteaded a ranch a few miles south of Duncan. Day called his outfit the Lazy B, and the ranch, despite an occasional drought, became one of the best known in Arizona. When he grew too old to run it any longer, he turned the 260-square-mile ranch over to his son Harry.

Sandra Day O'Connor on Chico at the Lazy B Ranch near Duncan
Courtesy
Sandra Day O'Connor

Harry Day, father of Supreme Court Justice Sandra Day O'Connor during an early day roundup at the Lazy B
Courtesy Sandra Day O'Connor

Harry Day's college education was interrupted by World War I. On the day he reported for duty, the war ended. His father died about the same time, and the ranch was facing financial ruin, so Harry returned to the homestead and never left. In 1927 he married Ada Mae Wilkey, the college-educated daughter of a prosperous cattle dealer from El Paso. Three years later a daughter was born. Ranch life was tough, especially on women and children. The cowpunchers slept in the house with the family until a bunkhouse was built in 1937, the same year plumbing was installed. Harry remained active in ranch operations until his death in 1984 at the age of 86. Harry and Ada Mae Day raised two daughters, Sandra and Ann, and a son, Alan. Both daughters were pretty, and although they went to school in El Paso, they spent their summers at the ranch. The story is still told around Duncan today that the young cowboys used to come from all over Graham and Greenlee counties on Saturday night just to look at Harry Day's daughters at some social function.

Sandra had always wanted to stay on the Lazy B and be a "cowboy," but her brother, Alan, was so much better at working cows she decided to get a college education, going off to Stanford, where she received a law degree. After graduation she married classmate John O'Connor and settled down to raise a family. When she began her own career as a lawyer, Sandra found many openings as a secretary but few firms wanted to hire a woman attorney. She persevered, however, and started her own firm in Phoenix. In the late 1960s she ran for the Arizona Senate and was elected. Eventually she became Senate Majority Leader, the first woman in American history to hold that post in a state legislature; however, she was destined for a wide career, so it was not a surprise to those who knew her, when Sandra Day O'Connor went to Washington, becoming the first woman to hold a seat on the United States Supreme Court.

Gripe

The old inspection station near the Arizona-New Mexico line was maintained to prevent the spread of plant disease and insect pests. Despite the good idea of plant inspection, weary motorists tended to resist the inconvenience of being stopped. When employees were thinking of a suitable name for the place, some clever wag suggested Gripe.

US 89
Prescott to Ash Fork

Fort Whipple

In 1863 General James Carleton, Union military commander, ordered Major Edward Willis and several companies of California Volunteers to set up a military post near where the Walker expedition had discovered gold in the Bradshaw Mountains a few months earlier. They established Camp Clark (for Surveyor General John A. Clark) at Del Rio Springs, in Chino Valley. The following May the post was moved, along with the territorial capital, eighteen miles south, to a site closer to the gold diggings at Granite Creek. Although the new post was sometimes called Prescott Barracks, it officially became Fort Whipple for General Amiel Whipple, who had recently fallen in the Battle of Chancellorsville. Whipple was the young engineer who surveyed Arizona along the thirty-second and thirty-fifth parallels during the 1850s.

During the 1860s Fort Whipple was a primitive post with a scattering of rough-hewn log cabins. Hostile bands of Yavapai and Apaches kept the military on constant alert. Post reports indicate that numerous punitive expeditions were sent out from the fort during these years. On January 22, 1870 Prescott editor John Marion, giving dates and locations, published a list of more than one hundred fifty citizens ambushed by Indians near Prescott. Despite the fact that people were being attacked within sight of Prescott, in 1871 department commander General George Stoneman recommended closing Fort Whipple. Citizen outrage prevented such action. Following the 1871 Camp Grant Massacre in southern Arizona, when citizens took matters into their own hands, Stoneman was replaced by General George Crook, the "fightin'est general" the army ever sent to Arizona.

Fort Whipple, condemned earlier, was rebuilt in 1872, but fire destroyed parts of the old fort during the next several years. Finally, in the 1880s army chief William T. Sherman recommended that frame and adobe buildings be built to replace the old ones.

Because of its mild climate and spectacular scenery, Fort Whipple was made the headquarters of Arizona's military department. The thriving community of Prescott offered amenities not found elsewhere in Arizona. Martha Summerhayes notes in her book on army life that the soldiers and their wives envied the ranking officers and their families who stayed at Whipple while others were sent to remote forts like Camps Verde, Apache, and McDowell.

Following the close of the Apache wars in 1886, the area around Fort Whipple quieted down. The post was abandoned in 1898, then reopened four years later. In 1913 it was closed again and remained closed until 1922, when the facility was turned over to the Public Health Service.

Granite Dells

The spectacular outcropping of salmon-colored granite boulders north of Prescott was a favorite rendezvous for war parties bent on mischief to miners and freighters going to and from Prescott. An earlier name was Granite *Dalles*, from a French trapper's description of a chasm or gorge. Another descriptive name, Point of Rocks, appears in early stories about the picturesque area. Nestled in the midst of a giant stone amphitheater is a tree-shrouded recreational area complete with a natural swimming pool set in among the boulders.

Chino Valley

During the historic 1853-54 survey, Lieutenant Amiel W. Whipple chose the name Chino Valley after the grama grass that carpeted the vast, windswept region. The Mexicans in the party called the range grass "de china," or "the chino," hence the name. The long, wide valley begins northeast of the Juniper Mountains near Seligman and stretches south all the way to Prescott Valley. The Verde River has its headwaters near Paulden, on the north side of the valley, along US 89.

During the 1820s mountain men like Ewing Young and Kit Carson had great success trapping beaver in this area. In 1829 following a successful season, the Young party split up near here; one group taking the furs to New Mexico, while Young and Carson went with another party on to California for another season of fur trapping.

The old narrow gauge railroad built in 1892 by William Andrews Clark ran from Jerome into Chino Valley, where it linked up with the Santa Fe line at what was called Jerome Junction. Special cars and engines had to be built to negotiate the twisting curves and switchbacks leading out of Jerome. One thirteen-mile stretch had one hundred sixty-eight curves, or as one old cowpuncher said, "more kinks 'an a cheap lariat." Local people quickly dubbed it the "world's crookedest railroad." Passengers claimed they could look out the window and see the engine passing them going the other way. In 1923 the name was changed from Jerome Junction to Chino Valley.

Del Rio Springs

East of US 89 along the Santa Fe line, is Del Rio Springs, the site of the original Fort Whipple. Soldiers camped at this site in 1864 prior to the establishment of a new Fort Whipple on the outskirts of the new territorial capital at Prescott. Territorial officials also set up a temporary capital at this site while they looked for a more suitable place closer to the gold prospectors on Granite Creek. After the troops withdrew, an ex-soldier named Robert Postle filed a claim at the site.

In 1867 a family of immigrants named Shivers passed through and stayed briefly. When the Shivers moved on, one of their daughters, fourteen-year-old Hannah, remained with Postle. They had several children before he died, leaving Hannah a widow at the age of nineteen. This remarkable young lady improved her homestead—she built a large, comfortable adobe house, and lived out her life at Del Rio Springs.

Following the fire that wiped out Prescott's business district in 1900 a water line was run out of the springs. A huge ranch was run by the Santa Fe Railroad in 1910—it was used to raise livestock for the Fred Harvey houses along the main line. Also, a train hauled water to both Ash Fork and Grand Canyon Village each day from the springs. An agreement existed between the company and the union that even during a strike, the water train would still haul water to the thirsty communities along the line. During the off season, mules from the Grand Canyon were pastured at the ranch while they recuperated from hauling tourists.

During the 1880s railroad promoter Tom Bullock built a short lived railroad from Prescott Junction (Seligman) to Prescott to link the latter up with the main line of the Santa Fe (see Seligman or Prescott Junction).

Paulden

The early settlers requested the name Spring Valley for their community, but for some reason the postal department refused the name and chose Midway Grocery. The name was changed again in 1926 at the request of the postmaster, Orville Pownall, whose son Paul had recently died of an accidental gunshot wound.

The tiny community, consisting of a store, motel, and truck stop, was bypassed when US 89 built a new stretch of road about a half mile away. The Lionel Gilpin family operated the store and post office for many years. Gilpin, brother of well-known Arizona peace officer Frank Gilpin, was also a deputy sheriff in Yavapai Conty for many years. In June 1969 he was with a group of lawmen pursuing an elusive prison escapee, Danny Lee Echard, in Chino Valley. Echard, known as the "Desert Fox," was shot to death near here in a gunfight, after he had killed highway patrolman Paul Marston.

Hell Canyon

During the 1950s a new highway took the thrill out of negotiating the twisting curves of Hell Canyon. Today motorists glide by hardly noticing the deep chasm.

The canyon was a favorite haunt for nomadic warriors during the Indian wars. Military records indicate a few skirmishes here, and several expeditions patrolled the area in search of elusive war parties.

A stage station on the line running from Ash Fork to Prescott was located in the canyon. The Tucson delegation to the Thirteenth Territorial Assembly passed through here on their way to Prescott in 1885, a roundabout trip as high waters in the Salt River caused the politicians to catch a train at Maricopa, then travel to Los Angeles and back to Ash Fork, where they boarded a stage to Prescott. Time was of the essence as they were desperately trying to bring the "capital on wheels" to Tucson once again. The stage was delayed by a raging snowstorm at Hell Canyon, so delegate Bob Leatherwood rode a mule to Prescott. He was carrying a satchel full of money, commonly used to throw festive parties which brought in votes. Leatherwood arrived too late; Prescott's happy political warrior Buckey O'Neill had "out-partied" the opposition, and Prescott retained the capital.

Jerome, a billion dollar copper town perched on the side of Cleopatra Hill
Courtesy Arizona Historical Foundation

US 89A
Prescott to Flagstaff

Jerome

Spanish explorers were the first to record the mineral wealth around the site that would one day become the "billion dollar copper camp" called Jerome. In 1583 Antonio de Espejo led a small expedition from his base camp at the Hopi villages into the Verde Valley where he located rich mineral outcroppings. When the conquistadore returned to Mexico, the silver specimens he displayed rekindled interest in resuming the explorations that had ended with Coronado's unsuccessful quest for gold forty years earlier.

In 1598 Governor Juan de Oñate, the great colonizer of New Mexico, sent Marcos Farfán to search for the lost mines reported by Espejo. Farfán returned with rich silver ore found in the vicinity of Prescott. Despite the success of Farfán's mission, Oñate didn't get around to exploring the area until 1604. The rough terrain and its remoteness made transporting ore too difficult, and the Black Hills kept their precious treasure for nearly three hundred years before a narrow gauge railroad made it economically possible to mine the area.

During the 1870s one of Arizona's most illustrious frontiersmen, army scout Al Sieber, worked claims on what became known as Cleopatra Hill. Sieber gave up his claims, never realizing their value until it was too late. In 1876, on the advice of Sieber, M. A. Ruffner and Angus McKinnon began working claims on Cleopatra Hill, marking the beginning of the modern era of the region. It is also claimed that the notorious Francisco "Pancho" Villa sold water to the early residents during his pre-revolutionary days.

Cone-shaped Cleopatra Hill, the reddish-hued mountain on which Jerome is precariously perched, was a freak of nature, a veritable treasure trove of gold, silver, and copper. Its reputation matches that of Cripple Creek and of Leadville, Colorado; of the Comstock Lode of Nevada; and of Tombstone. Before Jerome shut down in 1953, it was widely known as the "billion dollar copper camp."

Much of the recorded history of Jerome is hard to come by because disastrous fires around the turn of the century wiped out the town three times, destroying valuable records.

Among the modern-day prospectors to blaze a trail up Cleopatra Hill were John Boyd and the O'Dougherty brothers, John and Ed. They located claims at the future site of the fabulous United Verde Mine. Territorial Governor Fred Tritle and Bill Murray bought into this enterprise. In 1882 the Santa Fe Railroad finally reached Ash Fork, making the difficult task of hauling ore easier. When the partners ran short of money, they brought in New York financier Eugene Jerome as a backer. He put up $200,000, insisting that the community which sprang up nearby be named after him. Jerome, a cousin of Jennie Jerome, the mother of Sir Winston Churchill, never visited the city that eventually had a population of fifteen thousand. The operation became known as the United Verde, and in 1883 it produced $80,000 in silver before the vein played out. Furthermore, the cost of hauling the ore to Ash Fork had jumped to twenty dollars a ton. So by 1884 Jerome was on its way to becoming a ghost town. Fred Tritle was given most of the blame for the failure. Three years later he tried again, but transportation and labor problems doomed the project once more. Tritle, once a mining magnate, died bankrupt in Phoenix in 1906, the first of many victims Cleopatra Hill would claim over the next few years.

In 1888 Phelps-Dodge sent Dr. James Douglas (see Bisbee) to examine the site, which was up for sale. Eugene Jerome was asking $300,000 and assumption of all debts. Douglas, one of the most knowledgeable of mining men, was high on the property, but the tight-fisted owners of Phelps-Dodge, believing they had Mr. Jerome over a barrel, authorized Douglas to offer only $30,000. Meanwhile, William Andrews Clark, a Montana copper king, paid Jerome the huge asking price, having satisfied himself that the property was highly promising. Phelps-Dodge finally agreed to meet Jerome's price, but their offer came a day late—Clark had beaten them to the punch. Phelps-Dodge would acquire the property many years later, paying twenty-one million dollars, after millions of dollars of ore had already been extracted.

In 1892 Clark built a narrow gauge railroad into Jerome from Chino Valley (Jerome Junction). The road was so steep they could only pull five cars at a time. The only other link with the outside world was a treacherous wagon road up Yeager Canyon to Prescott. Clark was secretive to a fault, rarely delegated authority, and trusted no one, not even his accountant. It was said the diminutive copper king allowed his bookkeeper in New York to keep the left side of the ledger while he kept the right side in Jerome—only Clark knew what was on both sides. Fearing governmental knowledge of the wealth of his properties, Clark fired any employee who discussed the company's wealth with an outsider. He even fired any underground miner who talked to an above-ground worker about the richness of the ore in the United Verde Mine. If a local newspaper became too meddlesome, he withdrew his advertising and that of the town's businesses (which he controlled), and the newspaper failed within a week.

In the 1890s the United Verde was paying Clark dividends of three and a half million dollars a year. Clark was no philanthropist, preferring to keep his wealth in the family. He had two sons and two daughters, and following his death in 1925, they engaged in an epic feud over the division of his estate.

Clark had always wanted to be a United States Senator, so in 1899, he ran in Montana. After spending over a million dollars in bribes, he was elected, but he was never seated—the Senate Elections and Privileges Committee refused to seat him. Clark ran again in 1902 and won, but he served only one term before quitting—public service did not appeal to him.

In 1914 Clark spent two million dollars to establish the smelter town of Clarkdale, four miles downhill from Jerome. Workers and officials were able to rent residences on easy company terms. At the same time, he loaned three and a half million dollars to the Santa Fe Railroad to build a line into the new town.

Clark's son Charlie, who managed the United Verde, was just the opposite of his father. Charlie loved fast women, fast horses, and high stakes poker. It was said that at times he played for stakes as high as a million dollars. During his father's first race for the Senate, Charlie was chased out of Montana for political skulduggery.

About the time Arizona became a state Jimmy Douglas came to Jerome to speculate on the mines around Cleopatra Hill. Douglas, a son of Dr. James Douglas, was like Charlie Clark, a departure from a steady father. "Rawhide" Jimmy, as he was known, was a flamboyant wheeler-dealer. In 1912 he bought the Little Daisy Mine at the foot of

Cleopatra Hill. He spent a half million dollars the first year without success. Two years later his mine hit a vein of pure copper five feet thick, the richest ever found in American mining. In 1916 "Rawhide" Jimmy's United Verde Extension mined ten million dollars in gold, silver, and copper, over 75% of the total in profit.

"Rawhide" Jimmy Douglas was smelting more ore from the Little Daisy in one furnace than Clark was in three. Competition between the two copper kings was fierce, and the local citizens loved it, but neither side had an edge. If a worker was unhappy at one mine, he could quit and go to work for the other without having to move to another town.

The town took on a personality of its own during these years. Payday came once a month, and the mines closed briefly to let miners have time to spend their earnings (most of the businesses were owned by the mine owners or their relatives). At one time there were fifteen saloons and fifteen hundred residents, or one drinking establishment for every hundred people.

Jennie Banters was the town's most prominent and prosperous madam. It was said she was the wealthiest businesswoman in Arizona around the turn of the century. She was also the most resourceful. Once, when the town was having one of its periodic holocausts, she went to the volunteer hose company offering them lifetime free passes to her establishment if they would put the fire out at her place. It was said that the volunteers rose to superhuman efforts, as they charged up the hill and extinguished the flames. Hillside Jerome, with its wooden structures, burned three times between 1897 and 1899. Religious fanatics swore God was destroying Arizona's Sodom and Gomorrah.

George W. Hull, who owned the original townsite, is considered the "Daddy of Jerome." Hull waited until he was sixty-one to marry; however, the long wait did not guarantee marital bliss. In two years his wife divorced him, but several years later he tried again, this time with success. He retired at the age of seventy-six and sold the Hull Copper Company for a million dollars in cash. However, a mine stockholder sued him for mismanagement, and litigation held up the money. Hull had wanted to die a millionaire. He came close, dying on the witness stand but never knowing that the court would rule in his favor.

Other characters in Jerome include Dr. Lee Hawkins, a self-trained dentist, who was not really a doctor but liked the title and since his remedies were harmless, residents let him practice. Eventually he became a good dentist. Doc Hawkins was also an inventor of gadgets that usually did not work. Another Jerome character was undertaker W. P. Scott, who was once accused of picking gold from the teeth of his subjects and selling it for thirty dollars an ounce. The local magistrate, Lewis St. James, was totally deaf and could not hear testimony but knew most of the defendants personally, ruling in their favor. He also had the uncanny ability to know how much cash each was carrying and set a fine accordingly.

Mingus Mountain was named for Joseph and Jacob Mingus, two brothers who settled in the area in the 1880s and later operated a sawmill near the base of the mountain that is named for them.

In 1900 Clark built the fabulous Montana Hotel. Towering above the town, the plush hotel had two hundred rooms and served twice that many patrons in its massive dining room. The Montana burned in a spectacular blaze in 1915. In 1917 Douglas built the Little Daisy Hotel not far from his mansion, which was built the same year and is now a state park.

Housing was always a critical problem in Jerome. During World War I, fifteen thousand people were crowded into space enough for five thousand. Residents attached lean-to rooms to their houses and became landlords. It was said the workers lived in rotating shifts— they worked eight hours, slept eight hours then loafed the other eight. Three miners shared the same sleeping quarters, but had to take turns using the tiny rooms. Because they had nowhere else to go, miners used to walk the four-mile grade between Clarkdale and Jerome on cold winter nights just to keep warm.

Many residents aspired to become millionaires by investing in Jerome's mines. Con men dealing in fraudulent mine stocks were known to sell shares in non-existent Jerome mines to local people and be out of town on the evening train, before the residents realized they had been duped.

In 1920 the thirty-mile Prescott-Jerome highway was built, and members of the community no longer had to rely solely on the railroad for easy access to the "outside world."

World War I brought Jerome to its highest pinnacle of success. Between 1914 and 1920, the population reached fifteen thousand, making it Arizona's third largest city. In 1919 copper sold for thirty cents a pound. Huge stockpiles of copper at the end of the war sent the market plunging. By 1920 the price had dropped to twelve cents, and no copper was sold in the latter part of the year.

During tough economic times, the other businesses, fearing the miners were not spending enough money in their shops, tried to close down the saloons and parlor houses. However, as soon as times improved, the bawdy houses with their ladies of easy virtue and the drinking establishments were back in full swing. During Prohibition bootlegging became Jerome's biggest industry, next to copper.

Moralists, determined to make "Jerome a decent place to live" and fearing that the miners might spend some of their hard-earned cash on decadent vices, had every kind of card game outlawed—it was even against the law to watch a game of chance. One police roundup gathered eight tin horn gamblers, nineteen drunks and two notorious ladies, a disappointingly small haul for a city that prided itself on revelry.

The citizens rarely missed the opportunity to celebrate some festive occasion. On July 4, 1920 the town jail, which was reputed to have spikes in the floor to prevent prisoners from getting any sleep, was overflowing, so the town marshal chained twelve drunks to a huge mill wheel. Undaunted, prisoners picked up the wheel in unison and hauled it to the door of the nearest speakeasy, demanding an ax to widen the doorway so they could get in.

The final chapter of Jerome's illustrious story was about to begin. In 1925 William Andrews Clark died, leaving a vast fortune to his children to fight over. Both sons, Charlie and William, Jr., died before the court battle ended. In 1935 Phelps-Dodge bought the operation. In 1938 the Douglas-United Verde Extension played out but not before making a lot of people wealthy. The Josephine Tuttle, Edith, and Little Daisy shafts paid fifty million in dividends. "Rawhide" Jimmy Douglas died in 1949 a multi-millionaire.

Jerome never recovered from the stock market crash of 1929. A few years earlier, the United Verde Extension had discovered a rich body of ore directly beneath the town. Hundreds of thousands of tons of dynamite were used to wrest the ore from the mountain's clutches. Above ground, years of choking smelter smoke had destroyed the flora on the mountain. With nothing to hold the soil, Jerome began to slide. Despite hard times and the new catastrophe, Jerome's citizens never lost their sense of humor. Mayor Harry Mader coined a new phrase when he proclaimed "Jerome—a city on the move."

Jerome in the 1920s
Courtesy
Southwest Studies

Clarkdale (see Jerome)

The First Interstate Bank in downtown Clarkdale was, at one time, the Bank of Arizona. The building and its interior have not changed much since the day in 1928 when it was the scene of Arizona's biggest bank robbery up to that time.

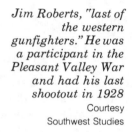

Jim Roberts, "last of the western gunfighters." He was a participant in the Pleasant Valley War and had his last shootout in 1928
Courtesy
Southwest Studies

On the morning of June 21 Earl Nelson and Willard Forester, two notorious Oklahoma outlaws, held up the bank, taking $40,000. As the two jumped into their getaway car, seventy-year-old Jim Roberts, the town constable, was making his rounds. One of the men fired a shot at the old man as the car sped away. The two Oklahoma outlaws did not know that the man they had fired on was one of Arizona's legendary gunfighters. Jim Roberts had tamed more towns than most people those days had ever seen. Before he became a peace officer in the 1890s, Roberts had been a participant in the famous Pleasant Valley War, and all agreed he was the deadliest gunman on either side. Later he became a deputy at Jerome, Congress, and Douglas— all tough towns. This time Jim calmly drew his Colt revolver and shot the driver, Forrester, through the head. The car careened off the road and came to a halt. Nelson climbed out of the car, took one look at Roberts standing there with both hands clasped around the handle of his nickel-plated six-shooter, and meekly surrendered.

Jim Roberts was a man of few words. After the incident he went home for lunch, later than usual. When his wife asked the usually punctual constable what had delayed him, Jim, never looking up from his plate, calmly replied, "Oh, there was a little trouble downtown." She did not learn of the shootout until later in the day, when some family friends came by to offer congratulations.

Clemenceau

There is not much left of Clemenceau today—it has been absorbed by the community of Cottonwood. The town was established in 1917 by "Rawhide" Jimmy Douglas as a smelter town. Originally it was called Verde, but the name was later changed to honor Georges Clemenceau, French Minister of War, a man much admired by Douglas. Clemenceau returned the honor by leaving the town a chaplet vase in his will. The vase never arrived, but the local high school has a letter announcing the gift.

The smelter closed in 1937, and the post office was discontinued in 1954.

Cottonwood

The first residents at Cottonwood were soldiers sent from Fort Whipple to protect settlers in the Verde Valley. Their headquarters was an adobe house near the Verde River. Later, when settlers arrived, they named the place in honor of large stands of cottonwood along the river. Later, the old adobe soldiers' quarters became the first school. The establishment of a post office in 1879 coincided with the settlers who first came to farm the fertile, but mosquito-infested valley.

Sedona

Sedona is one of those rare Arizona communities that takes its name from a woman, Sedona M. Schnebly. Ellsworth Schnebly named the town nestled among the sandstone cathedral-like monuments at the entrance to Oak Creek Canyon for his sister-in-law. From its humble beginnings in the early 1900s until the 1950s Sedona was one of Arizona's best kept secrets. After several Hollywood Westerns, including *Johnny Guitar* and *Broken Arrow*, the whole world knew about Sedona, and an influx of tourists was imminent.

The *Cowboy Artists of America* was founded in downtown Sedona at the Oak Creek Tavern. In 1965 Joe Beeler, a transplanted cowboy-artist from Oklahoma; George Phippen of Skull Valley, Arizona; Verde Valley resident Charlie Dye; and John Hampton, another cowboy artist of reknown, sat around a table and organized what has become the most illustrious group of artists in the world. These men set some lofty ideals in their charter: "to perpetuate the memory and culture of the Old West. . . ." and ". . . to insure authentic representa-

First meeting of the Cowboy Artists of America, June 23, 1965, at the Oak Creek Tavern in Sedona. Left to right Joe Beeler, Charlie Dye, John W. Hampton, George Phippen, and (back to camera) Robert McLeod
Courtesy Elizabeth Rigby
Photo © 1965

tion of the life of the West as it was and is."

Joe Beeler, a Sedona resident since 1960, says, "We wanted to maintain the integrity of artists like Charlie Russell." And they have succeeded. Members of this select group have shown their works throughout the world, making cowboy art popular and lucrative. Today these artists are earning what Charlie Russell used to call "dead man's wages" for their works. A recent cowboy art show in Phoenix drew two thousand viewers and grossed over $1.75 million. Beeler remembers the old days when he used to haul his paintings around in the back of an old station wagon and the only buyers were cattlemen whose life he so accurately depicted. Today, cowboy art enjoys unprecedented popularity by people from all walks of life. "Cowboy art is real," Joe explains; "people can interpret it themselves. They don't need the artist to stand there and tell 'em what it means."

Oak Creek Canyon

They call it "the Grand Canyon with a road." The winding, twisting highway built in 1929 presents one of the most scenic tours in Arizona. Before the road was built, settlers in the canyon kept wagons and teams on top of the east side of the canyon and climbed trails called ladders to the top for a trip into Flagstaff. They harvested crops and fished native trout out of the icy, clear waters, selling their wares in Flagstaff or hauling them out the south end of the canyon to markets at Jerome or Fort Verde.

The original settlers in Indian Gardens were the Thompson and

Oak Creek Canyon, 1931
Courtesy
Southwest Studies

Purtymun families. Jim Thompson moved to the Verde Valley in 1876 and started ranching. Not long after his arrival Al Sieber and his Apache scouts routed a band of Tonto Apaches at Indian Gardens. The crops of pumpkins and squash were still growing so Thompson decided to stake a homestead claim and take up farming. He built a log cabin on the site but did not move his family to the Gardens until 1887. His partner, Richard Wilson, was killed by a bear two years earlier in what is called Wilson Canyon today.

Another early resident in Oak Creek Canyon was Jesse Jefferson Howard, better known as "Bear" because of his prowess as a hunter. Howard, so the story goes, escaped from San Quentin, where he was serving time for killing a sheepherder. He escaped and came to Arizona sometime in the mid-1870s. Earlier his wife had died and left him with two youngsters, Jesse and Martha. One day while Howard was away, Tonto Apaches kidnapped the children. While making their escape, the war party accidentally ran into Howard and a party of hunters. The Apaches tossed the children into some cactus to cover their getaway.

Many years later Martha Howard married Steve Purtymun. They lived in several Arizona towns before moving to Oak Creek in 1896. In 1901 the entire student body at the Oak Creek school was named Thompson or Purtymun. Later, two Thompson girls married Purtyman boys. Descendants of the Purtymun-Thompson family are still scattered throughout the Verde Valley.

Colonel Hooker in patio of Sierra Bonita Ranch
Courtesy Arizona Historical Society Library

US 666
Interstate 10 to Interstate 40

About fifteen miles north of Interstate 10, Arizona 266 branches off and crosses the Pinaleno Mountains to the little community of Bonita, a word meaning "pretty" in Spanish.

Bonita was a rough place in the 1880s when the military post at Fort Grant was in its heyday. Soldiers were paid once every four months and came to Bonita to whoop it up. Ladies of easy virtue came from miles around on payday to help them spend their wages in the town's ten saloons. The population was about one thousand, including families of soldiers stationed at the fort. Class-conscious officers and their wives preferred to do their genteel socializing at Henry Clay Hooker's famous Sierra Bonita Ranch, in the Sulphur Springs Valley. The ranch, covering about eight hundred square miles, was the largest in Arizona at the time. It was a happy stopover for weary travelers, the hospitality and cuisine an Arizona tradition. The ranch was a storybook outfit, and many famous personalities considered their visit to Arizona incomplete without a social call at the Sierra Bonita. The ranch, located at an elevation of four thousand feet, was blessed with an abundance of water and lush grass. The ranch was known all over the West for its purebred cattle and fine racing horses. Hooker started in the livestock business during the silver rush to Nevada, when he bought a flock of five hundred turkeys in California and drove them over the Sierra Nevada Mountains, intending to sell them in Virginia City. While crossing the mountains, his less-than-bright birds stampeded over a cliff, and for a time it looked as though his investment had been lost. However, when Hooker reached the valley below, his flock had soared free and were waiting for him. At the silver camp, he sold the birds for five dollars apiece and bought a ranch in Arizona. Hooker is one of the few Arizona ranchers to be inducted into the National Cowboy Hall of Fame at Oklahoma City.

Sierra Bonita Ranch
Courtesy Arizona
Historical Society

Fort Grant, located on the southern slopes of the lofty Pinaleno Mountains, was established in 1873. Following the massacre of peaceful Apaches at Old Camp Grant, at the junction of Aravaipa Creek and the San Pedro River, and because of malaria problems, the army decided to relocate the post to a more healthful site. However, the soldiers developed another health problem at Fort Grant, venereal disease—two notorious bawdy houses posing as whiskey mills beckoned just outside the post.

The post was abandoned in 1895, but apparently a few hardy souls remained because the post office did not close until 1905. In 1908 President Teddy Roosevelt, miffed because Colonel Bill Stewart did not re-enlist after forty years of military service, exiled the officer to Fort Grant. Colonel Stewart's entire command consisted of a caretaker and a cook. Years later Fort Grant was used as a state reform school.

The Galiuro Mountains area, a spectacular range west of Fort Grant, is among the most primitive regions of the Southwest. It was in these mountains that Tom and John Power shot it out with a posse in 1918. The brothers were charged with evading the draft, and four lawmen were sent to bring them in. For mysterious reasons the posse, after surrounding the Power cabin, shot and killed Jeff Power, the boys' father, without warning. In the ensuing gunfight, three of the four peace officers were killed. Arizona's greatest manhunt followed, and the two brothers and a family friend, Tom Sisson, were captured just below the Mexican border by United States Cavalry. They were jailed at Safford amid much public outrage. The newspapers had already tried and convicted the two, and the trial was a mere formality. They were given life sentences and sent to the state prison at Florence. The brothers always maintained their innocence, insisting that the officers had shot and killed their father without identifying themselves and that they were acting in self-defense.

At parole hearings, relatives of the slain men protested vehemently, and the board refused to release the trio. Tom Sisson died in 1956, five years before the Power brothers were finally released—they had served forty-two years, the longest sentences in Arizona history. Old and bent when they left the prison, Tom and John spent most of their remaining years in this quiet area.

Clifton and Morenci

Henry Clifton was one of the first settlers to arrive in the Prescott area following the discovery of gold in 1863. A year later he entered politics in Yavapai County. As county recorder, he knew that most of the rich placers around Prescott had already been claimed; he also knew that the county extended all the way to the New Mexico border and that several claim applications from the San Francisco River area had been filed. Clifton, an incurable prospector, set out for the San Francisco River in 1865.

Clifton prospected this area and perhaps gave his name to the townsite. Others claim the town was named for the cliffs along the San Francisco River, which flows through town. Henry seems to have drifted over to the Silver City area and out of the pages of Clifton's history.

These miners and prospectors were not the first white men to visit the Clifton area—Francisco Vasquez de Coronado passed somewhere west of here in 1540; James Ohio Pattie and others trapped for beaver in the San Francisco River in the 1820s; in 1846 General Stephen Watts Kearny, Kit Carson, and a hundred dragoons followed the Gila on their way to California; Mace Greenlee prospected for gold here following the Civil War, giving the county a name when it was created in 1909; and in the early 1870s several men, including army

Old Chase Creek in Clifton, 1890s
Courtesy Arizona Historical Foundation

captain John Bourke and Jim and Bob Metcalf, reported rich copper ore in the area.

The Metcalf brothers had located copper outcroppings around Clifton while working as scouts for the army. In 1872 after the Apaches agreed to a peace treaty, the brothers returned to the area and filed claims on the Longfellow and Metcalf mines. In time these would be among the richest mines in the Southwest. J. N. Stevens and his brother Captain Jay Stevens, and Joe Yankie, arrived and located the Montezuma, Copper Mountain, Yankie, and Arizona Central mines. That same year these men organized the Copper Mountain Mining District. Since the nearest railroad was seven hundred miles away at La Junta, Colorado, transporting the ore was the most important concern except for the Mimbres Apaches, who claimed the area as their own.

Needing more capital to keep the Longfellow going, Bob Metcalf went to Las Cruces, New Mexico, where he made the acquaintance of Charles Lesinsky, proprietor of a stage station. The skeptical stationkeeper showed the ore samples to his brother Henry, experienced in mining. Henry strongly suggested they buy into the operation. Soon the Lesinskys had a controlling interest, and after a falling out, the Metcalfs sold them the rest of the stock.

Much of the ore mined in Arizona during the early 1870s was sent to Swansea, Wales, for smelting. This practice was not practical or profitable, so the Lesinskys built a crude smelter of adobe on Chase

Creek, using charcoal fuel made from mesquite wood. The ore was hauled by burro from the mine down to Chase Creek. The smelted ore was then hauled by ox train over the Santa Fe Trail to Kansas City, twelve hundred miles away. Many of these expeditions were attacked by Apaches and Comanches, the drivers killed and the oxen eaten. The copper ingots, being of no value to the raiders, were left behind to be retrieved by the next ore train.

Metcalf
Courtesy
Arizona
Historical
Foundation

The Copper Mountain Mine, located west of the Longfellow, had even greater potential for wealth. In 1872 a settlement called Joy's Camp, for Captain Miles Joy, a mineral surveyor, was established. Three years later, Eastern capital was raised to expand operations, and the Detroit Copper Company was created. Joy's Camp was changed to Morenci, for a town in Michigan.

In the late 1870s the Lesinskys built a narrow gauge railroad down Longfellow Hill to the smelter at Chase Creek. The empty ore cars were pulled up the incline to the mine by sturdy mules. On the return, the ore-filled cars, fueled by gravity, plunged headlong down the grade, with the mules getting a free ride in an empty ore car. In 1879 the Lesinskys had the first steam locomotive hauled into the area overland from La Junta. By 1880 both the Detroit Copper Company and Lesinskys' Longfellow were reaping great prfits. However, poor health and a fear of glutting the market caused the Lesinskys grave concern, so a year later they sold the Longfellow for two million dollars.

In 1881, because the Detroit Copper Company was in need of investment capital, Phelps-Dodge sent Dr. James Douglas to investi-

A Sunday outing at the Longfellow Tunnel, Clifton
Courtesy
Southwest Studies

gate the Clifton-Morenci area. Dr. Douglas was much impressed and wrote favorably to the New York-based firm, which put up the money for a share of the property. Then in 1895 William Church, longtime president of the Detroit Copper Company, decided to retire, selling his stock to Phelps-Dodge and giving them full control of the operation.

The Clifton-Morenci area would become, over the next half century, one of Arizona's greatest copper areas. Phelps-Dodge would begin a massive open-pit operation that would, in time, swallow up the picturesque city of Morenci. By the 1950s the Morenci Mine was the second largest in America and the fourth largest in the world.

About the same time the mines of this area were starting up, cattlemen were moving in. As the beef industry grew, ranchers had to begin branding cattle. There are many kinds of brands, and each has a name of its own. The brands are a cattleman's trademark and are registered in an official brand book. A brand is the key to ownership, and many cattlemen have named their ranches after a brand.

Cowboys who could neither read nor write quickly learned to name any brand whether it was letters or numbers. One Arizona rancher said, "A good cowboy could understand the Constitution of the United States were it written with a branding iron on the side of a cow."

One of Arizona's most enduring brands had its beginnings back in 1885, when Fred Fritz, Sr. settled along the Blue River, north of Clifton, and started raising cows. He was from a German settlement in south Texas, spoke English with a thick German accent, and could neither read nor write the English language. One day a brand inspector rode into the Blue River area and informed Mr. Fritz he had to register his brand. After filling out the necessary papers for the cattleman, the inspector handed Mr. Fritz a paper to sign. He scrawled an "X" in the proper place, then called over a couple of cowpunchers as witnesses. Neither could write his name, so each placed an "X" beside the boss's.

"Now," said the official, "you must draw your brand in the box at the bottom of the page." The cowman stared at the "signatures" a moment, then with slow deliberation marked three X's in the box, and the Triple X brand, one of Arizona's most famous, was born.

Life was not easy on the Blue River in those days. The renegade Apache bands were gone, but beef-killing bears were plentiful. One day in 1898 Fred Fritz came across one of his range cows that had been freshly killed by a grizzly. He jerked out a .45 revolver and fired at the bear, hitting it in the jaw. The animal charged, raking his four-inch claws the length of Fritz's body and ripping off chaps and clothes. Fritz was able to fire four more shots point blank, but this just seemed to make the grizzly more angry. Then Fritz lay still, and the bear backed off; however, each time the cowman tried to get up, the bear pounced on him. "He chawed on one end for a while and then he turned me around and chawed on t'other end," he said later. Fritz used his pistol as a club until it broke; he stabbed the bear with his knife until the blade snapped; and he tried unsuccessfully to set the bear on fire with his last weapon, a pocket full of matches. The struggle finally ended when a relative arrived with a rifle and shot the bear. Seven bullets were found in the carcass. Fritz never fully recovered from his injuries but lived another eighteen years.

They still run cows on the Blue River with three X's stamped on their hides, and Fred Fritz's son, Fred, Jr., continued to run the historic outfit until he retired in 1976. During the 1940s Fred Fritz, Jr., took time off from ranching to serve in both houses of the Arizona Legislature for a number of years. The popular cowman from Greenlee County was one of only three legislators in Arizona history to be elected both Speaker of the House and President of the Senate.

Clifton was still a raw town when society demanded the construction of a suitable place to lock up intractables. The result was a most unusual, escape-proof jail. Built in 1881, it was carved out of solid rock on the flood plain above the river. A hard rock miner was employed to gouge out the jail, and after being paid off he went on a binge at the nearest whiskey mill, Hovey's Dance Hall. Later that evening he proposed a toast to the world's greatest jail builder, and when no one would lift a glass in his honor, he proceeded to shoot holes in the ceiling of the hall. He was then escorted to the new jail for his misdeeds and thus became its first customer.

The Coronado Trail

This stretch of highway does not follow Coronado's trail, which was a precipitous route west of here. About nine miles north of Clifton lies the town of Metcalf, first settled in 1872, after gold was discovered in nearby Gold Gulch, two thousand people living here at one time. A mule-powered narrow gauge railroad linked the community with Clifton. Later the mules were replaced by a small locomotive. The engine was so light nobody became excited when it jumped the tracks—they just picked it up, set it back on the rails, and continued the journey.

Eighteen miles up the road from Metcalf and off to the right is the old Double Circle Ranch. When it was established in 1880, everything had come in by pack mule over several miles of rough terrain. On one occasion several Mexicans hauled a piano into the ranch. It was so heavy they could only carry it a few steps at a time. Another time four men wanted for a train robbery in Texas came to work for the Double Circle as cowboys. A posse, led by several Texas Rangers, trailed them to the ranch, and the outlaws chose to shoot it out—they were buried where they fell.

Further up the highway, Hannegan Meadow was named for Bob Hannegan, who ran cattle here briefly in the 1890s. A story is told that a reason for his hasty departure came from the way local people collected unpaid debts. Hannegan owed $1,200 to a couple of men and would not pay up, so they took him out and chained him to a tree until his relatives paid the debt in full.

Alpine

Alpine, located in some of Arizona's most spectacular high country, was originally called Bush Valley for Anderson Bush, the first settler. Three years later, in 1879, a party of Mormons arrived and renamed it Frisco for the San Francisco River. Finally, someone noticed the Swiss-like mountains, and the town was then named after Alpine, Utah. Jacob Hamblin, the greatest of all Mormon trailblazers of the Southwest, is buried here.

Nutrioso

Some of America's most famous fur trappers used to pass through this valley coming from Taos, New Mexico, to the White Mountains in the 1820s. *Nutria* means "beaver," or "otter," and *oso* is "bear" in Spanish. Mormon settlers arrived here in the 1870s, and a small fort was built in 1880.

Lyman Lake

The devastating floods that ravaged the Mormon settlements along the Little Colorado River in the 1870s were finally brought under control by a dam, but not without a struggle. In 1903 the original dam was washed out. A second one, named for Mormon bishop Francis Lyman, was swept away in 1915. Finally, the state contributed

$800,000 for an indestructible dam that has at last harnessed the river.

St. Johns

Early Mexican sheepmen crossed the Little Colorado at this site, calling the ford El Vadito, or the Little Crossing. There are two versions of the town's current name: one derives the name from the first woman resident, Maria San Juan; the other says it was named for San Juan's Day (June 24), which celebrated the beginning of the summer rainy season. The story is told that after Sol Barth won several thousand sheep and a few thousand dollars in a card game, he settled at this crossing. Hispanic and Mormon settlers located in the area in the early 1870s, the first Mormon colony a mile north. Because of flooding, the Mormons moved their community adjacent to that of the Mexicans, but for many years the two groups were not on friendly terms.

The Udalls, Stewart and Morris, were born and raised in St. Johns. Their father, Levi S. Udall, was one of Arizona's most prominent citizens and was for years a Justice on the State Supreme Court. Their grandfather, David K. Udall, was a leader in the first Mormon party of colonizers to settle at St. Johns. Both were basketball stars at the University of Arizona. After World War II, the two brothers returned to the University of Arizona and attended law school. In 1954 Stewart was elected to Congress. Six years later, President John F. Kennedy appointed him Secretary of the Interior. He was the first Arizonan to hold a cabinet post. Morris replaced his brother in Congress in 1961. "Mo," as he is called, has a folksy, homespun personality that has made him one of Washington's most popular politicians. In 1976 he ran a strong campaign for President in the Democratic primaries before losing out to Jimmy Carter.

Zuni River

A few miles north of St. Johns is the Zuni River. For hundreds of years this area has been held sacred by Indians of the Zuni pueblo of New Mexico, who believe the spirits of their ancestors reside here. In 1985 recognizing the area's religious significance for the Zuni, the state of Arizona declared the ground hallowed.

St. Johns, 1949
Courtesy
Southwest Studies

Concho, 1936 Courtesy Arizona Historical Foundation

Arizona 61

Concho

A few miles west of St. Johns is Concho. Concho means "shell" in Spanish, the shallow basin around the community inspiring the name. Among the earliest settlers here was sheepman Juan Candaleria of New Mexico. Arriving in 1866 he is considered to be the first white man to own sheep in northern Arizona. Candaleria raised fine merino sheep, known for their wool rather than their meat. His ranch was over forty square miles, the largest in this area. Juan's sons inherited the ranch, livestock, and town. The Mormons settled here a few years after the Mexicans arrived. A post office was established in 1881 under the name Erastus, for the apostle Erastus Snow. The Mexicans insisted on calling their village Concho, and in 1890 persistence paid off, as the Mormons agreed to bow to the wishes of the Mexicans.

Arizona 69
Cordes Junction to Prescott

Mayer

The thirty-six-mile road from Cordes Junction to Prescott skirts around the north end of the Bradshaw Mountains. The junction is just west of where Big Bug Creek joins the Agua Fria River. Big Bug was named by Prescott newspaperman John Marion for the dark, walnut-sized beetles that frequent the creek. Big Bug Creek meanders back and forth along Arizona 69, passing under the highway for the last time at Mayer.

Mayer was named for Jewish merchant Joseph Mayer, who arrived in 1882, opened a store, stage station, and saloon along the old wagon road from Prescott to Phoenix. Along with being town merchant, Joseph Mayer was a tourist-minded entrepreneur. An article published in the local newspaper in 1902 mentions his marketing "Indian toothpicks." In reality they were spines taken from prickly pear cacti.

During the latter part of the nineteenth century, the picturesque community on the banks of Big Bug Creek became a prosperous commerce center for the mining and farming ventures in the area. Mayer was the end of the line for the Prescott and Eastern Railroad until 1904, when Frank Murphy extended his narrow-gauge track to the south end of the Bradshaws.

The towering smokestack standing alone on the edge of town was the result of some best-laid plans that went awry. An optimistic developer planned a smelter on the site and let two contracts—one for a smokestack and the other for the smelter. Before the project began, the mine played out, and the developer tried to break the contract. The smelter builder accepted this bit of bad news with grace; however, the Weber Chimney Company was adamant. "A deal's a deal," they said stubbornly, and hired a crew of workmen at thirty-six cents an hour to fulfill the contract.

Poland Junction Road

In the early 1900s, the Prescott and Eastern Railroad ran a branch line into the rich Poland Mine. The junction of the tracks was near here. The mine was named for Davis R. Poland, who arrived in 1864 during the earliest days of the gold rush. He located the Poland Mine eight years later. Poland Junction, about five miles away, was as close to the mine as the railroad could get in the mountainous terrain. By 1902 Poland Junction was a bustling community with a post office, fourteen-room boarding house, and a general store. During its peak years Poland had a population of about eight hundred.

An 1,100-foot tunnel was cut through the mountains to the town of Walker, allowing ore from that community to be hauled by mule-drawn ore cars to the railroad at Poland Junction. Between 1900 and 1912 the Poland vein, located about eight hundred feet from the south portal, produced three quarters of a million dollars—mostly in silver. A miner's work week was long, and he drew little pay. In 1901 miners labored underground seven days a week for $2.25 a day. A dollar a day was taken out of that amount for food and lodging.

The post office discontinued service in 1913, a good indication that the mines and town were fading.

Humboldt

During the 1860s King Woolsey had a stamp mill on the Agua Fria River near here in the Big Bug Mining District. There was a new interest in gold prospecting between 1893 and 1907 due primarily to a drop in the price of silver. Arizona was the center of many wild and wooly promotional schemes during this period; it was said that the Iron King Mine sold more stock than ore. The mine did have excellent sources of gold and silver, along with some lead and zinc, but the technology had not been developed to produce the minerals profitably. However, the Iron King produced 1,253 ounces of gold and over 35,000 ounces of silver in 1907. The ore averaged about eight dollars a ton, but good times were all too brief. After the Panic of 1907 brought operations to a standstill, the mine was quiet until 1937, when it reopened with a one-hundred-ton mill. The demand for lead and zinc during World War II brought new life to the Iron King and Humboldt. In 1959 three million tons of ore were produced, making the mine the largest producer of lead and zinc in the state. The Iron King had finally fulfilled the dreams of its investors.

Humboldt, at its peak, was primiarily a smelter town for gold and silver. The town was named for German scientist and explorer Baron Alexander von Humboldt, who had predicted "the riches of the world would be found" here. By the late 1920s gold and silver mining in the area was on the wane, and the town began to take on the appearance of a ghost town; however, it boomed again after the Great Depression.

Dewey

In 1864 King Woolsey had a ranch along the Agua Fria River where Dewey is located. The ruins of the old town are still visible lying in a field a hundred yards north of the old highway.

In 1860 Woolsey arrived in Yuma, owning nothing more than his horse, saddle, rifle, pistol, and the clothes on his back. He took a job

King Woolsey, Prescott area rancher, prospector, and Indian fighter Courtesy Southwest Studies

Woolsey Ranch today Courtesy Jeff Kida

hauling supplies, investing his savings in mining ventures and buying a ranch at Agua Caliente on the Gila River. When gold was discovered in the Prescott area in 1863 Woolsey was among the first to arrive. He established a ranch on the Agua Fria and quickly gained reknown as a formidable Apache fighter. In 1864 a band of warriors went on a rampage in the Prescott area, driving off a few head of cattle. Woolsey organized a punitive expedition and trailed the Indians east into the Tonto Basin, then south into the area around Globe, where a battle was fought (see Fish Creek, Arizona 88 and Miami, US 60).

The fearless rancher became a hero for this and other expeditions against Indians. One memorable fight occurred in the fields surrounding the Dewey ruins when a war party of fifteen or twenty attacked Woolsey and two of his hired hands while they were hauling a load of hay. There was only one weapon, a double-barreled shotgun, among them. Woolsey told his helpers to hold the mules; at the same time he fired a round of buckshot into the on-rushing Apaches. He picked out the headman and dropped him from his horse with the other barrel. Seeing their leader on the ground, the rest of the band fled. As an example to other raiders, Woolsey dragged the leader's body to a tree and left it dangling. Journalist J. Ross Browne passed through here and noted the mummified, grotesque remains of the Apache. Woolsey was elected to the Territorial Legislature for five terms before his premature death in 1879.

Earlier, in 1867 Woolsey left his Agua Fria ranch and eventually wound up at the new settlement of Phoenix. During the 1870s he was the largest landowner in Phoenix and at the time of his death was considered one of Arizona's most prominent citizens.

In 1871 after Apaches drove nearly a hundred forty head of cattle from the ranch, noted Indian scout Jack Townsend organized a party of twelve frontiersmen from Prescott and set out to punish the raiders. They located the band feasting on beef in a remote canyon. A fierce fight ensued, and fifty-six Apaches were killed. Most of the cattle were returned, and Townsend's party suffered no casualties. Townsend's family had been killed and scalped by Indians, and he swore to get revenge, especially against Apaches. He usually went after them alone at night. Before he was ambushed and killed near the old Woolsey place, Townsend could claim responsibility for the deaths of fifty Apaches. It was said the Apaches held him in such high esteem as a warrior that as a tribute to his bravery, they did not mutilate his body but placed a blanket over it with stones at the corners.

In 1872 "Lord" Darrell Duppa operated a stage station called Agua Fria, and for a time the place was called Agua Fria Valley. The post office was closed in 1895, and when it reopened three years later, a new name had to be given. There was much patriotic fever over Admiral George Dewey's victory over the Spanish fleet at Manila Bay, so residents named the place in honor of America's newest war hero.

A short distance west of Dewey, in the vicinity of the Prescott Country Club, is the old Orchard Ranch, owned by famed poet-historian Sharlot Hall (see Prescott). Miss Hall moved to Prescott with her family in 1882 from the plains of Kansas. She was only twelve at the time, making the entire trip on horseback. A gifted poet, she wrote mostly about Arizona.

In 1907 she became the first woman in Arizona to hold a political office, when Governor Richard Sloan appointed her Territorial Historian. During the journey to Arizona in 1882, Sharlot had been thrown from her horse, suffering a lingering and painful spine injury. After Arizona became a state in 1912, she retired to the Orchard Ranch and remained there until the late 1920s, when she moved in to Prescott and began the project for which she is best remembered—the restoration of the Governor's Mansion. In 1981 Sharlot Hall was among the first group selected as members of the Arizona Women's Hall of Fame.

Arizona 73
Carrizo to McNary

Kinishba Ruins

The three-story-high Kinishba Ruins are among the best examples of the prehistoric Mogollon culture found in Arizona. In the 1930s Dr. Byron Cummings of the University of Arizona and his team of archaeologists restored a part of Kinishba, exacavated other ruins, and left a mound for future scientists to explore. It is estimated that as many as two thousand people lived in this two hundred-ten-room sandstone building between 1100 and 1300 A.D. The Mogollon people lived mainly in the central mountains of Arizona and are believed to have descended from the Cochise culture. About 2000 B.C. Cochise man cultivated the first crops of corn in Arizona. For mysterious reasons the Mogollon natives left this area in the early 1300s. Evidence indicates they moved to Casas Grandes, Chihuahua, in northern Mexico.

Fort Apache

Thanks in part to the silver screen, Fort Apache is one of the best-known military posts in the West. Although it was in one of the most remote parts of Arizona, it was important for its strategic location between the Apache tribes to the south and the Navajo nation to the north. During the waning days of the Apache wars in 1886 Chiricahua bands were gathered here, taken to Holbrook, and put on trains for Florida. At the time, Geronimo and his small band were still running free in Mexico. Lieutenant Charles Gatewood, interpreter Tom Horn, and two Apache scouts, Martine and Kayitah, entered the wily war chief's stronghold in late August and informed him that the Chiricahua had all been transferred to Florida. This news probably persuaded Geronimo to surrender.

The first military installation in this area was located here in the spring of 1870 by Major John Green, when he established Camp Ord at the end of a recently-constructed road into the land of the Coyotero Apaches. The name changed twice more that year—to Camp Mogollon and Camp Thomas.

According to some, the name was changed to Camp Apache after a friendly visit by the noted Chiricahua leader Cochise in February 1871, although this seems unlikely as Cochise was still on the warpath at the time and Camp Apache was far north of his bailiwick. A more likely explanation of the name change to Camp Apache is that the installation was in the middle of Apache territory; in 1879 Camp Apache became Fort Apache.

Apaches belonging to bands under the leadership of such men as Alchise, Miguel, Captain Chiquito, and Pedro were enlisted in the army as scouts in the campaign against other bands classified by the army as "hostile." These scouts had long and distinguished careers that lasted from General Crook's famous Winter Campaign of 1872 to the Geronimo Campaign of the 1880s. The hard-riding Apaches could track bees in a blizzard, and most historians credit them as being the most effective weapon in Crook's arsenal.

Despite the beautiful scenery, Camp Apache was a lonely, primitive duty station. Martha Summerhayes and her soldier-husband arrived at Camp Apache in October 1874. Her narrative gives a good description of the way it looked:

At that time (it was the year of 1874) the officers' quarters at Camp Apache were log cabins, built near the edge of the deep canon through which the White Mountain River flows, before its junction with Black River.

We were welcomed by the officers of the Fifth Cavalry, who were stationed there. It was altogether picturesque and attractive. In addition to the row of log cabins, there were enormous stables and Government buildings, and sutler's store. We were entertained for a day or two, and then quarters were assigned to us. The second lieutenants had rather a poor choice, as the quarters were scarce. We were assigned a half of a log cabin, which gave us one room, a small square hall, and a bare shed, the latter detached from the house, to be used for a kitchen. The room on the other side of the hall was occupied by the Post Surgeon, who was temporarily absent.

Our things were unloaded and brought to this cabin. I missed the barrel of china, and learned that it had been on the unfortunate wagon which rolled down the mountain-side. I had not attained that state of mind which came to me later in my army life. I cared then a good deal about my belongings, and the annoyance caused by the loss of our china

*Fort Apache in
the 1870s*
Courtesy
Southwest Studies

was quite considerable. I knew there was none to be obtained at Camp Apache, as most of the merchandise came in by pack-train to that isolated place.

In January Martha gave birth to a son, the first Anglo child born in these parts. Naturally, the baby was a great curiosity to whites and Indians alike:

All the sheepranchers and cattlemen for miles around came into the post. The beneficent canteen, with its soldiers' and officers' club-rooms did not exist then. So they all gathered at the sutler's store, to celebrate events with a round of drinks. They wanted to shake hands with and congratulate the new father, after their fashion, upon the advent of the blond-haired baby. Their great hearts went out to him, and they vied with each other in doing the handsome thing by him, in a manner according to their lights, and their ideas of wishing well to a man; a manner, sometimes, alas! disastrous in its results to the man! However, by this time, I was getting used to all sides of frontier life.

Several Apache women living on the reservation nearby came to pay their respects:

The seventh day after the birth of the baby, a delegation of several squaws, wives of chiefs, came to pay me a formal visit. They brought me some finely woven baskets, and a beautiful pappoose-basket or cradle, such as they carry their own babies in. This was made of the lightest wood, and covered with the finest skin of fawn, tanned with birch bark by their own hands, and embroidered in blue beads; it was their best work. I admired it, and tried to express to them my thanks. These squaws took my baby (he was lying beside me on the bed), then, cooing and chuckling, they looked about the room, until they found a small pillow, which they laid into the basket-cradle, then put my baby in, drew the flaps together, and laced him into it; then stood it up, and laid

383

it down, and laughed again in their gentle manner, and finally soothed him to sleep. I was quite touched by the friendliness of it all. They laid the cradle on the table and departed.

Most people are familiar with the Battle of Wounded Knee in South Dakota in 1890. Several years earlier, a Paiute Indian named Wavoka had blended his native religion with his adopted Christian teachings. It was believed that by dancing and performing other ceremonial acts, former leaders would be resurrected and come back to lead the downtrodden Indians again. This religion was picked up by the Plains tribes, who added ideas of their own. They were convinced they could bring great war chiefs like Crazy Horse back to life. They also believed in a ceremonial "ghost shirt" that the white man's bullets could not penetrate. Convinced they were invulnerable in their bullet-proof shirts, the warriors left the reservation. The 7th Cavalry was sent out to bring them back, and a confrontation developed, resulting in the massacre of Big Foot's band of Sioux at Wounded Knee Creek.

Few realize that a similar situation occurred here nearly a decade before the ghost dance craze. An Indian mystic named Nock-ay-del-Klinne had been mixing Apache and Christian religion, his message suggesting the return of two dead chiefs. His teachings were loose and could be interpreted to suit individual believers. Soon not only Apaches on the reservation but army scouts as well were coming under his spell. The military was becoming uneasy over the way the dances were affecting the natives and decided to put a stop to them. In the summer of 1882 Colonel Eugene A. Carr was sent to Cibicue from Fort Apache with a hundred seventeen men, including twenty-three Apache scouts, to arrest Nock-ay-del-Klinne. Geronimo, the eternal opportunist, was there and saw a chance to stir up trouble—he incited a riot over the arrest, and when the shooting ended, Nock-ay-del-Klinne had been killed. Eight soldiers, including Captain Edmund Hentig, were killed, and most of the Apache scouts, torn between alliances, sided with their own people. Later, three would be hanged and two more sent to prison at Alcatraz. On the return trip to Fort Apache, Carr's force was nearly annihilated by angry warriors. Uninformed Eastern journalists, believing they had another Little Big Horn, had a field day with the story. For a brief time Fort Apache was under siege. Will C. Barnes, a young soldier stationed at the post, slipped out and set up a lookout that kept the officers informed about the movements of the roving bands of warriors. Barnes was awarded the Medal of Honor for his bravery. Many years later he wrote stories about early Arizona and compiled the classic *Arizona Place Names*.

After Cibicue, the warriors rallied around a war chief named Na-ti-o-tish and rode into the Tonto Basin. Militia were raised in Globe to pursue the Indians. The group, well fortified with whiskey, stopped to take a siesta at the Middleton Ranch. No guards were posted, and while the so-called Globe Rangers were sleeping it off, several Apaches crept in and stole their horses. It was a long walk back to town for the humiliated heroes of Globe.

The rebellious Apaches were finally defeated on July 17, 1882 at Big Dry Wash north of Payson. The Apaches tried to set up an ambush, but crafty scout Al Sieber "smelled a rat" and set an ambush of his own. When the smoke lifted, about twenty Apaches, including Na-ti-o-tish, were dead. The battle marked the end of an era, for it was the last fought on Arizona soil.

V Western Arizona

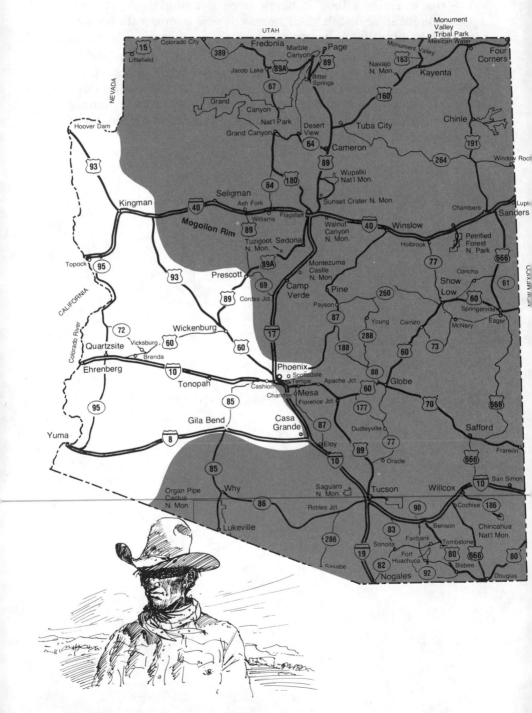

Gila Bend mule team
Courtesy
Southwest Studies

Interstate 8
(near Casa Grande) to Gila Bend

The new Interstate strikes boldly across desert country, heading almost straight for Gila Bend, sixty miles to the west. Before the arrival of the freeway system, this route was better known as Arizona 84 and was like all others in the area in that travelers were advised to carry extra fan belts and radiator hoses, and to hitch a canvas water bag to the car's door handle. Earlier trails followed paths of least resistance farther north. Weary travelers on the way to Yuma Crossing from Tucson went north to the Pima villages on the Gila River, where they bartered for supplies and rested their stock before venturing out across the desert to Gila Bend.

One of the most important sites on this trail was along the Gila River at Maricopa Wells. The place takes its name from wells in the area, and was a natural location for a stage station. The Wells was a favorite stopping place for thousands of immigrants on the Gila Trail. It was the last place to take on water and supplies before challenging the forty-mile desert crossing to Gila Bend. During these years a trading post was established for both natives and immigrants. Pima Indians living in the area raised crops of melons, corn, wheat, and barley, which they sold to travelers.

It is believed that the villages were visited by Father Kino in 1694 and again by Father Garcés in 1775. Kino had expressed a strong desire to build missions along the Gila, but the Spanish government would not give him support. In 1846 General Stephen Watts Kearny and his dragoons, guided by Kit Carson, rested briefly here before continuing their conquest of New Mexico and California. Captain

Philip St. George Cooke camped at this site in December 1846 while constructing a wagon road, which became known as the Gila Trail, to California.

Maricopa Wells was first used as a stage station by the short-lived San Antonio and San Diego Mail in 1857. This company secured an annual federal subsidy of $149,800 to haul mail and passengers semi-monthly over the 1,475 miles between San Diego and San Antonio. This stage route caused one disgruntled California newsman to complain that the line ran "from no place through nothing to nowhere." The line was perhaps better known as the "Jackass Mail" because the roads on some parts of the journey were impassable except by jackass.

In 1873 Maricopa Wells was linked to the outside world by a military telegraph. Today the town is located on the Maricopa Ak Chin Reservation, home of five hundred Papago, or Tono O'Odham, Indians.

The Butterfield Trail did not pass through Casa Grande. West of Picacho it veered northwest to Sacaton on the south bank of the Gila, then west to Casa Blanca, passing just south of Bapchule. The next stop after Casa Blanca was Maricopa Wells.

In 1879 the Southern Pacific began stretching its line east of Yuma through the rocky cuts and sandy arroyos of the Arizona desert toward Tucson, two hundred fifty miles away. Most of the construction was done by Chinese laborers, who toiled for a dollar a day. From their wages, they paid room and board. One observer wrote: "The Chinese are crowded there and work with monotonous industry that reminds one of the ants. These men appear to be neither happy nor miserable, just stolid and indifferent. It is plain that they move dirt more slowly than white men, but as they have no pipes to fill and no political reforms to discuss, they manage to get in a fair day's work before night falls."

The slow but industrious Chinese were able to lay more than a mile and a quarter of track a day. When the first sections of the line were opened, the passenger fare was ten cents a mile and freight rates were set at fifteen cents a mile per ton. At these rates one could ride at twelve miles an hour on a passenger train from Yuma to Tucson for just under twenty-three dollars on a trip that took one day. This was a bargain when compared to the sixty dollars one had to pay to ride a dusty, jostling stagecoach, which took three days and two nights of travel time.

On April 29, 1879 the Southern Pacific line reached Maricopa Station. Land speculators poured in with high hopes of quick sales, some lots selling for as high as a thousand dollars. Maricopa Station, located about eight miles south of the old Maricopa Wells stage station, became the terminus for travelers connecting by stagecoach with Phoenix, the upstart Salt River community thirty miles north, or with Tucson, nearly a hundred miles to the southeast. The proposed city of Maricopaville never reached the expectations of the developers, and eventually it was relegated to a railroad siding and called Heaton.

Later in 1887 a line would be extended to Phoenix from Maricopa Junction (not to be confused with Maricopa Station or Maricopa Wells). The word "Junction" was dropped in 1887, and the place was called Maricopa. The arrival of the railroad caused the old Butterfield station at Maricopa Wells to sink into oblivion. Maricopa Station became Heaton, leaving only one Maricopa. The fact that Maricopa is located in Pinal County instead of Maricopa County seems to be one more confusing place-name puzzle piece.

At Maricopa Wells the old road veers in a southwesterly direction until it reaches the Maricopa-Pinal County line near Enid. Here the old road parallels the Southern Pacific line and a dirt road.

Five miles northeast of Mobile, on the railroad line, was the old station at Desert Well. This was the only stop on the forty-mile desert crossing. The old adobe walls were still standing in the mid-1950s. West of Desert Well was treacherous Pima Pass, a dangerous ambush place. On the west side of the pass, the Butterfield company constructed a water tank, hauling water in from Gila Bend. The place was appropriately called Happy Camp. This trail was part of the Cooke Wagon Road, or Gila Trail, and was made famous by the Butterfield Overland Mail, which began operation in 1858. The trail runs roughly three to four miles north of the Southern Pacific tracks and as much as twenty miles north of Interstate 8 in some places. At the Maricopa Mountains they separate, the old road taking a more direct route through a range of the Maricopa Mountains and the new road dipping around the south end of the range. Both old and new roads then follow a more-or-less-direct route to Gila Bend.

Illustration from
The Narrative of
James O. Pattie, *an*
account of an Apache
attack. First written
material on Arizona
by Americans
Courtesy
Southwest Studies

Interstate 8
Gila Bend to Yuma

Near today's Gila Bend the southbound river makes a ninety-degree turn to the west and flows toward Yuma. During the early days, Gila Bend, or Big Bend as local people called it, was a welcome sight after a forty-mile desert crossing from Maricopa Wells to the east.

In 1774 Franciscan Padre Francisco Garcés reported a Papago *rancheria* at Gila Bend, which he named *Santos Apostales San Simon y Judas*. During the 1860s a group of white men raised grain to sell to miners in the Bradshaw Mountains to the north.

The location of the old Butterfield station is about four miles south of today's Gila Bend. It was burned by Indians in 1860 but was back in business soon after. Like Tucson and Fort Yuma, Gila Ranch was a timetable station. The reason for the shift to the present site was the location of the Southern Pacific Railroad line and station. Then, as now, when the road shifted, so did the town.

The stretch between Maricopa Wells across the "forty-mile desert" to Yuma Crossing and beyond to the coastal mountains, was the most tortuous on the entire twenty-four-day bi-weekly run of the Butterfield Overland Mail. The first history-making journey of the legendary stage line began at 6:00 P.M. on the evening of September 16, 1858. Waterman Ormsby, a reporter for the *New York Herald*, climbed aboard the first westbound stage at Tipton, Missouri, a hundred sixty miles west of St. Louis. The twenty-three-year-old journalist was the only "through" passenger, reaching San Francisco in twenty-three days, twenty-three and a half hours. His descriptive account of the journey is fascinating reading.

Stations spaced fifteen to twenty miles apart bore a litany of picturesque place names like Murderer's Grave, Oatman Flat, Flap-jack Ranch (where one of the amenities was a community bathtub), and Filibuster Camp.

Another traveler, William Tallack, kept a journal while traveling eastbound in 1860 along the one hundred-fifty-mile road between Yuma Crossing and Gila Bend. Tallack tells an interesting story of the trail:

> Breakfasted on venison at three A.M. at Stanwick's ranche on the Gila and, by special favor of the conductor had time for a plunge in the stream. On starting we noticed hereabouts the marks of several recent Indian campfires. A month subsequent to our visit here, two overland passengers, wishing to bathe in the Gila, and not having any extra time allowed for the stage to stop, borrowed horses from the ranche, had their bath, and rode after the others, overtaking them at the next station. But on the way they were assaulted by five Indians armed with bows and arrows. In self-defense, they killed three of the Indians, and so escaped to their fellow-travelers and the stage. . . .
>
> We took our next meal at two P.M. at Gila Bend. This station had been destroyed by the Indians only four months previously, but the inmates escaped. More than a hundred arrows were afterwards picked up around the spot. . . .
>
> At nightfall we reached the Pimo (sic) villages, a settlement of comparatively civilized Indians. . . . Near the station our attention was called to a "sweat-house," where the Indians get rid of fevers by a vapour-bath process.
>
> While our supper was preparing we washed in an Indian bowl formed of reeds, but quite watertight. Saucepans also of reeds are here made use of. They are filled with water, which is then boiled by dropping hot stones into it. . . ."

While many complained about the food, Tallack was more understanding. "The fare, though rough, is better than could be expected so far from civilized districts and consists of bread, tea, and fried steaks of bacon, venison, antelope, or mule flesh—the latter tough enough." In Arizona, amenities such as milk, butter, and fresh vegetables were scarce as horseflies in December. Usually passengers were served jerked beef, slumgullion, cornbread, beans, and black coffee. Jars of chili peppers and mustard provided added spice to the meal.

Little time was wasted at the stations. About two miles out, the driver blew a bugle to warn the hostler to have a fresh team of horses ready. Mail sacks were exchanged, and passengers headed for the outhouses. In ten short minutes, the stage was ready to roll again.

A century ago Gila Bend proudly boasted one of the West's most appropriately named saloons, "Whiskey, the Road to Ruin." Today that sign hangs over the false-front saloon at Pioneer, Arizona's living museum, north of Phoenix on Interstate 17. When US 80 was built across Arizona in the 1920s, Gila Bend was one of the few places where weary travelers could stop for water and gas. The auto repair and accessory business was the most lucrative in town. Residents still jokingly refer to this desert highway community as the "fan belt capital of the world."

Kenyons Station

The next stop west of Gila Bend was Kenyons Station, better known as Murderer's Grave. Actually, the name was given in 1873, several years after the Butterfield line closed, after a gang of cutthroats had tortured and killed the agent in an unsuccessful attempt to rob his station.

Painted Rocks

Painted Rocks may have been the natural marker that separated the Maricopa Indians from their arch rivals, the Quechans, or Yumas. There are many petroglyphs in the area, and they may have inspired Father Eusebio Kino to refer to the site in 1699 as Sierra Pinta, or Painted Mountains. The place was mentioned in 1754 by Father Jacob Sedelmayr and again by John C. Fremont in 1849.

West of Painted Rocks on the south bank of the Gila is Oatman Flat, the scene of one of Arizona's most grisly massacres. Here, on February 18, 1851 a Yavapai or Tonto Apache war party attacked a family of immigrants traveling alone on the Gila Trail. The lone survivors of the Oatman Massacre were two girls, Olive, twelve; Mary Ann, eight; and Royce Oatman's oldest son, Lorenzo, who was clubbed and left for dead. The rest were brutally slain, the wagon plundered, and the two girls carried off.

The girls were eventually traded to some Mojave Indians living along the Colorado. Mary Ann did not survive the ordeal, but Olive remained with the tribe. She was tatooed on her chin, as was the custom for Mojave women. Lorenzo recovered from his wounds and moved to California, but he never gave up hope of finding his sisters. In 1856 Henry Grinnell, an employee at Fort Yuma, learned of a white captive living with the Mojaves and decided to investigate. When the Indians denied having the girl, Grinnell let it be known that a large military force was planning to sweep through the valley searching for white captives. This news persuaded the chief to exchange Olive for some gifts, and a short time later a reunion was arranged with her brother. The ordeal of Olive Oatman became one of the most publicized events to have taken place on the Gila Trail. In 1857 a sensationalized account of the event was written by a preacher named Royal Stratton. Poor Olive was supposed to have gone crazy and died in an insane asylum soon afterward. In reality, Olive was not violated sexually and came through her ordeal as well as could be expected. She lived a long and full life, married, raised a family, and lived to the age of sixty-four.

The bodies of the rest of the victims of this massacre were buried where they had fallen, their graves noted by travelers along the Gila Trail for many years.

The Butterfield Overland Mail established a station at Oatman Flat in 1858. It is said the road ran right over the Oatman grave site. In 1865 pioneer cattleman Billy Fourr ran cattle in the area. His headquarters was an adobe structure about a quarter mile from the old station.

Agua Caliente ("Hot Water")

Jesuit Father Jacob Sedelmayr called this native *rancheria* Santa Maria del Agua Caliente and suggested it would be a suitable place for a mission. The priest noted that natives were using the warm mineral springs and mud for therapeutic purposes. These soothing medicinal hot springs have been a godsend for healthseekers from prehistoric to modern times.

In 1775 the great Franciscan explorer Father Francisco Garcés visited the natives in the area, and one of Arizona's most illustrious early pioneers, King Woolsey, settled here in 1865. Two years earlier, Woolsey accompanied the Joe Walker expedition when they found gold in the Bradshaw Mountains. During this time he also gained fame as an Indian fighter.

On the south side of the river, opposite Agua Caliente, was Burke's Station, named for its first agent, Patrick Burke. The station was part of the Butterfield Overland Mail line but fell into disuse after the line closed at the outbreak of the Civil War.

In 1864 the station was used to store government hay. It reopened in the 1870s with G. R. Whistler acting as agent. Whistler was murdered by the stableman, who was pursued and captured by King Woolsey. The man was hanged and left swinging from a limb for weeks afterward as a warning to other potential murderers—a common custom on the frontier before organized law enforcement took over.

During the twentieth century Agua Caliente has been a popular health resort. A few years ago someone had the idea Agua Caliente could be enlarged to accommodate more healthseekers. Dynamite was used to blast out a large bath area; however, the plan backfired when the springs disappeared into a deep underground cavern.

Stanwix Station

Stanwix Station was another stage stop along the Butterfield Overland Mail line. Stanwix Station is approximately nine miles northwest of present-day Stanwix (two miles west of Sentinel on Interstate 8). It was called Flap-jack Ranch and seems to have had a facility, natural or otherwise, for bathing. Established in 1858, Stanwix is claimed by some historians to be the site of the westernmost skirmish of the Civil War. (Other claimants of this honor are sites at Picacho and at La Paz, on the Colorado River.)

In January 1862 Confederate General Henry Sibley and his Texas army marched up the Rio Grande toward Santa Fe. At the same time, he ordered Captain Sherod Hunter and fifty-four cavalry troops to occupy Tucson. Accompanying Hunter was Colonel James Reily, whose mission was to open relations with Don Ignacio Pesqueria, governor of Sonora. The Confederacy had high hopes the Mexicans would assist the South by allowing supplies to come in through Mexico, thus avoiding the Union's naval blockade.

Hunter's Confederate cavalry occupied Tucson on February 28, 1862. A few days later Colonel Reily, along with Lieutenant James Tevis and twenty cavalrymen, rode south to Hermosillo. However, if the Mexicans had any plans to assist or sell supplies to the Confederates, they never had the chance to carry them through. As soon as word of the meeting leaked out, the Union ordered a warship to Guaymas. This "subtle" gunboat diplomacy was intimidating enough to make Pesqueria renege on any deal to assist the South.

Captain Hunter hoped to link up with Confederates in southern California to create an ocean-to-ocean Southern power. The plan failed when Union loyalists were able to control all of California. To make matters worse for Captain Hunter's small force, a large army of about two thousand volunteers, called the California Column, began moving toward Yuma Crossing. Hunter knew it was only a matter of time before his small force would have to evacuate Arizona, so the resourceful officer decided to create as much havoc as possible in the time that remained.

Advance units of the California Column were already establishing supply stations along the Gila Trail, so on March 3, 1862 Hunter led his troops to the Gila River, hoping to destroy as many Union supply posts as possible. At the Pima Villages, near Sacaton, Hunter captured Ammi White, a Union sympathizer. White owned a mill and was busy storing supplies for the Calfornians. Rather than destroying about fifteen hundred sacks of wheat, Hunter distributed them among the Pimas. He learned that the Butterfield stage stations between the Pima Villages and Yuma were being used to store hay, so he determined to burn as many haystacks as possible. Hunter succeeded in destroying fodder at six stations. His raiders came so close to Yuma Crossing that the ferry boat operations were suspended for fear the Texans would gain control of this strategic crossing. One wonders how much the course of history might have changed had the South made a stronger commitment to control this area.

Colonel James Carleton, the tough professional soldier in charge of the California volunteers ordered Captain William McCleave to take a small force and ride to Ammi White's flour mill at Casa Blanca (near today's Bapchule) and check out the activities of Captain Hunter's "band of renegades and traitors." The ambitious colonel even suggested McCleave take his small force to Tucson to capture the notorious Captain Hunter. McCleave, however inadvertently walked into a trap at Ammi White's flour mill, where Hunter, posing as White, took the Union officer and his nine-man patrol prisoner. McCleave was so chagrined at having been duped that he boldly challenged Hunter and his men to a bare-knuckle fight, the winner to go free. Hunter, who really had nothing to gain since he was already free, laughingly turned down the challenge. Lieutenant Jack Swilling of Hunter's command took White and the Union prisoners to Tucson. At the Old Pueblo the enlisted men were paroled, and White and McCleave were escorted to the Rio Grande. Eventually they, too, were paroled. (Paroling prisoners was common during the Civil War in the Southwest. Supplies were hard to get, and soldiers did not want the extra responsibility of foraging food for captives.)

An interesting sidelight to this story was that Lieutenant Swilling and Captain McCleave became well acquainted on the journey to the Rio Grande. Swilling told McCleave that before the war he had found gold on the Hassayampa River and presented his prisoner with a few nuggets as proof. After he was paroled and had rejoined Colonel Carleton, McCleave passed this information along to his commanding officer. The nuggets eventually found their way to Washington and helped influence the creation of the Territory of Arizona in 1863. Later Carleton met with ex-mountain man and army scout Joe Walker, who was now leading a party of prospectors, and suggested Walker check out Swilling's story about gold on the Hassayampa. On the way to Arizona, Walker met Swilling near Silver City, New Mexico. Swilling, who had deserted the Confederate cause, was eager to go prospecting on the Hassayampa and joined up with the Walker party, which found rich placers in the Hassayampa River country. Later, the city of Prescott, which sprang up nearby, became the first territorial capital of Arizona.

Captain William Calloway was ordered to take his troops to the

Gila River area to close down the Hunter threat. When one of Calloway's patrols ran into a small party of Confederates burning haystacks at the old Butterfield station at Stanwix, the Texans opened fire, wounding a Californian. Then the Confederates gave their Yankee pursuers the slip, heading toward Tucson. On the way back, Captain Hunter left a sergeant and nine enlisted men at the Butterfield station at Picacho, forty miles north of Tucson.

The exchange of shots which led to the wounding of Private Bill Semmilrogge at Stanwix Station has been called the westernmost Civil War skirmish, but a larger battle would occur a few days later at Picacho Pass.

Grinnell's Stage Station

The next station on the Butterfield Overland line was Grinnell's, named for the same Henry Grinnell who arranged the release of Olive Oatman in 1856. Like other buildings in this part of the country, it was made of adobe; it was built in 1858, the first year of Butterfield's operation, and closed in 1861 with the outbreak of the Civil War. The station was located two miles east of Texas Hill, near a bluff overlooking the Gila River. Years later, Grinnell's Station was marked on maps as Teamster Camp, or Texas Hill Station.

Mohawk/Peterman's Station

Peterman's Station is located about three miles northeast of present-day Mohawk. Sometime after the Butterfield line closed operations in 1861, the Mohawk station was built nearby. Nothing much remains of either station. Apparently the name Mohawk was used by some New Yorkers in honor of the New York Indian tribe. With the arrival of the Southern Pacific, Mohawk was moved a few miles south to its present location and called Chrystoval. In 1905 the name was changed to Mohawk.

Antelope Peak Station

Built in 1859, this adobe station located on the west side of Antelope Hill was a late addition on the Butterfield Trail, replacing Filibuster Camp, four miles to the west. A better source of water was the reason for the change.

Most of the old Butterfield stations are located north of the railroad and highway. At Antelope Hill the tracks of the Southern Pacific turn north, passing over the site of the old station and wiping out any remains. The site is just under two miles north of Tacna on Interstate 8.

Tacna

Tacna was originally located at Antelope Peak. With the arrival of the Southern Pacific in 1879, Tacna moved south several miles to its present location.

The name Tacna was supposed to have been a shortened version of a Greek priest named Tachnapolis, who came from California to work among the natives in the 1600s. This seems unlikely, a story perhaps begun in the fertile mind of Max B. Noah, who came to the area in the 1920s and opened a service station with a barrel of gasoline and a hand pump. He took the name from the old railroad siding of Tacna, where a post office was established in 1888 but which closed a decade later. Noah re-established the post office in 1927 and called it Tacna. When Noah's little community began to fade, the Tacna post office was moved four miles further east and called Ralph's Mill-Tacna, the Ralph being for Joe Ralph, who ran a small cafe for travelers on old US 80. The true origin of the name Tacna remains a mystery.

Filibuster Camp
(approximately one mile north of present-day Wellton)
The Butterfield Overland Station

Filibuster Camp was established in 1858 on the campsite of the ill-fated Crabb Expedition of 1857.

Filibusters were private armies of adventurers, or land pirates. During the mid-nineteenth century, bands of American *filibusteros* invaded parts of Mexico and Central America to establish private empires or republics. Among these filibusters was Henry A. Crabb, a politically ambitious opportunist, but in some respects he has been unfairly maligned by historians. Crabb married into a prominent Mexican family named Ainsa with family ties in Sonora, although most of the Ainsas lived in California. Crabb was invited by Ignacio Pesqueira to bring a thousand "peaceful" colonists to Sonora. In reality Pesqueira hoped to use Crabb and his men to help him overthrow Governor Manuel Gándara's regime and "liberate" the people

Filibuster Camp
Courtesy
Southwest Studies

of Sonora. In March 1857 Crabb recruited an army in Calfornia and set out for Sonora. By the time he reached Yuma Crossing, his force had dwindled to less than a hundred men; however, Crabb was determined to carry on. They camped about forty-five miles up the Gila River at the site of a future stage station, before turning south for the Mexican border town of Sonoita.

In the meantime Pesqueira had overthrown Gándara's government without the aid of the Americans. Crabb's untimely arrival provided the new governor with an opportunity to rally Sonorans to his side by declaring war on the "hated gringo bandits." He disavowed having any connection with the invaders and rallied loyal Mexicans: "Let them die like wild beasts. . . . Viva Mexico! Death to the Filibusters."

Outnumbered ten to one at Caborca, Crabb and fifty-nine of his men held out for six days before surrendering in exchange for safe passage back to the border. On April 7, the prisoners, with hands tied behind their backs, were lined up and shot in the back by firing squads, Crabb saved for last. Afterwards his head was cut off and placed in a jar of mescal and put on public display. Later, it was sent to Mexico City as testament of Pesqueira's loyalty. The deceitful governor was perceived by Sonorans to be a patriotic savior. The Sonorans did not bother to bury the bodies but left them to be devoured by village dogs and hogs.

Shortly afterwards, another party of sixteen Americans was captured, marched into Caborca, lined up before a firing squad, and shot. Their bodies were also left to the animals. A few days later, Mexican troops under Hilario Gabilando crossed the American border and executed four more members of the Crabb Expedition, men who had been ill and had not taken part in any of the fighting.

In Caborca the brutal and cowardly slaughter of the Crabb Expedition is celebrated to this day as a glorious victory.

Adonde

Adonde, Spanish for "where" is a railroad siding just east of Yuma, used as a watering stop in the days of steam locomotives. Although Adonde was an old stage station, it was not used by the Butterfield Overland line, since the Butterfield line had moved its transcontinental line several hundred miles north when the Civil War broke out. Other companies, such as Wells Fargo, picked up the slack in the 1870s and continued until the arrival of the Southern Pacific Railroad.

About a mile north of Adonde, on the south bank of the Gila River, was the old Butterfield station of Mission Camp. It was closed in 1859, when the company moved the station to Antelope Peak. The name Mission Camp is said to have been given because famed Jesuit Father Eusebio Kino had built a mission on the site, a highly improbable story—although Kino came through this area in the 1690s, he did not build any missions. The station was the scene of a triple murder on Christmas Eve, 1870, when three outlaws robbed and killed the cook, stage manager, and his wife.

Snively's Station

The last Butterfield Overland station east of Yuma Crossing on the 437-mile trek across Arizona was named for Colonel Jake Snively, a Texas frontier hero. In 1858 Snively discovered rich gold placers at this site, twenty miles up the Gila River from Yuma, the first important gold strike in Arizona history. A town materialized overnight and was soon filled with hundreds of miners, and soon others came to "mine the miners." World traveler J. Ross Browne, a writer who had great influence on Mark Twain, said of Gila City, "Enterprising men hurried to the spot with barrels of whiskey and billiard tables; Jews came with ready-made clothing and fancy wares; traders crowded in with wagons of pork and beans; and gamblers came with cards and Monte-tablès. There was everything in Gila City within a few months but a church and a jail. . . ." This Babylon on the Gila reached a peak population of about twelve hundred, and by 1861 prospectors were panning out $20 to $125 in gold dust a day. The placers were quickly exhausted, and when the gold ran out, so did the miners. The Gila River went on a rampage in 1862, rushing over its banks and washing out what remained of the town. Browne, who toured the territory in 1864, reported that all that remained of the once-prosperous boom town were "three chimneys and a coyote."

In 1879 the Southern Pacific built a siding a mile and a half east of the stage station and called it Dome, for the Castle Dome Mining District, or the nearby mountains of the same name. The station replaced Castle Dome Landing, on the river, as the shipping point for ore. As the railroads continued into the interior of Arizona, railroad sidings gradually replaced the old steamboat landings in this area. In the 1890s prospectors were still panning gold in the area, but hardrock mining had become far more important.

Dome, Arizona, former site of Gila City. Here in 1858 discovery of placer gold led to the state's first gold rush
Courtesy Arizona State Library

399

Fort Yuma and Jaeger's Ferry
Sketch by
J.R. Bartlett, 1852

Interstate 8
Yuma

Yuma

Yuma Crossing, located near the confluence of the Gila and Colorado rivers, was destined to play a major role for both Hispanic and Anglo-Americans. However, its importance goes back much further in time—it is believed that Indians began farming this rich land more than a thousand years ago. Included among these natives were the Quechan, Cocopah, and Mojave peoples. The Quechan are better known as the Yumas because of a misunderstanding by early Spanish explorers. One version has it that when the Spanish asked to meet with the native leader, a young man stepped forward and proclaimed himself a "Yuma," or son of the leader. The Spanish believed he was refering to the name of the tribe. Both the people and the river crossing would from that time forth be called Yuma. The most probable version says the name comes from the custom of building bonfires in the belief that the ensuing fire and smoke would bring rain. It is said the old Spanish word *Uma*, meaning "smoke," became Yuma and was applied to the Quechans.

These Quechan (Yuma) farmers were perhaps Arizona's first winter visitors. They farmed the flood plains during the winter and then escaped the hot, mosquito-infested summers by crossing the desert to the cool range of coastal mountains east of San Diego. However, when Spanish colonizers in the 1600s began coveting their farmlands, the Quechan took up full-time residency to protect their interests.

The earliest *entrada* of Spanish explorers came in 1540, when Hernando de Alarcón sailed three supply ships to the mouth of the Colorado. Alarcón was supposed to be hauling supplies for the Coronado Expedition on their quest for the fabled Seven Cities of Gold, but the geographical features of the land were separating the two Spanish leaders. At the mouth of the river Alarcón began a fifteen-day journey upstream with two small boats and twenty men. He named the stream Rio de Buena Guida, or River of Good Guidance. At the junction of the Gila, he was introduced to the natives as the "Son of the Sun," indicating that he wanted to make a positive impression, as the natives were sun worshipers.

Alarcón found no sign of the Coronado Expedition, but he did note that California was a peninsula, not an island, as was commonly believed. Since worms were feasting on his ships, he decided to leave the Yuma area. Before sailing, however, he left a message buried at the trunk of a large tree with these words carved on the trunk, "Alarcón came this far. There are letters at the foot of this tree."

Several months later Melchior Diaz, one of Coronado's officers, arrived at the Yuma crossing with twenty-five soldiers in search of Alarcón and located the messages but no supplies. The Quechans attacked Diaz and his men, but the Spaniards escaped. Diaz, one of Coronado's most valued officers, died on the return journey when he was thrown from his horse and impaled on his own lance.

The next Spaniard to visit the Yuma crossing was Juan de Oñate, the first governor of New Mexico. In 1604 he left the Rio Grande with thirty soldiers and two padres, heading west across Arizona, then down the Colorado River, hoping to find the Cities of Gold, or the fabled Northwest Passage. Instead, the party encountered some of Arizona's earliest tellers of tall tales. Modern-day yarnspinners have nothing on these natives, who told of fabulous Lake Copalla, where people adorned themselves with solid gold bracelets. Others spoke of a wealthy island ruled by a fat woman with big feet, whose subjects were all bald men. Nearby was a tribe of people with such large ears that several people could stand in the shade of a single ear; members of another tribe were reported to have only one foot; and still another tribe subsisted only on the smell of food. These strange people had unusual sleeping habits—one group slept in a tree, another slept under water, and a third never slept at all.

Oñate himself was guilty of spreading misinformation. Contrary to Alarcón's findings, he proclaimed California to be an island.

The next European to visit the Yuma crossing was the great Jesuit missionary Father Eusebio Kino. The tireless explorer made at least three journeys down the Gila to visit and hold Mass for fifteen

401

hundred natives living in the area. Kino, a skillful cartographer, refuted Oñate's claim that California was an island. Earlier he had seen peculiar blue abalone shells on the west coast of the Baja in California. These same shells were found among the Pima and Papago as trade items. Kino was convinced that traders used an overland route from California. Further exploration and interviews with headmen inspired him to make his historic proclamation: "California no es isla sino peninsula."

Lack of funding and resources prohibited Kino from establishing a mission at Yuma. Sixty years after the "Padre on Horseback" died, Francisco Tomás Garcés trekked across Kino's old "Camino del Diablo" to the Yuma crossing. The natives welcomed the humble Franciscan, and he established a mission, La Puerta de la Purisima Concepcion, on a bluff overlooking the confluence of the Gila and Colorado rivers, and another mission twelve miles upstream called San Pedro y San Pablo de Bicuner.

The new missions in Alta, California, under Father Junipero Serra, were struggling in the early 1770s and were in desperate need of an overland supply route from Mexico. Garcés convinced Juan Bautista de Anza, commandant of the presidio at Tubac, that a land route was feasible. In January 1774 an expedition left Tubac and traveled along the Camino del Diablo to the Yuma crossing. Anza, a third generation soldier on the Sonora frontier, proved to be an able statesman. He negotiated a treaty with Chief Palma of the Quechan to allow colonists to use the critical river crossing. Anza's expedition was a success, and he returned to the crossing a year later with two hundred forty colonists bound for California. For his great work, Anza was promoted to Governor of New Mexico. Unfortunately, the officers who followed him were not made of the same stuff. A government belt-tightening program drastically reduced funding for the Yuma crossing. Promises of lavish gifts to the Quechans were not kept, leading to Chief Palma's loss of prestige with his people. Lack of respect and Spanish abuses caused deep Indian resentment of the continued presence of the Spanish.

On the morning of July 17, 1781 the Quechans revolted, destroying Spanish missions and dwellings. The slaughter went on for two days, and when the bloodbath was over, fifty Spaniards, including the revered Father Garcés, were dead. Later, forty-eight captives (women and children) were ransomed back to the Spanish, but the overland road to California would remain closed for more than forty years.

The river people living near the Yuma crossing had little contact with whites until 1823, when Captain José Romero crossed overland to California. Romero, the commandant at the Tucson presidio following the Mexican Revolution, is remembered as the "Mexican Anza" for his accompishment. The fearsome reputation of the Yumas caused Romero and his party to bypass the crossing at Yuma and ford the Colorado near its mouth. Upon returning, he attempted to establish a trail north of the Yuma crossing but lost his way in the Mojave Desert, finally reaching Tucson in late 1825.

The first Anglo-Americans to penetrate the wilderness regions of Arizona were the fur trappers. Prior to their arrival in the 1820s, few people east of "the Wide Missouri" were even aware of the vast, uncharted lands that would be called Arizona forty years later.

The earliest written account of this area was the narrative of James Ohio Pattie, of Kentucky. Pattie's bigger-than-life story reads like a cross between dime-novel fiction and stage play melodrama. During his five-year Southwest odyssey, he braved Comanche lances to rescue naked women; fought grizzlies, mountain lions, and Apaches; survived a torturous desert ordeal; and vaccinated thousands against the scourge of smallpox.

Grieving over the loss of his mother in 1824, Pattie and his father, Sylvester, left the family farm in Kentucky and headed for St. Louis, where they outfitted themselves for a fur trapping expedition. It was the heyday of the fur trade, and soon they were bound for the pristine hunting grounds of New Mexico, arriving in Taos in the fall of 1825. Taos in those days was the favorite rendezvous of American and French trapping parties in the Southwest. It was also the launching pad for expeditions into Arizona. The Gila watershed was an untapped resource of beaver pelts, or "hairy bank notes," back when beaver hats were the fashion and the fur trade was one of America's greatest economic enterprises. The area was still part of the Republic of Mexico, and the Mexicans were not eager to see the increasing number of buckskin-clad Americans setting up business in Taos and Santa Fe.

The Patties were delayed in Santa Fe while trying to secure a Mexican license from Governor Antonio Narbona. The governor was reluctant and might not have granted permission had fate not intervened in a most dramatic way. A Comanche war party swooped down on Santa Fe and carried off some young women, including Governor Narbona's beautiful daughter, Jacova. The Patties, outraged at such barbaric behavior, organized a party of trappers and went off in hot pursuit. Since the Comanches were not accustomed to being followed, it was not difficult for the rescuers to circle around and set up an ambush. The unwary war party was emerging from a narrow gap when the trappers struck. The captive women had been stripped of their clothing, being forced to walk in advance of the main group.

When the shooting began the warriors momentarily forgot their captives and braced for battle. This gave young James and several friends time to ride in and make a heroic rescue. "The gratitude of such captives," he wrote, "so delivered, may be imagined. Fears, thanks and exclamations in Spanish were the natural expression of feeling in such a position." He removed his buckskin jacket and gallantly placed it on Jacova's bare shoulders, then returned her safely to her father in Santa Fe. Needless to say, the grateful governor had a change of heart, issuing the Patties and their friends a license for trapping in the "Helay," or Gila country.

The remote city of Santa Fe, resting on the gentle, piñon-studded slope at the foot of the towering Sangre de Cristo Mountains, had a population of five thousand in 1825. The fabled Santa Fe Trail had recently opened a flourishing trade between Mexicans and Americans, and with the arrival of merchants, trappers, and opportunists, the Southwest would never be the same. Mexican officials at first welcomed the interlopers, but soon began to realize that trappers would exploit the beaver-filled streams. Soon after Governor Narbona issued licenses to the Pattie party, the Mexicans toughened their trapping laws, placing heavy restrictions on American fur trappers.

Meanwhile the Patties and their friends were following the Rio Grande south to Socorro before heading west to the Santa Rita del Cobre mines (near today's Silver City, New Mexico), the last outpost of white civilization before the rugged Gila wilderness.

After a brief rest at Santa Rita, they went up the headwaters of the Gila, finding a wealth of beaver sign—the first night out they caught thirty beaver.

Next, the trappers headed north, up the San Francisco River, passing today's Clifton. In two weeks their packs contained the pelts of two hundred fifty beaver. They had even better luck farther down the Gila country. The San Pedro River was so full of beaver they named it "Beaver River."

One morning while James was scouting the area, he chanced upon a bear's den. Endowed with the recklessness of youth, he rigged a pine torch to the end of his rifle and foolishly entered the cave, coming face to face with a huge grizzly. In the dark, narrow confines of the cave, Pattie aimed his rifle at the shadowy figure and fired. Without waiting to see if his shot was on target, he ran toward the entrance, dropping his rifle along the way. Moments later, his courage regained, Pattie borrowed a rifle and re-entered the cave. The grizzly was dead, and it took four men to haul the carcass out. The fat, according to Pattie, yielded ten pounds of valuable grease. A few nights earlier, he'd had a similar encounter with a mountain lion which had sprung out of the darkness and landed on a log less than six feet from his bedroll. James grabbed his rifle and fired point blank, killing the animal with a head shot.

In April 1826 the Patties cached several thousand dollars worth of pelts near the San Pedro River and returned to Santa Rita; James then went on to Santa Fe to get more pack animals to haul out the unexpected treasure. However, when he returned to recover the cache of furs, he found that Apaches had found the pelts and stolen a year's trapping results. Despite the loss, the news started a rush of trappers to the Gila country.

In the fall of 1826 Pattie joined a party of French trappers led by Michel Robidoux and journeyed down the Gila to the junction of the Salt and Gila rivers (near today's Cashion). According to Pattie, they stopped at a village of Papagos (more likely nomadic Yavapais or Tonto Apaches). With a grand display of hospitality, the natives invited the trappers to spend the night. All agreed, with the exception of the suspicious James Pattie, who camped some distance away. During the night he was awakened by the sounds of violence and was soon joined by Robidoux and an unidentified Frenchman—the others had all been killed by their hosts. The three survivors traveled up either the Salt or the Gila and chanced upon Ewing Young's party. Young, a mountain man of reknown, took his group, along with the Pattie survivors, and returned to the site of the massacre, where they trounced the natives and burned their village.

Pattie remained with Young's outfit the rest of the season. They trapped up and down the Salt and Verde rivers, then followed the Gila to the Yuma crossing, becoming the first Americans to make this trip.

The first encounter between Ewing Young's trappers and the Yuma Indians seems to have been peaceful. Pattie wrote admiringly of the Indians:

We thence returned down the Helay (Gila River), which is here about 200 yards wide, with heavily timbered bottoms. We trapped its whole course, from where we met it to its junction with the Red River (The Colorado River). The point of junction is inhabited by a tribe of Indians called Umene (Yuman). Here we encamped for the night. On the morning of the twenty-sixth, a great many of these Indians crossed the river to our camp, and brought us dried beans, for which we paid them with red cloth, with which they were delighted beyond measure, tearing it into ribbons and tieing it round their arms and legs; for if the truth must be told, they were as naked as Adam and Eve in their birthday suit. They were the stoutest men, with the finest forms I ever saw, well proportioned and straight as an arrow. They contrive, however, to inflict upon their children an artificial deformity. They flatten their heads, by pressing a board upon their tender scalps which they bind fast by a ligature. This board is so large and light that I have seen women,

405

when swimming the river with their children, towing them after them by a string, which they held in their mouth. The little things neither suffered nor complained, but floated behind their mothers like ducks. . . .

Next, they went up the Colorado and past the Bill Williams Fork to the Mojave Villages, where a fight erupted between the natives and the trappers. The big guns of the trappers carried the day, but the cunning Mojaves stalked the intruders along the trail. One night a war party launched a barrage of arrows into the trapper camp. Pattie counted sixteen arrows embedded in his bedroll, but somehow he was unscathed. After losing a few men in skirmishes, the trappers split up and returned by separate paths to Santa Fe. Pattie took the scenic route—traveling by way of the North Rim of the Grand Canyon, across to the San Juan River, and then overland to the Mexican capital.

Once again bad luck plagued James Pattie. This time his furs were confiscated by Mexican officials, who claimed, under a new policy, the bundles were illegal contraband.

Undaunted, Pattie tried again in the fall of 1827. This time his father, Sylvester, joined the expedition. They trapped the Gila all the way to the Yuma crossing. This time the natives proved inhospitable, stealing their horses. Assuming the Mexicans would have a port city at the mouth of the Colorado, they loaded their furs in canoes and headed downstream. At the mouth of the Colorado, they found more Indians, also unfriendly. Their last desperate hope was to turn west and try to reach the California coast. When they reached the coast they were immediately arrested as trespassers and jailed in San Diego. Sylvester Pattie, weakened from the desert ordeal, died in his cell, but fortune was with young James—he negotiated his release by promising to vaccinate "thousands" of locals against smallpox.

In 1830 an older and wiser James Ohio Pattie returned to his old Kentucky home. Discouraged, weary, and financially ruined, he lamented, "The freshness, the visions, the hopes of my youthful days have all vanished, and can never return."

Pattie did not keep a journal of his Arizona adventure but relied on recall, telling his story to Reverend Timothy Flint, who edited it for publication. It was customary for the buckskin men to stretch their tales a bit, and Pattie was no exception. However, there was basis for fact in much of what he recalled, which provides an important piece of the history of the fur trade in Arizona.

It was quiet around the Yuma crossing until the Mexican War broke out in 1846. Expansionist-minded Americans were proclaiming it as our "manifest destiny" to be an ocean-to-ocean power. The real prize of this war was California. Colonel Stephen Watts Kearny's Army of the West, seventeen hundred strong, was given the assignment of taking both New Mexico and California. Kearny captured New Mexico without trouble, then setting out for California with three hundred dragoons.

Meanwhile, unknown to Kearny, soldiers, sailors, marines, and mountain men led by Captain John C. Fremont, Commodore John Sloan, and Commodore Robert Stockton had already seized California. Fremont ordered Kit Carson to take seventeen mountain men and ride cross-country to inform President James K. Polk of the successful takeover.

On October 6, 1846 Kearny and his dragoons met Carson and his men near Socorro, New Mexico. Since the legendary mountain man was familiar with the terrain, Kearny ordered him to hand his dispatches over to scout Tom Fitzpatrick and return to California with the dragoons. Next, Kearny sent two hundred dragoons back to Santa Fe and, with the reluctant Carson leading the way, set out for California.

Near the junction of the Gila and Colorado rivers, the dragoons met some Mexican *vaqueros* who informed Kearny that the Californians had staged a counterattack and that only the port city of San Diego remained in American hands. On November 25, 1846 Kearny's small army crossed the muddy waters of the Colorado and started for San Diego. In early December the dragoons, weary and worn from their desert crossing, had their first taste of battle at a place called San Pasqual. Kearny's dragoons were outnumbered but made a valiant two-day stand, until Carson, Lieutenant Edward F. Beale, and an Indian named Che-muc-tah were able to sneak through the enemy lines to notify the American forces in San Diego, who then came to the rescue of the battle-weary dragoons.

The Mormon Battalion, under the command of Captain Philip St. George Cooke, arrived at the Yuma crossing a few weeks after Kearny, on their roadbuilding mission. They were running low on supplies after an ill-fated attempt to navigate the Gila River with a supply raft. Twenty-five hundred pounds of flour, corn, and other supplies were lost when the craft sank in the unpredictable desert river. The resourceful Mormons rustled up bushels of mesquite beans, ground them up in their coffee mills, and made nutritious "mesquite patties."

On January 10, 1847 the Mormons crossed the muddy-red Colorado and continued their road-building expedition to California. The Mormon Battalion traveled more than a thousand miles in a hundred two days, the longest infantry march in American history.

Major Lawrence Graham, an iron-willed American officer, and his troops arrived at the Yuma crossing in late November 1848 on their way to California. He was accompanied by Lieutenant Cave Johnson Couts, a young West Pointer, who wrote an interesting account of the perilous expedition. Couts would return to the Yuma area in the 1850s with the Army Corps of Topographical Engineers.

Graham's troops built a boat to ferry the men, horses, and equipment across the cold, muddy waters. After a ceremonious launching, the craft sank. Eventually Graham's band forded the river and completed their march to California.

The war with Mexico ended with the signing of the Treaty of Guadalupe Hidalgo on February 2, 1848. Article V of the treaty stipulated that the boundary line separating the United States and Mexico (in the Yuma area) would be the Gila River. A straight line from the junction of the Gila and Colorado across to a point one marine league south of San Diego marked the boundary separating Upper and Lower California. The line would be surveyed by a joint commission from the United States and Mexico. Lieutenant Amiel W. Whipple, of the Army Corps of Topographical Engineers, was placed in charge of the American contingent. Lieutenant Cave Johnson Couts and a company of dragoons, along with a party of infantry, were assigned to Whipple as an escort. Couts, a gregarious, outgoing young officer, contrasted sharply with the quiet, studious Whipple. Needless to say, the two personalities clashed frequently.

In late September 1849 near the site where Fort Yuma would be established, Whipple set up his headquarters, and the boundary work began in earnest. Gold had been discovered in California the previous year, and thousands of argonauts were making their way to the gold fields, following the Gila Trail. This southern route, treacherous in the summer, was an ideal winter route. Lieutenant Couts's troops built a ferry pulled back and forth by a rope stretched across the river to transport the would-be millionaires across it. By December 10, 1849 Whipple had completed his survey between San Diego and Yuma.

Two years later Whipple returned to Arizona with civilian surveyor Andrew B. Gray to work on the Gila River boundary survey. By December 22, 1851 the westbound party had marked three hundred fifty miles of the river. Sixty miles east of Fort Yuma (a fort had been established on the California side a year earlier) the surveyors ran low on supplies. The work was halted, and the party headed for the fort to spend Christmas before going on to San Diego to re-outfit.

They arrived to find the post abandoned, being greeted by fifteen hundred hostile Yuma warriors. Some of the immigrants had been abusing the Yumas, and the natives had retaliated by seizing the two ferry boats. After learning the natives were planning an attack, Whipple and his party, fortified themselves and made ready for battle. It is believed that Whipple's defensive position was somewhere near where the territorial prison was later located. Christmas Eve was spent waiting for an attack that failed to materialize. The next day a delegation of natives approached and queried Whipple and Gray about money. To cross the river, Whipple offered to pay two dollars a person and one dollar apiece for each horse and mule.

The situation was becoming tense, when a young girl recognized Whipple as the man who had saved her life two years earlier. She had become lost in the desert, and Whipple had given her food and water and then presented her with a mirror. Whipple's humanitarian act probably saved the lives of his entire expedition. The mood of the natives shifted from hostility to open friendliness. Whipple's party was not only provided with supplies and transported across the river, but were given escort across the desert toward San Diego.

A major dispute arose over the location of the boundary in the Mesilla Valley of New Mexico. Also, the rough country north of the Gila River made the construction of a national road and a transcontinental railroad impossible, and Cooke's Wagon Road, or the Gila Trail, ran through Mexican territory south of the Gila. President Franklin Pierce sent James Gadsden to Mexico to negotiate a new treaty, and in 1854 the United States Congress ratified the Gadsden Purchase, which created new boundary problems. The new boundary was twenty miles south of the junction of the Gila and Colorado rivers and ran in a diagonal line southeast toward Nogales. This time Washington chose as head surveyor the able and experienced Major William Emory, of the Topographical Engineers as Boundary Commission. Emory split his group, sending Lieutenant Nathaniel Michler to Yuma to mark the diagonal line, while he worked west from El Paso. The two parties were to meet at Nogales. Michler was a capable officer, but the desert proved formidable. He was forced to retreat east along the Gila Trail to Tucson and then go south to Nogales to await the welcome summer rains that would fill the *tinajas* (water holes) along the way before attempting to mark the dreaded Camino del Diablo, or Devil's Highway. Michler kept a detailed expedition record that was published in 1857 with Emory's well-known *Report of the United States and Mexican Boundary Survey*. The scientific data and pictures of flora, fauna, geology, geography, and anthropology provided the first accurate information of the area and was praised by scientific groups around the world.

A civilian survey led by Andrew B. Gray and sponsored by the Texas Western Railroad Company passed through the Yuma area in

The Searchlight
docked at Yuma
circa 1880
Courtesy
Southwest Studies

1854. The proposed transcontinental line along the thirty-second parallel was the best all-weather route, but war clouds were looming on the horizon, and the southern line would be delayed until 1877, when the Southern Pacific finally reached Yuma.

During the gold rush the business of ferrying California-bound immigrants across the Colorado was indeed lucrative. Lieutenant Cave Johnson Couts built a temporary ferry in 1849 while providing military escort for Lieutenant Amiel Whipple's boundary survey party. A year later Dr. Abel Lincoln was charging a dollar a person and two dollars an animal while accumulating a sizeable bankroll. In three months he grossed sixty thousand dollars. Unfortunately for Dr. Lincoln, a notorious scalphunter named John Joel Glanton and his gang muscled in on the business. Not happy with controlling Lincoln's Ferry, Glanton and his greedy rogues decided to corner the market.

The Yuma Indians also had a flourishing ferry business and had hired a white man to operate a boat on their behalf. Glanton's men killed the operator and cut the ferryboat loose. Next, they began abusing Indians and robbing immigrants. On April 23, 1850 the natives set a trap and slaughtered Glanton and his gang. Unfortunately, the innocent Dr. Lincoln, caught in the melee, was also killed. It is believed that Glanton's treasure, probably fifteen thousand dollars in gold, was buried under a tree near the crossing and has never been found. However, another cache of gold was recovered by the natives. It was said that for the next few months, travelers were being overpaid for such items as shirts, hats, and pants.

A few men survived the Glanton Massacre and staggered into Los Angeles with lurid tales of the slaughtering of innocent whites at the

410

Yuma crossing. The story of Glanton's treasure was widely circulated, inspiring an opportunist named General Joe Moorhead to raise a band of a hundred forty-two militia to punish the Yuma Indians. This so-called Gila Expedition rode to the crossing in September 1850 under the guise of protecting newcomers and demanded that the natives hand over the treasure or he would give them a severe beating. The Indians chose to fight and gave Moorhead's marauders a sound thrashing. The militia then turned its attention to fleecing the homeward-bound Mexicans of gold they were taking home. Finally, California authorities ordered the militia home, but not before over $113,000 dollars in expenses had been charged to the state treasury.

Fort Yuma was established by Captain Sam Heintzelman in November 1850 to protect immigrants at the Yuma crossing. Several hundred unpredictable native warriors in residence around the crossing made life precarious, although more serious was the dry, desolate, and unforgiving desert that ranged for miles on both sides of the river.

Due to lack of supplies, the fort on the west bank of the Colorado was abandoned, Lieutenant Tom Sweeny and a small force being left behind. Sweeny, heavily outnumbered by the restive natives, moved his camp downstream six miles to Pilot Knob. In early December 1851 the lack of supplies caused the army to withdraw completely. The fort was re-occupied in February 1852 when Captain Heintzelman returned with a strong military force.

Captain Heintzelman ordered a series of punitive expeditions against the warrior tribes around the Yuma crossing, some of whom openly admitted attacking small, poorly-armed immigrants along the Gila Trail. By the end of 1852 most of the tribes, with respect for the strong military presence, agreed to cease their warlike activities against the whites. This, however, did not end the intertribal warfare. The long alliances between the Mojaves and Yumas, or Quechans, versus the Cocopah, Maricopa, and Pima brought on a series of bloody skirmishes. Finally, the latter lured the former into an ambush and inflicted heavy casualties. After that devastating loss, the Yumas settled down to a relatively peaceful co-existence at the crossing.

The high cost of freighting supplies overland from San Diego caused the government to explore the possiblities of navigating the Colorado River. In the fall of 1850 Lieutenant George Derby determined that the fort could be supplied by water, and one of Arizona's greatest nineteenth-century enterprises—steamboats on the Colorado—was born.

During their heyday, before railroads and massive dams drove

them out of business, steamboats with colorful sounding names like Esmeralda, Mohave, Cocopah, and Gila, hauled freight and passengers to riverport towns like Yuma, Ehrenberg, and Hardyville. They were skillfully piloted around sandbars and underwater snags by colorful captains like Jack Mellon and Isaac Polhamus.

The steamboats that played a major role in opening the remote regions of Arizona were not the floating mansions of Mark Twain's Mississippi. Their primary purpose was functional—to transport mining equipment and other supplies in and haul the rich ore out to freighters docked at Port Isabel, near the mouth of the Colorado. The larger boats had three decks with up to twenty staterooms to accommodate passengers. A first-class ticket from San Francisco to Yuma cost $90, while those traveling steerage could purchase a ticket for $40.

One of the finest and most vivid accounts of a voyage up the Colorado River was written by Martha Summerhayes in her classic book on army life *Vanished Arizona*. Mrs. Summerhayes arrived in Arizona in August 1874 as a young bride of an army officer. Her romantic image of frontier life quickly evaporated when she arrived at dismal Port Isabel. The incessant wind was "like a breath from a furnace." Following endless delays they boarded the steamer "Gila" and set out for Yuma. "After twenty-three days of heat and glare," Mrs. Summerhayes wrote, "and scorching winds, and stale food, Fort Yuma . . . Seemed like paradise." They remained at Yuma for several days before beginning the two hundred-mile journey up the Colorado to Fort Mohave. "When we departed, I felt, . . . we were saying goodbye to the world and civilization, . . . I could not help looking back longingly to old Fort Yuma."

The dreary days passed slowly; "and thus began another day of intolerable glare and heat. Conversation lagged; no topic seemed to have any interest except the thermometer, which hung in the coolest place on the boat; and one day when Major Worth looked at it and pronounced it one hundred twenty-two in the shade, a grim despair seized upon me, and I wondered how much more human beings could endure." Despite her footwear, the heat rising from the deck of the steamer burned Martha's feet.

The nearest ice cubes were hundreds of miles away, so fresh food was conspicuous by its absence. The menu, prepared by a creative Chinese cook, usually consisted of salted beef, canned vegetables, biscuits without butter, and pie made from preserved plums or peaches. Afternoon siestas were impossible because of the searing temperature and a night's slumber was a trade-off—the staterooms were hot and stuffy, but sleeping under the stars was hot and subject to aerial attacks by giant mosquitoes. Finally, eighteen days later, the weary travelers reached Fort Mohave.

In 1851 George Alonzo Johnson, a former seaman on Lake Erie, who had followed the gold rush to California, was contracted by the army to haul supplies by flat-bottomed barge from the mouth of the river a hundred twenty miles south. After fighting off a band of hostile Indians, Johnson lost a barge and the precious cargo disappeared in the river. Mule-drawn freight wagons had to be sent to the rescue, and it was four weeks before the supplies reached the fort. Captain Johnson's inglorious initiation to the temperamental Colorado River was a humbling experience. But persistence paid off—he would later return and become a major figure in the steamboat business for fifty years.

The first steamer to navigate the river was a sixty-five-foot sidewheeler named the *Uncle Sam*. It was a prefab affair shipped from San Francisco by schooner. Her pilot, Captain James Turnbull, and crew assembled it at the mouth of the Colorado. They started up the river in mid-November 1852 and did not reach Fort Yuma until two weeks later. The maiden voyage had been slowed by an earthquake that changed the river's channel. Regular stops had to be made for fuel, and since there were not any service stations (woodyards), all hands had to go ashore and rustle sticks of mesquite. The return trip was less eventful, taking only fifteen hours in the swift current.

The *Uncle Sam*, powered by a twenty-horsepower woodburning engine, could carry thirty-five tons of freight and could navigate in only twenty-two inches of water. Her career on the river came to an abrupt end the following year when she was accidentally sunk. The wooden hull was shrinking in the blistering desert sun, so one of the deck hands removed a bilge plug to soak the wood and make it swell. Water quickly filled the hold, and the *Uncle Sam* went down. The deck hands worked feverishly to raise her, but on the third try the ropes broke and the little steamer was pulled into the swirling current. Her skeletal remains were discovered sometime later lying bottom up in a slough.

But the *Uncle Sam* had proved that steam navigation on the unpredictable Colorado was possible and set the stage for what was to become Arizona's biggest commercial enterprise in the 1870s. In the fall of 1853 Captain George Johnson made his second attempt at conquering the river. This time he brought in a sidewheeler with a fifty-horsepower engine dubbed the *General Jesup*. The steamer measured a hundred four feet stem to stern and was twenty-seven feet wide. She could haul fifty tons of freight and needed only thirty inches of draw. The *General Jesup* was an immediate financial success; at $75 a ton, Johnson's Colorado Steam Navigation Company was soon grossing $20,000 a month. Business was so brisk that in 1855 he added another even larger craft, the hundred-twenty-foot-long *Colorado*.

The steamers traveled about thirty miles a day, tying up to the bank at sundown, since the unpredictable river made nighttime navigation too risky. As the business began to flourish, dozens of landings sprang up along the river. Small time entrepreneurs could make $5,000 a year supplying firewood for the paddlewheelers. Natives, who had greeted the arrival of the noisy contraptions with cries of "the devil is coming, blowing fire and smoke out of his nose and kicking the water back with his feet," soon became accustomed to the newfangled paddlewheelers and earned money by cutting firewood for fuel.

The so-called Mormon War in 1857 increased government interest in the area. Hard feelings between the United States and the Mormons developed after Washington-appointed territorial officials in Salt Lake City were being usurped by local representatives. Open hostility between Mormons and gentiles prompted President James Buchanan to order federal troops into Utah. Part of the occupation scheme was to transport soldiers and equipment by steamboat up the Colorado, the army having appropriated $75,000 for a survey to see how much of the Colorado was navigable.

Not one to miss an opportunity for adventure and business expansion, Captain Johnson offered to send the *General Jesup* upriver at a fraction of his cost for only $3,000 a month. The farsighted captain had another reason for wanting to survey the river—he had plans to open commerce with Utah.

His generous offer was refused, and the army went on a spending binge. An iron-hulled sternwheeler was assembled in Philadelphia, tested on the Delaware River (where it received poor grades), disassembled, and shipped to San Francisco via Panama. Then it was transported by schooner to the mouth of the Colorado. The expedition was led by Lieutenant Joseph C. Ives, a member of the legendary Army Corps of Topographical Engineers. Ives and his party reassembled the diminutive steamer—it was only fifty-four feet long—in chilly, gale-force winds and christened it the *Explorer*. She was not the most graceful steamer to navigate the Colorado; the expedition artist, Baldwin Möllhausen, called her a "water-borne wheelbarrow." The journey to Fort Yuma took ten days, and on the way the little steamer managed to hit most of the snags and sandbars on that part of the Colorado.

In the meantime, Captain Johnson had decided to explore the Colorado with his own steamer, the *General Jesup*. Accompanying him was a curious crew, including famed Indian scout Pauline Weaver, the old Yuma Chief Pascual, an army officer, and fifteen enlisted men. The later group had been sent to report on Mormon activities and on the Indians living upstream.

Captain Johnson took his paddlewheeler up the silt-laden Colorado as far as Pyramid Canyon, over three hundred miles above Fort Yuma. He determined correctly that the river was navigable all the way to the Virgin River; he then turned around and steamed downstream.

The following day, near today's Needles, they met Lieutenant Beale and his camels. Beale's beasts of burden had been great on the desert but had stubbornly refused to swim the river, so the meeting with the *General Jesup* was most fortunate. The camels were loaded on the steamer and ferried across to the California side.

On the return trip a few miles north of Fort Yuma the *General Jesup* hit a rock and sank in three feet of water. Her sister ship, the *Colorado*, was called to the rescue, towing the stricken steamer home for repairs.

Meanwhile, Lieutenant Ives continued his journey up the Colorado on the *Explorer*. After a friendly meeting with the crew of the southbound steamer, the *General Jesup*, near today's Parker, the little steamer traveled as far north as Black Canyon, the site of today's Hoover Dam, before it struck a large rock. While the crew made repairs, Lieutenant Ives boarded a small skiff and rowed another thirty miles to the mouth of the Virgin River. Johnson's theory was correct—during high water, steamboat navigation was possible all the way to the Virgin River. Eventually, the Mormons would establish port cities at Callville, now buried beneath the waters of Lake Mead, and Rioville, at the mouth of the Virgin River.

On the return trip, Lieutenant Ives decided to take the scenic route.

At Beale's Crossing, he and his men left the *Explorer* with its crew and traveled across Arizona to Santa Fe, New Mexico, and thence down the Rio Grande to El Paso. From there he hitched a ride on the Butterfield Overland Stage back to Fort Yuma. Concluding that the project was too expensive, he sold the *Explorer* to Johnson's Colorado Steam Navigation Company for $1,000.

Lieutenant Ives later published an account of his journey. Unfortunately, he praised his own efforts and failed to mention that Captain Johnson and the *General Jesup* had been the first to navigate the perilous Colorado above Fort Yuma. On the positive side, the *Ives Report* provides an excellent scientific study of the flora, fauna, geography, geology, and native cultures of the area.

The decline of the steamboat business began in 1877 with the arrival of the railroad at Yuma. Steamboats had several revivals during the next few years, but the building of Laguna Dam, above Yuma, in 1907 brought the enterprise to an end.

Following her historic voyage up the Colorado, the freakish-looking little *Explorer* was relegated to menial tasks. They removed her engine and turned her into a barge for hauling firewood on the Gila. She repaid the indignity in 1864 after some workmen had tied her to the trunk of a cottonwood tree. Making a last independent hurrah, she broke away and headed toward the Colorado, pulling the cottonwood tree behind. She drifted into a slough somewhere down-river and settled on the bottom. Eventually, the fickle Colorado changed its course, and the *Explorer* disappeared somewhere out in the shifting desert sands. Her desert burial ground was accidentally discovered nearly a quarter of a century later when a party of surveyors stumbled across a piece of iron hull sticking out of the sand.

L.J.F. Jaeger, merchant, ferryboat operator and one of Yuma's first citizens
Courtesy
Southwest Studies

Following the fiasco of General Moorhead's Gila Expedition, George Johnson started a ferry operation just south of Fort Yuma. Johnson decided to cast his lot with the more lucrative steamboat business and sold out to a hard working entrepreneur named Louis J. F. Jaeger, who first came up the river in 1853 as a cook on the steamer *General Jesup*. Jaeger survived a thrilling and almost fatal attack by a party of Yuma warriors, going on to establish a successful ferry operation and mercantile store near the site of today's Winterhaven, California. When the Butterfield Overland Mail stretched a line across Arizona in the late 1850s, Johnson became stationmaster at Yuma Crossing, feeding passengers and charging the stage five dollars to ferry across the river. By the time he sold out to the railroad in 1877, Jaeger had become one of the most prosperous and best-known personalities at Yuma Crossing.

The founding of the first town on the Arizona side is shrouded in fiction. Apparently Charles Poston, destined to go down as the "Father of Arizona," and a German engineer named Herman Ehrenberg reached Jaeger's Ferry but did not have money for passage. The ingenious Poston conceived a plan to survey a townsite which would be called Colorado City. He and Ehrenberg mapped out city lots and convinced the ferryman that he could get in on the ground floor of a real estate boom. For the sum of $25 (the exact price of passage), Jaeger could buy a choice city lot. According to Poston, the deal was consummated, passage was booked, and the future city of Yuma was born. It is true that Poston and Ehrenberg drew up the plans and registered them in California, but the rest seems to have come from Poston's fertile imagination.

Whatever its origins, a small community called Colorado City grew prosperous, the military, steamboats, immigrants, and gold strikes in the vicinity all playing a part in the success story. In 1858 the name was changed to Arizona City. During the Civil War the name was changed to Yuma, then back to Arizona City. Finally, in 1873 it was given the permanent name of Yuma.

Yuma continued to be an important center of commerce after the arrival of the railroad. Steamers loaded with cargo and passengers continued to plow their way up the Colorado River until the building of the great dams in the 1900s. The ferry continued to haul wagons, horses, and, later, automobiles until 1915, when a bridge was constructed.

One of the most colorful women who ever graced the old West was Sarah Bowman of Yuma. She did not fit the common frontier stereotype—calico dress, sunbonnet, and a youngster hanging on each arm with another tugging at her skirt. In fact, there was nothing common about Sarah. They called her the "Great Western," after the biggest sailing ship of her day. Since she stood 6'2", that didn't seem to bother her.

This redheaded woman with blue eyes was a Southwestern legend in her own time. She could literally sweep men right off their feet (and did on more than one occasion). Because of her bravery during the Mexican War at the Battle of Fort Texas, the soldiers affectionately dubbed her the "American Maid of Orleans." Some people may have questioned her morals—she had a long string of "husbands" during the war—but nobody ever questioned her bravery or generosity. During the seven-day bombardment of Fort Texas (later Fort Brown) by Mexican artillery, she dodged shells to serve hot coffee and soup to soldiers. Once she joined a battle charge, declaring that if someone would lend her a pair of trousers, she would whip the whole Mexican army all by herself.

Sarah Bowman was born in Clay County, Missouri, in 1812 and seems to have led an uneventful life until the war with Mexico broke out in 1846. When her husband volunteered for service, she came along as a cook and laundress. He became ill and was hospitalized, so Sarah left him behind and went on with the regiment to Fort Texas on the Rio Grande. During the siege of Fort Texas, she and nine other women, along with fifty men, were trying to hold out against a superior Mexican force until the arrival of General Zachary Taylor's army. Sarah was supposed to be sewing sandbags from soldiers' tents but opted for more hazardous duty, defiantly dodging bullets to bring aid and comfort to the troops, thus earning their everlasting admiration. When Taylor's army advanced into northern Mexico, she went with it, setting up hostels along the way. For Sarah it was truly a labor of love. Her husband died in the fighting around Monterey, but the redoubtable "Great Western" continued to be the belle of Taylor's army.

During the two-day Battle of Buena Vista, Sarah's commanding presence caught the attention of officers and men alike as she moved fearlessly around the battleground, serving hot coffee to the weary soldiers.

When the war ended, Sarah loaded her wagons and decided to ride along with Major Lawrence Graham's dragoons to California. When told that army regulations stated that a woman could not travel with the troops unless she was married to a member of the squadron, she gave a snappy salute and announced with great alacrity, "All right, I'll marry the whole squadron." She then climbed on her Mexican donkey and rode down the line shouting, "Who wants a wife with $15,000 and the biggest legs in Mexico! Come my beauties, don't all speak at once—who is the lucky man?"

A soldier named Davis took the challenge. "I have no objections to making you my wife," he said, "if there is a clergyman here to tie the knot."

"Bring your blanket to my tent tonight," she laughed, "and I will learn you a knot that will satisfy you, I reckon!"

Sarah's "marriage" to Davis did not last long; a short time later she cast her eyes on a man her own size and fell madly in love—for a while. Actually, she switched husbands several times along the way.

Sarah got sidetracked in Franklin (El Paso), Texas, and spent the next few months running an eating establishment that offered the customers other amenities not usually found in restaurants. Later, on the way to California, Sarah stopped at Arizona City (Yuma) at the Colorado River crossing and decided to set up business in a "dirt-roofed adobe house." Author Raphael Pumpelly noted in 1861 that Sarah was the only resident of the eight-year-old town. He described her as "no longer young," stating that she "was a character of a varied past. She had followed the war of 1848 with Mexico. Her relations with the soldiers were of two kinds. One of these does not admit of analysis; the other was angelic, for she was adored by the soldiers for her bravery in the field and for her unceasing kindness in nursing the sick and wounded. . . ."

Author-adventurer Captain James Hobbs described her as "liked universally for her kind, motherly ways. . . ." during the war. Another observer, Jeff Ake, said she always packed two pistols, and "she shore could use 'em." He went on to say admiringly, "She was a hell of a good woman." According to Ake's father, Sarah was "the greatest whore in the West."

Fort Yuma was evacuated briefly during the Confederate occupation, so when the soldiers prepared to march to San Diego, Sarah sent her "girls" home to Sonora and "followed the guidon" once more. She returned a few months later with the California Column but died in Yuma on December 22, 1866. Years later, when the fort was abandoned, her remains and those of soldiers who had died at that post were reburied at the Presidio in San Francisco.

Historians have used a lot of words, including "generous," "loyal," "devoted," and "brave," to describe Sarah Bowman, the "Great Western." The community of Yuma, however, pays her the greatest compliment, proudly calling Sarah Bowman their "first citizen."

The Colorado River went on a rampage in 1852 and wiped out the town of Yuma—a new town was built on higher ground, and by 1870 the population was over 1,100. In 1876 the infamous territorial prison was established on high ground overlooking the west bank of the Colorado River. Some of the West's most notorious men and women spent time behind bars at the prison, which had some of its cells carved out of solid rock.

Because of the long stretches of desert on each side of Yuma and because of Indians, who could "track bees in a blizzard," living along the river, escape was difficult; yet twenty-six of the 3,069 prisoners between 1876 and 1909 managed to escape and were not recaptured.

One of the prison's most illustrious prisoners was Pearl Hart, the "girl bandit." In 1899 Pearl and her boyfriend, Joe Boot, robbed the stage north of Florence. They were captured by a posse soon after and brought up for trial. Pearl stashed her tomboy clothes and appeared before the jury in delicate, feminine attire. She batted her long lashes and lifted her skirts to reveal a pair of well-shaped ankles. She was the consummate coquette and repentant sinner all rolled into one. The jury found Joe Boot guilty and Pearl innocent! The judge was so outraged he ordered her recharged for stealing the stage driver's six-shooter. This time the jury complied and found her guilty, sentencing her to the Yuma Territorial Prison. Joe escaped soon after and was not seen again, but Pearl became a celebrity. Journalists came from all over the nation to interview her, and Easterners were shocked that such a "refined lady" was behind prison bars.

After being released from prison Pearl had a brief show business career, before returning to Arizona, where she married a cowboy named Cal Bywater and settled down to a respectable life near Globe.

In 1909 the new prison was opened at Florence, and for a brief time the old prison was empty. In 1910 a fire burned the high school and for the next few years classes were held in the prison. The school colors of Yuma High are still black and white, and the school's teams are

1877 – Southern Pacific crews completing rail bridge across the Colorado to reach Yuma
Courtesy Arizona Historical Society Library

called the "Criminals." The prison fell into a state of ruin for many years before local citizens began a restoration program. It became a city museum in 1941 and a state park twenty years later.

Major floods in 1890, 1905, 1916, and 1920 devastated the town, but the residents of the crossing have a strong "sense of Yuma," and they keep recovering from these setbacks.

The most dramatic change in the history of Yuma Crossing came with the arrival of the railroad in 1877.

Naturally there was always cause for celebration with the arrival of a new railroad. Anyone who had crossed the desert on foot or on a horse or mule, or who had rocked and rolled on the leather-slung thoroughbraces of a stagecoach, or ridden in a wagon without shock absorbers was bound to appreciate the wonders of riding in a steam car.

In the spring of 1877 Arizona's citizens at Yuma were anxiously awaiting the arrival of the first railroad. Construction was delayed when the Southern Pacific, building eastbound from California, reached the Colorado River and ran into some Washington-style bureaucratic politicking. Earlier, permission had been granted from General Irwin McDowell to build the bridge at Yuma. However, the Secretary of War overruled the department commander, refusing to allow the railroad to cross a federal stream until some red tape was untangled. Permission was granted to build the bridge, but without railroad tracks.

Chinese workmen spent the hot summer months laying a grade while piledrivers were busily constructing a six-hundred-sixty-seven-foot bridge across the Colorado. On September 29, 1877 the bridge was completed except for the rails.

Major Tom Dunn, commander of Fort Yuma, had orders not allow any track laying on the bridge and he was determined to see that the railroad remained on the California side. He put his entire command, consisting of a sergeant and a private, on alert and posted a sentry at the entrance to the bridge.

At eleven P.M. the guard went off duty and within an hour, dark, shadowy figures appeared out of nowhere. With the stealth and cunning of an Apache war party, the gandy dancers began laying track across the bridge. All went well until about 2 A.M., when some careless pick and shovel men accidentally dropped a rail. The resounding clatter woke up the sleeping soldiers, and the three-troop garrison of Fort Yuma sprang into action. With bayonets fixed, Major Dunn and his men grimly stood their ground, the major bravely stationing himself on the tracks.

Suddenly, a rumbling sound came out of the darkness, and the major found himself staring into the headlights of a locomotive. Quickly deeming that discretion was the better part of valor, the major and his men made a hasty retreat to the confines of the fort.

At sunrise the next morning, Engine No. 31 came rolling into Yuma with her whistle screaming. The whole town turned out to witness the historic occasion. The locomotive crept slowly along, blowing off steam while the gandy dancers laid track ahead of her along Madison Avenue.

The Southern Pacific and the federal government accused each other of being highhanded in the matter. General McDowell was much chagrined and quickly reinforced Fort Yuma with a dozen more soldiers to thwart any further usurping of his military authority.

Engine 31, first locomotive in Arizona
Courtesy Arizona State Library

422

Interstate 10
Ehrenberg to Phoenix

Ehrenberg was one of those towns that owed its existence to the capricious Colorado River. Rich gold placers were discovered near here in 1862 by scout Pauline Weaver. Weaver and his friends made their discovery in Arroyo de la Tenaja on January 12, the Feast of Our Lady of Peace, providing inspiration for the name La Paz. Before the rush was over, about eight million dollars in gold was gathered in pans, rockers, and sluices.

At one time the town boasted fifteen hundred frontier citizens. But the gold played out, and the town dwindled to three hundred fifty-two residents, enough to be named county seat for Yuma County when Arizona became a territory in 1863. La Paz was given strong consideration as first territorial capital, but Prescott was selected instead. In 1870 the county seat was moved down the Colorado to Arizona City (Yuma). The records, property, and officials were transported by steamboat, something unusual in the Arizona desert. Actually, the downfall of La Paz had begun two years earlier when the river changed its course, leaving the river port of La Paz on dry ground. By 1870 Ehrenberg had replaced La Paz as a river port and was already boasting nearly two hundred fifty residents.

Among the first to arrive at the new gold strikes to seek their fortunes were merchants Mike and Joe Goldwater. These two Polish

Ehrenberg circa 1871, river port and supply point during the heyday of the steamboat business on the Colorado River
Courtesy Arizona
Historical Foundation

immigrants had come to California during the big gold rush and opened a mercantile store in the Mother Lode country. Hard times in California during the early 1860s caused Mike and Joe to pack their merchandise in a wagon and head for Arizona. La Paz, and later Ehrenberg, would be the main supply port for transporting goods to the numerous mining towns in the Bradshaw Mountains, including Prescott.

When the river left La Paz high and dry, the Goldwaters packed up again and moved to the new port six miles downstream. The town had been named in honor of German mining engineer Herman Ehrenberg, one of the first to locate rich mineral deposits in the new Gadsden Purchase area. Ehrenberg was shot to death in 1866 on the road from La Paz to San Bernardino, California. The storied Goldwater dynasty began from this hot and dusty town with a meandering street and a row of adobe houses facing the river and boat landing.

In time the Goldwater brothers would establish a chain of stores in Prescott, Parker, Tombstone, Bisbee, Contention, and Phoenix. One of Mike's sons, Morris, would later become mayor of Prescott and one of the territory's most prominent political figures. He is generally considered the "Father of the Democratic Party" in Arizona. One of Mike's grandsons and a nephew of Morris is Senator Barry Goldwater. Barry Goldwater was elected to the United States Senate in 1952 and was the Republican Party's nominee for President in 1964. Senator Goldwater was the father of the conservative movement that had its origin in the early 1960s, setting the stage for the dramatic conservative surge that swept the nation in the 1980s.

424

*Mike Goldwater,
early day merchant
at Ehrenberg and
Prescott,
grandfather of U.S.
Senator Barry M.
Goldwater*
Courtesy
Southwest Studies

Martha Summerhayes, a young army bride traveling up the Colorado River by steamer in 1874, painted a dismal, but true, picture of Ehrenberg. The fact that she had spent some time in Germany might have influenced her impressions.

One morning, as I was trying to finish out a nap in my stateroom, Jack came excitedly in and said: "Get up, Martha, we are coming to Ehrenberg!" Visions of castles on the Rhine, and stories of the middle ages floated through my mind, as I sprang up, in pleasurable anticipation of seeing an interesting and beautiful place. Alas! for my ignorance. I saw but a row of low thatched hovels, perched on the edge of the ragged looking river-bank; a road ran lengthwise along, and opposite the hovels I saw a store and some more mean-looking huts of adobe. . . .

But I did not go ashore. Of all dreary, miserable-looking settlements that one could possibly imagine, that was the worst. An unfriendly, dirty, and Heaven-forsaken place, inhabited by a poor class of Mexicans and half-breeds. It was, however, an important shipping station for freight which was to be sent overland to the interior. . . .

Quartzsite

Quartzsite was originally known as Tyson's Wells. Charles Tyson found water here in 1856 and built a fort on the site as defense against Mojave Indians. Later the place was used as a stage station on the road from Ehrenberg to Prescott. Martha Summerhayes, who writes a memorable account of her years on the Arizona frontier in her *Vanished Arizona*, gives her view of Tyson's Wells. She was traveling with a small military party from Prescott to Ehrenberg, camping at ranches along the road each night. The last night before reaching Ehrenberg was spent at Tyson's Wells. "We slept in our tent that night," she wrote, "for of all the places on earth a poorly kept ranch in Arizona is the most melancholy and uninviting. It reeks of every-

425

thing unclean, morally and physically." These were not the observations of a young bride fresh from the East—by this time Martha had experienced some of the most primitive conditions Arizona had to offer.

Tyson's Wells faded for a time but prospered again in the late 1890s, when prospectors began scouring the craggy, cactus-strewn hills nearby for gold. Since the postal authorities do not allow a branch to re-open with the same name, Tyson's Wells was dropped and the name Quartzite was suggested. Some bureaucrat misspelled the name by adding an "s." Today's Quartzsite is about nine miles east of the original site of Tyson's Wells.

On the outskirts of Quartzsite is a monument to one of the most unusual experiments undertaken in the history of the westward movement. In 1857 Lieutenant Edward F. "Ned" Beale, ex-Navy officer turned landlubber, charted a proposed railroad route along the thirty-fifth parallel using camels as beasts of burden.

Since American muleskinners could not speak Arabic and the stubborn camels would not learn English, Arabs were imported from the Middle East to handle the camels. The most famous of these Arab drivers was a Syrian named Hadji Ali, who soon became known as "Hi Jolly" to American drivers. He has been immortalized by a stone monument marking his grave, and by a folk song written in his honor by Randy Sparks and recorded by the New Christy Minstrels in the 1960s.

Somewhere in the desert between Quartzsite and the Yuma County line, near milepost 69, lies an outcropping of rich virgin ore known as the Lost Six-shooter Mine. In 1884 a man named Perkins, or Jenkins, or P. J. for short, was superintendent of the Planet Mines on the Bill Williams River and had just taken some prospective investors to the stage station at Tyson's Wells (Quartzsite). On the

Tribute to "Hi Jolly," the legendary camel driver of the 1850s
Courtesy Jeff Kida

way home, when P. J. was caught in a blinding sandstorm, he dismounted and holed up behind some rocks for protection. When the storm had passed, he looked around and discovered what all prospectors dream about but seldom see—a fabulously rich vein of ore with strings of glittering gold running throughout. He broke off a few specimens, filling his holster. He then left his six-shooter and overcoat as markers and set out across the desert in a northerly direction toward the Bill Williams River. P. J. and his horse had traveled for some time without water, and he figured the best way to reach his destination safely was to give his horse her head and she would lead him home. He was probably walking behind, holding onto the tail of his guide. The next day the horse showed up at the Planet Mine, but P. J. was nowhere to be seen. Searchers later found his body, half covered by sand near the old Bouse-Parker wagon road. Before dying, P. J. had scribbled this message in his notebook: "Found gold ledge by rocks 15 feet high. Two rocks alike. Knocked off some pieces. Very rich. Dust in air too thick to tell exact location. Think it is above ravine I come up 7 miles."

Very rich indeed! The specimens assayed out at $25,000 the ton. Prospectors searched for the cluster of tall rocks and the seven-mile ravine but both proved illusive. There were gold strikes in that part of western Arizona, but none in surroundings that fit P. J.'s description.

Litchfield Park

Litchfield Park started out as the Agua Fria Ranch. During World War I, the Allies were using Egyptian long-staple cotton in the manufacture of balloon tires. When cotton supplies were cut off by the German blockade, the Allies desperately needed a new source of the long, fibrous material. Arizona was found to be an ideal climate for growing long-staple cotton, so in 1916 the Goodyear Tire and Rubber Company purchased tracts of land along the normally dry Agua Fria River. Paul W. Litchfield, vice president of the company, gave his name to the site. The war created a great demand for cotton, not only for tires, but for uniforms, observation balloons, airplane fabric, and a host of other essentials of the war effort. Cotton produced around Litchfield and in other parts of the Salt and Gila river valleys brought unprecedented prosperity to cotton growers.

❄GLENDALE❄

*The new town of
Glendale put heavy
emphasis on the high
moral character of
its prospective
citizens*
Courtesy Arizona
Historical Foundation

US 60/Arizona 93
Phoenix to Wickenburg

Glendale

Glendale had its beginnings in late 1891 as a temperance colony on
a site selected by B. A. Hadsell, of Chicago, Illinois. The first residents were members of the Church of the Brethren in what was called
"Glendale Valley." The temperate and industrious settlers located on
a thirty-six-block townsite laid out on bare farmland outside of
Phoenix. By 1892 seventy families had arrived, naming their community Glendale, but nobody seems to know the origin of the name. A
long drought three years later caused some Glendale residents to
move to California. By 1911 a trolley service along Grand Avenue
linked Glendale to the territorial capital at Phoenix. At the height of
ostrich ranching, Glendale boasted a large number of prosperous
ostrich operations. Fashionable ladies wore the frowsy feathers on
their hats and bustles until the end of World War I, when styles
changed, bringing to a close the colorful era of "ostrich boys" and their
thundering herds.

428

Historically, Glendale was an agricultural community. A number of Japanese farmers settled in the area over the years, but greater impact came from refugees from Russian political oppression. In 1911 a large party of Russian colonists called Molokans purchased four hundred acres and began farming sugar beets. The Molokans were a dissident group that had broken off from Catholicism and the Russian Orthodox Church. The name is derived from the Russian word *moloko*, meaning "milk." The Orthodox Church branded these dissidents with the name because they drank milk on days that were forbidden by Church doctrine.

During World War I the demand for Pima long-stable cotton helped the settlers improve their economic situation, and by the end of the war two hundred Russian immigrants were living in Glendale.

Many descendants of old Russian families with names like Popoff, Treguboff, Tolmachoff, and Conovaloff still farm in the Glendale area and are a part of the rich agricultural heritage of Glendale.

Peoria

In 1896 four families, including that of Chauncy Clark, arrived here from Peoria, Illinois, and began farming. The main base of the economy over the next ninety years was citrus, cotton, melons, and other fruits. A dam made of brush, rocks, and dirt had been built on New River before Clark and the others arrived, but it washed out in a flood, causing most of the original settlers to abandon their farms.

In 1980 the population was only 12,307. Then Peoria was swept up by creeping suburbia and spread out beyond Glendale; four years later the population had more than doubled.

Glendale and Peoria, like many other communities in the Salt River Valley, used to be separated by huge tracts of farm land; however, today, motorists traveling along Grand Avenue (US 60/ Arizona 93) have to check the city limit signs to know when they are leaving one city and entering another.

El Mirage, Surprise, and Beardsley

These three agricultural communities were founded in 1937. One has only to use his imagination to guess how El Mirage was named; Surprise's origin is more complicated—local folklore says that early observers noted that "if it becomes a town, it'll be a surprise." This makes a good story, but in reality the name comes from settlers hailing from Surprise, Nebraska, who brought the name along.

Beardsley goes back to 1888, when Will Beardsley farmed the area, and the small community that grew up here took his name.

Wittman

In 1920 the railroad attached the name *Nada*, Spanish for "nothing," to a station located in the middle of nowhere. Although a few people took up residence, Nada, or Nadaburg, stuck for several years, until it was changed to Whittman in 1929. Five years later it was changed again, this time to Wittman, for a promoter of the ill-fated Walnut Grove Dam, on the Hassayampa River.

A tragic murder and robbery occurred here in 1886, when Barney Martin, his wife, and their three children were killed by three members of the Valenzuela gang. The charred remains of the Martin family were found in a shallow grave near the ranch. Sometime later the gang robbed and murdered three men hauling forty pounds of bullion from the Vulture Mine. A posse picked up the trail and followed it to Gila Bend, where they had a shootout with the gang. One of the murderers, Innocente Valenzuela, was killed, but the other two escaped to Mexico and were never caught. The gold was found wrapped in a blanket.

Morristown

Vulture Siding was the original name of Morristown. During the prosperous days of the historic Vulture Mine, ore was shipped by wagon across the desert to Vulture Siding railroad stop. Around the turn of the century, Vulture Siding was a junction for people traveling to the health resort of Castle Hot Springs, and for a time it was called Hot Springs Junction. The passengers had to travel in a leather-slung stagecoach across twenty-one miles of dusty, rock-strewn highway to reach the resort. The springs, located a few miles north in the Heiroglyphic Mountains, was a favorite gathering place for the wealthy, who sought to soothe their aching bodies in warm mineral waters. George Monroe and Ed Farley were among the first white men to use the warm waters to scrub themselves clean. The springs also doubled as a laundramat. It was said the hundred-sixty-degree water would, in five minutes, cleanse a pair of long johns that a prospector had worn for three months.

George Morris, owner of the Mack Morris Mine, was the first to take up residence at Hot Springs Junction, and the name changed, for the last time, to Morristown.

US 60
Wickenburg to Brenda

Heading west from Wickenburg, US 60 follows the old wagon road to Ehrenberg. The building of a railroad in the early 1900s was responsible for the founding of most of the desert communities along this route.

Aguila

Taking its name from a nearby mountain shaped like an eagle's beak, Aguila was a small station on the railroad line. The Mexicans called it *Pico de Aguila*. F. H. Kline tried to establish a community here in 1909, but the development failed.

Wenden

At the turn of the century, Otis Young wanted to name the town he founded Wendendale, for his farm in Pennsylvania. But the postal department preferred Wenden so that was what it became.

Salome

Dick Wick Hall, the "Sage of Salome," used to say the town, whose full name was "Salome Where She Danced," got its name in 1904, when Grace Salome Pratt removed her shoes to walk in the hot sand and wound up doing an Indian dance.

Hall, an entrepreneur who promoted everything from oil wells and gold mines to desert communities, was the one most responsible for making Salome one of the West's best-known small towns during the early 1900s.

Salome in the 1940s
Courtesy Arizona
Historical Foundation

Born Deforest Hall, he later changed his name to Dick Wick, the Wick being for Wickenburg. Leaving his Iowa birthplace because he could not stand the cold weather, Hall found his Shangri-la in the deserts of western Arizona. He opened a gas station at a forlorn place he called Salome. Bone-weary travelers were treated to a display of humorous signs plastered on the walls of the gas station and along the road for several miles in either direction. The signs joked about the many bumps and ruts, causing even the most cynical of travelers to grin. Hall's wit provided a welcome relief, helping travelers to endure the miserable automobile trip across the searing desert.

Although Hall's humor touched many travelers on the Los Angeles-Phoenix highway, his fame really began to spread with the publication of his mimeographed newspaper, called the *Salome Sun*. He published the paper solely for the purpose of breaking the monotony and cheering up his customers. He liked to say he did not care whether or not people paid him for his paper: "I don't need the money," he kidded merrily; "there's no place here to spend it."

Soon most of the civilized world knew of the seven-year-old frog out in Arizona that never learned to swim because "he didn't need to," and of the desert golf course that was 247 miles long with a par of 16,394. He called it the Greasewood Golf Links, bragging that some winter visitors spent the entire season playing just one round of golf. The clubhouse rented not only golf clubs but also camping equipment, horses, canteens, and maps.

Harcuvar

An old mining district located in this area was named Harcuvar for a Mojave word that roughly means "There's very little water to be found here," a name that would fit most southern Arizona communities.

Hope

There used to be a community named Johannesberg near here, but just when the community was being settled, a new highway was built (1920), and residents had to move to a new community they called Hope, because they hoped they would not have to move again. (In the early 1980s the highway moved again, but the people have not given up hope yet.)

Henry Wickenburg, discoverer of the Vulture mine near the town that bears his name
Courtesy
Southwest Studies

US 89

Wickenburg

They say that on the day Henry Wickenburg made his great Vulture Mine strike, he gazed at the sky and saw a vulture hovering over him. Another story says he threw a rock at his stubborn burro and it shattered, revealing a glittering interior. Although many of the West's famed mineral discoveries were found by accident, they generally came from hard work. A prospector might find "color" in his pan while washing out dirt in some rocky arroyo; next he would work his way up the wash, tracing the gold until it ran out; then he would backtrack, exploring the area looking for the gold's source. Wickenburg's strike came after rancher King Woolsey had suggested he check out the nearby Harquahala Mountains to the west. It was only a matter of time until the experienced prospector found his bonanza. Wickenburg's Vulture Mine was destined to be one of the richest gold strikes in the history of the West.

Henry Wickenburg was born Heinrich Heintzel in Austria in 1820 and came to America as a young man to escape political oppression. He changed his name and went to California to seek his fortune during gold rush days. Like many others, he worked his way back toward Arizona. Henry prospected central Arizona in 1862, then returned to La Paz, the new boom town on the banks of the Colorado River, where Pauline Weaver had made a gold strike earlier that year.

When Joe Walker led a party up the Hassayampa River in search of gold, a Mojave chief named Irataba acted as guide. They reached the river, which they called the "Haviamp," just below where Wickenburg is today and followed it up to its headwaters, just south of today's Prescott. Irataba warned them of the grave danger of entering the land of the Apaches, but the prospectors were not to be denied. Rich placers were found on Lynx Creek, Big Bug, Turkey Creek, and several other streams in the area.

That same year Pauline Weaver led the A. H. Peeples' expedition up the Hassayampa in search of the *madre del oro*. A few miles north of today's city of Wickenburg they found gold nuggets strewn across the top of a small mountain which they called Rich Hill. It is said the goldseekers pocketed $100,000 in nuggets the first few weeks on the site, which was to become the richest single placer strike in Arizona history and the richest single piece of real estate until the arrival of the developers of the twentieth century.

Henry Wickenburg set out on his own, following Woolsey's advice to explore the mountains west of the Hassayampa and finding his glory hole in a range twelve miles from the river. He also made the acquaintance of Charles Genung in 1864, another piece of good fortune. Genung knew hardrock mining (the Vulture was a lode mine; the gold was still attached to the ore as opposed to placer, or "free" gold). Henry wisely sold his ore for $15 a ton, and the buyer was responsible for the mining, transporting, and milling. All this was done at the river, where forty *arrastras* (mule-driven ore crushers) were operating.

Within a year after Wickenburg's discovery, a thriving community of two hundred was established on the banks of the Hassayampa and named Wickenburg in honor of the discoverer of the Vulture. Like all

Arizona prospectors
on Hassayampa
River
Courtesy
Southwest Studies

boom towns, the varied assortment of citizens included tin horn gamblers, shady ladies, saloonkeepers, and dreamers and schemers.

The residents of Wickenburg were so busy trying to strike it rich they did not have time to build a proper jail, so a large tree at the corner of Tegner and Center streets was used. Incorrigible characters were chained to the jail-tree until they sobered up or served their time in the shade of the old mesquite. One regular customer was George Sayers, a mountain of a man who bellowed like a range bull, even when sober. At one time George, who was known as the "King of Gunsight" (a small desert town from which he hailed), went on a tear. Finally several deputies subdued him, dragging him to the jail-tree. The mesquite was already filled to capacity, so George was chained to a huge log. The night was spent in deep slumber, but when daylight came, the "King of Gunsight" wanted a drink. His bellowing shook the nearby mountains and woke the town, but nobody came to his aid, so George shouldered the log, which would have put a pack mule to the supreme test, and hauled it to the nearest saloon, where he demanded and received a drink, no questions asked.

By 1870 the population in Maricopa's oldest community was nearly five hundred, not including countless drifters who came with the dust and went with the wind; Wickenburg had become the most important city in central Arizona. Phoenix, a tiny agricultural settlement on the banks of the Salt River, was created by residents of Wickenburg to grow feed for livestock and food for the miners.

Mining equipment for the Vulture was hauled by steamer up the Colorado to Ehrenburg, then hauled overland across the desert to the

Vulture Mine near Wickenburg, circa 1900
Courtesy
Southwest Studies

mine. Senator Barry Goldwater tells a story about a time when the company failed to pay their bills to his grandfather Mike—the iron-willed merchant rode over to the mine and took over the operation until he had collected enough money to satisfy the debt.

Mesquite wood was the chief fuel at the Vulture, and before long all the trees in the vicinity had been cut except for one venerable mesquite in the middle of the camp. It was kept as a hanging tree to thwart would-be highgraders. Highgrading (stealing ore from the mine) was always a serious problem. It has been estimated that as much as forty percent of the gold from the rich vein was stolen by miners. It is also said that more than twenty thieves were administered "suspended sentences" by Judge Lynch. During the first six years of operation, 2.5 million dollars in gold were taken out, and it is estimated that another million was highgraded. The Vulture went on to become the richest gold mine in nineteenth-century Arizona, producing close to twenty million before closing. It is said that the rock used in the construction of the old buildings would assay out at $20 a ton today; however, Henry did not capitalize on the potential riches—he sold four-fifths of his interest in the mine to Ben Phelps of Philadelphia for $85,000. Furthermore, Henry never received the money owed him, and a string of bad luck plagued the Austrian for the rest of his days. Henry committed suicide in 1905, when a flood wiped out his small farm, at the town named in his honor.

One of the most notorious acts of violence in Arizona history was the so-called Wickenburg Massacre of November 4, 1871. The stage to Ehrenberg was about nine miles west of Wickenburg when assailants unleashed a barrage of gunfire, killing driver Dutch John Lentz and five passengers, including a reporter for the *New York Tribune* named Frederick Loring. Two people survived the bloody massacre: Mollie Shepherd, a bawdy house madam carrying $40,000 from the sale of her bordello in Prescott, received a powder burn on the arm; and army paymaster William Kruger, who was taking a $100,000 payroll to California, received a gunshot wound in the shoulder.

Kruger claimed the attack had come from renegade Indians from Date Creek. Others believed it had come from either Mexican bandits or Americans dressed up to look like Indians. It seems unlikely that Indians committed the crime because the horses, harnesses, clothing, and ammunition were left at the scene—these items were valuable to the native bands and most certainly would have been taken. The $100,000 payroll, Miss Shepherd's $40,000, and a shovel were all that was missing.

As the case began to unravel, other evidence indicated it might have been an inside job. Most holdups or ambushes occurred in remote areas that provided concealment, yet this one was in open country. Kruger and Mollie, the two survivors, told conflicting stories of the attack. Kruger claimed he had held off nine Apaches for several hours with a six-shooter, but the bullet-riddled, blood-splattered stagecoach had been attacked from the front, rear, and on one side; Kruger's story was improbable since it is unlikely that the attackers would have put themselves in a crossfire. Also, there was no evidence of the Indians on the Date Creek Reservation spending an unusual amount of money following the robbery.

As investigators tried to piece the puzzle together, it began to look as though the culprits were Kruger and Shepherd. Prescott people claimed that Kruger was a regular customer at Mollie's place and that the two could have murdered the other six people, inflicted superficial wounds on themselves, and buried the loot. When the case against Kruger and Mollie proved too weak to press charges, the two went to California (where the story of the massacre had received front page attention in the newspapers) for a stint as celebrities. In Arizona General Crook nearly lost his life trying to punish the Date Creek Indians for the crime. The natives at Date Creek plotted to ambush the general while the two sides were gathered for "peace talks." The plan went awry when a friendly Hualapai tipped off the soldiers. Crook narrowly escaped death in the ensuing gunfire, and the renegades were soundly whipped and chased into the hills. Although some historians believe that a war party of Date Creek Indians attacked the stage, no evidence has been found to prove the claim.

Meanwhile, in California Kruger revealed in a newspaper interview that Mollie had died of wounds suffered in the massacre. When newsmen tried to check out the story, they found no record of Mollie's death. By the time they returned to Kruger's hotel, the ex-paymaster had checked out, his whereabouts unknown.

In December 1872 a man registered in a Phoenix hotel as William Kruger was cut down by a stray bullet fired during a fight between two customers. The victim's description fitted the William Kruger who survived the Wickenburg Massacre; Kruger, according to the hotel clerk, was on his way to the Wickenburg area to do some prospecting. The Wickenburg Massacre remains one of frontier Arizona's many unsolved murders.

During the mid-1920s Wickenburg became known as the "dude ranch capital of the world." About this time the Old West was rapidly fading from reality into romantic myth, and as Americans became more mobile, the lure of visiting a cow ranch inspired men like Jack Burden and Romaine Lowdermilk of Wickenburg to establish dude ranches. Much to the surprise of working cattlemen and their hired hands, Easterners would actually pay for the privilege of staying on a ranch, eating the chow, and "riding herd on the cows." Burden's "Remuda" and Lowdermilk's "KL Bar" were the first, and others soon followed. During World War II as many as twelve dude ranches were prospering around Wickenburg. The cowboys entertained guests around the campfire with their own authentic songs and poems, many of which were picked up by radio-singing cowboys in Hollywood and New York, bringing fame to punchers like Gail Gardner, Billy Simon, and Curly Fletcher.

The old "KL Bar" is still a dude ranch, and the picturesque old adobe buildings provide a picture of old Arizona cow ranches for winter visitors.

Prior to the completion of Interstate 17 in the mid-1960s the Wickenburg road was the only paved road connecting Phoenix with Flagstaff. Historically, Arizona's highways ran east and west, and Arizona's rugged central mountains and the Mogollon Rim isolated northern Arizona from the more populous regions to the south. To reach Flagstaff from Phoenix, a traveler usually went by way of Wickenburg, Prescott, and Ash Fork, and then east fifty-two miles to Flagstaff. The new Interstate 17 eliminated much of the highway traffic through Wickenburg; then the completion of Interstate 10 from the California line to the greater Phoenix area took the town off the main highway between Phoenix and Los Angeles.

It was just a little over a hundred years ago when the first railroads crossed Arizona, and twenty years later when many people in the territory had not yet ridden on a train, another marvelous marvel of the industrial revolution sputtered and jerked into the region. With the gas buggy came the demand for better roads. As late as 1926 there were only a hundred forty miles of paved roads in the entire state. A few miles west of Yuma travelers between that city and San Diego crossed the desert for several miles on wooden planks tied together with cable. Every time the sand shifted, the highway took a new course. It was said that service stations sold more shovels than

438

gasoline.

Slowly but surely automobiles were gaining acceptance in the wide open spaces of the West. In 1905 the great Apache war chief Geronimo allowed himself to be photographed hunting buffalo in a tin lizzie. A few years later Pancho Villa made a daring escape in a Model T. "Flivver rodeos" were being staged with cowboys bulldogging steers from running boards. One daring fellow drove a car into the Grand Canyon. The sturdy, durable machines were an improvement over horses, one convert said, because "you only needed to feed 'em when you use 'em." When one did break down, monkey wrench surgery and a little profanity were usually enough to get the machine running again. "Only trouble with them," Will Rogers said, "is you get there quicker than you can think of a reason for going there."

The public demand for better highways began in 1908, and to promote highway construction in the Southwest, road races were staged across the cactus-strewn desert between Los Angeles and Phoenix. These races combined all the elements of a Keystone Kops movie, a melodrama, and a convention of Jaycees. Legendary drivers like Lewis Chevrolet and Barney Oldfield, competing for the prestigious title of "master driver of the world," raced for $2,500 in prize money on roads that were no more than wagon trails. There were no filling stations and no garages, so drivers used an oversized gas tank and strapped extra parts on the running boards or behind the driver's seat.

The great Los Angeles to Phoenix road races that were staged between 1908 and 1914 represented two diverse points of view concerning the newfangled horseless carriages. One group saw the automobile as a plaything of the idle rich; the other, more visionary, proclaimed the time would come when everybody could afford to own one.

As they raced against time rather than each other, one route took the daring contestants out to Palm Springs, across the Colorado River by ferry, and then across the desert to Salome and into Phoenix.

The first race in 1905 took over thirty hours to complete. It roughly followed today's Interstate 10. The winner, Colonel F. C. Fenner, averaged 17.6 miles per hour over the five hundred-mile course in a steam-driven auto affectionately named "Black Bess."

Earlier in the day another race was run from Tucson to Phoenix. Six stripped down cars were ranked up at the old pueblo at 4 A.M. Two broke down somewhere between Tucson and Tempe, leaving the final four running hell-for-leather over the last twelve-mile stretch to the fairgrounds. It was opening day of the Territorial Fair and 10,000 people were on hand to see the thrilling finish of a race that had lasted

*Race driver Barney
Oldfield during one
of the "Cactus
Derby" road races
between Phoenix and
Los Angeles in the
early 1900s*
Courtesy
Southwest Studies

just under twelve hours. The winner, H. S. Corbett, in a Stoddard-Dayton, came in forty-five seconds ahead of T. A. Hendon's Reo.

During the next five years the Los Angeles—Phoenix race alternated between the Yuma and the Ehrenberg roads. Over the years, technology kept improving the speed and endurance of the racing cars, but the roads remained rock-strewn and rutted.

One of the most exciting races in this series was the one in 1914 which went from Los Angeles to Needles, over notorious Oatman Pass, east to Ash Fork, then south to Wickenburg, and on into Phoenix, a distance of seven hundred miles of potholes, sage, and arroyos. Rain, sleet, and snow turned the roads into a quagmire of mud and slush. Since the drivers raced against time and not each other, overnight stops were made in Needles and Prescott, where the autos were locked up for the night under guard in a local horse corral to keep mechanics from making repairs or sabotaging a competitor's machine.

Colorful Barney Oldfield, the grizzled, cigar-chomping "grand old man of racing" was one of the favorites. In 1914 he was the most famous driver in the world. Earlier, he had been suspended for taking part in an unsanctioned race against heavyweight boxer Jack Johnson, and now, at the age of thirty-six, he was making a comeback.

The promoters, which included the *Arizona Republican* (today's *Republic*), ballyhooed this race as the greatest yet. Dubbed the "Cactus Derby," it was over a hundred thirty miles longer than earlier races and took an extra day to run. Barney navigated the rutted roads made slick by the rain with the skill of an Arizona muleskinner. He eventually won, even though his Stutz-Bearcat blew a tire near

Kingman, forcing him to drive several miles on the rim. The car nearly sank while crossing New River outside Phoenix and had to be pulled out by a team of mules. Barney's first place finish at the Phoenix fairgrounds was overshadowed by the fifth place finisher, Bill Bramlett, who wobbled across the finish line with two fence posts spliced together to replace his Cadillac's broken steering system after the car had made a nosedive into an arroyo, one of several spectacular mishaps. A few hours earlier, he was driving on a circuitous old wagon road north of Wickenburg when his auto slipped off the rain-slick road, did a perfect barrel roll, and landed on all four wheels. A few miles later the Cadillac was nearly lost when it plunged into quicksand. Only seven of the original twenty starters reached Phoenix.

That evening there was a lot of oratory and boasting at the victory celebration. Enthusiasts predicted optimistically that all-weather, paved roads would someday cross the Southwest. But the most sagacious forecast that night in 1914 was that the auto would pass from being a plaything of the rich and a professional race driver's toy to becoming a standard fixture in American culture.

Congress
(three miles west of Congress Junction)

In 1883 Dennis May located the fabulously rich Congress Mine in the rugged foothills of the Date Creek Mountains and nine miles west of Pauline Weaver's Rich Hill discovery. The mineral-laden mountains between Wickenburg and Prescott yielded what was to be one of Arizona's greatest gold mines. "Diamond" Jim Reynolds, a Mississippi riverboat gambler with a flamboyant lifestyle, owned the mine in the late 1880s. He built a twenty-stamp mill, and by the time of his death in 1891 more than $600,000 in gold had been taken out.

Congress, 1889
Courtesy Arizona
Historical Foundation

441

Following the death of "Diamond" Jim, E. B. Gage, of Tombstone
fame, and railroad entrepreneur Frank Murphy, also a tycoon of
reknown, were instrumental in getting the Santa Fe to bring a
railroad through the area. By 1897 four hundred twenty-five men
were employed at the mine, and the rough-and-tumble city of Congress was at its peak. President William McKinley paid a visit to
Congress a few months before his assassination in 1901 to see the big
bonanza at first hand.

The economic importance of Congress is evidenced by the fact that
in the 1890s, the Santa Fe Railroad laid its Prescott to Phoenix line
just east of Congress, locating a stop at what was to become known as
Congress Junction.

Congress was in reality two towns—Mill Town and Lower Town.
Located at Mill Town were the mill, a hospital, homes for the
employers and employees, bunkhouses, and company offices. Lower
Town consisted of a series of buildings strung out along a canyon and
included saloons like the Red Front and Silver Dollar, boarding
houses, restaurants, churches, mercantile stores, and a varied assortment of other enterprises usually found around a boom town. The
only source of water in town was a small spigot in front of the
company store at Mill Town. Thirsty residents rolled an empty fifty-
gallon barrel up the hill each day, filled up, and let gravity carry it
down the hill to Lower Town.

In April 1898 the scarcity of water prevented volunteers from
fighting a fire that consumed the business district of Lower Town.
Another fire, two years later damaged several saloons, two restaurants, and a barbershop.

One day, not far from Congress, a pair of amateur outlaws using
feedsacks for masks stopped the Wickenburg stage and ordered all
the passengers to hand over their valuables. All six victims dug into

their pockets and handed over their cash, which amounted to some small bills and change. After ordering the passengers back into the stage, the robbers lit out, not realizing they had missed several hundred dollars by not searching the passengers themselves.

By the 1930s the boom times were long gone; nothing much was left but the tumbled walls of miners' cabins and abandoned stores and rusted mining equipment. Congress, by this time, was becoming better known as a sheep-shipping station. In 1938 the post office was relocated to Congress Junction on US 89.

Stanton, Octave, and Weaver

Two miles north of Congress Junction a dirt road leads off to the east toward the old ghost towns of Stanton, Weaver, and Octave. Eight miles east of Congress Junction, at the base of Rich Hill, is Stanton, named for Charles P. Stanton, one of the most ruthless, conniving scoundrels in Arizona history. He arrived in Arizona in the late 1860s and for a time worked at the Vulture Mine. Later he moved to Antelope Creek, near Rich Hill, and opened a store. Nearby, at Antelope Station, Yaqui Wilson operated a stage stop. About a half-mile away an Englishman named William Partridge was also running a stage station. Apparently the two were not-so-friendly competitors, so Stanton figured he could get a corner on all the business if some way could be found to build an open feud. The scheme worked, and in a gunfight, Partridge killed Wilson. The Englishman was tried for murder and sent to the territorial prison at Yuma. However, before Stanton could take over the Englishman's station, a silent partner named Timmerman appeared and sold the outfit to Barney Martin. Undaunted, Stanton hired a dangerous cutthroat named Francisco Vega and his band of rogues to kill Timmerman and Martin. After murdering Timmerman, the outlaws set out to get Martin, who had recently sold his cow ranch and was planning to use some of the money to send his family back east while he remained behind to remodel the stage station. In July 1886 the family set out for Phoenix in a wagon, but never reached their destination. A few weeks later their charred remains were found in the desert near Morristown. Since there were no witnesses willing to testify in the case, no charges were pressed.

Later that year Charles Stanton learned the moral lesson of living by the sword. Recently he had insulted the sister of one of Vega's henchmen, Cristo Lucero. On November 13, 1886 Lucero entered Stanton's store and filled him full of lead, no one lamenting his passing.

The town of Stanton, at its peak in the 1890s, had about two hundred residents, a five-stamp mill, a boarding house, a store, and various other businesses.

Weaver, about two miles east of Stanton, was named for famed scout Pauline Weaver. In 1863 the rugged explorer was hired to guide the Abraham Peeples' party into the nearby mountains. On top of what became known as Rich Hill, they found a fabulous pocket of gold nuggets just waiting to be picked up. Other rich placers were found along Weaver and Antelope creeks, and eventually, a community sprang up named for the great scout.

In December 1863 one of the white man's more humiliating battles with the Indians occurred a few miles from Weaver. The fracas began when a party of Mexicans who were out cutting grama grass for their burros found themselves surrounded by a fierce-looking war party. Deciding that discretion was the better part of valor, they surrendered their weapons, hoping the Indians would be merciful. They got their wish; however, the natives also wanted their clothes. The happy warriors rode off equipped with the Mexicans' clothes, weapons, and burros, forcing them to return to camp wearing nothing more than a sheepish expression and convinced that the braves had given them a "raw" deal.

Weaver took on a wild reputation around the turn of the century. About that same time the placer gold began to play out, and eventually the community was absorbed by the underground mining community of Octave.

Octave was a relative latecomer to this trio of ghost towns. Located adjacent to Weaver, it came into existence in the late 1890s, many years after the Rich Hill discovery. The mine was developed by eight entrepreneurs, hence the name Octave. Once the community of three thousand boasted a school, post office, grocery store, stage station, and general store. At one time the mine was said to be netting $50,000 a month; however, in 1942 the Octave Gold Mining Company shut down operations and demolished the buildings.

Yarnell

The highway up Yarnell Hill, a long precipitous grade that winds and twists its way to the top, has been tamed and straightened, even made into a one-way road in recent years; however, there was a time when it was one of the most treacherous stretches of road in Arizona. Yarnell, the hill and the community, were named for Harrison Yarnell, discoverer and operator of a mine nearby, who was among the first to settle in the area, arriving in the 1890s.

Kirkland Junction

Kirkland Junction lies four miles east of Kirkland, both named for William Kirkland, the first settler and one of Arizona's most illustrious pioneers. Kirkland moved his family to this valley in 1863 and established a stage station. The excellent meals provided at Kirkland's station made it a favorite stopping place for travelers. He farmed and mined in the area until 1868, when restlessness and Indian attacks caused him to move his family to Phoenix. An encounter with hostile warriors occurred one day when Kirkland was hauling a load of flour between Yuma and Wickenburg. He was stopped by a large band demanding a yoke of oxen. The Virginian obliged by giving them a small team, which made the braves angry. One charged with his lance and opened a deep wound from Kirkland's hand to his elbow. Kirkland pulled out his revolver, but other warriors jumped on him and held him down while the rest cut open the flour sacks, scattering the contents across the desert; they then made crude shirts out of the sacks, riding off and leaving Kirkland battered and bleeding. On another occasion he was stopped by a band of Indians, and a warrior demanded his shirt. When the brave tried to remove the garment, Kirkland shoved him away. Another warrior rode up behind and ran a lance into his back. Although the wound was painful, he refused to flinch, staring defiantly at his captors. Eventually, they tired of the game and rode away. Years later, at Fort McDowell, Kirkland recognized his old adversary, a one-eyed Indian. The brave gave the white man a hard, but respectful look, and said in Spanish, *"valiente capitan,"* or "brave captain."

Kirkland, a big strapping Virginian, came to Arizona in 1856 and the following year established a ranch at Canoa. He drove in a herd of cows from Mexico to become the first American in Arizona to engage in cattle ranching. He was in Tucson in 1856 the day the Mexican troops evacuated the town. It was Kirkland who climbed to the top of Edward Miles's store and raised the first American flag over what would later become Arizona. A few years later he married Missouri Ann Bacon in what was said to be the first Anglo-American wedding in Tucson.

Bill Kirkland was one of a few people who came to Arizona in the turbulent 1850s and lived into the twentieth century. One good reason for his longevity was that he refused to stay in an area when bands of natives went on the warpath. Kirkland proved his bravery on many occasions but knew when it was time to steer clear of trouble. "I've helped bury a lot of men," he used to say, "who insisted they had as much right to a place as the Indians did." He died in 1909, with his boots off.

Peeples Valley

In 1863 Abraham H. Peeples left California and joined the Arizona gold rush at La Paz. He organized a prospecting expedition and hired Pauline Weaver as guide. They made a big strike at Rich Hill that same year. Two years later, Peeples was ranching in the valley that bears his name. Charles Genung bought the ranch six years later, and Peeples moved to Wickenburg, where he became a saloonkeeper. Genung, a noted mining man, rancher, and Indian fighter, was among the first to arrive in Yavapai County in 1863 and was one of the area's most prominent citizens during the latter part of the nineteenth century.

The Hays Cattle Company, located in Peeples Valley, is one of Arizona's most historic ranches, the Bar-Muleshoe-Bar brand dating back to 1876. In 1912 Roy Hays bought the ranch, which included about five thousand cows and which is still run by the Hays family.

Prior to his death in 1973 Hays was one of the state's most prominent cattlemen, serving for years as president of the Yavapai Association. He was also an active committee member of the Arizona Association and was also a member of the national group.

US 93
Wickenburg to Kingman

Date Creek

The highway north of Wickenburg passes through the old Martinez Mining District in southern Yavapai County. The district was in the southwest region of the Date Creek Mountains, west of the Weaver District and northwest of Congress. The most productive mine in the district was the Congress Mine, which produced nearly eight million dollars between 1889 and 1910. Date Creek, incidentally, comes from the Spanish word *datal*, the fruit of the *opuntia* cactus (cholla), which grows in clusters like dates.

Camp Date Creek, a few miles north of the highway, was a military post established to protect the road between Ehrenberg and Prescott during the Apache Wars. For a brief period in the 1870s, it was also an Indian reservation.

Santa Maria River

Early Spanish explorers named this area, and Lieutenant Amiel Whipple followed their lead in 1854, when he explored here. Spanish explorer Juan de Oñate passed this way in 1604 in search of fabulous lost silver and gold mines. He followed the river to the Colorado, which he called Rio Grande de Buena Esperanza, or "Big River of Good Hope." His quest was hopeless, however, as he never found the treasure trove, only natives who filled his ears with tall tales of gold. According to Barnes's *Arizona Place Names*, Oñate called the Santa Maria *Rio de San Andr*és, for St. Andrew's Day (November 30), following the custom of naming a place in honor of the saint on whose day it was first visited.

Big Sandy River

According to Lieutenant Amiel Whipple, Joe Walker gave this muddy stream its name during his adventures in Arizona. There is some disagreement over its earlier names. Place name expert Byrd Granger mentions that Oñate called it the Rio San Andrés for St. Andrew's Day. However, Barnes's *Arizona Place Names* gives that name to the Santa Maria. Jesuit padre Jacob Sedelmayr came here in 1744 and called it Rio Azul, or Blue River. Whipple called it the Bill

Williams River. In reality, the Santa Maria and the Big Sandy merge at Alamo Lake to form the Bill Williams River.

Burro Creek

Army officers named Burro Creek in 1869. They did not say why, but it was probably because the area was populated by burros that had escaped from their sourdough partners or been turned loose for one reason or another.

Wikieup

Wikieup is a descriptive name for the temporary, dome-shaped brush dwellings built by Apaches, Yavapai, and their nomadic or *rancheria* peoples. Apparently, one was found at a spring where the small community on the western plain above the Big Sandy River would develop. Originally, the names Owens and Neal were used by local residents or relatives, but the names failed to last. For a time, settlers tried to use Sandy, but someone else was using that name, so Wikieup was accepted, even though misspelled (Wickieup is correct). Nearby Wikieup Canyon is sometimes marked on maps as "Wake Up" Canyon.

The mountains between Wikieup and the Colorado River were rich in minerals. A number of mines and mining camps, including Planet, McCrackin, American Flag, Signal, and Scatterville, dotted the area. North of Wikieup, Deluge Wash merges with the Big Sandy. Anyone familiar with Arizona's desert flash floods would agree that Deluge Wash is accurate in describing many of Arizona's desert arroyos.

US 93
Kingman to Hoover Dam

Santa Claus

Santa Claus is perhaps the best-known fast-blink community in America; however, as a metropolis it never materialized. Nina Talbot of Los Angeles, a three hundred pound woman billing herself as the "biggest real estate agent" in California planned a subdivision here, fulfilling a dream of building a Christmas village, with architecture to match, in the Arizona desert. Nina and her husband Ed took up residence at Santa Claus, where she delighted friends around the country with picturesque Christmas cards from Santa Claus, Arizona.

Santa Claus,
Arizona
Courtesy
Southwest Studies

Chloride

At one time two thousand miners lived at Chloride. That was in 1900, when a rich gold strike in the Cerbat Mountains brought in would-be millionaires convinced that Chloride sat right on top of the mother lode and that its streets would be cobbled with gold bricks. Chloride, named for the exposed ore that was laced with silver chloride, claims to be the oldest Anglo-American mining town in Arizona.

Cerbat is a Yuman word meaning "bighorn mountain sheep." The old ghost town of Chloride came into existence in 1860 and was important enough to become the Mohave County seat in 1871. Two years later it was moved a few miles south to Mineral Park, on the Hardyville-Prescott road.

Among the many mines in the Cerbat Range are included the Payroll, Golden Gem, Esmeralda, and Vanderbuilt. The richest mine in the Cerbat Range until the 1930s was the Golconda, located between Chloride and Kingman. By that time it had produced six and one-half million dollars in ore, mostly zinc. It was later surpassed by the Tennessee, near Chloride. Like most of the dozens of mines located in the Cerbat Range, the Tennessee did not become prominent until the Santa Fe Railroad came to Kingman in 1883. The major lode running through the Cerbat Mountains was the Elkhart, a mixture of lead, zinc and copper, with some gold and silver. This type of ore made separation complex and difficult. According to an optimistic newspaper article in 1899, the Merrimac Mine was producing high grade ore, the article claiming the Merrimac had a carload ready to ship that averaged five hundred ounces of silver and assayed at $100 a ton in gold.

449

In 1898 the Arizona Utah Railroad stretched from Kingman to Chloride and was cause for a celebration. A ballot was held to select the woman who would have the honor of pounding in the silver spike. She was also to receive a gold watch and chain valued at $25. Each voter had to pay ten cents for a ballot, the proceeds going to erect a new school for Chloride. The old one, it was claimed, was a tumble-down, leaky-roofed building with cracks in the walls big enough for coyotes to walk through. A drilling contest, the highlight of any celebration, was planned—contestants were expected to bore into a granite slab at a rate of "two drinks per minute." A fellow named Greely Clack, apparently a driller of some reknown, was representing the Kingman Ice Plant. The champion hundred-yard foot racer, Charley Bradley, was clocked, so the newspaper claimed, in the unbelievable time of seven seconds. Everyone was expected to enter a contest and the paper sardonically noted that poker would attract the most entrants.

In spite of the tremendous celebration, the railroad lasted only a few years. Still, Chloride could claim to be the first incorporated city in Mohave County; as the newspaper proudly proclaimed, ". . . the City of Chloride will be all the same . . . as New York."

Chloride continued to be a thriving community until mining went into a decline in the 1940s. The final blow came in 1947, when the Tennessee Mine shut down for good.

White Hills

White Hills is a ghost town a few miles east of US 93 on the road to Temple Bar. No part of Arizona of similar size had so many mines concentrated in such a small area; however, the ore was capricious, with rich pockets of silver mixed in with low grade ore. Some shipments, according to reports, averaged three thousand ounces to the ton. The mines eventually produced two or three million dollars in silver. Boom times in the White Hills began in 1892, when an Indian named Hualapai Jeff found a rich chunk of silver ore, and within a few months Mohave County had a prosperous new boom town consisting of three eating places, four saloons, a scattering of tents, and a population of two hundred. Two years later fifteen hundred residents crowded the town. Before a large corporation took over the mine, water was scarce, and thirsty residents were paying a dollar a barrel. By 1895 White Hills had electric lights, telephones, running water, and flush toilets—the largest town in Mohave County for a time.

Detrital Valley, on the west side of the highway, used to be called Death Valley Wash. Detritus, or loose material resulting from decomposed rock, characterized this area and provided inspiration for the name. Further south, but adjoining Detrital Valley, is Sacramento Valley, named by the California Volunteers in 1864. They prospected in their spare time and named their mining district the Sacramento, along with the valley separating the Black Mountains from the Cerbat and Hualapai ranges.

Hoover Dam

Throughout history, the Colorado River, last of the great rivers of America to be explored, devastated Mexico, southern California, and Arizona every time it went on a rampage. Floods in the 1890s, 1916, and 1920 made the roads in Yuma suitable only for submarine traffic. In 1905 the river sent its tempestuous waters hurling into the Imperial Valley and filled the Salton Sea. It took months and thousands of railroad cars filled with rock and dirt to rebuild the river banks and put the river back on course.

To harness the Colorado and to fill southern California's ravenous appetite for water and electricity, Congress passed the Boulder Canyon Project, which authorized a dam in Black Canyon. The original name was to be Boulder Dam, but two years later, the Secretary of Interior ordered the name changed to Hoover in honor of the President, respected more as an engineer than Chief Executive. When the Democrats came back in power in 1934, the name was changed back to Boulder and remained that way until President Harry Truman, in a grand gesture of non-partisan politics, changed it back to Hoover.

Chief engineer on the project was Frank T. Crowe, a man whose main mission in life was to build the largest dam in the world. In early 1931 Crowe put three thousand men to work in the eight-hundred-foot-deep canyon, where the temperature reached a hundred twenty degrees and the rock was hot enough to fry eggs. Daring workers with jackhammers hung hundreds of feet off the canyon floor, clearing rock debris before the concrete could be poured. Then they dumped sixteen-ton buckets of concrete into the forms every sixty seconds for the next two years, and when the job was finished, the dam was taller than a sixty-story skyscraper.

The dam's construction, at its peak, employed five thousand workers; ninety-six were killed on the project. The chief engineer was dubbed "Hurry Up" Crowe for his timesaving methods—he designed a lighting system that allowed crews to work around the clock. By 1935 construction on the forty-nine-million-dollar dam was finished (at the time the world's largest dam), Crowe having brought the project in two years ahead of schedule. Although first in size at the time, Hoover Dam now ranks fifty-second in the world.

When the lake began to form behind the dam, alarmists declared falsely that the tremendous weight of water would cause devastating earthquakes. The hundred-mile-long lake was named for Dr. Ellwood Mead, Commissioner of Reclamation during the building of Hoover Dam. Dr. Mead died on January 26, 1936, and a week later the lake was re-named in his honor. Up to then it had been called Lake Powell, for John Wesley Powell, who first explored the Colorado River. By volume, Lake Mead is the largest man-made lake in the western hemisphere.

US 95
Yuma to Interstate 40

US 95 leaves Yuma and runs parallel to Interstate 8 for ten miles, then turns north. It crosses the Gila River several miles west of Dome, which is the approximate site of Gila City, where Arizona's first great gold strike occurred in 1858. Northeast of Dome are the Castle Dome Mountains. Colonel Jake Snively and others staked unsuccessful claims in this area during the 1860s. During the mid-1870s ore was being mined and shipped to Castle Dome Landing and then hauled to Yuma by steamer. Today much of this area is located on a United States Army proving ground, and movement is restricted.

During the spring of 1942 General George S. Patton established a desert training center in western Arizona to prepare troops for the rugged campaign in North Africa. Patton was a tough tank commander from the old school, and the harsh desert was a good match for him. He wanted his training ground to be as rigorous and realistic as possible, and the desert proved equal to the task. Several soldiers died in the heat, but in the end the troops were to prove their mettle against the seasoned veterans of Rommel's Afrika Corps. Patton was always a stickler for spit, polish, and protocol, no matter what the circumstances. A story is told about a time he came on a man stripped to the waist working on telephone lines. Patton stopped his jeep and ordered the man to report at once. The worker casually walked up to the general, who snapped, "Stand at attention! What is your name and what outfit are you with?" Patton spiced up this interrogation with a few choice expletives. The man waited until Patton was finished, then replied, "My name is John Smith, my outfit is Mountain States Telephone Company, and you can go straight to hell."

West of US 95 the Colorado River meanders down to the Sea of

*La Fortuna, one of
Arizona's richest
and most enduring
gold mines*
Courtesy
Southwest Studies

Cortez. At the peak of the steamboat business, 1852-1877, paddlewheelers churned their way up and down the muddy Colorado, unloading freight and taking on firewood for their boilers at landings along the banks. Steamers were able to navigate the river as far north as Callville and Rioville, now buried beneath the waters of Lake Mead. Landings between Yuma and Ehrenberg included Laguna, Castle Dome Landing, Eureka, Norton's Landing, Clip, Rhodes Ranch (also known as Cibola), and Mineral City. Just north of Ehrenberg was a small landing and ferry crossing known as Olive City, named for Olive Oatman, the young white girl who was captured by Indians and held captive for several years in the 1850s.

On the east side of US 95 north of the Castle Dome range, are the Kofa Mountains. The Kofa range takes its name from the King of Arizona Mining Company, which used to stamp its "K of A" brand on company property, lending its name to the nearby Kofa Mountains. The King of Arizona Mine's active years of gold production came from 1896 to 1910. In 1897 a five-stamp amalgamation mill was built at Mohawk, thirty-five miles south of the mine. A cyanide plant to treat tailings was built a year later. The mine produced $3,500,000 in gold before it played out. The old mine, located in the southwest part of the Kofa Mountains, can be reached by taking the dirt road at Stone Cabin.

Although most maps refer to these mountains as the Kofas, old timers around Yuma and La Paz County call them by their original name, the S. H. Mountains. This name comes from the 1860s, when soldiers noted that the physical structure of some of the mountains resembled large houses with small buildings, better known as outhouses, in back. With a soldierly touch of bawdy humor, the mountains were dubbed appropriately. Later, as women came to the area,

453

initials were used in lieu of the full name. The women, of course, wanted to know what "S. H." meant; they were told discreetly that "S. H." stood for "Short Horn," a name that even appears on some maps.

Stone Cabin, thirty-eight miles north of the turn-off to Dome, was, according to *Arizona Place Names*, a stage station on the road between Ehrenberg and Yuma.

Another of the many anomalies for which Arizona is so well known is Palm Canyon, located on the west side of the Kofas, nine miles north of the Stone Cabin road. Here, in a narrow, red-rock canyon, a species of towering palm trees called *Washingtonia Arizonaica* grows, its origin a botanical mystery.

One of the most violent murders in Arizona history occurred in the desert not far from the Palm Canyon road. During the summer of 1978 the three sons of Gary Tison broke their father and Randy Greenawalt out of the Arizona State Prison, at Florence. Both men were convicted murderers. The gang then went on a killing spree, murdering four members of a family at Tyson Wash, west of US 95. Ironically, one of the murder victims was also named Tyson. Several weeks later one of the Tison boys was killed in a shootout, and the other members of the gang were captured. Gary Tison escaped capture, but died in the desert.

US 95 makes a beeline north of the Kofas to join Arizona 72 a few miles south of Parker. A few miles west on the highway that cuts through the Colorado River Indian Reservation, is Poston, thirty-two miles north of Ehrenberg. Charles Poston was a prime mover in Arizona's becoming a territory in 1863; as a reward, he was named first Superintendent for Indian Affairs, establishing this reservation in 1865.

Poston arrived in Arizona in the 1850s and is considered the "father of Arizona"; however, in the annals of Arizona history, the town's claim to fame is dubious and recent. Following the Japanese attack on Pearl Harbor, large numbers of Japanese-Americans were rounded up in California and transported to this desert area. The reasons for this relocation are debated to this day. Some say that authorities suspected an invasion on the West Coast and wanted to remove all Japanese residents for fear of fifth column activities; others trace the relocation back to gold rush days, when Orientals were deeply resented in California. Whatever the reasons, Poston became Arizona's third largest city, behind Phoenix and Tucson, when about twenty thousand Japanese were "relocated" to a community surrounded by barbed wire and guarded by United States Army troops. Ironically, some of the sons of these internees became members of the legendary 442nd Regimental Combat Team. This outfit, made up of Japanese-American soldiers was the most decorated unit in the American army during the Second World War.

Parker, 1940s
Courtesy
Southwest Studies

Parker

The original town of Parker was located four miles downstream from the present city. It was established in 1865, the same time as the Colorado River Indian Reservation, and named for United States Superintendent of Indian Affairs General Eli Parker. Parker, an American Indian, was a highly respected officer on General Ulysses S. Grant's staff during the Civil War and was one of those present when Lee surrendered at Appomattox.

When the Arizona and California Railroad built a bridge across the Colorado four miles north of Parker in 1905, the town moved to its present location.

Parker Dam, a few miles north of the town, is one of several built along the Colorado River since 1909. It was completed in 1938 but not before some interesting encounters took place between hostile factions. Arizona and California have maintained a long-running dispute over Colorado River water use. The Californians, with greater political clout in Washington, had usually called the plays, which infuriated Arizona Governor Ben Moeur, a crusty country doctor from Tempe. During the building of Parker Dam, which was designed to deliver some of Arizona's water to the West Coast, Governor Moeur, in a grand display of Arizona's claim to self-determination in water affairs, sent the Arizona National Guard to the east bank of the

Colorado. One night a few venturesome members of the Guard decided to cross to California to have a look around. In Parker lived a colorful woman named Nellie Bush, the first woman elected to the Arizona Senate during the 1920s and both an airplane and steamboat pilot. She was also the only woman to hold a license to pilot a steamer on the Colorado. Nellie was happy to oblige the Arizona "war effort," placing her two steamers, the *Julie B* and the *Nellie T*, at the disposal of the Arizona troops. The mission took place under cover of darkness, but the two craft became entangled and the red-faced "Arizona Navy" had to be rescued by their California arch-nemeses. Soon afterward the United States Supreme Court forced the Arizona Guard to make a hasty withdrawal to Phoenix.

Bill Williams River

Just north of Parker Dam is the confluence of the Colorado and Bill Williams rivers. Though seldom mentioned in history books, this area was the setting for much of Arizona's early history.

In 1604 Juan de Oñate, the great explorer-governor of New Mexico from 1598 to 1609, came through this area on his way to Yuma Crossing. During the 1820s fur trappers, including Ewing Young and James O. Pattie, plied these streams for beaver. The trapping was excellent, but the Mojave Indians proved formidable. After 1830 the mountain men generally avoided the area. Lieutenant Amiel W. Whipple, of the Army Corps of Topographical Engineers, also came here in 1854, when he was surveying a possible railroad route. He claimed the river was named for the noted "king of the free trappers," Bill Williams, by Joe Walker, a great mountain man in his own right.

Whipple's route took him across northern Arizona (they spent the Christmas of 1853 camped at the foot of the San Francisco peaks) to the headwaters of the Big Sandy River. The surveyors followed that desert stream down to where it joins the Bill Williams River and then turns west to the Colorado.

Another explorer of reknown, Francois X. Aubry, lent his name to an important shipping point at the mouth of the Bill Williams River. The settlement of Aubry was established in 1864 to honor the so-called "Skimmer of the Plains." Aubry, a French-Canadian, earned that title by riding horseback non-stop from Independence, Missouri, to Santa Fe, a distance of eight hundred miles, in the amazing time of five days and thirteen hours.

During his travels in Arizona in the 1850s, Aubry claimed to have encountered a tribe of Indians using rifle balls made of solid gold. He also reported selling a few shirts for $1,500 in gold and swapping a brok ı-down old mule for one and a half pounds of the yellow metal.

Aı ry established a prosperous freighting and livestock business betw ın New Mexico and California. Between 1852 and 1854 he mad two round-trip overland journeys between California and Sant Fe, driving thousands of sheep and hundreds of horses and mulı with wagons loaded with merchandise. He became convinced that ıe thirty-fifth parallel was an excellent site for a rail and wagon road ıubry remained a strong advocate of this idea despite the fact that e and his small party had two narrow escapes with Indians in Auk Valley (west of Seligman and near today's Flagstaff).

L ıtenant Amiel W. Whipple met the French-Canadian in Albuquerque in October 1853 and learned much from Aubry about the geographical features of the area he would have to cover in his historic expedition. At the time Aubry was launching another ambitious trip, driving fifty thousand sheep from the Rio Grande across northern Arizona, to sell in San Francisco. He completed this transaction and was back in Santa Fe in forty-three days.

Aubry's claims that the thirty-fifth parallel was the best route for a railroad was bound to create enemies among those who had vested interests in other possible routes. He became involved in an altercation in a Santa Fe *cantina* with Richard Weightman, a local attorney who favored a route along the thirty-second parallel. Aubry pulled a revolver, but Weightman was faster—he jerked out a bowie knife and drove it up to the hilt in Aubry's belly, killing the great "Skimmer of the Plains." Aubry's journals eventually reached Washington, where they received a great deal of attention, providing future explorers with valuable information on northern Arizona.

Aubry Landing lasted until 1865, when the copper that had been discovered in the nearby hills played out. The last vestiges of Aubry Landing are a single building that housed a post office, hotel, and local saloon, along with a steamboat cabin which had been converted into a house.

Lake Havasu City

Robert P. McCulloch, Sr. was a twentieth century visionary and entrepreneur reminiscent of those enterprising men of a century ago who developed mining ventures and irrigational oases in the arid wilderness.

Back in the late 1950s McCulloch was flying above the Colorado River in western Arizona looking for a place to test the outboard motors his company produced. Perched on a small desert peninsula jutting out into Lake Havasu was an old World War II emergency air strip. McCulloch liked the site and through some smart wheeling and dealing was able to purchase the piece of land for about $75 an acre. He later claimed to have envisioned a new city at the foot of the picturesque Mohave Mountains the moment he first laid eyes on the site.

Next, he teamed up with a Texan named C. V. Wood, who's major claim to fame was being the creative genius who developed the original Disneyland. The "dynamic duo" was a perfect match to create this new jewel in the desert. "Lake Havasu is McCulloch's baby," someone noted, "but Wood is the guy who spanked it and made it breathe." The dream started to become reality in the fall of 1960 when McCulloch flew Wood over the site and said, "Let's build a city." The rest is history. In 1980, the *Los Angeles Times* wrote: This city of 16,000 on the "West Coast" of Arizona is arguably, " the most successful free-standing new town in the United States..."

What really put Lake Havasu City on the map was the acquisition of London Bridge in 1968. It is only fitting that in this land of startling contrasts the strangest of all should occur. Legend has it McCulloch went to France and tried to buy the Eiffel Tower. Predictably, the French told him where to go. So he went to Italy and offered to buy the Leaning Tower of Pisa. He got the same response from the Italians. He tried the same thing in England — "Boy have we got a deal for you," the British exclaimed enthusiastically. The venerable bridge on the Thames with bullet-riddled piers from Luftwaffe gunners in World War II was unable to stand up under modern day traffic and had to be replaced. McCulloch offered $2,460,000, "a thousand dollars for each year of your age," and the British accepted.

The bridge was dismantled and the bricks numbered, hauled by sea to Los Angeles and by truck to Havasu City. The bridge was reconstructed, brick by brick, and a mile-long channel was cut through the peninsula creating a flow beneath the bridge for boat traffic. On October 10, 1971 the bridge was formally dedicated in the Arizona desert. Appropriately, the Lord Mayor of London, Sir Peter Studd, was in attendance.

Today, the spectacular London Bridge in Lake Havasu City is second only to the Grand Canyon as a tourist attraction in Arizona.

Arizona 72
Vicksburg to Arizona 95

Vicksburg was not named in honor of the city on the banks of the Mississippi as is often thought, but for Victor Satterdahl, who had a store here in 1906. When the post office was set up in his store, Satterdahl suggested Victor, but perhaps because of Victorville, California, postal officials thought the names were too similar and named it Vicksburg.

Bouse

Bouse, named for George Bouse a local developer, lay basking quietly in the hot desert sun from its founding in 1906 until World War II, when it became General George Patton's Desert Training Center.

Beginning in the summer of 1942, thirteen infantry divisions and seven armored divisions were assigned to the deserts of California and Arizona to undergo training in preparation for tackling Field Marshal Erwin Rommel's Panzer divisions in North Africa.

"The war in Europe is over for us," Patton said in 1942; "England will probably fall this year. It is going to be a long war. Our first chance to get at the enemy will be in North Africa. We can not train troops to fight in the desert of North Africa by training in the swamps of Georgia." He went on to say, ". . . the desert can kill quicker than the enemy." With that statement the wheels were literally set in motion. The first troop train arrived at the Bouse station on October 10, 1943. Trucks were waiting to haul the troops over twenty-three miles of rough dirt road to the new camp, and soon the denizens of the desert were sharing space with thousands of soldiers.

Bibliography

Acuff, Guy. *Akimult Aw A Tham, The River People: A Short History of the Pima Indians*. Casa Grande, Arizona: Casa Grande Centennial Ed., 1979.

Aguirre Yjinio. *Echoes of the Conquistadores*. Red Rock, Arizona: 1983. Published privately.

Ahnert, Gerald T. *Retracing the Butterfield Overland Trail through Arizona*. Los Angeles: Westernlore Press, 1973.

Arizona Highways. October, 1984. (Entire issue on Metropolitan Phoenix).

Arizona Highways. Prescott Centennial Issue—April, 1964.

Altshuler, Constance Wynn. *Chains of Command: Arizona and the Army 1856-1875*. Tucson: Arizona Historical Society, 1981.

Baeza, Jo (Jeffers). "Tales of the Little Colorado." *Arizona Highways*. September, 1965.

Bailey, Lynn R. *Bisbee: Queen of the Copper Camps*. Tucson: Westernlore Press, 1983.

Barnes, Will C. *Apaches and Longhorns*. Los Angeles: Ward Ritchie, 1941.

Bartlett, John R. *Personal Narrative of Exploration and Incidents*. Chicago: Rio Grande Press, 1854 (2 Volumes).

Bourke, John G. *On the Border with Crook*. New York: Scribner's, 1902.

Bourke, John G. *An Apache Campaign in the Sierra Madre*. New York: Scribner's, 1956.

Boyer, Glenn, ed. *I Married Wyatt Earp: (The Memoirs of Josephine Marcus Earp)*. Tucson: University of Arizona Press, 1976.

Breckenridge, Wm. *Helldorado*. Boston: Houghton Mifflin, 1928.

Brooks, Juanita. *Jacob Hamblin, Mormon Apostle to the Indians*. Salt Lake City: Westwater Press, 1980.

Brooks, Juanita. *John Doyle Lee: Zealot, Pioneer Builder, Scapegoat*. Glendale, California: A. H. Clark, 1972.

Brophy, Frank C. "The Mystery of San Xavier del Bac." *Arizona Highways*, March 1970.

Brandes, Ray. *Frontier Military Posts of Arizona*. Globe, Arizona: Dale Stuart King Publisher, 1960.

Browne, J. Ross. *Adventures in Apache Country*. New York: Harper Bros., 1871.

Byrkit, James. *Forging the Copper Collar*. Tucson: University of Arizona Press, 1982.

Carlson, Frances. "James D. Houck, the Sheep King of Cave Creek." *Journal of Arizona History*, spring, 1980.

Chamberlin, Samuel. *My Confession*. New York: Harper and Brothers, 1956.

Chaput, Donald. *Francois X. Aubry: Trader, Trailmaker and Voyageur in the Southwest*. Glendale, California: Arthur H. Clark Co., 1975.

Clarke, Dwight L. *Stephen Watts Kearny, Soldier of the West*. Norman: University of Oklahoma Press, 1961.

Cline, Platt. *Mountain Campus: The Story of Northern Arizona University*. Flagstaff: Northland Press, 1983.

Cline, Platt. *They Came to the Mountain: The Story of Flagstaff's Beginnings*. Flagstaff: Northland Press, 1976

Colton, James (Tom Kollenborn). *The Apache Trail*. Apache Junction, Arizona: Superstition Mountain Research Center, 1980.

Connor, Daniel. *Joseph Reddeford Walker and the Arizona Adventure*. Norman: University of Oklahoma Press, 1956.

Cooke, Philip St. George. *The Conquest of New Mexico and California in 1846-1848*. Chicago: Rio Grande Press, 1964.

Corle, Edwin. *The Gila: River of the Southwest*. New York: Rinehart and Co., 1951.

Cremony, John C. *Life Among the Apaches*. Glorieta, New Mexico: Rio Grande Press, 1868.

Crowe, Rosalie, and Brinckerhoff, Sidney. *Early Yuma*. Flagstaff: Northland Press, 1976.

Dobyns, Henry F., ed. *The Journal of Cave Johnson Couts*. Tucson: Arizona Pioneers Historical Society, 1961.

Dobyns, Henry F. *Spanish Colonial Tucson*. Tucson: University of Arizona Press, 1976.

Dunning, Charles H., and Peplow, Edward. *Rock to Riches*. Phoenix: Southwest Publishing Co., 1959.

Eason, Nicholas J. *Fort Verde: An Era of Men and Courage*. Sedona: Tonto Press, 1966.

Egerton, Kearney. *The Fascinating Fourteen ... Arizona's Counties*. Phoenix: The Branding Iron Press, 1977.

Egerton, Kearney. *Somewhere Out There ... Arizona's Lost Mines and Vanished Treasures*. Glendale: Prickly Pear Press, 1974.

Faulk, Odie B. *Destiny Road*. New York: Oxford University Press, 1973.

Faulk, Odie B. *Tombstone: Myth and Reality*. New York: Oxford University Press, 1972.

Favour, Alpheus. *Old Bill Williams*. Norman: University of Oklahoma Press, 1962.

Federal Writers Project. *Arizona*. Original work by Ross Santee, edited by Joseph Miller. New York: Hastings House, 1956.

Foreman, Grant, ed. *A Pathfinder in the Southwest*. Norman: University of Oklahoma Press, 1968.

Forrest, Earle. *Arizona's Dark and Bloody Ground*. Caldwell, Idaho: Caxton Printers, 1936.

Gilbert, Bil. *Westering Man: The Life of Joseph Walker*. New York: Atheneum, 1983.

Goff, John. *Arizona Biographical Dictionary*. Cave Creek: Black Mountain Press, 1983.

Goff, John. "Arizona's National Monuments." *Arizona Highways*. March 1978.

Granger, Byrd Howell, ed. *Will C. Barnes' Arizona Place Names*. Tucson: University of Arizona Press, 1979.

Granger, Byrd Howell. *Arizona's Names: X Marks the Place*. Tucson: Falconer Publishing Co., 1983.

Hall, Sharlot. *Pauline Weaver, First Citizen of Prescott*. 1934.

Harte, John Bret. *Tucson: Portrait of a Desert Pueblo*. Woodland Hills, California: Windsor Publications, 1980.

Heatwole, Thelma. *Arizona Off the Beaten Path*. Phoenix: Golden West, 1982.

Heatwole, Thelma. *Ghost Towns and Historical Haunts of Arizona*. Phoenix: Golden West, 1981.

Hinton, Richard. *The Handbook to Arizona*. San Francisco: Payot, Upham & Co., 1878. Reprinted 1954: Tucson, Arizona Silhouettes.

Hobbs, James. *Wild Life in the Far West*. Hartford, Connecticut: Wiley, Waterman and Eaton, 1872.

Hopkins, Ernest J., and Thomas, Alfred Jr. *The Arizona State University Story*. Phoenix: Southwest Publishing Co., 1960.

Johnson, Wesley. *Phoenix: Valley of the Sun*. Tulsa, Oklahoma: Continental Heritage Press, 1982.

Kessell, John. *Friars, Soldiers and Reformers: Hispanic Arizona and the Sonora Mission Frontier 1767-1856*. Tucson: University of Arizona Press, 1976.

Lake, Carolyn, ed. *Under Cover for Wells Fargo: The Unvarnished Recollections of Fred Dodge*. Boston: Houghton Mifflin, 1969.

LeCount, Al, ed. *The History of Tonto*. Punkin Center, Arizona: Punkin Center Homemakers, 1976.

Levine, Albert J. *From Indian Trails to Jet Trails*. Snowflake's Centennial History. Snowflake, Arizona: Snowflake Historical Society, 1977.

Lingenfelter, Richard E. *Steamboats on the Colorado*. Tucson: University of Arizona Press, 1978.

Lynch, John; Kennedy, John W.; and Wooley, Robert L. *Patton's Desert Training Center*. Council of Abandoned Military Posts. Fort Meyer, Virginia: 1982.

Lynch, Richard E. *Winfield Scott: A Biography of Scottsdale's Founder*. Scottsdale: City of Scottsdale, 1978.

Malach, Roman. *Chloride: Mining Gem of the Cerbat Mountains*. Lake Havasu City, Arizona: Locater Publications, 1978.

Marshall, James. *Santa Fe: The Railroad That Built an Empire*. New York: Random House, 1945.

Martin, Douglas. *Yuma Crossing*. Albuquerque: University of New Mexico Press, 1954.

Maxwell, Margaret. *A Passion for Freedom: The Life of Sharlot Hall*. Tucson: University of Arizona Press, 1982.

McCarty, Kieran. *Desert Documentary*. Tucson: Arizona Historical Society Historical Monograph, 1976.

McElfresh, Patricia Myers. *Scottsdale: Jewel in the Desert*. Woodland Hills, California: Windsor Publication, 1984.

McLaughlin, Herb, and McLaughlin, Dorothy. *Phoenix: 1870-1970*. Phoenix: Photographic Associates, 1970.

Merrill W. Earl. *One Hundred Steps Down Mesa's Past*. Mesa: Lofgreen Printing Co., 1970.

Meyers, John M. *The Last Chance: Tombstone's Early Years*. New York: E. P. Dutton, 1950.

Miller, Joseph, ed. *Arizona: The Last Frontier*. New York: Hastings House, 1956.

Möllhausen, Baldwin. *Diary of a Journey from the Mississippi to the Coast of the Pacific*. 2 vol. London: 1858.

Mulligan, R. A. "Apache Pass and Old Fort Bowie." *The Smoke Signal*. Tucson: Corral of Westerners. spring, 1965.

Murphy, Ira. *Brief History of Payson*. Payson, Arizona: Payson Roundup.

Myrick, David F. *Railroads of Arizona*. Vol. I & II. Berkeley: Howell-North.

Noble, Marguerite. "Payson—100 Years 1882-1982." *Payson Centennial*. Payson, Arizona: Rim Country Printery, 1982.

Northern Gila County Historical Society. *Rim Country History*. Payson: Rim Country Printery, 1984.

Ormsby, Waterman L. *The Butterfield Overland Mail*. San Marino: Huntington Library, 1955.

Patton, James. *History of Clifton*. Greenlee County Chamber of Commerce, 1977.

Plumlee, Tosh. "Arizona's Impossible Railroad." *Arizona Highways*. September, 1979.

Rolak, Bruno J. "History of Fort Huachuca, 1877-1890." *The Smoke Signal*. Tucson: Corral of Westerners. spring, 1974.

Ruffner, Lester. *All Hell Needs Is Water*. Tucson: University of Arizona Press, 1972.

Ruffner, Lester. *Shot in the Ass with Pesos*. Tucson: Tucson Treasure Chest Publications, 1979.

Rusho, W. L., and Crampton, C. Gregory. *Desert River Crossing: Historic Lee's Ferry on the Colorado River*. Salt Lake City: Peregrine Smith Inc., 1975.

Russell, Frank. *The Pima Indians*. Tucson: University of Arizona Press, 1975.

Ruxton, George Frederick. *Life in the Far West*, ed. Leroy R. Hafen. Norman: University of Oklahoma, 1951.

Salt River Project. *The Taming of the Salt*. Phoenix: Salt River Project, 1979.

Schellie, Don. "Tucson Turns 200." *Arizona Highways*. September 1975.

Schulty, Vernon B. *Southwesten Town: The Story of Willcox, Arizona*. Tucson: University of Arizona Press, 1964.

Sharkey, J. E. "Douglas-Agua Prieta." *Arizona Highways*. September 1975.

Sherman, James, and Sherman, Barbara. *Ghost Towns of Arizona*. Norman: University of Oklahoma Press, 1969.

Sonnichsen, C. L. *Billy King's Tombstone*. Caldwell, Idaho: Caxton Printers, 1942.

Sonnichsen, C. L. *Tucson: Life and Times of an American City*. Norman: University of Oklahoma Press, 1982.

Southwest Parks and Monuments Association. *Montezuma Castle*. Globe, Arizona.

Summerhayes, Martha. *Vanished Arizona*. Philadelphia: Lippincott Co., 1911.

Swanson, James, and Kollenborn, Tom. *Superstition Mountain: A Ride Through Time*. Phoenix: Arrowhead Press, 1981.

Theobald, John, and Theobald, Lillian. *Post Offices and Postmasters*. Phoenix: Phoenix Arizona Historical Foundation, 1961.

Theobald, John, and Theobald, Lillian. *Wells Fargo in Arizona Territory*. Tempe: Arizona Historical Foundation, 1978.

464

Thrapp, Dan. *Conquest of Apacheria*. Norman: University of Oklahoma Press, 1967.

Thrapp, Dan. *Al Sieber: Chief of Scouts*. Norman: University of Oklahoma Press, 1964.

Tinker, George. *Northern Arizona and Flagstaff in 1887*. Glendale, California: Arthur H. Clark Co., 1969.

Trafzer, Clifford E. *Yuma: Frontier Crossing of the Far Southwest*. Wichita: Western Heritage Books, 1980.

Trimble, Marshall. *Arizona: A Panoramic History of a Frontier State*. New York: Doubleday, 1977.

Trimble, Marshall. *Arizona Adventure*. Phoenix: Golden West, 1982.

Trimble, Marshall. *The CO Bar Ranch*. Flagstaff: Northland Press, 1982.

Trimble, Marshall. *In Old Arizona*. Phoenix: Golden West, 1985.

Tyler, Daniel. *A Concise History of the Mormon Battalion in the Mexican War*. Glorieta, New Mexico: Rio Grande Press, 1969 (First published in 1881).

Udall, Stewart. "In Coronado's Footsteps." *Arizona Highways*. April 1984.

Underhill, Ruth. *The Papago and Pima Indians of Arizona*. Palmer Lake, Colorado: The Filter Press, 1979.

Varney, Phil. *Arizona's Best Ghost Towns*. Flagstaff: Northland Press, 1980.

Verde Valley Pioneers Association. *Pioneer Stories of Arizona's Verde Valley*. 1954.

Wagoner, Jay J. *Early Arizona*. Tucson: University of Arizona Press, 1975.

Wagoner, Jay J. *Arizona Territory: 1863-1912*. Tucson: University of Arizona Press, 1970.

Walker, H. P., and Bufkin, Don. *Historical Atlas of Arizona*. Norman: University of Oklahoma Press, 1979.

Weiner, Melissa Ruffner. *Prescott's Yesteryears: Life in Arizona's First Territorial Capitol*. Prescott: Primrose Press, 1978.

Weiner, Melissa Ruffner. *Prescott, A Pictorial History*. Virginia Beach: Donning Co., 1981.

Whipple, A. W. *The Whipple Report*. Los Angeles: Westernlore Press, 1961.

Williams, Brad, and Pepper, Choral. *Lost Legends of the West*. Holt, Rinehart and Winston, 1970.

Wilson, Maggie. "Yoo Hoo, Old Friend: Reflections on a Copper Camp's Post." *Arizona Highways*. September 1983.

Woody, Clara T., and Schwartz, Milton L. *Globe Arizona*. Tucson: Arizona Historical Society, 1977.

Wyllys, Rufus K. *Arizona: The History of a Frontier State*. Phoenix: Hobson and Herr, 1950.

Young, Herb. *Ghosts of Cleopatra Hill*. Jerome Historical Society, 1964.

Young, Herb. *They Came to Jerome*. Jerome Historical Society, 1972.

Index

Acevedo, Lupe, 203
Ackimoel O'Odham (Pima Indians), 157
Acme, 290
Acquarius Mountains, 286
Adamana, 269
Adams, Billy, 250
Adams, Charles, 118
Adams, Jeff, 340
Adamsville, 118
Adonde, 398
Agua Caliente, 379, 393
Agua Fria Ranch, 427
Agua Fria River, 201, 376, 378-79
Agua Prieta, 75
Aguila, 431
Aguirre Cattle Company, 171
Aguirre, Don Pedro, 170-71
Aguirre, Don Yjinio, 171
Aguirre, Higinio, 171
Ackimoel O'Odham, 38
Ajo, 110-11
Ake, Jeff, 419
Alamo Lake, 277, 448
Alarcón, Hernando de, 401
Albuquerque, 457
Alcatraz,384
Alchise, 382
Aldrich, Mark, 6
Ali-Shonak, 144, 426
Alkali Tom, 347
Allande, Don Pedro de, Capt., 3-4
Allen Street, 60
Allen, Rex, 33
Allen, Rial, 216
Alpine, 294, 374
Altar Valley, 144-45
Alvarado, Hernan de, 128
Alvord, Burt, 28-30
American Flag, 448
American Mining and Trading Company, 111
Ames, Frank, 265
Amundsen, Andrew, 254
Anasazi, 269, 301-02, 322
Anderson, Ed, 203
Andrews, William, 354
Antelope Creek, 444
Antelope Hill, 177, 396
Antelope Peak, 397, 399

Antelope Peak Station, 396
Antelope Spring, 238, 246
Antelope Station, 180
Antonio, Juan, chief, 160
Anza, Juan Bautista de, Capt., 3, 49-50, 77, 402
Apache County, 310, 321
Apache Junction, 195-96, 218
Apache Leap, 198
Apache Pass, 104, 133-35, 137
Apache Spring, 141
Apache Trail, 201, 218, 220
Apaches, 38, 46-47, 51, 108, 197, 199, 221, 322,
    339, 341, 350, 353, 385
Apaches de Paz, 4
Aravaipa Creek, 368
Arivaca Ranch, 52
Arizola, 166
Arizona, 144
Arizona Canal, 52, 54, 173, 207, 219
Arizona Cantalope Queens, 202
Arizona Cattle Company, 240-41
Arizona Central Mine, 370
Arizona City, 417, 419, 423
Arizona Eastern Railroad, 91, 95, 346
Arizona Highway Patrol, 324
Arizona Improvement Company, 52
Arizona Lumber Company, 244
Arizona Miner, 328
Arizona National Guard, 435
Arizona Rangers, 76, 267, 342
Arizona Republican, 347, 440
Arizona Stage Company, 177
Arizona State College, 193
Arizona State Prison, 454
Arizona State Teachers College, 193
Arizona State University, 193, 203
Arizona Utah Railroad, 450
Arizona Women's Hall of Fame, 380
Arizona and California Railroad, 455
Arizona and New Mexico Railroad, 350
Arizona and South Eastern Railroad, 70
Arizona and Southwestern Railroad, 36
Armer family, 211
Army Corps of Topographical Engineers, 227,
    277, 279, 408
Army of the West, 21
Arroyo de San Bernabé, 286
Arroyo de la Tinaja, 423

467

Arthur, Chester A., President, 63
Ash, 348
Ash Canyon, 281
Ash Creek, 281
Ash Fork, 234, 241, 279, 281-82, 291, 355-56, 358, 438, 440
Ash Fork Hill, 279
Ash Fork Livestock Company, 281
Ashley-Henry Expedition, 259
Ashurst, 348
Ashurst, Henry Fountain, 318
Ashurst-Hayden Diversion Dam, 89
Atlantic & Pacific Railroad, 233, 236, 238, 240, 244, 261, 264, 274, 280, 283-84, 286
Aubry Landing, 457
Aubry Valley, 285, 457
Aubry, Francois X., 228, 235, 456-57
Avondale, 112
Avra Valley, 171
Ayers Lumber Company, 244
Ayers, Edward, 244
Azatlan, 183
Aztec Land and Cattle Company, 242, 265, 283
Azul, Antonio, Lt., 162
Babbitt, Billy, 241
Babbitt Brothers Trading Company, 243, 301
Babbitt, Bruce, 244
Babbitt, C. J., 241, 244
Babbitt, Dave, 241-43
Babbitt, George, 241
Babbitt, John, 244, 246
Babocomari Creek, 221
Baca Float #5, 102
Bacabi, 317
Bacon, Missouri Ann, 445
Ballinger, Jesse O., 254
Banters, Jennie, 360
Bapchule, 388
Barnes, Will C., 7, 271-72, 341, 384
Barney, Jim, 197
Barnum, Jim, 151
Barringer, Daniel, 253
Barth, Sol, 375
Bartlett, John R., 260
Bascom affair, 136
Bascom, George, Lt., 79, 104, 136
Bassett, Joe, 212
Battle of Big Dry Wash, 185
Battle of Bull Run, 22
Battle of Valverde, 103
Beale Camel Experiment, 230
Beale Camel Road, 263, 279
Beale Springs, 289, 343
Beale's Crossing, 16
Beale, Edward F., 231-33, 236, 249, 251, 260, 270, 279, 285-86, 289, 407, 415, 426
Beardsley, 429
Beardsley, Will, 429
Beautiful Valley, 311
Beaver Creek, 187
Becker, Julius and Gustav, 342
Beeler, Joe, 364-65
Beeline Highway, 14
Behan, Johnny, 63
Belderrain, Tomás de, Capt., 49
Bell, Harvey, 173
Bellemont, 274
Ben Nevis Mountain, 115
Benson, 21-23, 36
Benson, William B., 23
Betatakin Ruin, 301-02
Big Bug, 179-80

Big Bug Creek, 184, 376-77
Big Bug Mining District, 378
Big Cienega, 315
Big Dry Wash, 385
Big Johnny Gulch, 200
Big Rump, 216
Big Sandy River, 230, 236, 260, 277, 287, 447-48, 456
Big Valley, 214
Bill Williams Fork, 229-30, 236, 405
Bill Williams Mountain, 275, 278-79
Bill Williams River, 277, 287, 426-27, 447, 456
Biltmore Luxury Resort, 338
Bird Cage Theater, 65
Bisbee, 6, 67, 70-72, 75
Bisbee Deportation of 1917, 73
Bisbee Massacre, 62
Bisbee Mining Museum, 74
Bisbee, DeWitt, Judge, 70
Black Canyon, 176-77, 415, 451
Black Canyon City, 176
Black Canyon Highway, 217
Black Hills, 357
Black Mesa, 302, 318
Black Mountains, 234, 290, 292, 450
Black Queen Mine, 220
Black River, 341
Black, Joe, 108-09
Blanchard, Bill, 256
Blevins, Andy "Cooper," 223-24, 261-63
Blevins, Charlie, 225
Blevins, Hamp, 24
Blevins, John, 263
Blevins, Mart "Old Man," 223-24
Blevins, Sam Houston, 263
Bloody Tanks Wash, 199-200, 221
Blount, Alza, Mrs., 205
Blue River, 372-73
Bolger, Bill, 23
Bonelli, Daniel, 293
Bonita, 367
Boot, Joe, 420
Borglum, Solon, 335
Bosque Redondo Reservation, 304
Boston colonists, 237
Boulder Canyon Project, 451
Boulder Dam, 451
Bourke, John G., Capt., 8, 10-12, 98, 174, 370
Bouse, 438
Bouse, George, 458
Bovett, John, 32
Bowen, Albert, 17
Bowie, 33-34, 202, 346
Bowie Station, 34, 83
Bowie, George Washington, Col., 141
Bowman, Sarah, 417-19
Box Canyon, 344
Boyd, John, 358
Bradford, Pleasant, 215
Bradley, Charley, 450
Bradshaw City, 179
Bradshaw Mining District, 179
Bradshaw Mountains, 148, 178, 327-28, 353, 376, 390, 393, 424
Bradshaw, Bill, 179
Bradshaw, Ike, 179
Brady, Pete, 43, 111, 169
Bramlett, Bill, 441
Brannen, Dennis J., 245
Brannen, Patrick B., 245-46
Brannen, Peter J., 246
Brawley Wash, 44

Breakenridge, Billy, 219, 221
Brewery Gulch, 70, 71
Bridger, Jim, 259
Brigham City, 255
Bright Angel Camp, 299, 306-07
Bright Angel Trail, 305
Brocius, Curly Bill, 63, 78, 83, 85, 102, 142
Brockman, John, 92
Brooklyn, 115
Brooks, Juanita, 296
Brown, Ben, 348
Brown, Bob, 29
Brown, E. O., 206
Browne, J. Ross, 7, 52, 399
Brunchow, Frederic, 58
Buchanan, James, President, 414
Buckeye, 112
Buckhorn-Boulder, 220
Buckman, J. J., 288
Buckman, Thad, 288
Buckey O'Neill Hill, 74
Bueno, 179
Buenos Aires Ranch, 45, 171
Buffalo Soldiers, 123
Bullock Railroad Line, 283
Bullock, Tom, 283, 355
Bumble Bee, 178, 180
Bundyville, 325
Buntline, Ned, 259, 262
Burch, Bill, 213
Burden, Jack, 438
Burke's Station, 393
Burke, Patrick, 393
Burro Creek, 448
Burts, Matt, 28-30
Bush, Anderson, 374
Bush, Nellie, 217, 456
Bush Valley, 374
Bushman, John, 215
Butte City, 192
Butterfield Overland Stage Line, 26, 33, 35,
    119, 134-35, 170, 192, 389-90, 393-94, 396,
    398-99, 416-17
Butterfield Trail, 388
Butterfield, John, 6, 134
Bylas, 345
Byrkit, Jim, Dr., 183, 217
Byrne, T. D., 67
Bywater, Cal, 420
C O Bar Ranch, 243-44, 298
Caborca, 398
Cactus Derby, 440
Calabazas, 44-45, 48
Calabazas Land and Mining Company, 44
Caliente, 95
California Gold Rush, 31
California Volunteers, 7, 22, 137, 208, 328, 394,
    419, 451
Calloway, William, Capt., 395
Callville, 453
Calumet and Arizona Mining Company, 71-72,
    111
Calva, 344-45
Cameron, 298-99
Cameron, Ralph, 245, 298
Cameron, Niles and Burton, 245
Camino del Diablo, 402, 409
Camp Apache, 183, 185, 190, 354, 382
Camp Beale Springs, 289
Camp Carroll, 210
Camp Clark, 353
Camp Date Creek, 447

Camp Goodwin, 347
Camp Grant, 8, 98, 172, 182, 368
Camp Grant Massacre, 353
Camp Lincoln, 184
Camp Mogollon, 382
Camp O'Connell, 210
Camp Ord, 382
Camp Picket Post, 196, 198
Camp Pinal, 197-200
Camp Reno, 210-11
Camp San Carlos, 344
Camp Thomas, 382
Camp Verde, 183-86, 190, 256, 331, 354
Camp Wallen, 102
Campbell, Bill, 256
Canada del Oro, 172
Cananea, Sonora, 206
Candaleria, Juan, 376
Canoa, 53, 445
Cañon de los Embudos, 122
Canyon Diablo, 183, 244, 250-52, 335
Canyon Point, 313
Canyon de Chelly, 311
Cardenás, Garcia Lopez de, 128-29
Carleson, Fran, 272
Carleton, James Col., 7, 32, 137, 140, 327-28,
    353, 395
Carlisle Indian School, 319
Carr, Eugene A., Col., 384
Carrizo Creek, 341
Carrizo, 340
Carson, Kit, 158, 231, 259, 279, 311, 319-20,
    354, 369, 387, 407
Cart, Jim, 269
Carter, Jimmy, 325
Casa Blanca, 388, 395
Casa Grande, 63, 165, 330, 388
Casa Grande Canal, 166
Casa Grande National Monument, 117-18
Casas Grandes, Mexico, 381
Cashion, 12, 405
Cashman, Nellie, 61
Casteneda, Pedro de, 26, 127, 130, 196
Castillo, Alonza del, 126
Castle Dome Landing, 399, 452
Castle Dome Mining District, 399
Castle Dome Mountains, 452-53
Castle Hot Springs, 430
Castle Rock, 74
Cataract Canyon, 285
Cavalliere, George, 206
Cave Creek, 174, 273
Cerbat, 286, 449
Cerbat Mountains, 290, 449, 451
Cerro Colorado, 144
Cha-Lipun, 185
Chaco Canyon, 302
Chacón, Augustine, 30, 350
Chambers, 271, 311
Chambers, Charles, 271
Chandler, 119
Chandler Ranch, 119
Chandler, A. J., Dr., 119
Charbonneau, Jean Baptiste, 21, 163
Chase Creek, 371
Chatto, 120
Chavez Lake, 189
Chavez Pass, 183, 190
Chavez Trail, 181, 217
Chavez, Francisco, Lt. Col., 181, 183, 188-89,
    255, 271
Che-muc-tah, 407

Chenowth, J. M., 151
Cherry, 181, 183
Cherry, Norville, 181
Cheto, 272
Chevrolet, Lewis, 439
Chihuahua, 381
Chilleen, Ed, 178
Chilson, George, Lt., 210
Chinle, 311
Chino Valley, 284, 328, 354-56, 359
Chiquito, Captain, 382
Chiricahua, 322
Chiricahua Apache Reservation, 142
Chiricahua Apaches, 80-81
Chiricahua Cattle Company, 345
Chivaria, Juan, Lt., 162
Chloride, 448-50
Christopher Creek,312
Christopher, Isadore, 312
Chrystoval, 396
Church, William, 372
Churchill, Winston, 358
Cibicue, 312, 341, 384
Cincinnati, Ohio, 241-42
Clack, Greely, 450
Claiborne, Billy, 63
Clanton, Billy, 63
Clanton, Ike, 63, 83
Clanton, N. H., 142
Clanton, Tom, 12
Clark, Charlie, 359, 362
Clark, Chauncy, 429
Clark, John A., 353
Clark, Marion, 341-42
Clark, Sam, 111
Clark, William Andrews, 354, 358-62
Clark, William, Jr., 362
Clarkdale, 359, 361-62
Clay County, Missouri, 418
Clay Springs, 313
Clear Creek Junction, 184
Clemenceau, Georges, 364
Cleopatra Hill, 357-60
Cleveland, Grove, President, 84
Cliff Dweller Springs, 295
Clifton, 349-50, 369-70, 372-74, 404
Clifton, Henry, 216, 369
Cline, Christian, 212
Cline, George, 213
Cline, John, 212
Cline, Roxie, 212
Clip, 453
Cluff's Cienega, 315
Cluff, Oscar and Alfred, 315
Clum, John, 63, 343-44
Clyman, Jim, 259
Cochise, 28-29, 91
Cochise Mining and Milling Company, 33
Cochise stronghold, 43
Cochise culture, 381
Cochise, Chief, 22, 33, 79, 104-05, 120, 135-36, 138, 143, 237, 328
Coconino County, 47
Cocopah Indians, 400
Cocopah, steamboat, 411-12
Cody, Bill Buffalo, 97, 259
Cody, William, 315
Colcord, Bill, 14
Cole, Ben, Elmer, and Pink, 215
Colorado City, 324, 417
Colorado Plateau, 255

Colorado River, 207, 232, 277, 286-87, 289, 292-96, 330-31, 392, 400-01, 406-07, 409, 411, 414-16, 421, 423, 434, 451
Colorado River Indian Reservation, 454-55
Colorado Steam Navigation Company, 414, 416
Colorado, steamboat, 414
Colorados, Mangas, 137-40, 237, 344
Colossal Cave, 19
Colton, Harold S., 249
Columbia, 179
Columbus, New Mexico, 73
Colyer, Vincent, 182
Comaduran, Antonio, Lt., 5, 22
Comanches, 403
Commonwealth, 92
Compostela, 126
Comstock Lode of Nevada, 358
Concho, 376
Congress, 363, 441-43, 447
Congress Junction, 442-43
Congress Mine, 441, 447
Conkling, Roscoe, Senator, 168-69
Conner, Daniel, 137
Conovaloff family, 429
Contention, 59
Contention City, 100
Conway, 211
Cooke Wagon Road, 389
Cooke, Phillip St. George, Capt. 5, 21, 159-60, 163-65, 388, 407
Cooley, 315
Cooley Ranch, 314
Cooley, Corydon E., 314-15, 341-42
Cooley, Molly and Cora, 341
Coolidge, 117
Coolidge Dam, 89, 344
Copeland, Isaac, 197
Copper Belle, 94
Copper Canyon, 183
Copper Mountain Mine, 370-71
Copper Mountain Mining District, 370
Copper Queen Hotel, 73-74
Copper Queen Mine, 68-69, 70, 72, 74
Corbett, H. S., 440
Corbin Mill and Mining Company, 59
Corbin brothers, 59
Cordes, 180
Cordes Junction, 376
Cordes, John, 180
Cordoba, Miguel de Peralta de, 168
Corliss, Charles, Capt., 209
Cornelia Copper Company, 111
Coro, Chief, 103
Coronado National Memorial, 125
Coronado, Francisco Vasquez de, 21, 125, 127-28, 130, 305, 317, 357, 369, 401
Corral, Tomas and Cecilia, 206-07
Cosninos, 285
Cottonwood,364
Courtland, 91, 93-94
Couts, Cave Johnson, 408, 410
Covered Wells, 116
Cowboy Artists of America, 64, 330
Cowboy's Home Saloon, 76
Coyne, Patrick, 107
Cozzens, Samuel, 237
Crabb Expedition, 398
Crabb, Henry A., 397-98
Crawford, Emmett, Capt., 81-82
Crazy Horse, 384
Cremony, John C., Capt., 7, 138

Cripple Creek, 358
Crocker, Charles, 23
Crook Military Road, 182, 217, 314
Crook, George, General, 80-82, 84, 98, 120, 122,
    182-85, 188-89, 210, 314, 339, 343, 353, 437
Cross, Ed, 51
Crossing of the Fathers, 294, 300
Crowe, Frank T., 51
Crown King, 179-80
Cruz, Florentino, 63
Crystal Palace Saloon, 64
Cummings, Byron, 381
Cushing, Howard, Lt., 102, 199, 221
Cushman, Pauline, 89
Daggs brothers, 224
Date Creek, 210, 343, 437, 447
Date Creek Mountains, 441, 447
Davidson Canyon, 108
Davidson, O., 108
Davis, Jefferson, 227, 230-31, 235
Davis, Lew, 206
Day, Alan, 351-52
Day, Ann, 351
Day, Harry, 351
Day, Henry Clay, 351
DeArnett, L., 197
DeMille, Cecil B., 235
DeSchradt, Jack, 217
Deadman Flat, 297
Deadman Wash, 297
Del Muerto, 11
Del Rio Springs, 183, 282, 284, 328, 355
Delaney, Bill, 62, 71
Deluge Wash, 448
Derby, George, 411
Desert Land Act, 204
Desert Well, 389
Detrital Valley, 450-51
Detroit Copper Company, 371-72
Devine, Andy, 289
Dewey, 378, 380
Dewey, George, Admiral, 380
Diaz, Jose, Capt., 49
Dillon, John, 108
Dinetah, 323
Dolores, 39, 40
Dome, 399, 452, 454
Dominguez, Father, 300
Dorantes, Andres, 26
Dos Cabezas, 133
Dos Cabezas, Mountains, 26, 33
Double Buttes, 25
Double Circle Ranch, 374
Douglas, 27, 75-77, 363
Douglas, James, Dr., 69, 75, 202, 358-59, 371-72
Douglas, Jimmy, 359-60, 362, 364
Dowd, Dan, 62, 71
Downing, Bill, 28-29, 31
Dragoon, 23
Dragoon Mountains, 23
Drorbaugh, Walt and Elaine, 215
DuBois, R. C., Lt., 210
Dudleyville, 98
Dugas, Fred, 180
Duncan, 350-51
Dunlap, Three-finger Jack, 28-30, 99-100
Dunn, Jack, 67, 74, 121
Dunn, Tom, 421
Duppa, Bryan Philip Darrell, 149-50
Duppa, Darrell, "Lord," 174, 192, 379
Duquesne, 106
Dye, Charlie, 364

Dyke, Cleve Van, 200
Eagar, 316, 342
Eagar, John, Joe, and William, 316
Earp, Morgan, 12, 63, 143
Earp, Virgil, 63, 329
Earp, Warren, 31
Earp, Wyatt, 12, 63, 102, 143
Eastern Arizona Junior College, 349
Echard, Danny Lee, 356
Ehrenberg, 330, 412, 423-25, 440, 447, 453
Ehrenberg, Herman, 50, 111, 417, 424
El Camino del Diablo, 50
El Mirage, 429
El Morro, 299
El Paso, 416, 419
El Paso and Southwestern Railroad, 65, 70, 75
El Potrero, 45, 47
El Rancho Grande, 171
El Rancho de San Francisco, 171
El Tovar, 306-07
El Vadito, 375
Elam, Jack, 202
Elfrida, 95
Elías, José, 37
Elk, 294
Elkhart Lode, 234, 285, 288, 293, 324-25, 441,
    449
Elliott, Minnie, 206
Emory, William, Major, 37, 117, 158, 220, 409
Empire Mountains, 108
Empire Ranch, 18, 107
Enid, 389
Erastus, 376
Ernest W. McFarland State Park, 88
Escalante, Silvestre, Padre, 293, 300
Esconolea, Chief, 33, 135
Esmeralda, 12
Esmeralda Mine, 449
Espejo, Antonio de, 184, 188, 317, 337
Establecimientos de paz, 4
Esteban, 21, 126
Eureka, 453
Evans, Benton Jesse, 206
Ewell's Springs, 133
Ewell, Richard, Capt., 103, 133
Explorer, 415-16
Fair, James, Senator, 84
Fairbank, 56, 70, 99
Fairbank, N. K., 99
Fairview, 313
Farfán, Marcos, 184, 188, 317, 357
Farley, Ed, 430
Federal Highway Act, 278
Fenner, F. C., Col., 439
Fewks, J. Walter, Dr., 118
Filibuster Camp, 391, 396-97
Fillmore, Millard, President, 231
First Volunteer Cavalry, 35
Fish Creek, 199, 221
Fish Creek Hill, 218, 220
Fisher, Sarah, 333
Fitzgerald, F. Scott, 162
Fitzpatrick, Tom, 259, 277, 407
Flagstaff, 191, 213, 224, 234-35, 237, 239-40,
    242-43, 247-248, 289, 298, 305, 337, 348,
    365, 438
Flake, William J., 310
Flap-Jack Ranch, 391, 394
Flattop Site, 269
Fletcher, Curly, 438
Flint, Timothy, Rev., 406
Florence, 88-89, 201, 369, 420

Flower, Richard, 346
Floyd, J. W., 214
Fly, C. S., 82
Ford, John, 304-05
Forester, Willard, 363
Fort Apache, 256, 313-15, 340-41, 381, 383-84
Fort Apache Reservation, 343
Fort Bowie, 33, 83, 141
Fort Breckenridge, 137
Fort Buchanan, 23, 44, 79, 103, 133, 137
Fort Crittenden, 106, 108
Fort Defiance, 232, 294
Fort Rickerson, 241
Fort Grant, 27, 348, 367-68
Fort Huachuca, 120-22, 204
Fort Lowell, 7, 172
Fort McDowell, 148, 174, 194, 208-10, 339, 343, 445
Fort Misery, 328-29
Fort Mohave, 412-13
Fort Moroni, 241
Fort Rock, 288
Fort Sill, Oklahoma, 84
Fort Tejón, California, 233
Fort Thomas, 341, 347-48
Fort Utah, 194
Fort Valley, 237, 239
Fort Verde, 190, 210, 314, 365
Fort Whipple, 174, 185, 271, 328-29, 353-55, 364
Fort Wingate, New Mexico, 272
Fort Yuma, 236, 392, 408, 411, 415-16, 419, 421-22
442nd Regimental Combat Team, 455
Four Corners, 303
Fourr, Billy, 393
Fowler, Ben, 155, 219
Foy, Eddie, 65
Franciscans, 3, 38, 48, 54-55
Frederick, Al, 205
Fredonia, 324
Free and Easy Saloon, 30-31
Free, Mickey, 105
Fremont, Jessie, 259
Fremont, John C., 259, 392, 407
Fryer, Jere, Sheriff, 89
Frisco, 374
Fritz, Fred, 372-73
Fritz, Fred, Jr., 373
Frontier Days Rodeo, 334
Fry, 124, Fry, Oliver, 24
Fuller, Wes, 63
Gabilando, Hilario, 398
Gable, Clark, 389, 291
Gabriel, Pete, Sheriff, 89
Gadsden Hotel, 76
Gadsden Purchase, 37, 409
Gadsden, James, 5, 43, 103, 409
Gage, E. B., 442
Galeyville, 85
Galiuro Mountains, 368
Gallup, New Mexico, 321
Galvez Plan, 4-5
Galvéz, Bernardo de, Viceroy, 4
Galvéz, José de, General, 3
Ganado-Hubbell Trading Post, 320-21
Gándara, Manual Maria, 43-44, 398
Gándara, Manuel, 397
Garcés, Francisco Tomás Father, 3, 42, 49, 52, 54, 285-86, 299, 305, 316, 340, 390, 393, 398, 402
Garcia, Gilanin, Col., 43

García, Hilarón, Capt., 5
Gaden Canyon, 123
Gadine, 287
Gardner Canyon, 108
Gardner, Gail, 330, 438
Garland, Hamblin, 322
Gatewood, Charles B., Lt., 82-84, 123, 381
General Jesup, 414-17
Genung, Charles, 434, 446
George, Joe, 27-28
Geronimo, 79, 81-84, 108, 120, 122, 141, 186, 343-44, 381-82, 384, 439
Geronimo, Arizona, 346
Gila Bend, 291, 349, 387, 389-92, 430
Gila City, 399, 452
Gila Expedition, 411
Gila Ranch, 390
Gila River, 189, 207, 218, 279, 327-28, 387, 396, 398-400, 405, 407-09, 416, 452
Gila River Arts and Crafts Center, 157
Gila River Indian Reservation, 157
Gila, steamboat, 412
Gila Trail, 50, 159, 169, 227, 278, 387, 389, 393-94, 408-09, 411
Gila Valley, 201
Gila Valley Bank, 350
Gila Valley, Globe and Northern Railroad, 201
Gilbert, G. K., 253
Gillett, 175, 176
Gillett, Daniel B., 176
Gilpin, Frank, 336
Gilpin, Lionel, 356
Giovando, Ken, 203
Gird, Richard, 58-59
Glanton Massacre, 410
Glanton, John Joel, 410
Glass, Hugh, 259
Gleeson, 91, 94
Gleeson, John, 94
Glen Canyon, 299-300
Glendale, 428-29
Glidden, Joseph, 268
Globe, 26, 57, 200-01, 203, 212-13, 240, 346, 379, 385
Globe Mining District, 201
Globe Rangers, 385
Goddard, Charles, 176
Golconda Mine, 449
Gold Gulch, 374
Gold Road Mine, 291
Golden Gem Mine, 449
Goldfield, 220
Goldfield Mountains, 220
Goldroad, 290-91
Goldroad Pass, 291
Goldwater, Barry M., Senator, 424, 436
Goldwater, Mike and Joe, 423-24
Goldwater, Morris, 333, 424
Gonzáles, Ignacio Elías, Capt., 101
Goodfellow, David, 215
Goodfellow, George, 64
Goodwin, John, Governor, 145, 189, 271, 328
Goodyear Tire & Rubber Co., 427
Goulding, Harry and Mike, 304-05
Gowan, Davy, 215
Graham, Billy, 224, 272
Graham, Lawrence, Major, 408, 418
Graham, Tom and John, 223-25, 272
Graham-Tewksbury feud, 261
Grand Canal, 152
Grand Canyon, 236, 241, 255, 278, 285, 297, 299, 305, 325, 406, 439

Grand Canyon Village, 355
Grand Central, 59
Grand Central Mining Co., 99
Granger, Byrd, 447
Granite City, 329
Granite Creek, 328, 331, 333
Granite Dells, 334
Granjon, Henri, 55
Grant, Heber J., 313
Grant, Ulysses S., President, 98
Gray, A. B., 43, 408-09
Graydon, James "Paddy," 103-05
Grazhoffer, Juan, Father, 41
Greaterville, 107
Green Valley, 214
Green, John, Major, 382
Greenawalt, Randy, 434
Greenback Valley, 211
Greenlee, Mace, 369
Greenway, John C., 111
Greer, Americus Vespucius, 315
Greer, Christopher Columbus, 315
Grey, Zane, 313
Grinnell Stage Station, 396
Grinnell, Henry, 291, 392, 396
Gripe, 352
Groom, Robert, 329
Grover, Bert, 29
Guadalupe, 136
Guaymas, 36, 42, 394
Guévavi, 40-42, 45
Gunfight at the OK Corral, 63
Gunnison, John W., Capt., 260
Gunsight, 116
Gunsight Mountains, 116
Gurley, John, 330
Hackberry, 277, 287
Hadsell, B. A., 428
Halcro, Joe, 72
Hall, Deforest and Dick Wick, 431-32
Hall, Sharlot, 331, 333-34, 380
Hamblin Road, 295
Hamblin, Gunlock Bill, 324-25
Hamblin, Jacob, 253, 294, 299, 324, 374
Hamilton, Charles, 16
Hampton, John, 364
Hance's Tank, 305
Hance, John, 305, 307-09
Hancock, Louis, 142
Hancock, William, Capt., 151, 211-12
Hanna, Adam, 269
Hannegan Meadow, 374
Hannegan, Bob, 374
Hansen, Peter, 215
Happy Camp, 389
Harcuvar, 432
Hardscramble, 324
Hardscramble Mesa, 215
Hardy, William, 288
Hardyville, 288, 328, 330, 412
Harer, David, 212
Harquahala Mountains, 434
Harrington, William Dudley, 98
Harris, Dore, 338
Harshaw, 106
Hart, Pearl, 420
Harte, Bret, 234, 240, 347
Harvey girls, 257-58
Harvey House, 257, 281
Harvey, Fred, 256-57, 259
Harvey, John, 18
Harvey, William, Dr.

Hashknife, 242, 252, 255, 266-67
Hassayampa River, 327, 331, 395, 434
Hastings, 198
Havasupi Indians, 305
Hawikuh, 126
Hawkins, Lee, Dr., 360
Hayden, 195
Hayden's Ferry, 192, 195
Hayden, Carl, 176
Hayden, Charles T., 176, 192
Hays Cattle Co., 446
Hays, Ira, 162
Hays, Roy, 446
Heard , Dwight, 155, 219
Hearst, William Randolph, 101
Heber, 313
Heintzelman, Sam, 144, 411
Heiroglyphic Mountains, 430
Helena Canyon, 273
Hell Canyon, 356
Hendon, T. A., 440
Hentig, Edmond, 384
Herraras, Leon, 103
Heith, John, 62, 71
Hill, Walter J., 274
Hise, John and Frank, 213
Hislop, H. R., 18
Hobbs, James, 419
Hohokam, 147-48, 184, 186-87, 269
Holbrook, 228, 234, 242, 254, 261-65, 381
Holbrook, H. R., 261
Holliday, Doc, 63
Hon-Dah, 314
Honeymoon Trail, 299
Hooker, Henry Clay, 367-68
Hoover Dam, 289, 413, 451
Hope, 433
Hopi Indians, 128-29, 183, 188, 285, 298, 302,
    307, 316, 318
Hopi Mesas, 300
Hopi-Navajo land dispute, 320
Horn, Tom, 82-83, 123, 381
Horse Mesa, 222
Horse Mesa Dam, 339
Horsehead Crossing, 242, 261, 263, 270, 272
Horseshow Dam, 173
Hot Springs Junction, 430
Hotevilla, 317
Houck, 272
Houck, James D., 224, 271-72
House Rock, 294
How the West Was Won, 291
Howard, Jesse Jefferson, 366
Howard, Jesse and Martha, 366
Howard, John, Judge, 329
Howard, Oliver O. General, 98, 120, 142, 182,
    343
Howard, Tex, 62, 71
Huachuca, 101
Huachuca Mountains, 125
Huachuca Water Company, 63
Hualapai Indians, 285-86, 288-89
Hualapai Valley, 286
Hubbell, John Lorenzo, 320-22
Hudson Bay Company, 330
Hull Copper Company, 360
Hull, George W., 360
Humboldt, 378
Humboldt, Alexander von, Baron, 378
Hunt, Margaret, 332
Hunter, Sherod, Capt., 7, 137, 394-96

Hurning, Henry, 261
Imperial Valley, 451
Independence Rock, Wyoming, 299
Independence, Missouri, 456
Indian Gardens, 191, 365-66
Indian Springs, 285
Industrial Workers of the World, 73
Ingersoll, Robert, 168-69
Inspiration Mines, 199-200
Interstate 40, 284-85
Interstate Defense System, 278
Irataba, 434
Irion, Robert A. "Old Man," 199
Irish, Fred "Cap," 194
Iron King Mine, 378
Irwin, B. J. D., Dr., 23
Isaacson, Jacob, 36
Ives, Joseph C. Lt., 227, 236, 270, 306, 415-16
Jack, 135
Jack's Canyon, 217
Jackass Mail, 6
Jackson, David, 5, 259
Jackson, M., 112
Jacob Lake, 294, 309
Jacobs, Bill, 224-25
Jaeger's Ferry, (also spelled Iaeger), 417
Jaeger, Louis, 417
Janos, 139
Jeddito Mesa, 319
Jeff, Hualapai, 450
Jeffords, Tom, 120
Jenerez, Joe, 290
Jerome, 281, 350, 354-55, 357-59, 361-63, 365
Jerome Junction, 354-55
Jerome, Eugene, 358
Jerome, Jennie, 358
Jesuit Expulsion, 42, 54
Jesuits, 3, 38-39, 41-42, 48, 54
Jicarilla Apaches, 322
Johannesberg, 433
Johnson, 25
Johnson, Andrew and Sam, 312
Johnson, George, 412-14, 417
Johnson, Jack, 440
Jones, Celeste Marie, 196
Jones, Hugh, 72
Jonesville, 194
Josanie, 81
Joseph City, 254
Joshua tree, 292
Joy's Camp, 371
Joy, Miles, 371
Juan, Mathew B., 119, 162
Juniper, 313
Juniper Mountains, 354
K L Bar, 438
Kabotie, Fred, 270
Kachina Point, 270
Kachinas, 319
Kaibab, 309
Kaibab National Forest, 294
Kanab, Utah, 254
Kayenta, 302
Kayitah, 83-84, 381
Keams Canyon, 319
Keams, Thomas V., 319
Kearny, Stephen Watts, General, 21, 158, 231, 331, 344, 369, 387, 407
Keet Seel, 302
Keller, Ignacio, Padre, 41
Kelley, Dan, 62, 71
Kelton, 95

Kennedy, John F., President, 375
Kenyons Station, 392
Kern, Ben, 277
Kern, Richard, 277
Ketchum, Black Jack, 35, 351
Kibbey, Joe, 219
Killeen, May, 95
Killeen, Mike, 95
Kimball, Heber C., 313
Kin Tiel, 272
King, Carlos III, 41, 49, 54
King of Arizona Mining Company, 453
Kingman, 234, 285, 288, 293, 324-25, 441, 449-50
Kingman, Lewis, 288
Kinishba Ruins, 381
Kino, Eusebio, Father, 21, 36, 39, 40-41, 43, 48, 50, 53-54, 77, 100-01, 103, 114, 117-19, 144, 340, 387, 392, 399, 401-02
Kinsley, Edward, 264
Kinsley, Henry, 265
Kirker Jim, 239
Kirkland, 445
Kirkland Junction, 445
Kirkland, Bill, 6, 53, 105-06, 151, 349, 444
Kirkland, May Ellen, 151
Kirkland, Missouri Ann, 151
Kitchen, Dona Rosa Verdugo, 46-47
Kitchen, Pete, 45-47, 53
Kitt Peak National Observatory, 114
Klagetoh, 311
Kline, F. H., 131
Kofa Mountains, 453
Kohls Ranch, 312
Kolb, Ellsworth and Emory, 306
Kruger, William, 436-38
L'Amour, Louis, 266
La Cienega, 20
La Junta, Colorado, 370
La Paz, 328, 331, 423-24, 434, 446
La Puerta de la Purisima Concepcion, 402
Laguna, 453
Lajoie, Helene, 261
Lajoie, Jean Baptiste, 261
Lake Copalla, 40l
Lake Mary, 241, 244
Lake Mead, 289, 293, 415, 452-53
Lake Mohave, 288
Lake Powell, 294, 299-300, 452
Lake San Carlos, 344
Lake Superior and Arizona Mine, 198
Lake, George, 254
Lakeside, 313
Lamy, Jean Baptiste, Archbishop, 50, 55
Lane, Jake, 214
Langloiz, Adolph, 35
Las Vegas, 289
Laskey, Jesse, 235
Lavender, Harrison, 73
Lawton, Henry, Capt., 84, 122
Lazovich, Teddy, 203
Lazy B, 351
Leal, Antonio, 2
Leatherwood, Bob, Mayor, 13, 356
Leavitt, Dudley, 325
Lee's Ferry, 254, 295
Lee, John Doyle, 295-96
Lee, Willard, 315
Lehi, 56, 194
Lehi Pioneers, 194
Lentz, John Dutch
Leroux Springs, 237, 260

Leroux Wash, 259
Leroux, Antoine, 21, 163, 188, 228-30, 236, 259-61, 277, 279
Leroux, Will, 261
Lesinsky, Charles, 370-71
Lesinsky, Henry, 370
Leslie, Frank Buckskin, 95-96, 143
Lewis, Thomas Cooper, 281
Lewisohn Brothers, 200-01
Liberty, 112
Lincoln, Abel, 410
Lincoln, Abrahan, President, 89, 328
Lindbergh, Charles A., 289
Linde, 313
Lipan Apaches, 322
Litchfield Park, 427
Litchfield, Paul W., 427
Little Colorado River, 190, 215, 237, 241-42, 251, 254-55, 261, 270, 299, 305, 310, 315, 327, 374-75
Little Colorado River Valley, 194
Little Daisy Hotel, 361
Little Daisy Mine, 359-60
Little Red Schoolhouse, 205
Littlefield, 293
Llunas, Juan Antonio, 158
Logan, 115
Loggers Jamboree, 214
Lombard, Carole, 289, 291
Long, Bill, 197
Long Valley, 214
"long walk," 304, 311
Longfellow Mine, 370-71
Lombard, Carole, 289, 291
Long, Bill, 197
Long Valley, 214
Longfellow Mine, 370-71
Lopez, Garcia, 305
Lopez, James, Sgt., 202
Lordsburg, New Mexico, 25
Loring, Frederick, 436
Los Angeles, 289, 300, 410
Los Nogales de Elías land grant, 36-37
Lost Dutchman Mine, 195-96, 218, 220
Lost Pick Mine, 177-78
Lost Six-Shooter Mine, 426
Lount, Sam, 152
Lousy Gulch, 215
Lovin, Henry, 290
Lowdermilk, Romaine, 438
Lowell Observatory, 247-48
Lowell, Percival, Dr., 247-48
Lucero, Cristo, 443
Lucky Cuss, 58-59
Lupton, 234, 273
Lupton, C. W., 273
Lyman, Lake, 374
Lyman, Francis, 374
Lynch, Dick, 206
Lynx Creek, 333, 434
Machebeuf, Josef, Father, 50, 55
Mack Morris Mine, 430
Mackey, John, 115
Mader, Harry, 362
Madison Square Garden, 212
Madonna of the Trail, 343
Magma Copper Company, 198
Maine, 275
Mammoth, 98, 220
Mammoth Mine, 98
Manje, Juan Mateo, Lt., 117
Many Farms, 311-12

Marana, 171
Marana Army Air Field, 171
Marble Canyon, 295
March of Tears, 210
Marcus, Josephine Sarah, 63
Maria del Agua Caliente, 393
Maricopa, 389, 411
Maricopa Ak Chin Reservation, 388
Maricopa County, 151
Maricopa Indians, 119, 160, 162, 392
Maricopa Junction, 389
Maricopa Mountains, 389
Maricopa Station, 388-89
Maricopa Wells, 387-90
Marion, Flora, 332
Marion, John, 189, 332, 353, 376
Mars Hill, 238, 247
Marston, Paul, 356
Martin, Barney, 430, 443
Martín, San Juan de, Father, 41, 48
Martine, 83-84, 381
Martinez Mining District, 447
Maryville, 194
Mason Valley, 199
Mason, Charles, 196-97
Maurel, Andre, 202
Maus, Marion, Lt., 82
Mavine, Arch, 220
Maxwell, Will, 342
May, Dennis, 441
Mayer, 179-80, 376-77
Mayor, Joseph, 377
Mays, Isaiah, 348
Mazatzal Mountains, 208, 210-11
McCleave, William, Capt., 395
McClintock, James, 193, 219
McCormick, Richard C., Governor, 118, 328-29, 332
McCoy, Hank, 72
McCracken, 57-58, 448
McCreery, James, 265
McDowell, 194
McDowell, Irvin, General, 208, 421-22
McFarland, Ernest W., 38
McGuire, Eugene, 138
McGuireville, 183, 188
McKay, Alexander, 115
McKinley, William, President, 263, 442
McKinnon, Angus, 357
McLaury, Tom and Frank, 63
McMillan Ranch, 238
McMillan, Charlie, 338
McMillan, Thomas F., 238
McMillanville, 338
McNary, 315
McNary Lumber Company, 315
McNary, James G., 315
McNeal, 75
Mead, Ellwood, Dr., 452
Meek, Joe, 317
Megargee, Lon, 206
Mellon, 293
Mellon, Jack, Capt., 293, 412
Menager, Joe and Louis, 114
Mendoza, Antonio, Viceroy, 126
Moenkopi, Wash, 254
Merrill, Philemon, 56
Mesa, 193-95, 204, 217, 221
Mesa Verde, 303
Mesaville, 195
Mescal Springs, 102
Mescalero, 322

Mesilla Valley, 409
Metcalf, 373-74
Metcalf Mine, 370
Metcalf, Jim and Bob, 370
Meteor Crater, 253
Mexican Water, 303, 310
Mexico and Colorado Railroad, 75
Miami, 198-200, 203
Miami Copper Company, 199-200
Miami Flat, 199-200
Michler, Nathaniel, Lt., 409
Middendorf, Bernardo, Padre, 2
Middleton Ranch, 385
Midway Grocery, 355
Miguel, 382
Miles, Nelson, General, 82-84, 122-23
Millennial City, 324
Miller, "Two Guns," 250
Miller, Sam and Jacob, 332-33
Mills, Billy, 319
Millville, 278
Milton, Jeff, 29, 99-100
Mineral Belt Railroad, 240
Mineral City, 453
Mineral Creek, 199
Mineral Park, 449
Mingus Mountain, 361
Mingus, Joseph and Jacob, 361
Mission Camp, 398-99
Missouri River, 259
Mix, Tom, 86-87
Mobile, 389
Moenave, 299
Moenkopi, 254, 301, 316
Moeur, Ben, Governor, 113, 455
Mofford, Rose Perica, 202
Mogollon, 269, 381
Mogollon Rim, 183, 211, 213, 217, 240, 278, 312,
   327, 438
Mogollon, Juan Ignacio Flores, 213
Mohave, 412
Mohave County Airport, 239
Mohave Lake, 289
Mohawk, 453
Mohawk Station, 396
Mojave Desert, 403
Mojave Indians, 236, 286, 291, 392, 400, 411,
   456
Mojave villages, 230, 406
Möllhausen, Heinrich Baldwin, 227-30, 271,
   415
Monroe, George, 430
Montana Hotel, 361
Montezuma Castle, 186-88
Montezuma City, 189
Montezuma Mine, 370
Montezuma Well, 188
Monument Valley, 304-05
Moons, Jack, 17
Moore, Billy, 112
Moorhead, Joe, 411
Morenci, 350, 369, 371-72
Morenci Mine, 372
Mormon Battalion, 5, 21-22, 34, 56, 163-65,
   169, 189, 259, 295, 331, 407
Mormon Cattle Company, 239
Mormon Flat, 222
Mormon Stope, 220
Mormon War, 414
Mormons, 194, 285, 292-93, 296, 299, 303, 310,
   315, 317, 324, 342, 348-49, 374, 376, 415
Morris, George, 430

Morrison, Samuel Elliot, 125
Morristown, 430, 443
Mortenson, Niels, 313
Moss, John, 290
Mossman, Burt, 30, 266, 350
Mount Baldy, 255
Mount Trumbull, 325
Mountain Meadows, 296
Mountain View Hotel, 97
Mowry Mine, 106
Mowry, Sylvester, Lt., 51, 106
Mt. Ord, 210
Mt. Taylor, 323
Mucho, Ganado, 320
Mule Mountains, 57, 67
Mule Pass Tunnel, 74
Mulheim Brewery, 74
Munds Park, 191
Munds, James, 191
Munson, Bill, 349
Munsonville, 349
Murderer's Grave, 391-92
Murphy, Frank, 179-80, 377, 442
Murphy, Patrick, 132
Murphy, William J., 152, 155, 204
Murphyville, 205
Murray, Bill, 358
Museum of Northern Arizona, 238
Na-ti-o-tish, 185, 335
Narbona, Antonio, 403-04
Narbona, Jacova, 403-04
Nachez, 122
Naco, 130-31, 134
Naco "blitzkrieg" of 1929, 132
Naco, Sonora, 130-31
Nacozari, Sonora, 75, 130
Nadaburg, 430
Nana, 120
National Cowboy Hall of Fame, 268, 338, 368
Nauvoo, Illinois, 310
Navajo Campaign in 1864, 273
Navajo County, 261, 310
Navajo Mountain, 323
Navajo National Monument, 301
Navajo Ordinance Depot, 274
Navajo Springs, 270
Navajos, 270, 294, 298, 304-05, 320-22
Neal, 448
Neal, Curley Bill, 86, 97
Neal, Jim, 95-96
Needles, 292-93, 440
Needles, California, 230, 284, 415
Nelson, Earl, 363
Nelson, Price, 216
Napomucino, Felix, 101
New River, 174-75, 429, 441
New Virginia, 115
New York Herald, 390
New York Tribune, 436
Newberry, J. S., 270, 306
Newlands Act of 1902, 154
Newman, Jack "Black," 200
Newton, Uncle Charlie, 338
Niza, Fray Marcos de, 21, 126-27
Noah, Max B., 397
Nock-ay-del-Klinne, 340-41, 384
Nogales, 36-37, 43, 45, 409
Norris, Lee, 336-37
North Rim, 309, 406
Northern Arizona University, 203, 245, 248
Northern Gila County Chamber of Commerce,
   217

Northwest Passage, 126, 129, 184, 305
Norton's Landing, 453
Norton, John, 219
Nutrioso, 374
O'Connor, John, 352
O'Connor, Sandra Day, 351-52
O'Conor, Hugo, Col., 3, 77
O'Dougherty, John and Ed, 368
O'Neill, Buckey, 252, 305, 335-36, 356
O'Rourke, John, 143
Oak Creek Canyon, 191, 364-65
Oak Creek Tavern, 364
Oatman, 290-91
Oatman Flat, 391-93
Oatman Hill, 234
Oatman Massacre, 392
Oatman Pass, 292, 440
Oatman, John, 291
Oatman, Mary Ann and Lorenzo, 392
Oatman, Olive, 291, 392, 396, 453
Obed, 254-55
Octave, 443-44
Octave Gold Mining Company, 444
Ohnesorgen Stage, 27
Ohnesorgen, William, 23
Oklahoma, 102
Old Dominion, 201-02
Old Spanish Trail, 300
Oldfield, Barney, 439-40
Oliva, Juan Marie de, Lt., 3
Olive City, 179, 453
Omer, 342
Onacama, 260-61
Oñate, Don Juan, 235, 317, 357, 401-02
Oñate, Juan de, 184, 188, 316, 401, 447, 456
Oracle, 97
Oracle Junction, 86
Oraibi, 301, 316-19
Orangedale, 205
Orchard Ranch, 380
Ord, E. O. C., General, 210
Ore Belle, 179
Organ Pipe National Monument, 110
Orme, John, 155, 219
Ormsby, Waterman, 390
Ortiz, Tomás and Ignacio, 52
Oury, Granville, Mrs., 20
Overgaard, 313
Owen, Jim, 294
Owens, 448
Owens, Perry, 262-63, 272
Packard Store, 211, 213
Packard, Florence, 212
Padilla, Juan, 261
Page, 299, 300
Page, John C., 300
Painted Desert, 270
Painted Desert Inn, 270
Painted Mountains, 392
Painted Rocks, 392
Paiute Indians, 293, 296, 309
Pajarito, New Mexico, 321
Palatkwapi Trail, 183, 217
Paleo-Indians, 147
Palm Canyon, 454
Palma, Chief, 402
Palominas, 130
Pantano, 19-20
Papago (also Tono O'Odham) Indians, 38, 114, 148, 157, 161, 388, 405
Paradise, 85
Paradise Valley, 173-74, 205, 273

Paradise Verde Irrigation District, 173
Parke, John G., Lt., 26, 32, 124, 340
Parker, 415, 454-56
Parker Dam, 287, 455
Parker, Eli, 455
Parker, Fleming, 336-37
Parks, 275
Partridge, William, 443
Pascual, Chief, 415
Patagonia Mine, 106
Pattie, James Ohio, 117, 158, 305, 369, 403-06, 456
Pattie, Sylvester, 403, 406
Patton, George S., General, 452, 458
Paulden, 354-55
Payroll Mine, 449
Payson, 213-15, 217
Payson, Louis, Senator, 214
Peabody, Endicott, 61
Peach Springs, 285, 336
Peach, Alfred and Frances, 216
Peach, Tuffy, 213
Pearce, 91-93, 143
Peavine, 284
Pecos River Reservation, 311
Pedro, 341, 382
Peeples, Abraham H., 331, 434, 444, 446
Peeples Valley, 446
Peloncillo Mountains, 351
Penrod, 314
Penrod, Bill, 313
Peoria, 429
Peralta Mine, 177
Percheron, 313
Perez, Ignacio, Lt., 77
Perkins, P. J., 426-27
Pershing, 348
Pershing, John "Blackjack," General, 73, 183
Pesqueria, Don Ignacio, 394, 397-98
Petrified Forest National Park, 269-70
Pfefferkorn, Ignaz, Padre, 41
Phelps, Ben
Phelps-Dodge, 69, 72-73, 202, 358, 362, 371-72
Phippen, George, 330, 364
Phipps, Johnny, 313
Phoenix, 12, 148, 150, 152-56, 201, 204-06, 214, 284, 289, 324, 350, 378, 389, 435, 438-41, 445
Phoenix Union High School, 207
Phy, Joe, 89
Picacho, 166, 170, 396
Picacho Pass, 169, 396
Picket Post, 197
Picket Post Butte, 199
Pierce, Franklin, President, 409
Pilot Knob, 411
Pima, 348
Pima Indians, 38, 148, 157, 159-62, 206, 208, 218, 387, 411
Pima Pass, 389
Pima Revolt in 1751, 49, 54
Pimeria Alta, 38-39, 41-42, 48-49, 53, 157
Pinal Apaches, 199, 201
Pinal City, 197-98
Pinal Creek, 200-01
Pinal Mountains, 199-200
Pinal Ranch, 199
Pinaleno Mountains, 367-68
Pine, 215-16
Pine Creek, 215
Pine Grove, 180
Pine Springs, 278-79

Pinedale, 278, 313
Pinetop, 313-14
Pinto Creek, 199
Pioneer, 391
Pioneer Saloon, 214
Pipe Spring, 254
Pipe Springs National Monument, 324-25
Piper, Ed, 196
Planchas de Plata, 144
Planet, 448
Planet Mine, 427
Pleasant Valley, 214, 223-24, 272, 310, 313
Pleasant Valley War, 214, 261, 363
Pluto, 248
Point of Rocks, 353-54
Poland, 179-80
Poland Junction, 377
Poland, Davis R., 179, 377
Polhamus, Isaac, 412
Polk, James K., President, 407
Popoff family, 429
Port Isabel, 412
Portal, 85
Porter, David, 231
Postle, Robert, 355
Poston, 454
Poston's Butte, 90
Poston, Charles, 50-52, 90, 111, 144, 417, 454
Potero Creek, 45
Powell, 293
Powell, John Wesley, 294-95, 297, 300, 305, 309, 452
Power, Jeff, 368
Power, Tom and John, 368-69
Pownall, Orville and Paul, 355
Pozos de San Basilio, 285
Pratt, Grace Salome, 431
Prescott, 12, 15, 153, 217, 223, 272, 281, 283, 288, 327, 329, 330-33, 336-37, 353-56, 369, 276, 424, 438, 440, 447
Prescott and Central Arizona Railroad, 284, 333
Prescott and Eastern Railrod, 377
Prescott Barracks, 353
Prescott Junction, 283-84, 355
Prescott, William Hickling, 329
Preston, Scott, 299
Pueblo Revolt of 1680, 316-17, 319
Puerco Ruin, 269
Pumpelly, Raphael, 419
Punkin Center, 211, 213
Purtyman, Clara Thompson, 191
Purtymun, Steve, 366
Pyramid Canyon, 415
Pythian Castle, 74
Quartzsite, 425-26
Quechans, (see also Yuma Indians), 392, 400, 402
Queen Creek, 199
Quiburi, 100-01
Quijotoa, 115, 144
Ralph, Joe, 397
Ramirez, Alferez Juan Matheo, Lt., 21
Ramos, Caroline, 329
Rasalia, Maria, 261
Reagan, Ben, 197
Reavis, James Addison, 166-68, 177, 346
Reavis, Sofia, 167, 169
Reclamation Act of 1902, 221
Red Crossing, 293
Red Lake, 301
Red Rock, 170-71, 293

Redlands, 348
Reily, James, Col., 394
Reno Pass, 211
Reno, Jesse, General, 212
Represso, 86
Reynolds, Jim Diamond, 441
Rhoades, 275
Rhodes Ranch, 453
Rich Hill, 331, 434, 446
Rich, George, 277
Richardson, Hubert, 298
Rickerson, C. L., 241
Ricketts, L. D., Dr., 202
Rigney, 313
Rillito Creek, 172
Ringo, Johnny, 63, 142-43
Rio Grande, 404, 416, 457
Rio Grande de Buena Esperanza, 447
Rio Puerco, 242, 270
Rio Rico, 43
Rio San Andres, 447
Rio Verde Canal Company, 173
Rio de Buena Guida, 401
Riordan, Timothy, Michael, Dennis, 244-45
Rioville, 415, 452
Roberts, Jim, 223-25, 363
Roberts, Mose, 263
Roberts, Tom, Capt., 137-38, 140
Robidoux, Michel, 405
Robles Junction, 113
Robles, Bernabe, 113
Robles, June, 113
Rock Point, 311
Rock Springs, 176
Rogers, Will, 17, 89, 163, 258, 439
Romero, José, 402-03
Rommel, Erwin, Field Marshal, 458
Runquillo, Manual, 45
Rowood, 112
Roosevelt, 212
Roosevelt, Teddy, President, 78, 84, 188, 222, 321, 335, 368
Rose, Johnny, 205
Rosecrans, George, Lt., 164
Roskruge, George, 114
Round Valley, 342
Route 66, 234, 278, 284, 290
Royal Stratton, 393
Rubenstein, John "Popcorn," 205
Rubí, Marquis de, 3, 49
Rucker, John A., Lt., 67
Ruffner, Lester "Budge," 338
Ruffner, George Sheriff, 335-38
Ruffner, M. A., 357
Ruggles, Levi, 88
Rupert, Jake, Col., 240
Rush, Charles, 332
Russ House, 61
Russell Gold and Silver Mining Company, 25
Russell, Charles M. (or Charlie), 365
Ruth, Adolph, Dr., 196
Ruxton, George Frederick, 276
Rye, 211
Rye Creek, 211
Rynning, Tom, 76-77
S. H. Mountains, 453
Sacajawea, 21
Sacaton, 119, 388, 394
Sacramento Valley, 286, 451
Sacramento Wash, 290
Safford, 349, 369
Safford, A. P. K., 59, 349

Salado Indians, 218
Salcido, Pablo, 350
Salome, 431-32
Salome Sun, newspaper, 432
Salpointe, Jean Baptiste, Father, 55
Salt River, 152, 154, 192, 207, 211, 219, 405
Salt River Canyon, 208, 339
Salt River Indian Reservation, 160
Salt River Project, 219
Salt River Valley, 147-48, 160, 194-95, 204,
    219, 273
Salt River Valley Water Users Association,
    155, 173-74
Salton Sea, 451
Sam Heintzelman Mine, 144
Sam, Jim, 89
Sample, Red, 62, 71
San Antonio-San Diego Stage Line, 6, 133, 388
San Augustin de Oiaur, 2
San Augustín del Tucson, 4
San Bernardino, 82, 424
San Bernardino Springs, 81
San Bernardino land grant, 77
San Blas, 231
San Carlos Apache Reservation, 210, 340,
    343-45
San Carlos Reservation, 135
San Cosmé de Tucson, 2
San Diego, 407-09, 411, 419
San Francisco, 50, 390, 419, 457
San Francisco Mountains, 228, 235, 237, 240,
    298, 319, 327, 456
San Francisco River, 369, 374, 404
San Gabriel de Guevavi, 38, 103
San Ignacio del Babocomari grant, 101
San José De Sonoita, 103
San José de Tumacacori, 40-42, 48
San José del Tucson, 2
San Juan River, 406
San Juan de las Boquillas y Nogales Grant, 101
San Juan, Maria, 375
San Marcos Hotel, 119
San Pablo, 192
San Pasqual, 231, 407
San Pedro River, 368, 404-05
San Pedro Station, 22
San Pedro y San Pablo de Bicuñer, 402
San Simón, 34-35, 201
San Xavier del Bac, 2, 5, 22, 53-54
San Ignacio de la Canoa, 52
Sanders, 272
Sanders, C. W., 272
Sanford, George B., Capt., 118
Sangre de Cristo Mountains, 404
Santa Claus, 448
Santa Cruz, 100-01
Santa Cruz de Terrenate, 100
Santa Fe Railroad, 70, 233, 235, 237, 252, 257,
    263, 272, 277-78, 305, 355, 359, 442
Santa Fe Trail, 371, 404
Santa Fe, New Mexico, 192, 236, 271, 300,
    327-28, 403-04, 406-07, 416, 456-57
Santa Maria River, 277, 287, 447-48
Santa Rita, 44, 405
Santa Rita Hotel, 7, 45
Santa Rita del Cobre, 404
Santee, Ross, 32, 345
Santos Apostales San Simón y Judas, 390
Sasabe, 145
Satterdahl, Victor, 458
Saunders, Art, 272
Sawyer, Frenchy, 149

Sayers, George, 435
Scarborough, George, 342
Stagecoach, 305
Starlett, John, 313
Scatterville, 448
Schell, Asbury, 212
Schieffelin Hall, 65
Schieffelin, Al, 57-58, 65
Schieffelin, Ed, 56-60, 121
Schnebly Hill, 191
Schnebly Road, 190
Schnebly, Ellsworth, 191, 364
Schnebly, Sedona, 191, 364
Schnebly, Theodore C., 190
Scott, George Washington, 204
Scott, W. P., 361
Scott, Winfield, 204
Scottsdale, 204-06, 208
Searchlight, 410
Sedelmayr, Jacob, Padre, 41, 392-93, 447
Sedona, 190, 364-65
Segesser, Philipe, Padre, 41, 48
Seligman, 283-84, 354
Seligman brothers, 265, 283
Sells, 114
Sells, Cato, 114
Semmilrogge, Bill, 396
Senator, 179
Serra, Junipero, Padre, 402
Serrano, don Fernando, 145
Seven Cities of Gold, 126, 401
Sharlot Hall Museum, 329, 334
Shaver, Ellen, 151
Shea, James A., 173
Shenfield Railroad Camp, 288
Shenfield, Conrad, 288
Shepherd, Mollie, 436-37
Sherman, William T., General, 121, 354
Shiver, Hannah, 355
Shivwits Indians, 294
Short Creek, 324
Shotwell, A. J., 111
Showlow, 278, 341, 343
Showlow Creek, 313
Shumway, 310
Shumway, Charles, 310
Sibley, Henry, General, 394
Sieber, Al, 70, 212, 357, 366, 385
Sierra Anchas, 208, 211
Sierra Bonita Ranch, 32, 367
Sierra Madre, 81, 350
Sierra Nevada, 327
Sierra Pinta, 392
Sierra Vista, 123-24
Signal, 448
Silver City, New Mexico, 201, 395
Silver Creek, 310
Silver Gert Mining Company, 116
Silver King, 196-98
Silver King Mine, 218, 220
Silver Queen, 198
Silver Queen Mining Company, 198
Simon, Billy, 438
Simpson, James, Lt., 235-36
Sinagua Indians, 184, 187-88, 249, 297-98
Sipapu Canyon, 298
Siphon Canyon, 134, 141
Sisson, Tom, 368-69
Sitgreaves Mountain, 275
Sitgreaves, Lorenzo, Capt., 228, 230, 235-36,
    260, 279, 286
Skeleton Canyon, 79, 83

Skeleton Cave, 340
Skull Valley, 364
Slaughter, John, Sheriff, 28, 64, 75, 77-78
Sloan, John, 407
Sloan, Richard, Governor, 380
Small, 95
Smalley, George, 347
Smiley, George, 263
Smith's Station, 148
Smith, A., 107
Smith, Belle, 274
Smith, Bill, 342
Smith, Duncan, 351
Smith, F. W., 274
Smith, Jedediah, 259, 293
Smith, Jesse, 348
Smith, John Y.T., 148, 152
Smith, Joseph, 310
Smith, Lot, 254, 256
Smith, Marcus, 348
Smith, Non-Assessable, 23
Smith, Van, 329
Smithville, 348
Snively's Station, 399
Snively, Jake, Col, 399, 452
Snow, Bud, 31
Snow, Erastus, 301, 310, 324, 376
Snowflake, 310
Sobaipuri Indians, 2, 41, 100, 103
Socorro, 404, 407
Solomon, Isador E., 349-50
Solomonville, 349-50
Sonoita, 103, 398
Sonoita Creek, 40, 44, 102, 105
Sonora, 36, 75
Southern Pacific Railroad, 13, 26-28, 33, 35, 70,
    91, 95, 168, 202, 277, 388-90, 396-97, 399,
    410, 421-22
Southwest Forest Industries, 315
Sparks, 95
Sparks, Randy, 426
Speed, Billy, Ranger, 31
Spence, Pete, 63
Spendazuma, 346-47
Spider Web, 298
Spring Valley, 355
Springer, Henry, 342
Springerville, 316, 342-43
Standard, 313
Stanton, 443-44
Stanton, Charles P., 443
Stanwix Station, 394, 396
Star Valley, 312
Starr, John, 312
State Highway Commission, 217
Steel Dam, 279
Steen, Enoch, Major, 44, 103
Steinbeck, John, 234
Steinfield, Albert, 17
Steins Pass, 28
Stevens, J. N., 370
Stevens, Jay, 370
Stevenson, James, 249
Stewart, Bill, Col., 368
Stewart, Luella, 325
Stewart Mountain Dam, 222
Stewart, Reid, Lt., 108-09
Stewart, Sam, 214
Stiga, Casper, 41
Stiles, Billy, 28-30
Stilwell, Frank, 12, 63
Stinson, Jim, 310

Stinson, Katharine, 16
Stockton, Robert, Commodore, 407
Stone Cabin, 453-54
Stoneman Grade, 196-97
Stoneman Lake, 183, 189-90
Stoneman, George, General, 22, 98, 182, 189,
    197, 199, 208, 353
Stonewall Jackson, 338
Stowell, Belle, 96
Strawberry, 216
Strawberry School House, 216
Stringtown, 193
Strobel, Oscar, Jr., 206
Sublette, "Frenchy," 259
Sugarloaf Mountain, 210
Sullivan, 196-98
Sulphur Springs Valley, 27, 75, 367
Summerhayes, Jack, 208
Summerhayes, Martha, 14, 185, 188, 190, 208,
    256, 310, 314, 354, 382-83, 412, 425
Sun Devils, 194
Sunflower, 210
Sunrise, 315
Sunset, 254-55
Sunset Crater, 187, 297
Sunset Crossing, 183, 188, 256
Sunset Pass, 217
Superior, 197
Superstition Mountains, 177, 195, 208, 218, 220
Supply, 231
Surprise, 429
Swansea, Wales, 370
Sweeny, Tom, 411
Swetnam, James, 184
Swilling Irrigation Canal Company, 148
Swilling's Ditch, 149
Swilling, Jack, 148, 150-51, 395
Swisshelm, John, 95
Switzer Mesa, 238
Sycamore Creek, 208, 210
Sykes, Charlie, 44
Tacna, 396-97
Taddock, Ben, 291
Tafolla, Carlos, 342
Talbot, Ed, 448
Talbot, Nina, 448
Tallack, William, 391
Taos, New Mexico, 260, 403
Taylor, 310
Taylor family, 77
Taylor, John, 310
Taylor, Zachary, General, 418
Teal, John, Private, 139-40
Teamster Camp, 396
Teec Nos Pos, 303
Tempe, 148, 192-95, 204-05, 225, 439
Temple Bar, 450
10th Cavalry, 123
Tennessee Mine, 449-50
Tevis, James, Capt., 33, 394
Teviston, 34
Tewanima, Louis, 319
Tewksbury, Ed, John Jr., Jim, Frank, 223-25
Tewksbury, Eve, 224
Tewksbury, John, Sr., 223-24
Texas Hill, 396
Texas Hill Station, 396
Texas Western Railroad Company, 409
Thatcher, 349
Thatcher, Moses, 349
Theodore Roosevelt Dam, 154-55, 193, 201,
    218-19, 221

Third Mesa, 316-17
Thomas, George, General, 347
Thomas, Marjorie, 205-06
Thompson, Jim, 366
Thompson Ladder, 191
Thompson, W. Boyce, 198
Thorpe, Jim, 319
Tiger, 180
Timmerman, 443
Tinker, George, 240
Tip Top, 176, 179
Tip Top Mine, 176
Tipton, Missouri, 390
Tison, Gary, 454
To the Last Man, 313
Tolmachoff family, 429
Tom Mix Memorial, 86
Tom Reed Mine, 291
Tombaugh, Clyde, W., 248
Tombstone, 28, 56-57, 59-62, 66, 344, 358
Tombstone Canyon, 70
Tombstone Consolidated Mines Company, 45
Tombstone County Court House, 66
Tombstone Epitaph, newspaper, 44
Tombstone Mine and Milling Company, 59
Tonalea, 301
Tonto Apaches, 184, 201, 208, 210-11, 218, 271, 405
Tonto Basin, 184-85, 210-13, 215, 379, 385
Tonto Creek, 154, 211, 219
Tonto Dam, 219, 221
Tonto Jack, 221
Tonto Natural Bridge, 215
Top of the World, 198
Topete Revolution, 131
Topock, 290, 292-93
Tortilla Butte, 220
Tortilla Flat, 220
Total Wreck, 108
Tough Nut, 58-59
Tovar, Pedro de, 128-29, 305, 317
Town Ditch, 149
Townsend, Jack, 379
Treaty of Guadelupe Hidalgo, 5, 42, 120, 168, 408
Treguboff family, 429
Trittle, Fred, 358
Troup, Bobby, 234, 250
Trujillo, Fito, 203
Truman, Harry, President, 451
Truman, William "Stammering Bill,"
Trumbull, Rose, 206
Truxton, 286
Tuba City, 301
Tuba, Chief, 316
Tubac, 3, 49-52, 402
Tucson, 1-3, 5-10, 12-15, 26, 33, 50, 57, 97, 113, 153, 192, 194, 328, 356, 387, 394-95, 403, 409, 439
Tully and Ochoa, 172
Tune, Mima, 200
Turkey Creek, 180, 434
Turnbull, James, 413
Turquoise Mining District, 91, 95
Tusayan, 128, 317
Twain, Mark, 134, 201, 399
24th and 25th Infantry Regiments, 123
Twin Buttes Archaeological District, 269
Two Guns, 250
Tyler, Daniel, Sgt., 164
Tyson's Wells, 425-26
U.S. Boundary Hotel, 104

Udall, David King, 325, 375
Udall, Levi, 325, 375
Udall, Morris, 325, 375
Udall, Stewart, 325, 375
Uncle Sam, steamboat, 413-14
Under the Tonto Rim, 313
Union Park, 213-14
United Verde Mine, 334, 358-60, 362
University of Arizona, 15, 193, 203, 375
Utahville, 194
Utley, Albert J., 205
Utleyville, 205
Vaca, Alvar Nuñez Cabeza de, 125
Vail, 18
Vail, Ed, 18
Vail, Walter, 18
Vale of Tempe, 192
Valentine, 286
Valentine, Robert O., 286
Valenzuela, Innocente, 430
Valley National Bank, 350
Vanderbuilt Mine, 449
Vega, Francisco, 443
Venta Mesa, 311
Vercamp, Gerald, 242-43
Verde, 364
Verde River, 183, 208, 216-17, 328, 354, 364
Verde Valley, 191, 357, 366
Verde Water and Power Company, 173
Verdugo, Francisco, "Pancho," 46
Vermillion Cliffs, 295
Vicksburg, 458
Victorio, 120, 344
Villa, Francisco, "Pancho," General, 76, 123, 130-31, 156, 358, 439
Villapando, Anna Maria, 261
Villapando, Don Pablo, 260-61
Virgen, Thomas, 293
Virgin Mary, 329
Virgin River, 293, 415
Virginia City, 115
Vivian Mining Company, 291
Volunteer Spring, 274
Vosburg, John, 59
Vucichevich, Rad and Johnny, 203
Vulture Mine, 430, 433-34, 443
Vulture Siding, 430
Wah-Poo-eta, 216
Wahwcap Canyon, 252
Walker, 179, 310, 377
Walker Creek, 303
Walker, Joe, 158, 180, 277, 327-28, 393, 395, 434, 447, 456
Walker, John G., 303
Walker, William, 33, 43
Walnut Canyon National Monument, 249
Walnut Creek, 250
Walnut Grove Dam, 430
Walpi, 183, 318
Walt Disney, 33, 194
Waltz, Jacob, 196, 218
Ward, John, 104
Warner, Jonathan, 5
Warner, Soloman, 6
Warren, 69, 73
Warren Mining District, 72-73
Warren, George, 67-68
Washington Camp, 106
Washington, John, Col., 273
Waters, "Thick-lipped Joe," 256
Watervale, 61
Wattron, Frank, 263

Wauba-Yuba, 286
Wavoka, 384
Way, Phocion, R., 6, 8
Wayne, Henry, Major, 231
Wayne, John, 305
Weaver, 443-44
Weaver Creek, 444
Weaver District, 447
Weaver's Needle, 196
Weaver, Pauline, 21, 117, 158, 163, 259, 277, 330-31, 415, 423, 434, 444, 446
Weedin, Tom, 168
Weekly Arizonian, newspaper, 51
Weightman, Richard, 457
Weiner, Melissa Ruffner, 332
Wells Fargo, 281
Wenden, 431
West Turkey Creek, 142
Western Apaches, 322
Westinghouse, George, 106
Wetherill, John and Louisa, 302-03
Wham Robbery, 348
Wham, Joseph, Major, 348
Wheeler Survey, 220
Wheeler, Grant, 27-28
Wheeler, Harry, Capt., 31
Whipple, Amiel W., Lt., 227, 229, 232, 236, 249 251, 260, 269-70, 279, 287, 292, 305, 328, 353-54, 408-10, 447, 456-57
Whiskey Row, 330
Whistler, G. R., 393
White Hills, 450
White Mountain Apaches, 211
White Mountain Reservation, 343
White Mountains, 315
White, Ammi, 394-95
White, Ruby, 130
Whitlow Crosing, 194
Whitside, Sam, Capt., 121
Why, 110
Wickenburg, 216-17, 331, 431, 433, 435, 440, 445-47
Wickenburg Massacre, 436, 438
Wickenburg, Henry, 433-34
Wide Ruins, 311
Wikieup, 448
Wikieup Canyon, 448
Wilkey, Ada Mae, 351
Willcox, 19, 25-26, 28-29, 31-33
Willcox Playa, 32
Willcox, Orlando B., General, 27
Williams, 234, 275, 278, 281, 284, 305
Williams Air Force Base, 119
Williams, Bill, 158, 275, 277, 279, 456
Williams, Hank, 58
Williams, Mollie, 95-96
Willis, Edward B., 270, 328, 353
Wilson Canyon, 366
Wilson, George and Martha, 193
Wilson, Maggie, 202
Wilson, Richard, 366
Wilson, Yaqui, 443
Window Rock, 322
Windsor Castle Livestock Growers Association, 325
Winged Victory, 133
Winona, 250
Winslow, 228, 234, 244, 254-56, 273, 284
Winslow, Edward, General, 256
Winslow, Tom, 256
Winter Campaign of 1872, 382
Winterhaven, California, 417

Wittman, 430
Wood, Leonard, Capt., 122-23
Woodhouse, Samuel W., 236
Woods Canyon, 313
Woods, Jack, 313
Woody, Clara, 199
Woolsey, King, 199, 201, 211, 216, 221, 340, 378, 393, 434
Worth, Major, 413
Wupatki National Monument, 187, 297
Wylie Way Camp, 309
Yampai Indians, 230, 235, 286
Yankee Stadium, 212
Yankie Mine, 370
Yankie, Joe, 370
Yaqui Indians, 156
Yarnell, 444
Yarnell Hill, 444
Yarnell, Harrison, 444
Yavapai Valley, 286, 353
Yavapais, 184, 208-10, 218, 271, 339, 392, 405
Yeager Canyon, 359
Yoas, Bravo Juan, 28-29, 99-100
Yosemite National Park, 327
Young, Brigham, 254, 293, 295, 310
Young, Ewing, 158, 259, 277, 279, 354, 405, 456
Young, George U., 220
Young, John W., 239-41, 261, 317
Young, Otis, 431
Youngsberg, 220
Ysario, Manual, 329
Yucca, 292
Yuma, 43, 50, 378, 388, 390, 399-400, 408-10, 412, 416-17, 419, 422, 438, 440, 445, 451-53
Yuma Crossing, 387, 390-91, 394-95, 398-400, 402, 407, 410, 421, 456
Yuma Indians, 236, 392, 405, 410-11
Yuma Territorial Prison, 30, 96, 252, 420
Zenos, 195
Zulick, Conrad, 283
Zuni River, 375
Zuni, New Mexico, 306, 375
Zuni Indians, 126-27